Matriarchs

Matriarchs

Great Mares of the 20th Century

BY

EDWARD L. BOWEN

FOREWORD BY

SETH HANCOCK

THE BLOOD-HORSE, INC.
LEXINGTON, KENTUCKY

ISBN 1-58150-022-X

Printed in The United States

First Edition: August 1999

1 2 3 4 5 6 7 8 9 10

TABLE OF Contents

Cover: Detail from the 1953 painting by
Milton Menasco of *La Troienne and her foals*

Foreword

My family has been involved in Thoroughbred breeding for more than a century and has been lucky enough to deal with some outstanding stock, both for ourselves and our clients. I have been asked to comment on broodmares and female families. From experience, you might assume that we would have established strong conclusions about how things are done and what approach is taken. To the contrary, I would warn anybody against trying to rely on a set of hard, fast rules that you can always depend on holding true. For example, I have seen good broodmares in all shapes and sizes.

However, each decision about breeding has to be based on something rather than chance. So, it may be useful to observe patterns that tend to repeat fairly often over generations. Generally, I believe in the old saying that the family is stronger than the individual. Connected to that line of reasoning is the fact that the racing record alone is not always a true measure. When you attempt to judge the breeding potential of a filly, I believe it is important to have as much information as possible. A filly might have run only three times and not gotten much done and yet still have had ability. An extreme example for Claiborne has been the mare Special. She only ran once and was unplaced, but I believe my father learned she was a bleeder. A lot of things can come up that keep a horse from showing its real potential, such as accidents or being with a trainer who just is not successful.

Every breeder is faced with decisions about when to give up on a mare. I would say, in general, that if a mare is from a good producing family, you might wait and see the first couple of foals. If you like them, then you would want to go on with that mare, but if you didn't, you would be ready to make the call to get rid of her.

Also, the whole matter of a strong family can change. Nothing lasts forever. There have been good producing families for Claiborne Farm that we have very few mares from anymore, because the family sort of died out. Sometimes, though, they will come back. Again, there are exceptions to every rule, but I would say that if the first and second dams have not done much, I would not rely on even a good third dam being enough to make the mare. Of course, it depends on your budget. If you are at a sale on a small budget, you might look at a mare like that and try to figure why the first and second dam had not followed through with the family's success and what could be done that might work.

The age of a mare is something I think is important. A study done at Claiborne Farm showed that a high majority of stakes winners came from mares that were not older than fourteen and had not had more than six foals. After "fourteen and six," they tended to hit a little wall when it came to foaling runners. However, I don't think the daughters of an older mare have less chance of being good producers themselves.

On the subject of mares' age, this is also something that can have an effect on a stallion's career. I have heard it said that one reason Secretariat had less success than many people expected was that he was bred to a lot of mares bred "too fine." Well, if there was a problem with Secretariat it was not mares bred "too fine," but the fact that everybody wanted to send their best, proven producer to him. You might think nothing could be better for a young stallion than to get a concentration of proven mares, but this means so many of those mares' best producing years were behind them instead of in front of them. Ideally, you would like to have a spread of mares, including a lot of them young enough that you could tell what was working and then react to it. That is a plus in having a stallion privately owned instead of syndicated. You can set the fee so you can pick and choose.

Another example of patterns being meaningful, but not ironclad, is in what some people call "sire families." I think most of the time a good family is a good family, not a good "filly family" or good "sire family." On the other hand, I admit I wouldn't be doing cartwheels to get a stallion from the Bourtai family, although it was one of our best over a long period of time.

Another subject breeders face is inbreeding. Some of Claiborne's best families have come from mares my father bought in England, and we still try to buy mares over there that might be outcrosses to all the Northern Dancer and Mr. Prospector lines. It is difficult to find mares from those old English families, though. When I see a horse inbred 3 x 3 to Raise a Native, I kind of shudder. But I also think it makes a difference which individual horses are involved. If part of the inbreeding is to Native Royalty, I would not be as worried, because I don't think he was a true Raise a Native. The same is true of Alydar. He ran one and a half miles and was pretty sound and not a typical Raise a Native. An example from the Northern Dancer line was Nijinsky II. He was a big, massive horse, about as far in type from (his sire) Northern Dancer as you could find, so I would not be as bothered by inbreeding to Northern Dancer if one of the horses close up was Nijinsky II.

The mares described in *Matriarchs: Great Mares of the 20th Century* came from a variety of backgrounds and had a wide range of racing success, but they turned out to be very successful and important as producers.

Breeders the world over strive, and hope, for just such a mare. They don't come along often, and the only advice I would ever give to anyone who comes up with a mare like that is to remember not to get to feeling smart — just feel lucky.

Seth Hancock   *Claiborne Farm, Paris, Kentucky*

Great Mares of the 20th Century

Introduction

horoughbred fillies launch their public lives as dainty debutantes, athletes in waiting, as they prance in what Degas described as "nakedly nervous" anticipation for the race.

Whether their competitive days single them out as star runners or they toil amid the sorority of obscurity, many of them recede into private lives to be matrons. While our minds know them to be "mere" animals, our hearts respond to the soft dignity of the eye, the quiet confidence of the protectress, as a broodmare lives the rhythms of motherhood — struggle to bear, the stolidity of nurture, the inevitability of separation. As this process is repeated — both directed by and indifferent to the commands of man — some few broodmares create lasting influence.

In that uplifting ritual of seeking to breed a nobler member of an already noble breed, we chance upon the exceptional. The jargon of the Turf styles them first as producers, then stakes producers, then Blue Hens. Some few give their genes to prosperity, and in so doing command an enduring reverence.

The mares addressed in this volume were special, and they collectively dodge the instinct to generalize or explain. Some were hard raced, some hardly raced, some not raced at all. Some were champions while others were simply dreadful in meeting the specific demands of being racehorses. Some brought lofty pedigrees; others created their own. We resist any implication of trying to unravel the pedigree mystery. These are true stories but are not presented as lectures. We are gratified in recalling what happened; there is no arrogance implied as to explain why.

Selection of mares for inclusion in this volume created an understanding of the English racing journalist Peter Willet for his naming of the book *Great Racehorses of the World*. Not *The Greatest*, not even *Some Of The Greatest*. Just *Great Racehorses of the World*. A review of broodmare records reminded us of, or uncovered, more candidates than we had anticipated. A breeder who owns a mare which has foaled, say, three stakes winners, is entitled to the notion that he/she has something special here. A breeder whose mare foaled five, or six stakes winners, is beyond even the suggestion that this is not one of the greatest of all times. To the inevitable, and indignant, trumpeting of such mares which are not profiled herein, we can only prepare to say often, "you have a point."

The record pointed us to far more of these mares than could be accommodated at any but the most superficial level if such a book were to be held within decent bounds. (Books of 500 or so pages invite such phrases as "weighty tome" and should be about philosophy, or history, or actresses — not filled by the raptures of a fellow lucky enough to have fallen for racehorses as a pre-teen.)

The parameters agreed upon with the editor, Jacqueline Duke of *The Blood-Horse*, were that the subjects included would be dams of American foals in the 20th Century, although impact abroad is included as part of many great mares' records. In addition, the general criteria were that mares to be included had produced a number of successful runners, perhaps one great one and some supporting cast, or else a wondrous number of stakes winners; moreover, the presence of the resulting female family should have traversed several generations so that the phrase "lasting influence," while trite, would at least be accurate. Since there were far more of these than could be included, we also added to the mix a desire for geographic variety, farm/breeder variety, and a range of eras within the century. Mares from farms such as Claiborne or Calumet could fill a book on their own, as could mares based in Kentucky or any of several other states.

In the main, the intent was to describe the subject mares' impact on racing and breeding history over about four generations — the span familiar in many pedigree presentations — but the lingering waft of quality rendered irresistible the urge to bring up a few examples extending several more generations from the wellspring. The seventh dam might not be the dominant factor of a Derby winner of the 1990s, but the constancy within a family is sometimes compelling.

What we have, then, is a group of twenty-four Matriarchs. Like Mr. Willet, we do not project them as the twenty-four greatest of the 20th Century, and yet we feel the comfort of certainty that each worked her wonders on the Thoroughbred breed.

Edward L. Bowen *Lexington, Kentucky, 1999*

Alcibiades

Alcibiades, a Kentucky champion of the late 1920s, became the fourth dam of an Epsom Derby winner some four decades later. She was also the dam of a champion colt whose offspring included two Horse-of-the-Year honorees. The degree to which Alcibiades has always been accepted as a sentimental figure, as well as a factually distinguished one, stems in part from the family whose farm and lives she touched. She was bred and raced by Hal Price Headley, and the Headley family, along with the Hancocks and a few others, is one which has remained prominent in Kentucky racing over many years and several generations.

There is a diversity of abilities and knowledge among men such as Hal Price Headley that harks back to the image of gentry in the old country — fellows who got their hands dirty on the farm one moment, dealt with sophisticated business matters the next, and managed to keep sportsmanship at least a part of the mix throughout. In America, a Southern personification of such true-life characters is equally at home in the foaling barn, tobacco barn, or board room. The breed, the sport, and the business of the Turf are concurrent beneficiaries.

The stories handed down about Hal Price Headley include the adventure of a fourteen-year-old lad sent by his father with the crack horse Ornament and sixteen others to the St. Louis World's Fair in the early days of the 20th Century. His father was Hal Pettit Headley, who had been a serious Thoroughbred breeder around Lexington since about 1890. Young Hal Price got the horse bug early and surprised his father by buying a mare named Tweedledum for $420 at a livery stable auction. The teenager had secured a loan from his grandfather.

From such agrarian environment, Headley was delivered in due time to the halls of Princeton. A young man is sent to such enclaves to get an education, and Headley did: He saw a horse race for the first time when he hied off to the Gravesend track on Long Island to see his father's Beacon Light finish second to Superman in the 1907 Brooklyn Handicap.

His father's stroke forced the young Hal Price into management of the family's Kentucky farm, and the timing could not have been worse for business. The ban on gambling in New York scuttled racing there for a few years, and the commerce of Kentucky breeding was highly dependent on New York racing. Headley at one point called himself broke, but racing came back, and so did he. He accomplished that most ingenious of responses to the circumstance of having ambition but no money, to wit, forming a partnership with a fellow who had both. He and William Baldwin Miller purchased the stallion Uncle for $38,000, an enormous amount at the time.

Outstanding runners sired by Uncle and bred by Headley and Miller included Motor Cop and Uncle's Lassie (see Courtly Dee chapter). Headley was back on his feet, and on his way. By 1923, as these "hardboot" Lexington stories go, he was in a position to bet about $5,000 on his imported mare Chacolet when she defeated In Memoriam in the Latonia Kentucky Special. The purse was $49,350, and the payoff on the bet was 21-1. Other horsemen have made such scores, then frittered away the spoils. Headley was too smart to foul up: He bred eighty-eight stakes winners from 1916 until he dispersed in 1953.

Hal Price Headley was also an organizer, and an organization leader. He was still in his twenties when he became first president of the Kentucky Thoroughbred Horse Association, whose bulletin was the forerunner of *The Blood-Horse*, and years later he was involved in the establishment of the American Thoroughbred Breeders' Association, which purchased the publication. Headley helped support the Saratoga yearling sale, recognizing its importance, but when wartime restrictions altered the equation, he was instrumental in the creation of a Kentucky alternative. Perhaps most important of all, he was one of the visionary founders of Keeneland, the racetrack that was created amidst the Depression to replace Lexington's century-old Kentucky Association track which had closed. The understated majesty of Keeneland owes its character to a very few sportsmen, none more important in its nurturing than Headley. (On the practical side, one of Headley's daughters, Alice Chandler recalls that Headley in the early days of Keeneland races "used to sit in the box and figure the handle, because he wasn't sure they were going to be able to keep the track open the next day." Another of Headley's daughters is Alma, who along with late husband, Louis Lee Haggin II, has continued to articulate the founders' image as to what should be done at Keeneland.)

Headley had played out some of these roles and would be facing others at the stage of life when he bred Alcibiades, a foal of 1927. The filly was sired by Supremus, who succeeded his own sire, the inbred Domino-line stallion Ultimus, at Headley's Beaumont Farm. The dam of Alcibiades was the imported Regal Roman, a mare by Roi Herode. Regal Roman traced back to the distinguished mare Santa Brigida.

The naming of a filly Alcibiades promulgated various judgments. Writing in Derrydale Press' first volume of *Famous Horses of the American Turf* (for 1930), Neil Newman called her "the atrociously named Alcibiades." Headley himself enjoyed recalling that during the filly's career some stentorian racing writer hectored that "the original Alcibiades was neither 'Regal' nor 'Roman' but was a drunken Greek." History and myth be damned, the filly was named because time was running out and one of the Headley staff had augmented the household nickname for the aforementioned Alice from "Alcie" to "Alcibiades."

Alcibiades the filly came out at two in 1929 and won four of seven races. Her triumphs included the Debutante and Clipsetta Stakes, and, challenging colts, she was second to Desert Light, with Gallant Knight third, in the Kentucky Jockey Club Stakes. Historians have ranked her as the champion two-year-old filly of the season, which predated balloting for such division titles by seven years. This status might seem suspect based on the regional record, but for the inability for any of the Eastern fillies to put together a series of victories in their circuit's traditional targets.

At three, Alcibiades was again reckoned best of her age and sex division. She scored in two of the most important filly events of her era, the Kentucky Oaks and Arlington Oaks, and, given the limited opportunities for fillies in those days,

SUPREMUS, b, 1922	Ultimus, 1906	Commando, 1898	**Domino** / Emma C.
		Running Stream, 1898	**Domino** / Dancing Water
	Mandy Hamilton, 1913	John o' Gaunt, 1901	**Isinglass** / La Fleche
		My Sweetheart, 1904	Galeazzo / Lady Chancellor
REGAL ROMAN, ch, 1921	Roi Herode, 1904	Le Samaritain, 1895	Le Sancy / Clementina
		Roxelane, 1894	War Dance / Rose of York
	Lady Cicero, 1913	Cicero, 1902	Cyllene / Gas
		Ste. Claire II, 1904	**Isinglass** / Santa Brigida

ALCIBIADES, ch m, 1927

ALCIBIADES, ch, 1927-1957. Bred by Hal Price Headley (Ky.). Raced 2 yrs, 23 sts, 7 wins, $47,860. Champion 2yo and 3yo filly. Won Kentucky Oaks, Clipsetta S, Debutante S, Arlington Oaks; 2nd Kentucky Jockey Club S; 3rd Latonia Oaks, Illinois Oaks, Hawthorne Gold Cup, Arlington Matron H. Dam of 8 named foals, 7 rnrs, 7 wnrs, 4 sw.

1932: Best Butter, ch g, by Mad Hatter. Raced 5 yrs, 57 sts, 9 wins, $2,820.

1933: **SPARTA**, b f, by St. Germans. Raced 4 yrs, 60 sts, 12 wins, $33,170. Won Shawomet S, Latonia Oaks, Mary Dyer H, Nursery S; 2nd Warren H, Ashland S, Detroit Derby; 3rd Ashland S, Ladies H, What Cheer H, Constitution H. Dam of 7 foals, 5 rnrs, 3 wnrs. Granddam of **ROYAL FAN**, **NAVY BRASS**, **Far Pacific**, **Sly Ami**.

1934: Agathon, b c, by Pharamond II. Raced 1 yr, 4 sts, 1 win, $750.

1935: **MENOW**, dk b c, by Pharamond II. Raced 2 yrs, 17 sts, 7 wins, $140,100. Champion 2yo colt. Won Massachusetts H, Futurity S, Potomac H, Withers S, Champagne S; 2nd Blue Grass S, Washington Park Futurity; 3rd Preakness S, Havre de Grace H. Died 1964.

1937: **SALAMINIA**, ch f, by Man o' War. Raced 4 yrs, 26 sts, 5 wins, $36,580. Won Alabama S, Ladies H, Gallant Fox H. Dam of 11 foals, 11 rnrs, 10 wnrs, including **ATHENIA** ($105,710), **LIBBA** ($23,025), **Salason** ($96,980), **Aegina**

($42,400), **Athenian** ($34,180), **White Cross** ($17,460), **Pella** ($16,550). Granddam of **HAFA ADAI**, **FIRM POLICY**, **GEORGIAN**, **ASSEMBLYMAN**, **DELTA SAL**, **TURN TO SAL**, **Greek Jab**, **Aesthete**, **Attica**, **Deadlock**, **Old Bag**, **Affectation**, **Trouble Agin**.

1944: Hipparete, dk b f, by Pharamond II. Raced 2 yrs, 15 sts, 4 wins, $8,850. Dam of 13 foals, 10 rnrs, 8 wnrs, including **RASH STATEMENT** ($218,022), **PILLOW TALK** ($42,470), **OUT TALK** ($32,771). Granddam of **Ave Valeque**, **Abdicating**. Died 1968.

1946: **LITHE**, b f, by Pharamond II. Raced 4 yrs, 62 sts, 10 wins, $187,415. Won Demoiselle S, Comely S, Beverly H, Arlington Matron H (twice), Clang H (ETR, Was, 7 furlongs in 1:21.40); 2nd Cleopatra H, Vineland H, Vosburgh H, Top Flight H; 3rd Washington Park H, Beverly H, Vineland H, Clang H, New Rochelle H, Matron S, Royal Oak S, Misty Isle H. Dam of 8 foals, 7 rnrs, 5 wnrs, including **SUPPLE** ($79,770), **Mountain Greenery** ($23,045). Granddam of **GENTLE KING**, **WHAT A GENT**, **LITHIOT**, **MONOLITH**, **Lancastrian**, **Panicum Repens**, **Carry Ruler**, **Bold Lithia**. Died 1975.

1950: Last of All, dk b f, by Rico Monte. Unraced. Dam of 8 foals, 7 rnrs, 4 wnrs. Granddam of **Wald**. Died 1970.

spent much of the year chasing the colts. The Kentucky Oaks was revered, as it is today, but while it was always intended to be the filly counterpart to the Kentucky Derby, it was not run the day before. In Alcibiades' year, the Oaks was the closing day feature of the Churchill Downs meeting, being run on May 31, or fourteen days after the Derby. Alcibiades ran in both. She was in front after a half-mile in the Derby, before falling back to tenth behind Gallant Fox.

In addition to her two Oaks victories, Alcibiades placed in the Illinois Oaks and Latonia Oaks, as well as the Arlington Matron and Hawthorne Gold Cup. In the Gold Cup, she was given the stern assignment of facing not just males, but top-class older ones, and she acquitted herself well in finishing third to as grand a horse as Sun Beau.

Alcibiades' last race was in the Latonia Championship. It is interesting to note that, even though Gallant Fox that year followed Sir Barton as second winner of what is known as the Triple Crown, that sequence of Kentucky Derby, Preakness, and Belmont Stakes was not yet set in the Turf world's consciousness as a unit. The aforementioned journalist and historian Newman referred that year to the Latonia Championship as "the last of the three-year-old classics." This was owing to its one and three-quarter-mile distance mirroring that of the St. Leger, the last classic of the prototype, in England. At any rate, Alcibiades was churning along in front in the Championship before rupturing a tendon. She was pulled up and did not race again, going home with a mark of twenty-three starts, seven wins, and earnings of $47,860. She was to produce eight foals, of which her seven starters all won and four won stakes. Such a record begs the question of what might have been without her atrocious run of bad luck in mid-career when she went a half-dozen years in succession without a surviving foal.

Quality and Fashion

Alcibiades' first foal was the Mad Hatter gelding Best Butter, a 1932 foal who won nine races in fifty-seven starts from three through nine and earned $2,820. Then came Sparta, a St. Germans filly born in 1933. Sparta won the Latonia Oaks and three other stakes and was second to Myrtlewood in the first Ashland Stakes to give that enduring race a splendid inaugural in Keeneland's first year. (The Ashland was not then written only for three-year-olds, and Sparta came back to be third in the event at four the next season.) Sparta won twelve of sixty races and earned $33,170 from two through five. She had seven foals, of which five raced and three won. Her daughter Buddy Kenney became the dam of stakes winner Navy Brass and second dam of Pass the Brandy and Hasty Honey. Sparta's daughter Pitcher, by Shut Out, foaled the Colonial Handicap winner Royal Fan.

In 1934, Alcibiades foaled the Pharamond II colt Agathon, who won once in four races and earned $750. The next Pharamond II—Alcibiades colt, foaled in 1935, was the champion Menow. Pharamond II was typical of an American trend which was unfolding during that time, the importation of European stallions to replace reliance on the traditional American sire lines. There were some high-profile importations, such as Blenheim II, but Headley was among the majority of breeders in that he could not deal for the very top echelon. When he visited Lord Derby's stud to dicker over a price on Pharamond II, he was reaching for the top in pedigree, more than he knew. Pharamond II (Phalaris—Selene, by Chaucer) was a full brother to Sickle and would later become a half-brother to the great Hyperion. Headley was accepting reality insofar as racing record was concerned, for Pharamond II had managed two modest victories from eleven starts. Still, the asking price was £10,000.

Headley looked into Pharamond II's darkened stall late one autumn day at the Derby stud in England and could barely make out a shadowy form bedded knee-deep in straw. The artful hardboot commercing with the peerage, Headley resisted asking for the horse to be brought out, because, he said, he "didn't want Lord Derby's men to learn how interested I was." Headley returned to Lexington, from whence he sent word that, "If Lord Derby would not be insulted, I would like to offer 4,000 pounds." At forty percent of the asking price, Headley had himself a new stallion prospect.

Menow, the second Pharamond II—Alcibiades colt, was a late foal, but was in action relatively early in his two-year-old season. He won three of his six races, his two stakes being the Champagne, in which he defeated fellow future sire Bull Lea, and the Futurity, which he won by four lengths. Menow was voted champion two-year-old of 1937.

Headley, of course, was keen to have Menow excel at the fresh, young Keeneland track, and the champion reappeared there, winning a sprint in the spring. Thereafter, he lost twice at Keeneland to Bull Lea, and by the time he went to the post in the Kentucky Derby, he was 8-1. Showing his old speed, he led for longer in the race than his dam had, but after being in front for a mile fell back to fourth behind Lawrin. Bull Lea fared worse, finishing eighth. It was not a lovely showcase for the pair of future stallions.

Menow was no longer contending for a championship and never was successful at one and a quarter miles, but he did win three major races at three: the Withers, Potomac Handicap, and Massachusetts Handicap. The MassCap was the occasion of a Headley family yarn — actually two:

(1) Daughter Alice's memory, handed down from the cherished discourse of many a jovial Headley-table meal no doubt, centered on the wisdom of her father. Upon his arrival at Suffolk Downs, Headley noticed that the harrow seemed somewhat redundant in its path. He discerned that these laps were intended to dry out the path in front of the storied War Admiral. Headley thereupon instructed jockey Nick Wall to use Menow's natural speed away from the gate and pursue the favored path around the track.

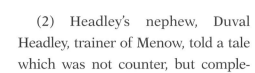

Alcibiades

(2) Headley's nephew, Duval Headley, trainer of Menow, told a tale which was not counter, but complement, to the above. The day before the race, Hal Price Headley was to accompany him to the track. It was the elder Headley's pre-voiced opinion that Menow needed nothing more than a slow move; the trainer felt a sharp blow-out was in order. Possessing a share of the same craftiness genes as his morning companion and recognizing that the dual titles of "Uncle Price" and "owner" gave a certain advantage to the other court, Duval had coached his exercise rider to ignore any signals from the infield as Menow was sent through his work. When owner Headley glanced at his watch and ordered the rider to slow down, trainer Headley went through a pre-arranged histrionic, after which he pretended to decry the rider's ability, judgment, and perhaps his ancestry.

The next afternoon, all choreography complete, Menow strolled.

The previous year's Triple Crown winner, War Admiral, giving twenty-three pounds in actual weight to the younger winner, finished fourth. Seabiscuit's team bypassed the opportunity to contest the race in the off going (delaying his long-awaited meeting with War Admiral until his triumph in the Pimlico Special that fall). Otherwise, Menow's victory might have achieved even a higher place in upset history.

Later in the year, Menow finished third behind Seabiscuit in the Havre de Grace Handicap, from which he came back lame in both forelegs. He was retired to Headley's Beaumont Farm with a record of seven wins in seventeen races and earnings of $140,100. Although of a pedigree dominated by foreign horses, Menow was well suited to the speed orientation of America, as he had proven as a runner and would prove as a sire. He got thirty-two stakes winners before his death at twenty-nine in

1964 (Bull Lea died the same year). Menow sired three champions: juvenile filly champion Askmenow; Preakness-Belmont winner Capot, co-Horse of the Year in 1949; and 1953 Horse of the Year Tom Fool. Bred by Duval Headley, Tom Fool was purchased for $25,000 by John Hay Whitney and Joan Payson's Greentree Stable and was a champion at two. At four, Tom Fool authored one of American racing's more glorious campaigns, going unbeaten in ten starts, sweeping the New York Handicap Triple (Metropolitan, Suburban, Brooklyn), and toting up to 136 pounds in doing so. Tom Fool in turn sired the multiple champion and important sire Buckpasser.

Another Kind of English Derby

Alcibiades had no foal in 1936, missing for the first time, then in 1937 produced a filly by the immortal Man o' War. Named Salaminia, the filly won two of the historic events for her division, the Alabama Stakes and Ladies Handicap. In the Alabama, she defeated the year's three-year-old filly champion, Fairy Chant, and in the Ladies she beat her again, as well as defeating older mares. Additionally, Salaminia took on older males and beat them going one and five-eighth miles in the Gallant Fox Handicap.

The tough Salaminia ran twenty-six times, all at three in 1940, won five races, and earned $36,580. In the stud, Salaminia was also exceptional, foaling the stakes winners Athenia and Libba. Athenia, by Pharamond II, also won the Ladies, as well as three other stakes, and was second in the Kentucky Oaks. Libba, by Sir Damion, won the Hurricane Handicap and produced the stakes winner Assemblyman (by Menow).

Athenia herself was a link to one of the noblest moments of the family. In addition to foaling the Washington Park Futurity winner Georgian, she had four stakes-placed foals. One was Affection,

dam of stakes winner Swiss Cheese. The star among Athenia's foals, however, was Attica, dam of Sir Ivor. Sir Ivor was bred by Alice Headley Chandler, one of several of Headley's family who also made their mark in the racing world. Headley had given her Attica. Mrs. Chandler, whose husband is veterinarian and international horseman John Chandler, operates Mill Ridge Farm on a portion of the old Beaumont property.

Attica was by Mr. Trouble, a Mahmoud stallion Headley had acquired and a horse of some success, but bothersome personality. Mr. Trouble was "a hot stallion, bred hot," Mrs. Chandler once told *The Blood-Horse*. "He was hell-bent on suicide every day of his life, the only horse, I believe, Daddy ever insured." In Attica, Mr. Trouble sired a quirky mare who placed in a pair of important stakes, and Mrs. Chandler sought to counter some of the attitude when she sent the mare to Sir Gaylord ("I think of him as phlegmatic"). Attica had five Sir Gaylord foals, one of which was Sir Ivor.

Purchased for Raymond Guest at Keeneland in 1966 for $42,000, Sir Ivor was sent abroad by his sporting owner who for a time was the American ambassador to Ireland. Turned over to trainer Vincent O'Brien, Sir Ivor developed into a high-class two-year-old. In an experimental strategy — with distant echoes today in Dubai — O'Brien sent Sir Ivor to a warm winter climate, in Italy, rather than remain in Ireland. Whether it helped or not, Sir Ivor made history the following spring when Lester Piggott brought Guest's colt along in a startling rally to land England's greatest prize, the Epsom Derby.

Alcibiades' great-great-grandson was the first American-bred winner of the Derby since Never Say Die in 1954. What had been an historic rarity would now become a flood tide, and Sir Ivor's proving of his bloodlines' ability to stay one and a half miles was a significant moment in an enduring pattern of American-breds' success abroad. Within the next decade, in the Epsom Derby alone, would come Nijinsky II (1970), Mill Reef (1971), Roberto (1972), Empery (1976), and The Minstrel (1977). Sir Ivor later proved an exceptional sire of good fillies, among them Optimistic Gal and Prix de l'Arc de Triomphe winner Ivanjica.

Alcibiades' daughter Salaminia was also the second dam of Firm Policy, a Princequillo filly of high mettle who won the Alabama, Mother Goose, Monmouth Oaks, and others for E. Barry Ryan in the early 1960s. Other stakes winners descending from Salaminia include Troublepeg, Delta Sal, Raise a Man, Turn to Sal, Mugatea, Patchy Groundfog, Bold Roll, and Prince Mab.

Lean Years, Then More Success

By 1938, as the dam of champion Menow, Alcibiades had proven a gem in the Headley broodmare band. If her naming did not really connote Greek legend, it might as well have, for the most inventive of ancient Greek gods or playwrights could hardly have contrived a more forceful reversal of fortune: Alcibiades had no surviving foal until 1944. She was not bred for 1938; then a full sister to Menow died as a foal in 1939; she was barren for 1940; another full sister to Menow died young in 1941, and the mare was barren again for 1942 and 1943.

Finally, in 1944, Alcibiades foaled Hipparete, another Pharamond II filly, who would be the first horse Alice Chandler ever had in her own name. ("She didn't have the greatest legs in the world, and Daddy, thinking she'd never get to the races, gave her to me when I was eighteen.") Hipparete was a moderate race mare, but just getting her to the races was a bonus, and she did win four of fifteen races and earned $8,850. She foaled three stakes winners, one of which was the exceptional Ambiorix filly Rash Statement. Bred

Alcibiades

in the name of Alice and raced in the father's name, Rash Statement achieved two sentimental triumphs for the family. At two in 1959, she won the Alcibiades Stakes, the race named for her granddam which had been inaugurated at Keeneland in 1952. What had quickly become the most important distaff race at the Kentucky track, the Spinster Stakes, was begun in 1956, and Rash Statement came back at three to win it, too, defeating Indian Maid and champion Royal Native. The 1960 Spinster was held on a day when Keeneland's silver anniversary was celebrated at a special dinner. Rash Statement's eight wins in fifty-five starts also included the Delaware Oaks, and Oaks Prep, and she placed in the Coaching Club American Oaks. The filly earned $218,022. Rash Statement foaled stakes-placed Abdicating and the dam of Canadian juvenile filly champion Seraphic.

Hipparete's daughter Pillow Talk was sired by the aforementioned, and well-named, Mr. Trouble. It is not within the purview of this volume to speculate upon what might motivate the name Pillow Talk for a filly by Mr. Trouble. It might be complimentary, or it might not. Be that as it may, the filly was another nice one bred by the daughter and raced by the father. In the spring of 1957, Pillow Talk aroused hopes for a win in the Kentucky Oaks. She won the Oaks Prep, but then was beaten into second by Lori-El in the Oaks itself. Pillow Talk did win the Black-Eyed Susan Stakes and also placed in the Delaware Oaks. She won three of eleven races and earned $42,470. Pillow Talk's stakes-placed filly Ave Valeque then foaled Ciao, winner of the Pocahontas Stakes and in turn the dam of four stakes winners of the 1980s and 1990s: Secret Hello, Silent Account, Hadif, and By Your Leave.

Hipparete's third stakes winner, the filly Out Talk, was a 1963 foal by Ambiorix. She won a pair of stakes and foaled the dams of stakes winners Island Chatter and Revivalist. Hedge, Koluctoo Bay, and Frost Free are among other stakes winners descending from Hipparete.

Lithe and Supple

Alcibiades again had no foal in 1945, marking the seventh time in eight years there was no harvest. In 1946, she foaled her final stakes winner in Lithe, another by Pharamond II. This filly won ten of sixty-two races and earned $187,415. She won a half-dozen stakes from two through five, including two runnings of the Arlington Matron. In 1953, Headley decided it was time to sell, and he held a dispersal at Keeneland in which thirty-four mares were sold for $672,400, an average of $19,776. Lithe brought a record for a broodmare sold at auction in the United States to that time, going for $85,000. Bull Hancock of Claiborne Farm bought the filly on behalf of John S. Phipps, outbidding Ivor Balding, who was representing C. V. Whitney. During the sale, Athenia matched the previous record when purchased for $72,000.

After the sale of the mares, most of the horses raced by Headley were leased from his children. One of them was Lithe's 1953 foal, who was a wean-ling at the time of the dispersal. She was another by Mr. Trouble. Named Supple, she won the Princess Pat Stakes two years later. Lithe foaled stakes-placed Mountain Greenery, and winner Gentle Ruler, dam of stakes winners Gentle King and What a Gent. Another of Lithe's daughters, Lithia, foaled two stakes winners by Ribot in Lithiot and Monolith. Stakes winners of the 1990s descending from Lithia include Lookin for Romance, Vladivostok, and Brass Scale.

Alcibiades, of course, was withheld from the Headley sale. She had had her last foal three years earlier and was not bred thereafter. She lived as a pensioner to the age of thirty in 1957. Headley died in 1962.

After Lithe in 1946, Alcibiades had no foal for three years, then produced the well-named Last of All, in 1950. Last of All was by the good Argentine import Rico Monte. Alcibiades' last foal was unraced and had eight foals, seven of which raced and four won.

In 1999, seventy-two years after the foaling of Alcibiades, Mrs. Chandler can look over her fields at Mill Ridge and still spot a couple of mares tracing directly back to the taproot mare — a Headley family in one sense that is almost family in another. ❖

Almahmoud

lmahmoud does not strictly fit the profile of most of the mares whose names are chapter titles in this volume. She did not produce multiple major winners, but she did foal one high-class stakes winner who herself became a major producer, and Almahmoud's stakes-placed daughter Natalma foaled Northern Dancer. Thus, as second dam of one of the great stallions of the century, and also of another major sire in Halo, Almahmoud would certainly be no apologetic member of the club. As we shall see, there also are many important horses in the world with Almahmoud buttressing their female line.

For many years, it was canon among Kentucky breeders that no better opportunity for success could be devised than somehow getting hold of a "Whitney mare." This label was applied to members, and their produce, of the broodmare band developed and nurtured over three generations of distinguished breeders: William Collins Whitney, Harry Payne Whitney, and C. V. Whitney. It was the last of that human male line of sportsmanship and industry who bred Almahmoud.

The filly was sired by Mahmoud, the 1936 Epsom Derby winner whom C. V. Whitney had imported to stand at his Lexington farm. The dam of Almahmoud was Arbitrator, an unraced daughter of Mother Goose, the 1924 Futurity winner for

whom one of the present day New York Filly Triple Crown races is named. By Chicle—Flying Witch, Mother Goose was a full sister to the speedy Whichone, winner of the Champagne, Saratoga Special, Whitney Stakes, Withers, and others, and the colt that goaded Gallant Fox into defeat at the hands of 100-1 Jim Dandy in the storied Travers Stakes of 1930.

In addition to Almahmoud, Arbitrator produced the Will Rogers Stakes winner Burra Sahib and the Test Stakes winner Dispute.

There was no Kentucky horseman of the 1940s more savvy than Henry Knight, who owned Almahurst Farm in Kentucky and had an entire night of the Saratoga yearling sale devoted to his consignment. Knight purchased Almahmoud from Whitney as a yearling in 1948, but the lure of a broodmare tomorrow was no match for the lure of a good deal today to Knight's way of thinking. Knight wheeled her back in his Saratoga melange, and she brought $15,000 from T. D. Taggart.

The buyer died soon thereafter and, while Almahmoud topped his estate's dispersal the next spring, she had not appreciated in market value. Bidding the $15,000 that time was William Helis, in whose colors the filly won a division of the Colleen Stakes at two later that year. At three, Almahmoud won one additional stakes, taking the one and one-sixteenth-mile Vineland Handicap at Garden State.

The field of thirteen fillies and mares included the older champion Bewitch. That the high-strung, moody Almahmoud's general form did not often place her in front of such exalted company is illustrated by her 50-1 odds for that event. In two seasons, Almahmoud ran eleven times, won four races, and earned $32,760.

Following Helis' death, none other than Henry Knight bought her again when he purchased the broodmares, yearlings, and racing stock from the Helis estate.

In 1953, Almahmoud produced her first foal, a filly by Cosmic Bomb. Eugene Mori, whose primary renown in racing was as head of management at Hialeah and Garden State Park, bought the filly, later named Cosmah, for $7,000 on the advice of Olin Gentry, who, like Knight, was a hardboot Kentucky horseman of the time and had run Idle Hour Farm for Col. E. R. Bradley. At two, Cosmah won the Astarita Stakes when the most striking juvenile filly of the moment, Dark Vintage, was disqualified for interference. If Cosmah's only stakes victory might seem a bit of luck, her other performances in major races that year easily validated her quality. She placed in two of the best races in America for two-year-old fillies: the Gardenia and Frizette.

At three, Cosmah was second in the Gazelle and Pageant, and she won a total of nine races from thirty starts and earned $85,525.

It was when Cosmah was two that Knight, who was in poor health, decided to disperse his bloodstock. A sale was held in a tent at one of his Kentucky farms, Coldstream, that November. Among the young horsemen whom the childless Knight had befriended was Danny Van Clief of Virginia. In later years, Van Clief cited his gratitude to Knight, "who taught me more about commercial breeding than anyone else. He was just a super, super guy."

Van Clief operated from his Nydrie Stud in the lovely horse country outside Charlottesville, Virginia, and also became a prominent Saratoga consignor as well as a member of a body with considerable history — the Virginia legislature. (A son, D. G. Van Clief, has kept the family name prominent and, as of the late 1990s, is president of the Breeders' Cup, chairman of Fasig-Tipton Company, still operates Nydrie, and somehow managed to take on the pivotal role as interim CEO of the National Thoroughbred Racing Association when the industry called.)

Knight told Danny Van Clief as his dispersal neared, "if you're going to buy any mare, you ought to buy Almahmoud — if you've got the money."

Van Clief took heed: His mentor was steering him to the center ring, but it was not a place for amateurs.

The Virginian took a deep corporate breath and placed a figure of $50,000 on Almahmoud. It took $7,000 more than that to win the bidding, but he bought her nonetheless.

A few months later, he sold an interest to his aunt, Mrs. E. H. Augustus, who also owned a Virginia farm, Keswick.

A Halo, and Other Symbols

Cosmah, of course, had been instrumental in raising the price of the mare Almahmoud. As a producer, Cosmah also continued to add to the prestige of the family.

First of Cosmah's foals to emerge as an outstanding runner was her 1961 Tim Tam filly whom Mori sold privately to Seven-Up bottler Anthony Imbesi. Named Tosmah, she flashed incredible speed and, but for finishing unplaced in the Gardenia of 1963, would probably have been the unanimous champion two-year-old of her sex. She won the Astarita, Mermaid, and Frizette that year, and she shared the championship honor with Gardenia winner Castle Forbes.

		Blandford, 1919	Swynford Blanche
	Blenheim II, 1927		
		Malva, 1919	Charles O'Malley Wild Arum
MAHMOUD, gr, 1933			
		Gainsborough, 1915	Bayardo Rosedrop
	Mah Mahal, 1928		
		Mumtaz Mahal, 1921	The Tetrarch Lady Josephine
ALMAHMOUD, ch m, 1947			
		Chance Shot, 1924	Fair Play Quelle Chance
	Peace Chance, 1931		
		Peace, 1927	Stefan the Great Memories II
ARBITRATOR, b, 1937			
		Chicle, 1913	Spearmint Lady Hamburg II
	Mother Goose, 1922		
		Flying Witch, 1917	Broomstick Fly by Night II

ALMAHMOUD, ch, 1947-1971. Bred by C.V. Whitney (Ky.). Raced 2 yrs, 11 sts, 4 wins, $32,760. Won Vineland H, Colleen S. Dam of 8 named foals, 8 rnrs, 6 wnrs, 2 sw.

1953: **COSMAH**, b f, by Cosmic Bomb. Raced 3 yrs, 30 sts, 9 wins, $85,525. Broodmare of the Year in 1974. Won Astarita S; 2nd Gazelle H, Pageant S, Gardenia S; 3rd Frizette S. Dam of 15 foals, 10 rnrs, 9 wnrs, including **HALO** ($259,553, gr. I), **TOSMAH** ($612,588, champion 2 and 3yo filly and older female), **FATHERS IMAGE** ($173,318), **MARIBEAU** ($20,925). Granddam of **CANNONADE, CIRCLE HOME, HEEREMANDI, NAZOO (Ire), REXSON, MURIESK, LAKE COMO, LA GUIDECCA, SINGLE COMBAT, MIZNAH (Ire), WASSL TOUCH, MATCHLESS NATIVE, DEL SARTO, Ring of Truth, Magloire, Tridessus**.

1954: Twins born dead.

1955: Barren.

1956: Armistice, ch g, by Citation. Raced 3 yrs, 16 sts, 1 win, $3,765. Died 1960.

1957: **Natalma**, b f, by Native Dancer. Raced 2 yrs, 7 sts, 3 wins, $16,015. 3rd Spinaway S. Dam of 14 foals, 12 rnrs, 10 wnrs, including **NORTHERN DANCER** ($580,647 Horse of the Year and champion 2yo colt in Can, champion 3yo colt), **NATIVE VICTOR** ($71,711), **REGAL DANCER** ($51,570), **BORN A LADY** ($57,544), **Nostrum** ($52,226), **Northern Native** ($19,150), **Arctic Dancer** ($2,500), **Tai** ($11,615). Granddam of **LA PREVOYANTE, ARROWTOWN, COUP DE FOLIE, Lady Bonanza, Northern Sister**. Died 1985.

1958: Retinoscope, ch c, by Helioscope. Raced 2 yrs, 14 sts, 0 wins, $1,400. Sire of 2 foals, AEI 0.69. Died 1964.

1959: FOLK DANCER, ch g, by Native Dancer. Raced 5 yrs, 56 sts, 10 wins, $44,595. Won Swynford S.

1960: Nash, b g, by Nashua. Raced 6 yrs, 43 sts, 11 wins, $30,745.

1961: Bubbling Beauty, ch f, by Hasty Road. Raced 2 yrs, 2 sts, 0 wins, $0. Dam of 12 foals, 8 rnrs, 2 wnrs, including **ARCTIC TERN** ($244,097, Fr-I). Granddam of **SANGRIA, Current Winner, Meadow Mist**. Died 1991.

1966: Ramadan, gr c, by Native Dancer. Raced 3 yrs, 26 sts, 1 win, $4,306. Sire of 100 foals, AEI 0.95. Died 1979.

1969: Barren.

At three, Tosmah defeated colts in the Arlington Classic, beat older fillies in the Beldame, and won seven other stakes to reign as champion three-year-old filly. She continued as a major winner at four and five, and again defeated colts, this time in the John B. Campbell Handicap. Tosmah won twenty-three of thirty-nine starts, earned $612,588, and was elected to the National Museum of Racing's Hall of Fame. Alas, she was a problem mare and got but one minor stakes winner among her four foals.

Cosmah and her 1962 Ribot foal were purchased from Mori by John R. Gaines, who was establishing Gainesway Farm as one of the leading Thoroughbred nurseries in Kentucky and the world. Gaines soon began selling high-priced sale yearlings out of Cosmah, although he then entered into a deal with John Olin for a partnership sale arrangement that took some of them out of the public bidding sphere.

Cosmah's 1962 Ribot colt, Maribeau, won the Fountain of Youth Stakes at three. Cosmah's next foal, the 1963 Swaps colt named Fathers Image, teased the Turf world into expecting great things. While those did not materialize, he did eventually become a decent stakes winner after placing at two in the Arlington-Washington Futurity and Pimlico Futurity.

In 1966, Cosmah foaled another Ribot foal, a filly who was to be named Queen Sucree. She was a modest winner, but produced Cannonade, who won the 100th Kentucky Derby for Olin in 1974. Cannonade was sired by Bold Bidder, who had been champion older horse of 1966, racing for Gaines, Olin, and John W. Hanes. Both Bold Bidder and Cannonade were trained by Woody Stephens.

Queen Sucree, who lived into her 30s, produced three other stakes winners: Circle Home, Wassl Touch, and Del Sarto. Also, her Gallant Man filly Kennelot helped launch the successful breeding and racing operation of Henryk de Kwiatkowski, for whom she foaled the Kentucky Derby and Belmont runner-up Stephan's Odyssey.

Other produce of Cosmah's female descendants include the dual turf female champion Flawlessly and the champion French miler L'Emigrant.

Cosmah's 1969 colt, by the dominant two-year-old champion and classic sire Hail to Reason, has proven one of the most resilient of modern Thoroughbreds. His pedigree placed his yearling price at $100,000, when he was purchased from breeder Gaines at the 1970 Keeneland July sale by the predominant yearling buyer of the time, Charles W. Engelhard.

Trained by MacKenzie Miller, Halo emerged as a stakes winner in the one and a half-mile Lawrence Realization at three, after which Hollywood pro-

ducer Irving Allen bought him for $600,000 from Engelhard's widow. Sent to Allen's Derisley Wood Stud in England, Halo soon showed himself to be a cribber, a circumstance the English horsemen of the time tut-tutted over far more than their American cousins. The deal was off.

Returned to racing, Halo proved he could get more than a fence plank between his teeth. Taking the bit, too, he won one of the most important grass races in the United States, the United Nations Handicap, by which time he had been purchased by E. P. Taylor. Sent to the Maryland division of Taylor's Windfields Farm, Halo soon established himself as a major sire. He eventually was moved to Stone Farm in Kentucky.

Halo twice led the American sire lists and got Kentucky Derby winners Sunday Silence (Horse of the Year) and Sunny's Halo, as well as Goodbye Halo, Glorious Song, Devil's Bag, and others.

More From Almahmoud

Although all the foregoing glories from Almahmoud's first foal, Cosmah, had not unfurled by the late 1950s, the mare's status was clearly on the rise by the time her yearling filly appeared in the Saratoga sale ring of 1958. This was Natalma, a 1957 filly by the great, once-beaten Native Dancer. Between Cosmah and Natalma, Almahmoud had lost twins, was barren once, and foaled a moderate winner with a noble name, Armistice, by Citation.

Natalma, bred by Danny Van Clief and Mrs. Augustus, attracted the notice of Windfields Farm owner E. P. Taylor and one of his trainers, Horatio Luro. This was, of course, more than a decade before Taylor bought Halo.

The word "reserve" is indigenous to the auction market, but, as Danny Van Clief recalled for *The Blood-Horse* in 1983, it was "preserves" that figured into the selling of the Native Dancer—Almahmoud filly.

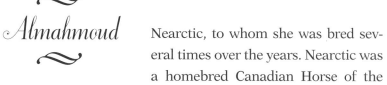

Almahmoud

"We used to take a house with my aunt every year at Saratoga," he explained. "Eddie Taylor and Horatio Luro came to breakfast one morning when they had been looking at Natalma, and we had these tomato preserves that our cook, Rosa Page, had made. They both gorged themselves on tomato preserves and hot bread, and I always attributed the sale of Natalma to that breakfast — I'm sure that was why they came back and looked at her one more time."

Whatever his motivation, Taylor paid $35,000 for the filly. At two, she beat the high-class Irish Jay to the wire in the Spinaway at Saratoga, but was disqualified to third. The following year, Luro was preparing her for the Kentucky Oaks when she suffered a chip in a knee. Natalma was retired with three wins in seven races and earnings of $16,015.

Repeatedly over the half-century or so that E. P. Taylor pursued the breeding and racing game, the saga of Windfields Farm was of families being gradually raised in stature from the minor league status Ontario racing once occupied to more exalted realms. Mares by stallions such as Chop Chop and Menetrier might be turning out minor stakes winners or being bred to regional stallions (in the international picture) in one generation, then be adorning pedigrees of high-priced yearlings and major winners some years later. Queen's Statute, for example, foaled her first stakes winner to the cover of Epic, whose King's Plate in 1949 was worth $11,060. Her foals of a decade later were by Northern Dancer and included the dam of Awaasif, she the dam of Epsom Oaks winner Snow Bride, in turn the dam of unbeaten Epsom Derby-Prix de l'Arc de Triomphe winner Lammtarra.

The fields of Windfields of Oshawa, Ontario, were fertile, indeed. On occasion, however, especially from the 1950s on, Taylor chose to buy at or near the top. Natalma was an example, and so was

Nearctic, to whom she was bred several times over the years. Nearctic was a homebred Canadian Horse of the Year for Taylor, but his dam, Lady Angela, by the great Hyperion, had topped the Newmarket December sale when George Blackwell bought her for Windfields in 1952. Moreover, Nearctic was the result of a cover of Lady Angela by Nearco, who reigned supreme in Europe as the sire of Nasrullah and other top horses.

Taylor in those days annually conducted a gentlemanly combination cocktail party and yearling sale at Windfields. The scheme was that every horse had a set, announced price, and once prospective buyers had milled around and agreed to meet the prices of half the candidates, the sale was closed. Taylor was happy to keep what was left to race himself. In 1962, the higher prices included $25,000 for the Nearctic—Natalma yearling, but he was a little thing, blocky and powerful, while hardly the beau ideal for the owner looking for a classic Thoroughbred with the potential to stay.

So, on that summer day, Taylor's guests got a few drinks and a look at the colt who would give his name to an era. The name was Northern Dancer, and the little colt proved swift and game enough to win the Kentucky Derby for Windfields in a record 2:00 in 1964, as well as the Preakness and Queen's Plate. He was Canada's Horse of the Year as well as North America's champion three-year-old. He won fourteen races in eighteen starts and earned $580,647.

At stud, first at Windfields in Canada and then at Taylor's Maryland division, Northern Dancer had profound influence. The frequent availability of his yearlings at Keeneland vaulted the summer sale there to a singular place atop the international bloodstock market, while his early crops also converted the Canadian Thoroughbred Horse Society yearling sale at Woodbine from minor league to world class. He got three Epsom Derby winners: The

Minstrel, Secreto, and Nijinsky II, England's only Triple Crown winner of the last six decades. Moreover, Nijinsky II followed suit in siring classic winners such as Ferdinand, Golden Fleece, Caerleon, Green Dancer, Shahrastani, and Lammtarra.

Other sons of Northern Dancer included Lyphard, Storm Bird, Danzig, El Gran Senor, Vice Regent, Nureyev, and Sadler's Wells. Northern Dancer led the American sire list in 1971 and the broodmare sire list twenty years later, and he was leading sire four times in England. His total of 146 stakes winners for a time was the all-time record, until passed by Mr. Prospector's total.

As might be expected, Natalma did not produce the likes of Northern Dancer again, but she foaled three other stakes winners among a total of ten winners from fourteen foals. They were Native Victor (by Victoria Park), Born a Lady (by Tentam), and Regal Dancer (by Grey Monarch). Natalma's four stakes-placed runners included Northern Dancer's full sister Arctic Dancer, who to the cover of Buckpasser produced La Prevoyante. Unbeaten in twelve races at two in 1972, La Prevoyante was Canada's Horse of the Year as well as Eclipse Award winner among two-year-old fillies in the United States.

Spring Adieu, Natalma's 1974 filly by Buckpasser, is the second dam of the inbred international sire Danehill, by Danzig. Raise the Standard, Natalma's 1978 Hoist the Flag filly, was unraced, but her own Halo filly, Coup de Folie, was a group winner in France and followed the family legend of multiple production; Coup de Folie is the dam of French juvenile champions Machiavellian and Coup de Genie, plus two additional group winners. Moreover, Raise the Standard is the dam of Bonita Francita, whose three stakes winners

include European-raced Orpen (by Lure), and American-raced Jules (by Forty Niner).

The Last Almahmouds

In 1958, the year after she foaled Natalma, Almahmoud foaled the non-winner Retinoscope, by the indifferent stallion Helioscope. Then came the modest stakes winner Folk Dancer, a Native Dancer colt who was gelded — an unlikely occurrence had the tea leaves been readable. Next came Nash, a gelding by Nashua and eventual winner of eleven races, then Bubbling Beauty, who was an unplaced Hasty Road filly. Bubbling Beauty managed to add yet more luster to the family as the dam of the French group I winner Arctic Tern (by Sea-Bird II), sire of Bering. Bubbling Beauty also is the third dam of the Japanese $2-million-plus earner Eishin Guymon, by Seattle Dancer.

Almahmoud, who had become sole property of Mrs. Augustus, had no more live foals until 1966. She was barren to, in succession, Hill Prince, Bald Eagle, Sir Gaylord, and Tom Fool. In 1966, she had her last foal, the winner Ramadan, a Native Dancer colt.

James Radney, Mrs. Augustus' farm manager, said some years later that the mare had been clean and breeding sound all that time and he could not attribute her sparse production in later years to any particular problem. She had been arthritic for some time, a condition relieved by Butazolidin, and for some years she had her stall bedded with dry cane stalks instead of straw because of allergies, although she was able to graze without problems.

Almahmoud developed navicular disease and was euthanized in 1971 at the age of twenty-four. She had proven again that the unique vein of Thoroughbred blood known as the "Whitney mares" remained potent, and prolific. ❖

Aspidistra

To a young W. L. McKnight growing up in Wheat, South Dakota, horses represented the struggle of daily existence on the family farm. Getting away from horses, and the farm, to seek his fortune was more likely a boyhood fantasy than was breeding and racing one of the most sensational Thoroughbreds in American history. Nevertheless, McKnight did both.

McKnight saved enough of his earnings from a job threshing grain to head for the big city — Duluth, Minnesota passing for such in his frame of reference. He attended business school there, then joined the struggling Minnesota Mining and Manufacturing Company. He did not found 3-M, as it later became known, but he took it to great heights, eventually rising to president and board chairman. One of the 3-M scientists/inventors developed a sticky product which McKnight figured out could be marketed with a bit of flourish from his personal heritage. Hence, Scotch Tape.

McKnight's status at Minnesota Mining and Manufacturing, added to his own personal investments, saw him listed in *Fortune* magazine's survey of wealthy Americans by 1957. That year also coincided with McKnight's 70th birthday. A group of employees scratched their heads over what to give the boss, and someone came up with the idea of a racehorse. Horses had long since passed from the role of albatross in McKnight's mind. McKnight's association with horses, and horse racing, was later recalled by Everett Clay, who for many years had viewed the world from his perch as head of publicity for Hialeah Race Course. When McKnight and his pal Bill Webster got to going to the races to make $2 bets — if there is a Scotsman's closeness-with-a-dollar quip in McKnight's tale, here is the place — Clay suggested they would have a fine time getting in to the races "free" if they had owners' licenses. By 1958, McKnight had made heavy investments in racing, purchasing the fine imported stakes winners Munch and Meeting.

The collective suck-up by his staff in 1957, however, led to a far more successful investment than a battalion of bloodstock agents or pedigree gurus likely would have contrived. The trainer John Sceusa was given the charge of finding a horse for the boss. As the tale has been handed down, he had $6,500 to spend, and did he ever spend it well. Sceusa landed for McKnight the three-year-old filly Aspidistra, and in so doing he unwittingly procured the future dam of Horse of the Year Dr. Fager and sprint champion Ta Wee, and ancestress of such as Holy Bull and Unbridled.

Aspidistra herself was indirectly the product of a bit of judgment by the sage Kentucky horseman J. Howard Rouse. As manager of the Kentucky division of King Ranch, Rouse took note of the impressive form of the young filly Tilly Rose at Keeneland in 1950. He pressed his feeling upon his boss, Robert J. Kleberg Jr., the head of King Ranch and himself an astute geneticist in cattle and horses. For the then rather kingly sum of $25,000, King Ranch purchased Tilly Rose from Warren Douglas. At three the following spring, Tilly Rose won a division of the Prioress Stakes, and at four she added another stakes triumph, in a division of the Colonial Handicap. She was retired with seven wins in twenty-three starts and earnings of $45,017.

Tilly Rose's was a pedigree of achievement without stardom. She was a daughter of Tilly Kate, a Draymont filly who won the Hotel Gibson Handicap at three in 1938. Tilly Kate in turn was out of Teak, a Tea Caddy filly who won the $2,000 Rex Handicap in 1926. A theme of recurring persistence pervaded this female family, as if the feminine genes were overachieving: Teak was one of only two stakes winners sired by Tea Caddy; Teak's daughter Tilly Kate was the only stakes winner sired by Draymont; Tilly Kate's daughter Tilly Rose was one of two stakes winners sired by Bull Brier.

Tilly Rose foaled Aspidistra in 1954 and died without producing any other foals. Rouse had been correct in his assessment of Tilly Rose, but that had produced little on behalf of his boss, King Ranch. Tilly Rose's filly was sired by Better Self, a Bimelech stallion who had won ten stakes races, including the Saratoga Special, Yankee, Carter, Gallant Fox, and Saratoga Handicaps. Better Self sired fourteen stakes winners, including the important Phipps-family filly and mare Lady Be Good.

Aspidistra did not race at two. By the time of her debut at three at Fair Grounds in New Orleans, in the winter of 1957, she had been acquired to race in the name of E. H. Lane. On Jan. 30, she finished ninth in an allowance event. Clarence Picou rode her to her first victory in her second start, and the busy filly won again in her seventh race, on March 6. By September, she was racing in the name of Monte Preston, who

earlier had been listed as her trainer, but not her owner. She had been moved up to the feature of a weekday at Hawthorne, where she finished sixth of eight behind the stakes winner Nirgal Lad.

It was at that point that 3-M employees had secured the services of trainer John Sceusa to find a birthday present for Mr. McKnight. The deal was struck, and Aspidistra next appeared in the name of McKnight's fledgling Tartan Stable. She was entered for a $6,500 claiming tag, perhaps, or perhaps not, signifying that McKnight had no qualms about passing on a birthday gift. She made two more starts, finishing her one-year career on Oct. 16, 1957, at Sportsman's Park, finishing third and again available to be claimed for $6,500. She had won two of fourteen races and earned $5,115.

The next year, Munch and Meeting provided McKnight with his first stakes wins as an owner, and the Minnesota industrialist was soon busy establishing Tartan Farms in the burgeoning breeding industry around Ocala, Florida. He hired Gallant Man's trainer, John Nerud, who not only trained the Tartan horses but also was instrumental in developing the farm and bloodstock. The energetic young Irishman John Hartigan came aboard to carve a farm out of the added acreage adjacent to that purchased originally from Bonnie Heath, and Tartan began a steep, confident, climb to the top. Once enveloped by the Thoroughbred industry, McKnight went the whole route. In addition to his farm, he became the chief owner of Calder Race Course, which extended the South Florida racing season through the year and pioneered racing versions of AstroTurf as a surface over which Calder horses raced for more than two decades.

The Tumbles of Destiny

Any contemporary observer of the career and early death of Tilly Rose, along with the obscure racing experience of her daughter, Aspidistra, presumably would have regarded it all as a meander-

		Black Toney, 1911	Peter Pan / Belgravia
	Bimelech, 1937		
		La Troienne, 1926	**Teddy** / Helene de Troie
BETTER SELF, b, 1945			
		War Admiral, 1934	Man o' War / Brushup
	Bee Mac, 1941		
		Baba Kenny, 1928	Black Servant / Betty Beall
ASPIDISTRA, b m, March 25, 1954			
		Bull Dog, 1927	**Teddy** / Plucky Liege
	Bull Brier, 1938		
		Rose Eternal, 1925	Eternal / Rose of Roses
TILLY ROSE, br, 1948			
		Draymont, 1925	Wildair / Oreen
	Tilly Kate, 1935		
		Teak, 1923	Tea Caddy / Fricassee

Aspidistra, b, 1954-1978. Bred by King Ranch (Ky.). Raced 1 yr, 14 sts, 2 wins, $5,115. Dam of 13 named foals, 11 rnrs, 10 wnrs, 4 sw.

1959: Barren.

1960: Perplexing, b f, by Esmero. Raced 2 yrs, 24 sts, 4 wins, $9,520. Dam of 6 foals, 5 rnrs, 4 wnrs, including **Interest Due** ($24,410), **Loss Wages** ($7,543). Granddam of **Frustrate**. Died 1972.

1961: **A. DECK**, b c, by First Cabin. Raced 7 yrs, 86 sts, 23 wins, $126,185. Won Ponce de Leon S; 3rd Florida Breeders' S.

1962: **CHINATOWNER**, b c, by Needles. Raced 4 yrs, 30 sts, 10 wins, $83,305. Won Canadian Turf H (T); 2nd Edgemere H (T); 3rd Appleton H (T). Died 1968.

1963: Aforethought, dkb/br c, by Intentionally. Raced 3 yrs, 24 sts, 5 wins, $40,645. Sire of 169 foals, AEI 0.67.

1964: **DR. FAGER**, b c, by Rough'n Tumble. Raced 3 yrs, 22 sts, 18 wins, $1,002,642.

Horse of the Year, champion sprinter (twice), turf male, and older male. Won New Hampshire Sweepstakes Classic (NTR, Rkm, 10 furlongs in 1:59.80), Hawthorne Gold Cup H, Arlington Classic S, Californian S, Washington Park H (NWR, AP, 8 furlongs in 1:32.20), Suburban H (ETR, Aqu, 10 furlongs in 1:59.60), United Nations H (T), Rockingham Special S, Vosburgh H (twice; NTR, Aqu, 7 furlongs in 1:20.20), Roseben H, Whitney S, Cowdin S, Withers S, Gotham S, World's Playground S; 2nd Champagne S, Brooklyn H; 3rd Woodward S.

1965: Captivate, dkb/br f, by Intentionally. Raced 2 yrs, 7 sts, 2 wins, $12,097 Dam of 4 foals, 4 rnrs, 3 wnrs. Died 1974.

1966: **TA WEE**, dkb/br f, by Intentionally. Raced 3 yrs, 21 sts, 15 wins, $284,941. Champion sprinter. Won Vosburgh H, Miss Woodford S, Fall Highweight H (twice), Prioress S, Comely S, Hempstead H, Regret H, Correction H, Interborough H (twice), Test S, Jasmine S; 2nd Gravesend H, Distaff H; 3rd Mimosa S. Dam of 5 foals, 5 rnrs, 5 wnrs, including **GREAT ABOVE** ($331,377), **ENTROPY** ($293,999), **TAX HOLIDAY** ($254,938), **TWEAK** ($148,597). Granddam of **CINTULA**. Died 1980.

1967: Slipped.

1968: **Highbinder**, b c, by Rough'n Tumble. Raced 4 yrs, 29 sts, 9 wins, $129,304. 2nd Vosburgh H (gr. II), Withers S, December H; 3rd Saranac S, Toboggan H. Sire of 124 foals, AEI 0.91.

1969: Magic, dkb/br f, by Buckpasser. Unraced. Dam of 10 foals, 10 rnrs, 9 wnrs, including **MAGNIFICENCE** ($149,243), **Belocolus** ($201,952), **Faces Up** ($336,771). Granddam of **TAYASU TSUYOSHI**, **COOLAWIN**, **PENTELICUS**, **Willingness**. Died 1984.

1970: Barren.

1971: Weyand, dkb/br c, by Prince Taj. Raced 2 yrs, 19 sts, 2 wins, $21,760. Sent to NZ 1976. Died 1980.

1972: Barren.

1973: Quit Me Not, dkb/br f, by Bold Reason. Raced 1 yr, 2 sts, 0 wins, $0. Dam of 11 foals, 8 rnrs, 6 wnrs. Granddam of **JUDGE T C**, **MISS PROSPECTOR**.

1974: Pollinize, dkb/br c, by Buckpasser. Unraced. Sire of 214 foals, AEI 0.46.

1976: Barren.

1977: Auraria, dkb/br c, by Minnesota Mac. Raced 2 yrs, 9 sts, 3 wins, $45,320. Sent to Ven 1982.

1978: Barren.

ing sequence of no great import. The racing class of Tilly Rose put her in the upper ranks of her breed, but events thereafter did little to suggest much in the way of lasting fame.

Looking back, however, there might be imagined an almost eerie pattern and pull toward the family's deep entrenchment within a central theme, and the name of that theme is Florida. In addition to McKnight's settling on Florida for his breeding and racing endeavors, there were numerous other, oblique connections to the newly developed industry of the Sunshine State:

(1) Tilly Rose was one of only two stakes winners sired by Bull Brier; the other was Menolene, older half-sister of the first Florida-bred champion, Needles;

(2) When Aspidistra opened a long early lead in the second race she won, the filly she held off by a neck was Rumpled; Aspidistra years later was covered by Rumpled's full brother, Rough'n Tumble, and thus conceived the Florida-bred champion Dr. Fager;

(3) Rough'n Tumble had been sent into Florida with the acquiescence of McKnight's fellow Minnesotans, Mr. and Mrs. Harold Genter, and it was Mrs. Genter who years later purchased Tartan Farms-bred Unbridled, winner of the 1990 Kentucky Derby; Unbridled is inbred to both Aspidistra and Rough'n Tumble.

Aspidistra, a name that refers to plants of the lily family, had her first foal in 1960. Her status at the time was reflected by the obscurity of her mate, the Argentine-bred stallion Esmero, who had not, nor ever did, sire a stakes winner. Aspidistra's first foal, Perplexing, won four of twenty-four races to earn $9,520 and foaled a pair of stakes-placed winners.

Then, in both 1961 and 1962, Aspidistra foaled stakes winners. They were A. Deck, a First Cabin colt who won the 1964 Ponce de Leon Stakes among twenty-three wins from eighty-six starts for earnings of $126,185, and Chinatowner, a Needles colt who won the Canadian Turf Handicap at Gulfstream Park among ten wins from thirty races for earnings of $83,305. In 1963, Aspidistra produced the first of her foals by the high-class runner Intentionally, whom Tartan had acquired. Named Aforethought, the colt won five of twenty-four races and earned $40,645.

These were but teasers for the main course. In 1964, Aspidistra produced a colt by Rough'n Tumble. The stallion was the Genters' former Santa Anita Derby winner, who had begun his stud career in Maryland, then had been moved by Joe O'Farrell to Ocala Stud Farms in Florida (see chapter on Iltis).

The 1964 colt, Dr. Fager, was named for the neurosurgeon who had operated on Nerud after a grave head injury. The colt showed flash and fire early, and while he proved more or less amenable to being controlled by mankind, he was never truly harnessed. Prodigious speed was his calling card, and on occasion his downfall.

At two in 1966, Dr. Fager flashed to victory in the World's Playground and Cowdin Stakes, but got caught up in a wasteful speed duel and went under to Successor in the Champagne. Successor was voted the champion two-year-old. Nerud discerned that getting one and a quarter miles out of the headstrong Dr. Fager was not necessarily the best goal for early spring, and he bypassed the Kentucky Derby even after Dr. Fager defeated the rising star Damascus in the one-mile Gotham. Dancing around the Triple Crown totally, Dr. Fager raced away from Tumiga in the Withers, then was sent travelling to score in the Arlington Classic, New Hampshire Sweepstakes, and Vosburgh Handicap.

By autumn, Damascus had assumed the role of pro-tem champion three-year-old, with wins in the Preakness and Belmont and runaway triumphs in the American Derby and Travers. When Damascus and Dr. Fager at last met again, they were joined by the previous season's Horse of the Year, the great

Buckpasser. The race was the Woodward Stakes, and the meeting of three horses of such quality recalled the Bold Ruler-Gallant Man-Round Table Trenton Handicap of a decade earlier.

Dr. Fager was not mature enough to take the two-ply strategy of pacemakers which Damascus and Buckpasser's trainers threw at him. In the final furlongs of the one and a quarter-mile Aqueduct event, he was no match for Damascus, who drew off to an astonishing ten-length victory over a less-than-perfect Buckpasser.

At four, Dr. Fager strode to the top of his game. He still could be brought down by Frank Whiteley's strategy of sending Hedevar rushing out to taunt him into wasteful early speed, while Damascus sat back waiting to pounce. With Hedevar in the race, Damascus ran down Dr. Fager while getting five pounds to win the Brooklyn Handicap, but without Hedevar around, Dr. Fager had defeated the other colt handily in the Suburban.

Standing even up with his archrival was not what distinguished Dr. Fager's four-year-old season, however. In addition to winning the Suburban, he turned in a series of astounding performances, each underscoring some particular aspect of his arsenal. The sheer speed of Dr. Fager was on display when he carried 134 pounds and raced the mile of the Washington Park Handicap in 1:32 1/5 — a world mark that stood for three decades. The hardiness of the colt was seen to advantage when he crossed the country to make his only start in California a winning one, taking up 130 pounds to win the Californian Stakes early in his campaign.

The audacity of Nerud — born of his confidence in the colt — called upon the versatility of Dr. Fager when he was asked to race on grass for the only time and toted 134 pounds to victory in the one and three-sixteenths-mile United Nations. The colt's reputation was reflected in his 1-20 odds when he

Aspidistra

rolled home in the Whitney, and sheer power was on display in the last start of his life, when he rushed through his second Vosburgh Handicap, this one under 139 pounds for the seven furlongs.

Winner of seven races from eight starts at four, Dr. Fager swept the boards: Horse of the Year, champion older male, champion grass horse, champion sprinter. In three seasons, the son of a gift horse had won eighteen of twenty-two races and earned $1,002,642. He went to stud at Tartan, and, despite dying young, at twelve, begot thirty-five stakes winners. He was the leading sire in U.S. earnings in 1977.

A Little Sister to be Proud Of

After foaling Dr. Fager, Aspidistra went back to Intentionally for the next two years. In 1965, she foaled the filly Captivate, who won a pair of races from seven tries and earned $12,097. Then, in 1966, Aspidistra foaled her fourth stakes winner, and second champion, in Ta Wee. The sire Intentionally had first attracted notice when he upset the previously unbeaten First Landing in the Futurity Stakes of 1958. For the next three years, he continued as a useful stakes winner and then, acquired as a sire prospect by Tartan, Intentionally ended his racing days with a flourish by winning the Palm Beach and Seminole Handicaps at Hialeah. Ironically, he was the sire of the Genters' Tartan-foaled In Reality, who took a backseat to Dr. Fager.

Ta Wee came to hand for trainer Scotty Schulhofer, who was training the Tartan horses after Nerud left the day-to-day backstretch duties in his management role with the McKnight enterprise. Dr. Fager had won the Vosburgh in 1967 and 1968, and as a three-year-old of 1969, Ta Wee kept the family string alive, defeating older males in the event in an audacious display of feminism. She gave three pounds of actual weight to the accomplished West Coast runner Rising Market, who dead-heated for second with Plucky Lucky. In the 1969 Fall Highweight Handicap, Ta Wee carried 130 pounds to defeat King Emperor (131), and she also numbered the Test Stakes, Miss Woodford, and Interborough Handicap among the eight stakes she won. Ta Wee was champion sprinter of 1969.

At four, Ta Wee carried her prowess to extremes, and Tartan never flinched. She won five of seven races from May through October, culminating with two final victories over males — and the racing secretary at Aqueduct. To win the Fall Highweight, she took up 140 pounds and outran Towzie Tyke, giving him nineteen pounds. In the Fall Highweight, as its name implies, runners are supposed to carry exceptional weights; that is what gives the race its distinction. Next, however, came the six-furlong Interborough, a "normal" handicap, but the Fall Highweight mentality lingered and Ta Wee was assigned 142 pounds. McKnight and Schulhofer may have blinked, but they didn't buckle: Ta Wee accepted the assignment and won at 3-5, giving runner-up Hasty Hitter twenty-nine pounds.

Ta Wee had won five of seven at four and was champion sprinter a second year. She was retired with fifteen wins in twenty-one starts and earnings of $284,941. She and Dr. Fager were both later elected to the National Museum of Racing's Hall of Fame in Saratoga Springs, New York.

To a similar extent as was true of Dr. Fager, Ta Wee's excellence was transferable from the racetrack to the foaling barn. She had six foals, of which five were winners and four were stakes winners. To the cover of the sentimentally named Tartan stakes winner Minnesota Mac, Ta Wee produced the graded sprint stakes winner Great Above as her first foal. Great Above later became renowned further as the sire of 1994 Horse of the Year Holy Bull and broodmare sire of two-time sprint champion Housebuster.

Ta Wee also foaled Entropy, a 1980 What a Pleasure colt who won the Sporting Plate and Coaltown Stakes, and Paumonok Handicap; Tax Holiday, a 1977 What a Pleasure filly who won the Petrify and Treetop Stakes; and Tweak, a 1976 Secretariat filly who won the Fair Lawn Stakes.

Unbridled Tapestry

To return to the log of Aspidistra, she slipped a foal in 1967, then in 1968 foaled a full brother to Dr. Fager, by Rough'n Tumble. Named Highbinder, this colt flashed impressive speed and class and, while he never won a stakes, he placed in five, including the family favorite, Vosburgh, and the Withers. Highbinder won nine races from twenty-nine starts and earned $129,304.

In 1969, nine years after she had foaled an Esmero filly, Aspidistra produced a filly by the four-time champion Buckpasser. Named Magic, the filly was unraced, but she lengthened, and broadened, the influence of the family. Magic had nine winners among ten foals. Only one was a stakes winner, Magnificence, but several of Magic's daughters became successful producers. Magic's daughter Magaro foaled the 1995 Japanese Derby winner Tayasu Tsuyoshi as well as the consistent graded grass stakes filly Coolawin.

Aspidistra's daughter Magic also foaled Charedi, by In Reality, and therein developed another extraordinary lyric of the ongoing melody. Charedi foaled Pentelicus, a Fappiano colt who won stakes and has become an important Florida sire. Charedi also produced Gana Facil, who emerged as the dam of two grade I winners, including Kentucky Derby winner Unbridled.

Unbridled was bred by Tartan Farms and foaled in 1987, nine years after McKnight's death had put management of the farm in the hands of his daughter and son-in-law, Mr. and Mrs. James Binger. It also was in 1987 that the Bingers decided to disperse their breeding stock, and Unbridled was purchased at Fasig-Tipton Kentucky as a weanling by Frances Genter Stable.

The interlocking loops of this tapestry were complicated, but cozy:

(1) Unbridled's sire was Fappiano, a brilliant racehorse who was bred and raced by Nerud on his own account; Fappiano's second dam, Grand Splendor, was another remarkable Florida broodmare bred by Tartan Farms.

(2) Unbridled's dam, the Le Fabuleux mare Gana Facil, was out of a daughter of In Reality, and In Reality had been bred and raced by Frances Genter Stable. It was the Genter horse Rough'n Tumble who was so instrumental in the rapid progress of Florida breeding and who was the broodmare grandsire of the aforementioned Fappiano.

(3) Frances Genter Stable purchased Unbridled for $70,000 as a weanling in the Tartan dispersal and raced him to victory in the 1990 Kentucky Derby and Breeders' Cup Classic, collecting an Eclipse Award for the three-year-old champion. Unbridled became an immediately successful addition to this yarn, siring Kentucky Derby winner Grindstone in his first crop, and his other early runners include champion filly Banshee Breeze, plus grade I stakes winners Unbridled's Song and Manistique.

Adding more glamour to the Gana Facil strand of the story, the year after she foaled Unbridled, she produced another Fappiano colt, Cahill Road, who broke down as he won the grade I Wood Memorial.

Perhaps the most ironic episode in the family history since Aspidistra defeated Rough'n Tumble's sister occurred in the 1996 Kentucky Derby: Grindstone, son of Tartan-bred Unbridled (who was inbred to Aspidistra) got up to win by the barest of margins from Cavonnier, whose dam, Direwarning, was out of Magic's daughter Mazurka, and thus traced in tail female to Aspidistra as well.

In 1970, Aspidistra was barren, then in 1971 she foaled a colt by Prince Taj. (Rough'n Tumble had died in 1968.) The Prince Taj colt, Weyand, won once in nineteen races to earn $21,760, and was sent to stud in New Zealand. Barren again in 1972, Aspidistra foaled the Bold Reason filly Quit Me Not in 1973. Quit Me Not was unplaced, but was a consistent producer of winners. In 1974, Aspidistra foaled the unraced Buckpasser colt Pollinize, then missed two years before producing her last foal, a Minnesota Mac colt named Auraria. Winner of three races from nine starts, Auraria earned $45,320 and was sent to stand in Venezuela.

Aspidistra died at twenty-four in 1978. McKnight died the same year, at ninety. ❖

Banquet Bell

Within a dozen years, Banquet Bell became the dam of one dual American classic winner and the second dam of another. Earlier, a daughter had been a champion and, in turn, became so important a producer in her own right that she was named Broodmare of the Year.

Primary beneficiary of this concentration of class was the Darby Dan Farm of the Galbreath family. John W. Galbreath spent a long life exemplifying the best in that genre called The Great American Success Story. Beginning in real estate in his native Columbus, Ohio, Galbreath left a positive mark on the business and architecture of his beloved community and also ventured far afield. He had various aspects to help him name his horses: Roberto was named for Roberto Clemente, the great player for the Pittsburgh Pirates, which Galbreath owned; Bramalea was named for a community in Canada which Galbreath's company developed.

Galbreath also developed a high regard for Thoroughbred racing. He first established Darby Dan Farm, a sprawling operation outside Columbus where his family grew up in a pastoral setting to complement the example of energetic, honest business which was Galbreath's hallmark. Darby Creek ran through the property, and Galbreath's young son was named Dan: Hence Darby Dan Farm.

For some time, Galbreath dealt in bloodstock some levels below the top, although he had a modicum of success. He moved into the big leagues when he acquired a large portion of Col. E. R. Bradley's Idle Hour Stock Farm, which had been renowned as one of the best Thoroughbred operations in Kentucky. Col. Bradley, who won four Kentucky Derbys, died in 1946.

Galbreath also employed Col. Bradley's farm manager, the sage Kentucky horseman Olin Gentry, who thus spent the vast majority of his career nurturing crop after crop of well-bred foals on the same bountiful Bluegrass property. Once he had committed to dealing at the top, Galbreath was adventuresome as well as willing to make major investments. In sport as in business, he recognized few geographic restrictions. After Ribot emerged as the great, unbeaten champion of Europe in the mid-1950s, Galbreath leased him for five years early in the horse's stallion career for $1,350,000. This was more than the total sale of the first million-dollar stallion, Nashua, only five years earlier. In the 1960s, Sea-Bird II emerged with a similar reputation in Europe, and Galbreath leased him, too, for $1,500,000.

At home, Galbreath's major acquisitions included an expensive draft from the broodmare band formerly so productive for the Brookmeade Stable of Isabel Dodge Sloane. Mrs. Sloane's

		Sickle, 1924	Phalaris / Selene
	Unbreakable, 1935		
		Blue Glass, 1917	Prince Palatine / Hour Glass II
POLYNESIAN, br, 1942			
		Polymelian, 1914	Polymelus / Pasquita
	Black Polly, 1936		
		Black Queen, 1930	Pompey / Black Maria
BANQUET BELL, ch m, 1951			
		Bruleur, 1910	Chouberski / Basse Terre
	Pot au Feu, 1921		
		Polly Peachum, 1913	Spearmint / Lindoiya
DINNER HORN, ch, 1937			
		Bull Dog, 1927	Teddy / Plucky Liege
	Tophorn, 1932		
		Leghorn, 1919	Celt / Tuscan Red

BANQUET BELL, ch, 1951-1984. Bred by Ira Drymon (Ky.). Raced 2 yrs, 15 sts, 1 win, $9,472. Won Gulfstream Turf Club Dinner S. Dam of 11 named foals, 8 rnrs, 6 wnrs, 2 sw.

1956: Barren.

1957: Ponder Heart, ch f, by Ponder. Raced 1 yr, 9 sts, 0 wins, $0. Dam of 4 foals, 3 rnrs, 1 wnr.

1958: **PRIMONETTA**, ch f, by Swaps. Raced 3 yrs, 25 sts, 17 wins, $306,690. Champion Older Female. Broodmare of the Year in 1978. Won Alabama S, Delaware Oaks, Spinster S, Molly Pitcher H, Falls City H, Regret H, Miss Woodford S, Prioress S, Marguerite S; 2nd Monmouth Oaks, Spinster S, 3rd Beldame S. Dam of 7 foals, 6 rnrs, 6 wnrs, including **CUM LAUDE LAURIE** ($405,207, gr. I), **PRINCE THOU ART** ($167,902, gr. I), **MAUD MULLER** ($138,383, gr. II), **GRENFALL** ($19,467). Granddam of **DANCE O'MY LIFE**, **High Honors**.

1959: Barren.

1960: **CHATEAUGAY**, ch c, by Swaps. Raced 4 yrs, 24 sts, 11 wins, $360,722. Champion 3yo colt. Won Kentucky Derby, Belmont S, Jerome H, Blue Grass S; 2nd Preakness S, Roseben H; 3rd Dwyer H, Travers S. Sire of 314 foals, AEI 2.47. Sent to Japan 1972.

1961: Banquet Beau, b c, by Gallant Man. Raced 2 yrs, 5 sts, 1 win, $3,360. Sire of 45 foals, AEI 0.89. Died 1970.

1962: Rameses, ch c, by Swaps. Raced 2 yrs, 20 sts, 2 wins, $8,260. Sire of 223 foals, AEI 0.53. Died 1989.

1963: Luiana, ch f, by My Babu. Unraced. Dam of 16 foals, 14 rnrs, 7 wnrs, including **LITTLE CURRENT** ($354,704, champion 3yo colt, gr. I), **PRAYERS'N PROMISES** ($188,924, gr. I), **WATER DANCE** ($112,826). Granddam of **ANJIZ**, **NABEEL DANCER**, **TURKISH TRYST**, **ALMAZYOON**, **Sutter's Prospect**, **Veritas**. Died 1987.

1964: Barren.

1965: Peace Prize, ch c, by Swaps. Raced 1 yr, 3 sts, 0 wins, $0. Sire of 90 foals, AEI 0.39.

1966: Banquet Circuit, ch c, by Swaps. Raced 2 yrs, 6 sts, 2 wins, $11,125. Sire of 194 foals, AEI 0.78. Died 1994.

1967: Grand Heritage, ch c, by Swaps. Raced 2 yrs, 13 sts, 1 win, $6,725. Sire of 76 foals, AEI 0.35.

1968: Barren.

1969: Pickaway, ch c, by Bold Ruler. Unraced. Sire of 120 foals, AEI 0.58.

1970: Barren.

1971: Jawn, ch f, by Graustark. Unraced. Dam of 7 foals, 5 rnrs, 3 wnrs. Granddam of **PICHY NANY**, **Silver Jauna**.

1972: Barren.

1973: Barren.

1974: Not bred.

1975: Not bred.

1976: Not bred.

champion Sword Dancer also stood at Darby Dan, as did the major winner Summer Tan, who had raced for the second Mrs. Galbreath prior to the couple's marriage. Galbreath never divested himself of the Ohio division of Darby Dan, and even dealing at the level he had achieved in Kentucky, he retained connections to his Columbus background. One of the stallions at the Kentucky Darby Dan was the sprint champion Decathlon, who raced for Robert J. Dienst. Galbreath and the Diensts had been associated years before, and one of Darby Dan's early stakes winners was named Darby Dienst.

Another key, and expensive, acquisition was the great horse Swaps. Bred in California, by the savvy cowboy Rex Ellsworth, Swaps had carried his breeder's colors to an upset victory over Nashua in the 1955 Kentucky Derby. At four in 1956, Swaps swept through an incredible series of major races, shredding world records along the way with an aplomb that bordered on nonchalance. Ellsworth was a successful rancher, but he was not in a position to turn down offers involving six zeroes (so long as there was at least one other figure to the left). Galbreath came calling. The owner of Darby Dan soon bought a half-interest in Swaps for a flat $1,000,000.

That autumn, Swaps suffered a fractured cannon bone, and his career suddenly was over. The Horse of the Year's life hung in the balance for a time, and his survival was aided by use of a stall sling provided by Sunny Jim Fitzsimmons, trainer of Swaps' great rival Nashua.

Long before inter-hemisphere shuttling of stallions became a trend, Ellsworth had the unusual idea for the time of standing Swaps in alternate years in California and Darby Dan. Mrs. Galbreath, however, paid Ellsworth another $1,000,000 for the other half of Swaps, and the horse was stationed at Darby Dan alone during his glory years. Swaps later was syndicated and moved to Spendthrift Farm, where, coincidentally, Nashua also stood.

The Bargain Mare

Among the early positive results from such major outlays were the foals of Banquet Bell, who herself had represented a more modest, but not inconsiderable, investment. Banquet Bell was bred in Kentucky by Ira Drymon and was of sufficient appeal to be included in the summer yearling sale at Keeneland in 1952. She was by Polynesian, the 1945 Preakness Stakes winner. Polynesian's most extraordinary contribution to the breed was siring the great racehorse and international stallion Native Dancer. The gray Native Dancer already had turned heads in winning his first two starts as a two-year-old by the time of the Keeneland sale that summer.

Gentry was not working for Galbreath yet, but was operating on another portion of the old Idle Hour property, running Danada Farm for Daniel Rice. He was at liberty to do some consulting work for others, and he liked Polynesian blood, especially that of the stallion's third dam. This was the Kentucky Oaks winner Black Maria, who, by Gentry's retelling, had been lost to Col. Bradley because of the unauthorized sale of her dam, Bird Loose.

Galbreath bought the Polynesian filly for $9,000, which was slightly more than twice the national average for all yearlings sold at auction that year. The purchase was certainly dwarfed by Darby Dan's later acquisition of the second-highest-priced yearling of the year, a $46,000 Roman filly at Saratoga.

The $9,000 Polynesian filly, who was to be named Banquet Bell, was out of Dinner Horn, whose sire, Pot au Feu, was a moderately successful sire in Europe and the United States. Dinner Horn was tough enough to make seventy-one starts in five seasons, and she won twenty races. Her own dam, Tophorn, was a winner by leading sire Bull Dog and also had foaled 1945 Selima Stakes winner Athene.

Banquet Bell was the only one of Dinner Horn's four winners to become a stakes winner. She achieved that mark at the outset of her career, in a division of the Gulfstream Park Turf Club Dinner Stakes in 1953.

That success did not presage others, and after two seasons she had a career record of fifteen starts, that single victory, and earnings of $9,472. In fact, on two occasions at three she was available to any gimlet-eyed buyer who might have noted her running twice for a price, $6,000 once and $4,000 once.

Unclaimed, Banquet Bell quickly staked a claim of her own, that as a distinguished broodmare. She did not produce her first foal until 1957, when she foaled a filly by Kentucky Derby winner Ponder. This filly was unplaced. Banquet Bell went next to the court of the newly acquired Swaps, and the resulting foal, a lengthy, lovely chestnut filly named Primonetta, became the sire's first stakes winner late in 1960 when she won all four of her races, capped by the one and one-sixteenth-mile Marguerite Stakes at Pimlico.

That hint of big things to come for Darby Dan and trainer James Conway blossomed the next year. Primonetta won a pair of the most important races for three-year-old fillies, the Alabama Stakes and Delaware Oaks. She had remained undefeated until the Monmouth Oaks in midsummer, when she was edged by the good filly My Portrait. In a tough filly division, Primonetta defeated Bowl of Flowers in the Alabama, but lost to that filly in the Spinster. Bowl of Flowers also had won the Coaching Club Oaks, and the Spinster clinched her a championship.

The following year, however, Primonetta reigned as champion older filly or mare. She closed that campaign with a win in Keeneland's Spinster, over Royal Patrice and Firm Policy, and Churchill Downs' Falls City Handicap. Earlier, she had taken the Molly Pitcher and Regret at Monmouth Park. She was retired to Darby Dan with a career record of seventeen wins in twenty-five races and earnings of $306,690.

Primonetta herself became a Broodmare of the Year and produced four stakes winners. Her 1974 Hail to Reason filly Cum Laude Laurie, continued

Banquet Bell

the tradition of winning top races, including her own edition of the Spinster as well as the Beldame, Ruffian, and Delaware Oaks.

Primonetta's 1972 Hail to Reason colt, Prince Thou Art, was another star briefly, but a frustrating one. In the winter of 1975, he took on the aura of a first-rate Kentucky Derby contender when he caught the previously unbeaten Foolish Pleasure to win the Florida Derby. Prince Thou Art never could duplicate that effort, although his stretch runs continued to tantalize as he was placed in the Blue Grass and Travers.

Primonetta's two other stakes winners, Maud Muller and Irish-raced Grenfall, were both by Graustark. That handsome sire shown brightly in the history of Darby Dan, and his blood continues as a valuable resource for the farm which is now run by one of John W. Galbreath's grandsons, John Phillips. Graustark was sired by Ribot and was out of Flower Bowl, dam of Primonetta's one-time nemesis Bowl of Flowers. Flower Bowl had been part of the Brookmeade purchase.

It was noted above that Ribot originally had been scheduled to stay in America only for five years. By the time that contract had expired, however, the horse's habits such as rearing and pawing at the top of his stall, or attacking a tree, led to the veterinary conclusion that it was unsafe and unwise to attempt to transport him across the Atlantic. A new deal was struck, and Ribot remained at Darby Dan until his death at twenty in 1972.

Graustark was the most spectacular Darby Dan-bred among Ribot's battalion of important sons and daughters. Although injury ended his career, and unbeaten streak, in the 1966 Blue Grass Stakes, he had wrapped about himself an aura of greatness which carried over into his stud career.

In the Graustark—Primonetta filly named Maud Muller, Darby Dan had another homebred good enough to win in top company, although not quite of championship caliber. Maud Muller won both the Gazelle Handicap and Ashland Stakes and placed in the Mother Goose and Coaching Club American Oaks.

Primonetta proved a mare of remarkable longevity. Eventually, she was pensioned to the Ohio division of Darby Dan, where her birthdays were observed with annual ceremonies. She lived to the age of thirty-five.

The First Classic Winner

In the autumn of 1962, when Primonetta was securing her championship, her full brother, and look alike, Chateaugay, was following a development path similar to her early career. James Conway had to deal with an airway obstruction with Chateaugay, but after a laryngotomy the colt came forward. Chateaugay won two of five as a juvenile and by the following spring was able to interject himself square-ly into the Kentucky Derby picture nine days before the classic by gaining a narrow win over Get Around in the Blue Grass Stakes. Darby Dan, at that time, had never won a classic race, and doing so was a stern task, for the three-year-olds of that spring were a for-midable cast. Galbreath's former partner Ellsworth had the unbeaten favorite in Candy Spots. Cain Hoy Stable's two-year-old champion of the previous year, Never Bend, had lost none of his brilliance, and Greentree Stable's No Robbery (also by Swaps) had won the Wood Memorial and also was undefeated.

Braulio Baeza, contract rider for Darby Dan, rode a classic race in a classic. He was on a horse whose very existence — as was true of Galbreath horses in general — had been contrived with such moments in mind. He rode from behind, but with confidence, and Chateaugay stormed into the lead in the upper stretch and outran Never Bend to win by slightly more than a length. Candy Spots was third.

During the week of the Preakness, Chateaugay drew gasps when he seemed to get away from his exer-cise rider one morning and darted through a workout obviously more demanding than Conway had in mind. In the second jewel of the Triple Crown, he was beaten soundly by the rebounding Candy Spots.

The Belmont Stakes during part of the 1960s was run at the new Aqueduct, because historic Belmont Park had been condemned and was undergoing rebuilding. (Galbreath's construction company executed the Aqueduct project.) Chateaugay ratified his Derby success with a two and a half-length victory over the 1-2 Candy Spots. The Darby Dan colt later added the Jerome Handicap and was the champion three-year-old of 1963. Thus, the bold Darby Dan initiatives had resulted in consecutive championships, and with full siblings. Chateaugay had desultory results in two start-and-stop campaigns thereafter and was retired with eleven wins in twenty-four starts and earnings of $360,722.

Few stallion careers have been as strange as that of Swaps. In his early crops, the 1956 Horse of the Year begot Primonetta, Chateaugay, the champion filly Affectionately, and No Robbery. Representing the Hyperion male line and with the backing of one of the up-and-coming Kentucky farms, he seemed destined for an exemplary career, as evidenced by his siring the first $100,000-plus North American yearling, at Keeneland, and also a record-priced Saratoga filly at $90,000. Then the string of important winners dwindled unmistakably. Chateaugay, perhaps hampered by the growing apprehension about Swaps, was not a successful sire in the aggregate, although he got the good handicap horse True Knight and also sired the dam of Epsom Derby winner Henbit and the second dam of Kentucky Derby winner Grindstone. After several years at stud here, Chateaugay was exported to Japan.

The Family's Next Classics

Banquet Bell got no further stakes winners, but her influence did not end. She foaled six winners among

Banquet Bell

eleven foals, but one of her most important was an unraced filly by My Babu foaled in 1963. She was named Luiana, and she produced sixteen foals, of which fourteen raced and seven won. Most important of the foals out of Luiana was Little Current, her 1971 colt by the imported French superstar Sea-Bird II.

Little Current fit the Darby Dan mold. Lean, racy, late developing, he came along at three, eleven years after Chateaugay and seven years after Proud Clarion had given Galbreath a second Derby winner. Little Current did not win the Derby, but he scored two wonderfully similar triumphs in taking the Preakness and Belmont Stakes by seven lengths each, and was the champion three-year-old colt of 1974. The Darby Dan horses of that time were trained by Lou Rondinello.

The year marked the 100th anniversary of the Kentucky Derby, and that distinction — plus the fact that it followed by one year the rollicking season of Secretariat and was, by and large, a wide open race — generated the largest crowd (163,000-plus) and largest field (twenty-three) in the race's history. A classically bred stayer whose trump card was stamina coming from behind had every chance to be impeded by rush-hour traffic in such a circumstance, and Little Current had his share of problems before closing from seventeenth to finish fifth.

We have always held that what happens in a race is more compelling than what might have happened, and Little Current, after all, was 22-1. Still, there was justification, on late evenings before the flickering fireplace, for John Galbreath and his children, Jodie (Phillips) and Dan, to chew over the concept that, but for Chateaugay's wild work before the Preakness and Little Current's bobbing-and-weaving Derby trip, Darby Dan might have matched Belair Stud and Calumet Farm as breeders-owners of two Triple Crown winners. Banquet Bell thus would have enjoyed unique status as the dam of one and the second dam of another!

Galbreath did not lack for distinction, however. When Roberto won the 1972 Epsom Derby, the master of Darby Dan became the first breeder-owner in history to win that fundamental English race as well as the Kentucky Derby. That uniqueness was not invaded until 1993, five years after Galbreath's death, when Sea Hero won the Kentucky Derby to add his name to Mill Reef's Epsom Derby in the record of Paul Mellon. (This newcomer hardly detracted from the neighborhood.)

After Little Current, Luiana produced the grade I stakes-winning filly Prayers'n Promises, by Foolish Pleasure, and the additional stakes winner Water Dance, by Nijinsky II. Prayers'n Promises in turn foaled Anjiz, a Nureyev colt who won stakes in England and returned to set a sizzling track record of 1:07 4/5 for six furlongs at Keeneland in the 1993 Phoenix Breeders' Cup Handicap.

Another foal of Prayers'n Promises is Nabeel Dancer, a 1985 Northern Dancer colt who was a group winner in France and placed in important races in England and Ireland. Anjiz and Nabeel Dancer added a concentrated expression of speed to a family whose pride of place had always stemmed from the stamina and quality for the classics and other distance races, for which they were bred. ❖

Best in Show

 est in Show's influence has been so prolonged that her offspring have markedly enhanced her status over the seventeen years since she was named Broodmare of the Year. When honored in 1982 by the Kentucky Thoroughbred Owners and Breeders, Best in Show was the dam of four stakes winners, of which her most recent, Blush With Pride, had just won that year's Kentucky Oaks and three other stakes. At the time, Best in Show also was known to be the second dam of El Gran Senor, but the latter as yet was neither a European classic winner nor international sire. Still to be produced from Best in Show's female descendants were Breeders' Cup Mile winner Spinning World, French/English high-weight Xaar, and American grade I winner Yagli.

Within the family history of all horses (or humans for that matter) are millions of untold scenes in the drama of genetics which affect their destiny. Few such dramas are as evident as a circumstance surrounding Colin, the unbeaten hero of the 1908 Belmont Stakes who would become sire of the third dam of Best in Show. Colin was a shy breeder and begot only eighty-one foals from twenty-three crops. Such a record hardly suggests maximum opportunity to be a link in an enduring sire line. As inheritable traits go, a tendency toward infertility is certainly undesirable. Sheer numbers are a part of most of the lasting sire lines, the volume enhancing opportunity for a few individuals

to rise to the top and carry on the lineage. Despite the lack of numbers in the case of Colin, however, the line survived, and flourished. There kept cropping up in each generation one son, or sometimes two, to carry on important success. In recent generations, this small band of intrepid genetic couriers has included Ack Ack, Youth, Broad Brush, and Concern.

As for daughters, Colin's eighty-one foals included Herd Girl, the third dam of Best in Show. A foal of 1917, Herd Girl foaled the 1929 Hourless filly Late Date, who won twenty-one races, including a half-dozen stakes, from 112 races and earned $37,325. Late Date in turn produced the Beldame and Arlington Matron winner War Date and the lesser stakes winner Beau Busher. Stolen Hour, dam of Best in Show, was a full sister to Beau Busher, being by Mr. Busher. Mr. Busher was a full brother to the great filly Busher (War Admiral—Baby League). Stolen Hour won six of thirty-eight races and was stakes-placed, earning $32,220. She became a jewel in the small broodmare band of market breeder Philip Connors, for whom she foaled the Kentucky Jockey Club Stakes winner Journalist and stakes-placed Reckless Driver, in addition to Best in Show.

Best in Show was Connors' 1965 filly from Stolen Hour. She was by Traffic Judge, whom Woody Stephens trained to win the Woodward, Withers, and Ohio Derby, for Clifford Mooers in 1955. After Mooers' death, Traffic Judge raced for

TRAFFIC JUDGE, ch, 1952	Alibhai, 1938	Hyperion, 1930	Gainsborough / Selene
		Teresina, 1920	Tracery / Blue Tit
	Traffic Court, 1938	Discovery, 1931	Display / Ariadne
		Traffic, 1923	Broomstick / Traverse
STOLEN HOUR, ch, 1953	Mr. Busher, 1946	War Admiral, 1934	Man o' War / Brushup
		Baby League, 1935	Bubbling Over / La Troienne
	Late Date, 1929	Hourless, 1914	Negofol / Hour Glass II
		Herd Girl, 1917	Colin / Torpenhow

BEST IN SHOW, ch m, April 29, 1965

BEST IN SHOW, ch, 1965-1990. Bred by Philip Connors (Ky.). Raced 2 yrs, 27 sts, 5 wins, $53,880. Broodmare of the Year in 1982. Won Comely S. Dam of 17 named foals, 12 rnrs, 9 wnrs, 4 sw.

1970: Sex Appeal, ch f, by Buckpasser. Unraced. Dam of 16 foals, 10 rnrs, 7 wnrs, including **EL GRAN SENOR** ($502,819, champion 2 and 3yo colt and miler in Eng, 2yo colt in Ire, Eng-I, Ire-I), **TRY MY BEST** ($83,393, champion 2yo colt and miler in Ire, 2yo colt in Eng, Eng-I), **SOLAR** ($16,249), **Compliance** ($2,007, in Ire). Granddam of **DR JOHNSON, BLU CARILLON, D'ARROS (Ire), NAPOLI, TRY MY SEGNOR, Devonwood, Tandra Gee, Olympic Majesty (Fr), Devilish Ninja**.

1971: Top Thespian, b c, by Pia Star. Raced 6 yrs, 99 sts, 9 wins, $38,214.

1972: **Star of Bagdad (GB)**, b f, by Bagdad. Raced 2 yrs in Eng, 11 sts, 1 win, $4,056. 2nd Princess Margaret S. Dam of 8 foals, 7 rnrs, 2 wnrs. Granddam of **Bridal Toast**.

1973: **MALINOWSKI**, b c, by Sir Ivor. Raced 3 yrs in Eng and Ire, 5 sts, 2 wins, $27,190. Champion 2yo colt in Ire. Won Ladbroke Craven S (Eng-III); 2nd William Hill Dewhurst S (Eng-I). Sire of 313 foals, AEI 1.02.

1974: Preferred Position, ch c, by Buckpasser. Raced 4 yrs, 36 sts, 3 wins, $53,205. Sire of 95 foals, AEI 0.44.

1975: **Minnie Hauk**, b f, by Sir Ivor. Raced 1 yr in Ire, 4 sts, 2 wins, $8,552. 2nd Cornelscourt S, Fasig-Tipton C.T.B.A. Stakes. Dam of 12 foals, 8 rnrs, 8 wnrs, including **CHIEF CONTENDER (Ire)** ($178,172, Fr-I) **AVIANCE (Ire)** ($43,766, Ire-I). Granddam of **CHIMES OF FREEDOM, IMPERFECT CIRCLE** (dam of **SPINNING WORLD**, champion in Fr) , **LIKELY STORY, Piquetnol, Falak**.

1976: Show Lady, b f, by Sir Ivor. Unraced. Dam of 13 foals, 11 rnrs, 8 wnrs, including **GREAT REGENT** ($133,112), **Diamond Syl** ($38,796). Granddam of **HURRICANE SKY, UMATILLA, Best Dancing, Sal's Shuttle**. Died 1992.

1977: **MONROE**, b f, by Sir Ivor. Raced 2 yrs in Eng and Ire, 8 sts, 3 wins, $34,422. Won Ballyogan S (Ire-III); 2nd Gallaghouse Phoenix S (Ire-I), Mulcahy S (Ire-III), Castleknock Sprint S. Dam of 14 foals, 13 rnrs, 11 wnrs, including **XAAR** ($462,359, champion 2yo colt in Eng and Fr, 3yo colt in Eng, Fr, and Ire, Eng-I, Fr-I), **MASTERCLASS** ($248,926), **DIESE** ($109,867), **ILE DE JINSKY** ($134,841), **Esquire** ($45,157, in Eng, Ger, and Ire), **Didicoy** ($80,977, in Eng and Ire). Granddam of **DIDINA (GB), ZANTE (GB), Victorian Style (GB)**.

1978: **GIELGUD**, ch c, by Sir Ivor. Raced 1 yr in Eng, 4 sts, 1 win, $56,635. Won Laurent Perrier Champagne S (Eng-II); 3rd Royal Lodge S (Eng-II). Sire in Japan. Sent to Aust 1981.

1979: **BLUSH WITH PRIDE**, ch f, by Blushing Groom (Fr). Raced 2 yrs, 16 sts, 6 wins, $536,807. Won Kentucky Oaks (gr. I), Santa Susana S (gr. I), Ashland S (gr. II), Golden Harvest H (gr. IIIT); 2nd Spinster S (gr. I), Santa Ysabel S, Turkish Trousers S (T); 3rd Mother Goose S (gr. I). Dam of 10 foals, 7 rnrs, 6 wnrs, including **SMOLENSK** ($227,806, Fr-II), **BETTER THAN HONOUR** ($161,580, gr. II). Sent to Ire 1997. ($650,000 keejul yrlg).

1980: Key Player, b c, by Sir Ivor. Raced 1 yr, 4 sts, 2 wins, $22,000. Sire of 42 foals, AEI 0.86.

1981: Star of the Show, ch f, by Alydar. Raced 1 yr, 1 st, 0 wins, $0. Died 1983.

1982: Gold Cup, ch c, by Alydar. Unraced. Sire of 38 foals, AEI 0.72. Died 1987.

1983: Nijinsky's Best, ch f, by Nijinsky II. Unraced. Dam of 6 foals, 3 rnrs, 2 wnrs, including **YAGLI** ($1,145,071, gr. I). ($2,100,000 keejul yrlg).

1984: Ride Sally Ride, ch f, by Super Concorde. Unraced. Dam of 1 foal, 1 rnr, 1 wnr. Died 1989.

1985: Ch c, by Nijinsky II. Died 1986.

1986: Barren.

1987: Perfect Isn't Easy, ch f, by Saratoga Six. Raced 1 yr, 4 sts, 0 wins, $750. Dam of 3 foals, 3 rnrs, 2 wnrs.

1988: Barren.

1989: Show You Care, ch f, by Peterhof. Raced 2 yrs, 3 sts, 0 wins, $480. Died 1995.

1990: Barren.

Lou Doherty, and won the Metropolitan and Suburban Handicaps in his last two starts at five in 1957. Traffic Judge's best offspring included Delta Judge, Traffic, Traffic Mark, Rest Your Case, and Court Recess. Traffic Judge was by Alibhai—Traffic Court, by Discovery, and was a half-brother to Preakness winner Hasty Road.

Connors consigned Best in Show to the 1966 Keeneland summer sale, where she was purchased by Norman Woolworth for $25,000. Woolworth, who raced her in the name of Clearview Stable, sent the filly to trainer Jack Skirvin, and she made her debut on May 10, 1967. She was seventh in a field of ten, and her progress was slow. The Traffic Judge filly did not place until her fifth race and did not break her maiden until her tenth, when she defeated the former record-priced yearling filly Many Happy Returns ($177,000) going six furlongs at Aqueduct.

After the maiden race victory, Best in Show was unplaced in her next two races before running third at seven furlongs and at a mile. Perhaps reading into this that she would be better as distances got longer, Skirvin entered her in the Gardenia Stakes, one of the juvenile filly division's most important races, going one and one-sixteenth miles. Best in Show went off at 50-1 and finished tenth of eleven. Thus, she had a single victory from fifteen starts at two.

Skirvin's hope that she would be a stakes filly was encouraged by her winter at Hialeah. She won her first two races, then was second to Sweet Tooth (dam of Alydar) in a one-two finish of future Broodmares of the Year. Rested for two months, Best in Show won again at Aqueduct, then was moved back into stakes company. Although sent off at 10-1 because of the strength of the field for Aqueduct's seven-furlong Comely Stakes, Best in Show rallied late and nipped King Ranch's Bold Ruler filly Heartland, with Gardenia winner Hasty Matelda third.

Best in Show then ran into a character neither she nor other three-year-old fillies of 1968 could handle; she finished fourth in the one-mile Acorn as Dark Mirage launched her successful bid to become the first winner of the New York Filly Triple Crown. Skirvin made no move toward the remaining races in the series. In fact, he kept Best in Show out of stakes company until her last race, and she did nothing to enhance the status she had earned in the Comely. The filly failed to win from five allowance races, then was last when attempting one and one-eighth miles against older fillies and mares in the Firenze. Best in Show carried 108 pounds to winner Politely's 131. The filly had won five races from twenty-seven starts and earned $53,880.

Appeal As a Broodmare

After Best in Show's final race, she was purchased by Anne Forsythe, the breeder of her first seven foals. The first of these was the Buckpasser filly Sex Appeal, who was unraced and then foaled seven winners from sixteen foals. Three of Sex Appeal's foals won stakes in Europe, and two were champions.

El Gran Senor, Sex Appeal's 1981 Northern Dancer colt, was champion two-year-old of both England and Ireland in 1983, when he won the Dewhurst Stakes and National Stakes. The following spring, he won the classic Two Thousand Guineas and was just beaten by Secreto in the Epsom Derby. He was ranked the top miler and top three-year-old in England. Moreover, he underlined his stamina by winning the Irish Sweeps Derby over The Curragh's testing one and a half-mile course. El Gran Senor was sent to stud in America, and his first renown was negative, as he indicated restricted fertility and got only fourteen foals in his first crop. Despite that early tremor, as if a distant echo from Colin, El Gran Senor has sired more than forty stakes winners, including Breeders' Cup Sprint winner Lit de Justice, English and Irish Two Thousand Guineas winner Rodrigo de Triano, and Strub winner Helmsman.

Best in Show's first daughter, Sex Appeal, also is the dam of Try My Best, another Northern Dancer colt who also won the Dewhurst and was champion two-year-old in both England and Ireland in 1977. Try My Best was champion miler at three in Ireland. Now at stud in Japan, Try My Best is the sire of more than thirty stakes winners, including Breeders' Cup Mile winner Last Tycoon and Prix de l'Abbaye de Longchamp winner My Best Valentine.

Another foal from Sex Appeal was the Irish stakes-winning Halo filly Solar, herself granddam of major winners on both sides of the Atlantic. Compliance, another Northern Dancer colt from Sex Appeal, placed in stakes and became the sire of the Irish Two Thousand Guineas winner Fourstars Allstar and his full brother Fourstardave, both millionaires.

Best in Show's second foal, born in 1971, was by the good handicap horse Pia Star. Named Top Thespian, he won nine of ninety-nine races and earned $38,214. Next came the 1972 Bagdad filly Star of Bagdad, who was sent to England and placed in the Princess Margaret Stakes. Star of Bagdad won once in eleven starts and earned the equivalent of $4,056.

In 1973, Best in Show produced a colt by the Epsom Derby and Washington, D.C., International winner Sir Ivor. Named Malinowski, the colt brought $92,000 at the Keeneland summer yearling sale. Sent abroad like Star of Bagdad, Malinowski won his debut at The Curragh in Ireland, then was second to Wollow in the Dewhurst Stakes in England. This was enough to earn him top weight on Ireland's two-year-old free handicap for 1975. At three, Malinowski won England's group III Craven Stakes. He won two of five races and earned the equivalent of $27,190.

Best in Show's 1974 colt by Buckpasser was named Preferred Position. He won three of thirty-six races and earned $53,205. Next came another Sir Ivor foal, the 1975 filly Minnie Hauk. Also sent abroad, she placed in a pair of Irish stakes. She won two of four races and earned $8,552. In 1993, Minnie Hauk foaled a colt by the great Irish-based Northern Dancer stallion Sadler's Wells. Named Chief Contender, he won the group I Prix du Cadran. Minnie Hauk also is the dam of Aviance, a Northfields filly who won Ireland's group I Heinz 57 Phoenix Stakes and in turn foaled Chimes of Freedom, an English and Irish group I winner and European highweight three-year-old filly. Chimes of Freedom later foaled North American stakes winner Tomisue's Indy.

This branch of the Best in Show family is very current. Aviance also is the dam of the Riverman filly Imperfect Circle, who was a stakes winner and group I-placed in England. Imperfect Circle is the dam of the brilliant miler Spinning World, a Nureyev colt who capped his career by winning the 1997 Breeders' Cup Mile. Spinning World, great-great-grandson of Best in Show, was the highweight older horse at seven to nine-and-a-half furlongs in France and the top three-year-old in Ireland in the same distance category. His wins abroad included the group I Jacques le Marois and Prix Moulin de Longchamp as well as the Irish Two Thousand Guineas. Spinning World won eight of fourteen races and earned $1,734,477 before entering stud at Ashford Stud in Kentucky. (His distant kinsman El Gran Senor also stands at Ashford.)

Best in Show was returned to Sir Ivor and foaled the filly Show Lady in 1976. Show Lady, who was a $175,000 Keeneland summer sale yearling, was unraced. She foaled Great Regent, winner of Canada's Cup and Saucer Stakes, and became the second dam of group I Australian winners Hurricane Sky and Umatilla.

New Owners, More Stakes Winners

After producing seven foals without missing a year for Mrs. Forsythe, Best in Show was purchased by Darrell and Lindy Brown, owners of Stonereath Farm outside Paris, Kentucky. She was one in a package of four mares the market breeders bought at the time

"Mrs. Forsythe relied on Charlie Kenney (a respected Kentucky horseman from Coldstream and Stoner Creek Studs), and when he died she decided to sell out," Mrs. Brown told *The Blood-Horse* in 1982. "She and Dr. Forsythe, who live in North Carolina, had two top mares — this one and Joans Paris — but I thought their others might be hard to sell. So, over several months, we made an arrangement to buy all their horses."

If taking some lesser luminaries with their first draft pick was a burden, Best in Show lightened it. The first three foals she produced for the Browns all became stakes winners and the best of them raced for the Browns and Mrs. Brown's father.

The first Stonereath bred was another Sir Ivor filly, foaled in 1977. By then the price of Best in Show's yearlings had tripled from earlier days, and the filly brought $300,000 at the Keeneland summer sale. Best in Show was still producing for a pipeline abroad, and this filly, named Monroe, won the group III Ballyogan Stakes and placed in group I company in Ireland. Monroe raced for two years and won three of eight races, earning $34,422.

Monroe has become a major producer in her own right. She is the dam of four stakes winners: Xaar, Masterclass, Ile de Jinsky, and Diese. Xaar, by Zafonic, was the champion two-year-old in both France and England after winning group I races in both countries in 1997. In 1998, he added a country, as topweight in England, France, and Ireland among three-year-olds in the distance category of nine-and-a-half furlongs. Several other stakes horses descend from Monroe.

In 1978, Best in Show foaled another Sir Ivor foal, this one the colt named Gielgud, who brought $235,000 at the Keeneland summer sale. After his

obligatory trip across the Atlantic, Gielgud won the group II Champagne Stakes in England. That was his only win from four races, and he earned $56,635.

Best in Show's 1979 filly represented a new cross for the mare. The filly, named Blush With Pride, was in the first crop by the flashy French-based miler Blushing Groom, soon to prove an extraordinarily gifted and versatile sire of important horses on both sides of the Atlantic. Best in Show's chestnut filly helped him establish that record. At Keeneland in the summer of 1980, the rapidly rising star trainer D. Wayne Lukas bid $650,000 for the filly, acting on behalf of Mrs. Brown's father, Leonard Firestone. At last, Best in Show would have a foal trained to race in America.

Lukas took plenty of time with Blush With Pride, and in the winter and spring of 1982, she ruled briefly as the pro tem leader of the three-year-old filly division. In the interim, the Browns had purchased her privately from Firestone. Blush With Pride won the Santa Susana on the West Coast before Lukas sent her to Kentucky, where she won both the Ashland at Keeneland and Kentucky Oaks at Churchill Downs. All three were grade I events. Blush With Pride was unable to sustain her form long enough to gain championship honors, although she placed in the Mother Goose and Spinster Stakes. She won six of sixteen starts and earned $536,807.

Blush With Pride's first foal, by Nijinsky II, brought $3.2 million as a yearling. He was the moderate winner Dancing Groom. Blush With Pride, however, is the dam of two stakes winners, the 1998 Demoiselle Stakes winner Better Than Honour and the French group II winner Smolensk.

Best in Show was fourteen when Blush With Pride was foaled. The Browns decided to retain an interest in her next several foals, syndicating a portion of their ownership. In 1980, Best in Show foaled Key Player, another Sir Ivor colt. He won two of four races and earned $22,000. Then, in 1981 came Star of the Show, an Alydar filly who was unplaced in her only start and died at two. The bad luck with Alydar continued the next year, as Best in Show's 1982 colt, Gold Cup, by the same sire, never raced.

Best in Show had no further foals by Blush With Pride's sire, Blushing Groom. Brown recalls that her late foaling date set up a sequence in which he was reluctant to use the Blushing Groom share. The mare's mates remained top class, however. In 1983, she foaled Nijinsky's Best. That filly was sired by Nijinsky II and, while she was unraced, she represents one of the up-to-date connections of the mare to current racing and breeding. Nijinsky's Best is the dam of Yagli, a Jade Hunter colt who is a grade I grass stakes winner and was runner-up in the 1998 Breeders' Cup Turf to champion Buck's Boy.

Best in Show's 1984 filly was Ride Sally Ride, a Super Concorde filly who was unraced, and her 1985

Best in Show

foal was a Nijinsky II colt who died early. In 1986, the word barren was affixed to Best in Show's produce record for the first time, following sixteen consecutive years of production. She missed only one year, for at twenty-two in 1987 she foaled the Saratoga Six filly Perfect Isn't Easy. Neither was winning; the filly was unplaced in four starts, earning $750.

Best in Show was barren again in 1988, but at twenty-four had one more foal, by the English/Irish juvenile stakes winner Peterhof. Named Show You Care, the filly was unplaced in three races, earned $480, and died as a young mare. Best in Show was barren for the spring of 1990, but at twenty-five that year got in foal to Rahy. Late that year, however, her condition prompted the decision to euthanize her, and she was buried at Stonereath.

Best in Show thus had had eighteen foals in twenty-one years. Twelve of them raced, nine won, four won stakes, and six of her ten daughters (to live) produced stakes winners. ❖

Blue Delight

T he distaff bloodline represented by Blue Delight broke into the stakes winner column in 1915 and has been producing stakes horses without interruption ever since. As would be expected, any number of links upon a chain spanning most of a century could be singled out to give her name to this enduring success. Blue Delight is chosen here in part because she represented a great leap forward insofar as the class of horse the family produced. She was prolific in her production of class in runners and in future broodmares.

Long before a fellow named George Strait set female hearts aflutter and recorded a stable full of country music hits, a little guy with the same sounding name but different spelling was making his way at the racetracks. As a youth, this George Strate had galloped Imp, an Ohio-bred snuggled into folksy legend as "My Coal Black Lady." Around the turn of the century, Imp was roaming about the Midwest and East, doing such things as running fifty times at three and beating the Eastern swells in the Suburban Handicap at five. (Some two decades later, Strate trained the whirlwind Inchcape.)

So, Strate knew a good one when he saw it, and he probably recognized that Washoe Belle was no Imp. Nevertheless, when he gave jockey Johnny Bullman a leg up on the Sweep filly for the Denver Juvenile Stakes of 1915, he was about to set into motion a marked upward momentum for her family. Washoe Belle became a stakes winner that day, earning $670 for George Wingfield's Nevada Stock Farm. Sent eastward, she was unable to win again and on occasion raced for a claiming tag.

Washoe Belle produced four stakes winners, of which Ruddy Light stood out as one of the top juvenile fillies of 1923 when she won the Clipsetta Stakes. Ruddy Light, in turn, also foaled four stakes winners in Chicleight, Siskin, Hygro, and the high-class Errard, the last-named foaled when Ruddy Light was twenty-one years old.

Chicleight, Ruddy Light's first foal, won the 1928 Pimlico Nursery and five other races. To that juncture, the family was more noted for precocity and speed than for ruggedness or longer distance capability. The stratagem of breeding upward via a high-class stallion with both of those qualities — so seemingly simple, yet misleadingly so — on this occasion worked as if genetics were nothing more than a chapter in a basic logic course.

The introduction of more quality in bloodlines was possible in part because both Ruddy Light and Chicleight had been acquired by John Marsch, who operated a small stable out of Chicago and did so on a high plane. Marsch, owner of back-to-back Belmont and Washington Park Futurities winners in the full brothers Occupation and Occupy, kept his mares in Kentucky with Thomas Carr Piatt. The

43

		Black Toney, 1911	Peter Pan / Belgravia
	Black Servant, 1918		
		Padula, 1906	Laveno / Padua
BLUE LARKSPUR, b, 1926			
		North Star III, 1914	Sunstar / Angelic
	Blossom Time, 1920		
		Vaila, 1911	Fariman / Padilla
BLUE DELIGHT, br m, 1938			
		Spearmint, 1903	Carbine / Maid of the Mint
	Chicle, 1913		
		Lady Hamburg II, 1908	Hamburg / Lady Frivoles
CHICLEIGHT, br, 1926			
		Honeywood, 1911	Polymelus / Honey Bird
	Ruddy Light, 1921		
		Washoe Belle, 1913	Sweep / Grace Commoner

BLUE DELIGHT, br, 1938-1966. Bred by John Marsch (Ill.). Raced 3 yrs, 24 sts, 10 wins, $51,615. Won Arlington Matron H, Cleopatra H, Cinderella H, Princess Pat H, Joliet S, Arlington Lassie S; 3rd Beverly H, Cinderella H, Falls City H. Dam of 10 named foals, 10 rnrs, 6 wnrs, 5 sw.

1945: Blue World, b c, by Whirlaway. Raced 1 yr, 1 st, 0 wins, $0.

1947: **ALL BLUE**, br c, by Bull Lea. Raced 4 yrs, 43 sts, 7 wins, $93,710. Won San Antonio H; 2nd American Derby, Inglewood H, Sheridan H, Whirlaway S. Sire of 176 foals, AEI 1.06. Died 1965.

1948: Whirling Lark, ch f, by Whirlaway. Raced 1 yr, 1 st, 0 wins, $0. Dam of 10 foals, 10 rnrs, 8 wnrs, including **GO LIGHTLY** ($143,497), **Morning After** ($62,185). Granddam of **DYNANITE, JEWEL OF THE NIGHT, PRINCE TERRELL, TENDERLY YOURS, Abdul, Chincoteague, Long Term, Dimpled Imp, French Light, Mistress Sophie**. Died 1972.

1949: **REAL DELIGHT**, b f, by Bull Lea. Raced 2 yrs, 15 sts, 12 wins, $261,822. Champion 3yo filly and handicap female. Won Kentucky Oaks, Coaching Club American Oaks, Beldame H, Arlington Matron H, Modesty H, Arlington Matron S, Beverly H, Black-Eyed Susan S, Cleopatra S, Ashland S. Dam of 10 foals, 10 rnrs, 9 wnrs, including **SPRING SUNSHINE** ($61,370), **PLUM CAKE** ($43,901), **NO FOOLING** ($20,105). Granddam of **Sweet Tooth, PLUM BOLD, SUGAR PLUM TIME, LONESOME RIVER, LUCKY SO N' SO, RAISE A CUP, Helixiv, Daranstone, La Lea**. Died 1969.

1950: **BUBBLEY**, dk b f, by Bull Lea. Raced 4 yrs, 34 sts, 7 wins, $91,480. Won Kentucky Oaks, Vanity H, Pollyanna S, Debutante S; 2nd Milady H, Ashland S, San Mateo Matron H, Lafayette S. Dam of 6 foals, 4 rnrs, 4 wnrs. Granddam of **FERROUS, WHO DUZZIT, Wave Forever**. Died 1964.

1951: **Turk's Delight**, ch c, by Alibhai. Raced 3 yrs, 22 sts, 7 wins, $59,550. 2nd Santa Anita H, San Marcos H. Sire of 154 foals, AEI 0.94. Died 1970.

1953: **PRINCESS TURIA**, ch f, by Heliopolis. Raced 3 yrs, 31 sts, 13 wins, $250,800. Won Kentucky Oaks, Delaware H, Acorn S, New Castle S, Cleopatra H, Black Eyed Susan S; 2nd Coaching Club American Oaks, Oaks Prep; 3rd Delaware Oaks, Wilmington H, Jersey Belle S. Dam of 9 foals, 6 rnrs, 5 wnrs, including **TURN TO TURIA** ($73,601, gr. II), **FORWARD PASS** ($580,631, champion 3yo colt), **Ever On** ($118,009). Granddam of **NATIVE HERITAGE, Real Proud**. Died 1975.

1954: Barren.

1955: **KENTUCKY PRIDE**, dk b c, by Bull Lea. Raced 5 yrs, 54 sts, 13 wins, $89,041. Won Royal Poinciana H; 2nd Bahamas S, Paumonok H, Everglades S; 3rd Arch Ward Memorial H, Clang H, Hurricane H. Sire of 172 foals, AEI 1.37.

1956: Barren.

1957: Dictum, dk b c, by Citation. Raced 1 yr, 7 sts, 0 wins, $34. Sire of 42 foals, AEI 0.54.

1958: Barren.

1959: Delidore, b f, by Commodore M. Raced 1 yr, 1 st, 0 wins, $0. Dam of 2 foals, 2 rnrs, 1 wnr.

1960: Barren.

1961: Not bred.

two men sent Chicleight to Blue Larkspur for the first time in 1935, and the resulting foal was the colt Lightspur.

A stakes winner at two and three, Lightspur suffered a broken leg in a race late in his second campaign and had to be euthanized. Lightspur was one of a number of unfortunate animals whose high-visibility travails might have tainted the reputation of Blue Larkspur had not the stallion had such a fine racing career and such success at turning out other winners. In addition to Lightspur's tragic end, the Blue Larkspur colt Benefactor, with whom Col. E. R. Bradley reportedly expected to win a fifth Kentucky Derby, went wrong in the autumn of his two-year-old season. Sky Larking, another Blue Larkspur colt, won the Hopeful Stakes of 1937 but soon thereafter broke a leg in the Champagne Stakes and was euthanized.

There were, of course, many pluses in Marsch's determination to send Chicleight to Blue Larkspur several years in succession. As a race horse, Blue Larkspur had been widely hailed as among the best of the 100-plus stakes winners from Col. Bradley's Idle Hour Stock Farm. The celebrated Turf historian John Hervey regarded Blue Larkspur as "the most beautifully gaited runner we have seen in forty years and more."

Blue Larkspur was not one of his famous owner's four Kentucky Derby winners, but his standing suffered little on that score because of the tale that just prior to the Derby his trainer was undergoing an emergency appendectomy and the assistant trainer neglected to fit the colt with mud caulks against the muddy conditions.

Blue Larkspur had been a good two-year-old before being kicked and running unplaced in the Futurity. At three in 1929, he overcame his Derby fourth and was seen as the best of his crop. He showed the speed expected of the Domino sire line when he won the one-mile Withers, but showed none of the stamina deficiencies often associated with the line when he added the one and a half-mile Belmont. He also won the Arlington Classic before bowing a tendon in training at Saratoga. Blue Larkspur was brought back at four, when he added two more important Chicago races: the Stars and Stripes Handicap and the Arlington Cup. It is no wonder a Chicago businessman with an interest in horses, such as Marsch, would have had a high and lingering regard for Blue Larkspur.

Winner of ten races from sixteen starts and earner of $272,070, Blue Larkspur entered stud at Idle Hour in 1931. His pedigree included some of the building blocks which Bradley and farm manager Olin Gentry employed repeatedly over the years — inbreeding to strong individuals while dealing with high-class families and sire lines. Blue Larkspur was by Black Servant and out of the North Star III mare Blossom Time. The latter had won the Pimlico Futurity and was one of five stakes winners produced from Bradley's imported English stakes winner Vaila. The close inbreeding in Blue Larkspur's pedigree was to the mare Padua, she of a noted English family. Padua was the second dam of both Vaila and Black Servant.

Kentucky horsemen's confidence in Blue Larkspur as a sire prospect was abundantly rewarded, as he sired fifteen percent stakes winners and ranked among the top ten broodmare sires for seventeen consecutive seasons. His daughters included Myrtlewood, Bloodroot, and Bee Ann Mac, and running offspring of his daughters included Twilight Tear, Durazna, Be Faithful, and Cosmic Bomb.

The Delights Begin

When the ill-starred Lightspur was two, Chicleight foaled a Blue Larkspur filly, who was named Blue Delight. The filly was presented to Mrs. Marsch to race in her colors, and Blue Delight and the other Marsch runners were trained by Roscoe Goose, forever famed for having won the 1913 Kentucky Derby on the 91-1 shot Donerail.

Contemporary descriptions have it that Blue Delight was a strong filly, standing over considerable ground at slightly more than sixteen hands and resembling her sire. She raced at two, three, and four, winning ten of twenty-four races and earning

$51,615. At two in 1940, Blue Delight won in her second attempt and soon was graduated into stakes class. Her first effort for added-money produced a win over colts in the Joliet Stakes, which was something of a family tradition as the event had been won in 1930 and 1931 by Siskin and Hygro, half-siblings to Chicleight. Blue Delight held on to defeat the colt Swain, who then went on to win the Arlington Futurity.

The Marsch filly's first race after the Joliet was a prep for the Arlington Lassie, which at that time was the second-richest among juvenile filly races, surpassed only by the Selima. She finished unplaced and was sent off at 14-1 for the six-furlong Lassie itself. Flashing front-running speed of :22 4/5 for the first quarter-mile and :46 3/5 for a half-mile, Blue Delight had a strong field defeated early and won by daylight over Misty Isle in 1:12 4/5. The track was such that the speedy colt Roman had taken almost as long to win another six-furlong test earlier in the day.

Blue Delight was laid up thereafter with a sore ankle and ran no more at two. She was ranked at 114 pounds on the Experimental Free Handicap, seven pounds below topweight Level Best, but below no other filly.

At three, Blue Delight won only a pair of overnight races and placed in two stakes, but at four she was one of the top runners in the Midwest. She won four of eight, including the Arlington Matron, Cleopatra, Cinderella, and Princess Pat Handicaps. She was kept in training at five, but bowed a tendon that spring and was retired.

Marsch decided to divest himself of his Thoroughbred holdings and in 1946 sold his broodmare band, which had grown to about twenty, to Henry Knight. A well-known Kentucky breeder and seller, Knight was ever ready to follow an incoming deal with an outgoing one, and he knew of a fellow who liked good race fillies, especially if they were by Blue Larkspur. This was Warren Wright Sr., who had transformed his father's Calumet Farm from a Standardbred operation to a prominent Thoroughbred establishment and had won a Triple Crown and a pair of Kentucky Derbys by the mid-1940s.

Although Olin Gentry worked for Bradley, he used to tell of Wright trying to lure him away. Gentry never went to work for Calumet, but recalled helping Wright buy mares from time to time. "Blue Delight was for sale for $25,000 and her sister for $15,000," Gentry recalled years later. "I told Mr. Wright I thought he should take Blue Delight. He asked why we were paying $25,000 for her instead of $15,000 for her sister. I told him, 'Mr. Wright, if it weren't for Blue Delight you would never even have heard of the other one.'"

With Calumet's acquisition of Blue Delight, the brood of Washoe Belle had climbed many steps from Denver and was now ready to contribute to the most remarkable phase of dominance the modern American Turf has seen.

Even before Marsch sold her, Blue Delight had been to Calumet. Her first two foals were both by farm stallions. The first was Blue World, a 1945 foal by Calumet's Triple Crown winner Whirlaway. He brought $15,700 as a yearling and was winless in his only start before his death. Blue Delight had no foal in 1946, but the following year produced a colt by Bull Lea.

Wright already had made a number of important and productive decisions: Entering the syndicate which imported the English stallion Blenheim II (sire of Whirlaway), and hiring Ben A. Jones as Calumet's trainer. No decision was to cast the halo of Calumet into wider arcs than did Wright's purchase of Coldstream Stud's Bull Dog—Rose Leaves colt at the 1936 Saratoga yearling sale. For $14,000,

Calumet bought Bull Lea, a colt good enough as a runner to win the Blue Grass Stakes and Widener Handicap and great enough as a stallion to beget three Kentucky Derby winners, lead the sire list five times, and leave pervasive influence as a four-time leading broodmare sire.

The first of Blue Delight's four foals by this great sire was All Blue, the aforementioned colt foaled in 1947. He won the San Antonio Handicap and placed in the American Derby, but in the context of the Calumet outfit trained by Jones and his son Jimmy, this drew scant note.

In 1948, Blue Delight foaled a Whirlaway filly named Whirling Lark. She was unplaced in her only start, but produced the stakes winner Go Lightly. The smattering of stakes winners which trace to Whirling Lark attest to a certain longevity in the genes. The 1990s stakes winner Strawberry Wine was foaled forty-four years after Whirling Lark, but only two generations separate them.

In the spring of 1948, Blue Delight was returned to the court of Bull Lea. That was the same spring when the greatest among many champions by Bull Lea, Citation, was embarking on a Triple Crown sweep amid a peerless campaign of nineteen wins in twenty races — enough to convince jockey Eddie Arcaro he was the greatest horse he had ever ridden and enough to convince Ben Jones he was the greatest racer anyone had ever seen.

Blue Delight's Bull Lea filly born the following year was to be named Real Delight. It was duly reported later in the trade press that Calumet manager Paul Ebelhardt wrote in "could be another Twilight Tear" on his report following initial appraisal of the hours-old filly. This was extravagant praise, but he did not miss the mark by far.

Real Delight was one of those rare Thoroughbreds that one can say was a "great" filly without fear of sullying an adjective that has enjoyed, among most horsemen, a rare respect even in an age of hype. Of course, the newcomer in racing may be forgiven to affixing the word "great" to this Derby winner or that streaking star, but, for the most part, an internal whisper of warning upbraids the speaker who is tempted to call a horse great on insufficient evidence.

Moreover, Real Delight must have been an emotional godsend for Calumet. Warren Wright Sr. had died late in 1950 and his widow had determined to carry on the farm and stable. Her resolve was girded by the knowledge that Wright had decided to keep Citation in training at six with the notion that he could become the first Thoroughbred to earn $1 million in purses. Despite an injury which had scuttled his entire four-year-old campaign and had rendered the Triple Crown winner something less than his best, Citation was tantalizingly close to that unprecedented seven-figure mark. He went over the goal in winning the Hollywood Gold Cup in the summer of 1951 and was thereupon retired.

In the spring of 1952, Hill Gail emerged as Calumet's fifth Kentucky Derby winner, and in the three-year-old filly division, Real Delight did her part with a championship campaign of eleven wins in twelve starts. Wright's widow had remarried, wedding the Hollywood producer and charming raconteur Adm. Gene Markey. The success of Calumet in 1952 must have given her great confidence that she had done the right thing by taking on responsibility for the farm and stable. The year marked the eighth of the twelve times the stable led the national earnings list from 1941 through 1961. It also was the sixth of eleven consecutive years that Calumet would lead the breeders' list in earnings and one of a Calumet total of fourteen seasons atop that list.

At two, Real Delight developed a splint near enough to the knee that Jones chose not to run her. The following year, she came out early, a large-framed filly who at full growth was said in Evan Shipman's *American Racing Manual* review to stand seventeen hands, but was placed at two inches

Blue Delight

shorter by Joe Estes in *American Race Horses* of 1952. (Whether one prefers to believe a fellow who used to drink with Ernest Hemingway at the Cafe des Lilas like Shipman or a scholarly editor of *The Blood-Horse* like Estes must remain a personal matter.)

Whatever her physical height, Real Delight towered over her contemporaries. Three consecutive wins and a luckless second primed her for a sequence of races that for many years was recognized as the filly counterpart to the Triple Crown. This series involved the Kentucky Oaks, Black-Eyed Susan Stakes, and Coaching Club American Oaks. The distances ranged from one and one-sixteenth miles up to one and three-eighths miles for the CCA Oaks. Real Delight won them all.

Sent next to Calumet's rich summer quarry, Chicago, she underwent a bizarre experience which seemed out of tune with the times. In 1952, Real Delight was the target of someone at Arlington Park, who flung an astringent substance toward her in the paddock prior to the Arlington Matron. Her groom took the brunt of the attack, but Real Delight was said to have suffered a welt on her neck. Undeterred, she went out and gave weight to her field and won handily.

As early as July 16, Real Delight began to face older fillies and mares, giving away weight (not just by the scale of weights, but actual pounds) to distinguished fields, including older female champion Sickle's Image. Real Delight had some close calls, but continued to win. Carrying 126 pounds and giving nine pounds to Sickle's Image, she outgamed the latter to win the Modesty Handicap by a head in 1:35 3/5, widely acclaimed as the fastest time for a mile any three-year-old filly ever had recorded under such weight.

Off that effort, Real Delight improved. She was in the midst of a streak of fifteen consecutive stakes efforts without a loss for the Calumet team, and,

taking up 129 pounds while again racing at a mile, she gave eight to Sickle's Image and carried regular rider Eddie Arcaro to victory in the Beverly Handicap with a mile in 1:34 4/5. Aesthete, under 105, was beaten a head, with Sickle's Image third.

For the Beldame in New York, Real Delight was assigned 126 pounds by the widely respected handicapper John B. Campbell and was set to give older distaff champion Bed o' Roses eight pounds by scale going nine furlongs. The meeting did not materialize. Despite its quality, the Beldame had an overflow field, and the two highest weights were drawn into separate divisions of the one and one-eighth-mile test. Both won, Real Delight scoring in her division over Marta, La Corredora, Kiss Me Kate, and Busanda, giving large chunks of weight to them all.

Early in the year, Real Delight had lost a race when an apprentice was asked to substitute for Arcaro. Otherwise, Real Delight might have gone twelve for twelve at three. As matters stood, she had won eleven of twelve, the last eight in succession. Whether the cachet of being undefeated would have enhanced further the perception the racing world had of her is not to be determined. Possibly it would have, for she might not have made the three starts at four which placed her career mark at twelve wins in fifteen starts. She lost her first start at four, then won a second Arlington Matron, but next finished unplaced for the only time in her life, telling Jones something was amiss, and she was quickly sent home.

Real Delight's 1952 campaign earned her championship honors for three-year-old filly and handicap female. She earned a total of $261,822.

Manager Ebelhardt's comment about the young Real Delight invites comparison to Twilight Tear. Both were eagerly accepted as among the eleven Calumet horses elected to date in the National Museum of Racing's Hall of Fame in Saratoga

Champion Alcibiades was an incomparable producer for the Headley family. She was the dam of juvenile champion Menow (left), and the fourth dam of the Epsom Derby winner Sir Ivor (below).

Almahmoud

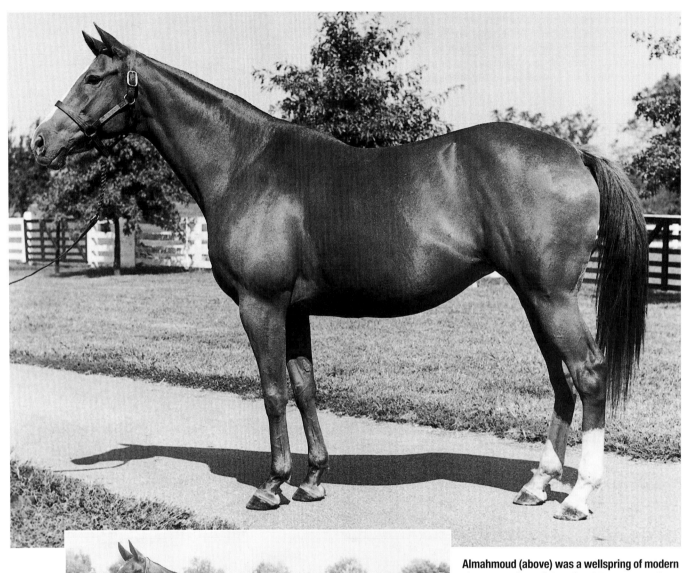

Almahmoud (above) was a wellspring of modern sire power through her daughters, among them Cosmah (left), who bears a striking resemblance to her dam.

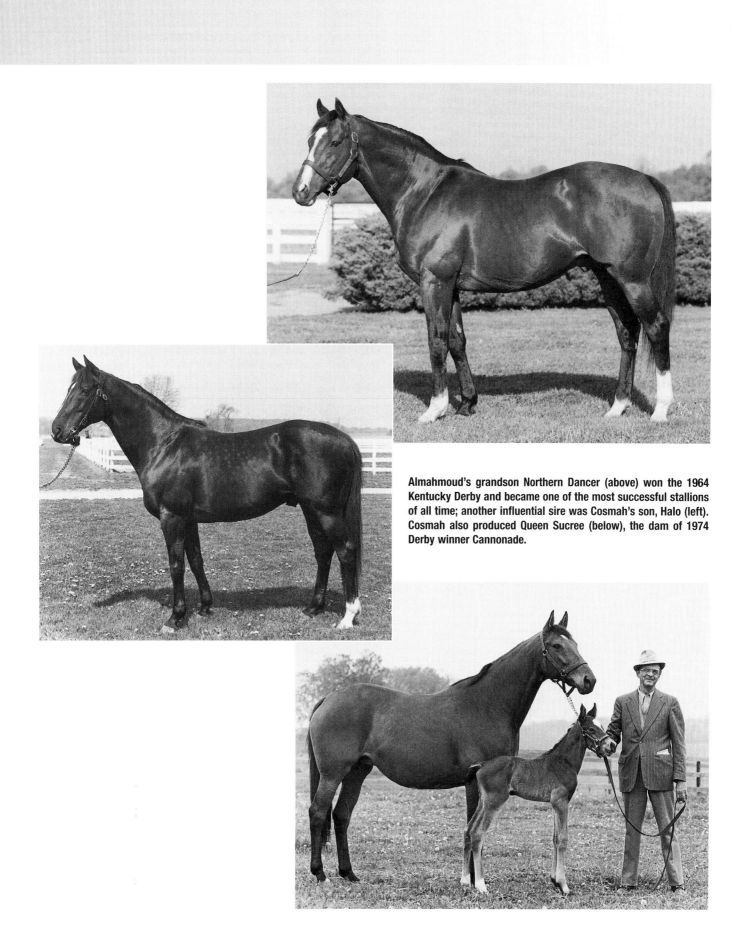

Almahmoud's grandson Northern Dancer (above) won the 1964 Kentucky Derby and became one of the most successful stallions of all time; another influential sire was Cosmah's son, Halo (left). Cosmah also produced Queen Sucree (below), the dam of 1974 Derby winner Cannonade.

Aspidistra

Aspidistra, who helped put the Florida breeding industry on the map, is shown above with her champion daughter Ta Wee (right); descendant Gana Facil (left) produced 1990 Kentucky Derby winner Unbridled.

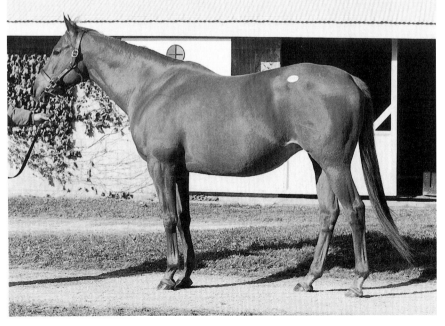

Banquet Bell (above) won only once in fifteen starts, but she became the foundation mare for John W. Galbreath's Darby Dan Farm; her daughter Primonetta (top, right) was a champion and stakes producer. Banquet Bell was the second dam of champion Little Current (right), who won the 1974 Preakness and Belmont.

Best in Show

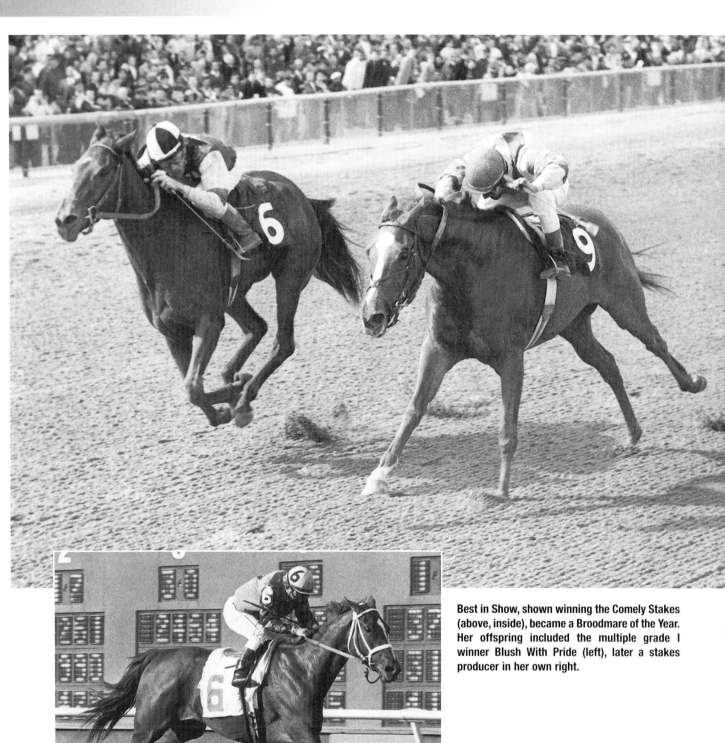

Best in Show, shown winning the Comely Stakes (above, inside), became a Broodmare of the Year. Her offspring included the multiple grade I winner Blush With Pride (left), later a stakes producer in her own right.

Blue Delight

Blue Delight (below) raced with distinction for three seasons, then became a stellar producer for Calumet Farm. Her daughter Real Delight (right) was a champion and top broodmare.

Blue Delight

Blue Delight was the third dam of Sweet Tooth (above), who produced Calumet stars Alydar (below, winning the 1978 Whitney Stakes), and his half-sister, champion Our Mims (left).

Springs, New York. In 1944, Twilight Tear, also by Bull Lea out of a Blue Larkspur mare, had a similar three-year-old season. She had a few more victories, but a few more losses, winning fourteen of seventeen. What puts Twilight Tear slightly ahead, we believe, is that she defeated colts, most stunningly in her runaway win over older champion Devil Diver at weight-for-age in the one and three-sixteenths-mile Pimlico Special. Such a win can be considered comparable to a three-year-old filly in the 1990s context if, say, Sky Beauty had concluded the year of her New York Filly Triple Crown by winning the Breeders' Cup — not the Distaff, but the Classic!

The Road to Alydar

A prejudice is attached in some circles against a big, rugged race mare's likelihood of becoming a successful producer. Applying a judgment of what a large, masculine type of female must connote, and adding Federico Tesio's warning about racing sapping a horse's inherent vitality, followers of this theory soldier on through the generations. They have a tough time, however, dealing with a Real Delight.

The mare had ten foals. All raced, nine won, and three were stakes winners: Plum Cake, Spring Sunshine, and No Fooling. If toughness is an undesirable trait for a female to have and pass along, succeeding descendants of Real Delight were somehow able to overcome it.

Real Delight's first stakes winner was the Ponder filly Plum Cake, who won the Jasmine Stakes at Hialeah. When she in turn went to stud, her contributions grew. It was often assumed when Calumet fell on lean times during the 1960s and 1970s that it had depended too heavily on Bull Lea and when he was gone, so was the magic. This is inaccurate, for Wright and later Mrs. Markey for many years made a practice of reaching out to successful stallions on other farms. By the dawn of the 1970s, the Phipps family's Bold Ruler had become a phenomenally suc-

cessful stallion. Unlike most top sires of the era, he was privately owned instead of syndicated, and, in contrast to the management of top sires today, few of his yearlings were consigned to the auction ring.

The Phippses and Bull Hancock, at whose Claiborne Farm Bold Ruler stood, developed a fine way to give other breeders access to the eight-time leading sire while at the same time recruiting new and high-class bloodlines for the Phipps broodmare band. With no fee involved, a breeder could send a mare to Bold Ruler for two years, the breeder to get one foal and Ogden Phipps and/or Mrs. Henry Carnegie Phipps to get the other. On such a sequence, for instance, Ogden Phipps got the filly The Bride while Meadow Stable made off with a colt named Secretariat.

Whatever the individual arrangement, Plum Cake was sent to Bold Ruler in 1971, the year the sire had come back to Claiborne after treatment for cancer at Auburn University and was able to stand one last season before his death. In 1972, Plum Cake foaled the filly Sugar Plum Time, who raced for Ogden Phipps' daughter, Cynthia, and won the Firenze, Maskette, and New York Handicaps. Sugar Plum Time also foaled stakes winner Christmas Bonus.

While the dramatic aspect of being in Bold Ruler's final crop — courtesy of excellent veterinary care and management — surrounded Sugar Plum Time, two earlier Bold Ruler foals from Plum Cake had perhaps more lasting influence. One was Plum Bold, who won the Juvenile Stakes and National Stallion Stakes for Calumet and later was the leading sire of South Africa. The other was Yule Log, who foaled Cynthia Phipps' homebred Christmas Past, a Grey Dawn II filly who won the CCA Oaks en route to three-year-old championship honors of 1982.

Pride of place among Plum Cake's foals in terms of impact, however, goes to her 1965 filly by the homebred Calumet stallion On-and-On (by Nasrullah). This was Sweet Tooth, who placed in the Alcibiades Stakes at two. In 1977, Sweet Tooth's Herbager filly, Our Mims, won what might earlier have been seen as the family birthright — the Coaching Club American Oaks. It was part of a campaign devised by young John Veitch, son of Hall-of-Fame trainer Syl Veitch and the latest in a caravan of trainers who had been summoned to follow, in turn, the Jones boys at Calumet. The victory was instrumental in Our Mims' recognition as the champion three-year-old filly.

Times, by then, had changed, and changed again. As alluded to earlier, Calumet had fallen onto hard times. Then came 1977, and not only Our Mims but her strikingly handsome half-brother, Alydar, emerged as major winners for Veitch and the aging Markeys.

Alydar was a son of Raise a Native, and his great rival, Affirmed, was a grandson of the same stallion. The days when Calumet stars also were by Calumet stallions might have been in the past, but tracing to Bull Lea gave the success a bit of succor from history. Revered in the hearts of Kentuckians was the bright, sun-polished spring day of 1978 when the Markeys, eyesight failing, were driven to the track rail at Keeneland. Jockey Jorge Velasquez steered Alydar to the outside where he greeted Mrs. Markey with Latino gallantry: "Here's your baby, my lady. Isn't he pretty?"

Alydar came home by thirteen that day, and although he was beaten in each of the Triple Crown races by Affirmed, he fired anew the hearts who had loved Calumet runners of the past. Alydar earned nearly $1 million, and the low tide of Calumet was swept away, mercifully, for the last years of both Adm. and Mrs. Markey.

Alydar came back to the farm to author a great success. His parade of major winners included Alysheba, Criminal Type, Easy Goer, Strike the Gold, Althea, and Miss Oceana. Alydar led the national sire list in 1990. By then, however, J. T. Lundy, who

Blue Delight

had married the granddaughter of Warren Wright Sr., had been entrusted with management of the jewel of the Bluegrass and had consigned it into a free fall to bankruptcy. Even the death of the majestic Alydar would be subject to hints of dark deeds.

In 1992, Henryk de Kwiatkowski, a sporting horse breeder, came forward to rescue the farm by purchasing it at public auction.

More Delights, Blue and Real

The history of the female family addressed here has many more elements. In 1957, Real Delight foaled a filly by Helioscope, he a high-class handicapper but not a particularly successful sire. Nevertheless, this foal, Heliolight, would earn a part in the ongoing story. Heliolight produced the stakes winner Lonesome River, but her Chieftain filly of 1967 would earn more renown. Named Minnetonka, she never got to the races, but produced four major winners in Eminency, Katonka, Barrera, and Phaedra. Moreover, among the foals from that generation of descendants was Minnetonka's 1971 Minnesota Mac filly Roundup Rose, dam of the 1980 Preakness winner Codex.

We return now to the subject mare of the chapter, Blue Delight. In 1950, the year after she foaled Real Delight, Blue Delight produced another Bull Lea filly, named Bubbley. Like her more exalted full sister, Bubbley won the Kentucky Oaks, which was among four stakes triumphs of her career.

In 1951, Blue Delight's foal was not by Bull Lea, but by the highly fashionable Spendthrift Farm stallion Alibhai. Named Turk's Delight, this colt never won a stakes, but was second to Bobby Brocato in the 1956 Santa Anita Handicap.

Blue Delight had no foal in 1952. Then, in 1953, she foaled a filly by Heliopolis, a leading sire and a son of the great English stallion Hyperion. Named Princess Turia, the filly became Blue Delight's third

Kentucky Oaks winner and also won the Black-Eyed Susan (nee Pimlico Oaks). Only a second to Levee in the CCA Oaks prevented her from duplicating her half-sister Real Delight's sweep of the old filly Triple Crown. Princess Turia's run in the 1956 Acorn Stakes resulted in one of the most unusual results of any major stakes in history: She dead-heated for first with a stablemate, Calumet's Beyond. Princess Turia at four defeated champion Pucker Up in the Delaware Handicap, which in the 1950s ranked as at least the equal of any other filly and mare event.

If the Princess Turia/Beyond Acorn was unique, it was nothing in terms of sensationalism compared to the Kentucky Derby of Princess Turia's son Forward Pass. In 1968, Forward Pass, a Calumet homebred by On-and On, was second to Dancer's Image under the wire in the Kentucky Derby, but a protracted legal battle over medication ultimately disqualified the apparent winner and made Forward Pass a record eighth Derby winner owned by Calumet. Forward Pass won the Preakness with no asterisk, but was second in the Belmont to Stage Door Johnny. That pair shared championship honors at three.

In 1954, the aging Blue Delight was barren, but in 1955 she foaled another stakes winner by Bull Lea, a colt named Kentucky Pride. In the winter of 1958, Kentucky Pride flashed into classic contention, but was soon eclipsed by stablemate Tim Tam, who won the Derby and Preakness. Blue Delight was barren in 1956, foaled the unplaced Citation colt Dictum in 1957, and was barren again in 1958. Her final foal was Delidore, an unplaced filly by Commodore M., but typically the ancestress of her own packet of winners, with a smattering of black type. Blue Delight's death was recorded in 1966. She was the dam of ten foals, of which six won and five were stakes winners. ❖

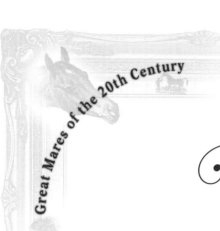

Boudoir II

 icomte Gabriel de Fontarce was a worldly European, with business interests in such exotic outposts as Egypt and Brazil. He owned an estate in the French countryside, where with a fine sense of feudal patronage, he occasionally brought in a personally selected Suffolk Punch stallion and made it available for his tenants' mares. The Vicomte entered racing in 1911 and kept his mares at the Highclere estate of fellow world traveler, Lord Carnarvon, grandfather of the present Carnarvon, who is racing manager for Queen Elizabeth II.

The highlight of Vicomte de Fontarce's racing career was the victory of his filly Brownhylda in the Epsom Oaks of 1923. Seventeen years later, the Vicomte and his advisers had made two exceedingly astute purchases, but he was by then in his 75th year and in declining health and thus was in no position to benefit from them. For a time in 1940 and 1941, as recalled in the *Bloodstock Breeders' Review* of the second year, Vicomte de Fontarce owned both Boudoir II and Uvira II, whose modern descendants were to include Graustark, Majestic Prince, A.P. Indy, Summer Squall, and a flotilla of other distinguished racers and producers. Uvira II disappointed in her two starts at two in 1940 for Fontarce, and he had her sold on to Sir Thomas Dixon. The next spring, she won the Irish Oaks. Boudoir II, likewise, had been sold, to The Curragh

trainer Cecil Brabazon, for whom she came within a head of winning Ireland's other filly classic of 1941, the Irish One Thousand Guineas.

Fontarce died in 1941. If he had lived longer and held on to the two classic fillies, the tales of their impact might well have been more slanted toward Europe. Had such eventuality transpired, the good Vicomte arguably might today be spoken of as one of those astute horsemen who wade through the maze of equine genetics and emerge with gleaming trophies and their implied wisdom.

As matters actually transpired, both Uvira II and Boudoir II were destined to sow their richness in North America. (Uvira II's career is summarized in the chapter on her daughter Missy Baba.)

Boudoir II was bred by C. Leigh and was a gray in the first crop of the Aga Khan's spectacular gray 1936 Epsom Derby winner, Mahmoud. Imported to Kentucky, Mahmoud became the sire of seventy stakes winners, and he led the sire list in 1946 and the broodmare sire list in 1957. Edging into the top of the latter list was no small accomplishment; Mahmoud ended a string of fourteen years that one of the full brothers Sir Gallahad III or Bull Dog had been the leading broodmare sire. The next four years belonged to Bull Dog's son Bull Lea.

In addition to Boudoir II, Mahmoud's distinguished daughters in the stud included Almahmoud, second dam of both Northern Dancer and Halo.

Neither the dam nor second dam of Boudoir II was a successful race mare. Boudoir II's dam was the Clarissimus filly Kampala, who was unplaced at two, and the next dam was the Prince Palatine mare La Soupe II, who was unraced. Boudoir II won only one race from twelve starts, all in Ireland, but her near victory in the Irish One Thousand Guineas was an indication of racing class well above average. The filly had won her second race at two, a five-furlong sprint at Phoenix Park, to become the second winner for Mahmoud. She raced in the name of R. L. Rogers. By the time she reappeared at three, the dealing had been done and she ran in Brabazon's name. In an incident with bizarre overtones to her family's future, she fell in her first race at three. Unhurt, she rebounded next with her fine effort in the Guineas, but in an active season never did win a race at three and only twice more finished as high as second. She earned a total of 358 pounds and in November was purchased at Goffs autumn sale in Dublin for 340 guineas in the name of F. F. Tuthill.

During the early 1940s, movie magnate Louis B. Mayer of Metro-Goldwyn-Mayer was actively acquiring horses. Among his purchases abroad were Boudoir II and the Aga Khan's Hyperion colt, Alibhai, who was unraced because of broken sesamoids. Alibhai and Boudoir II were taken to the Mayer ranch in Perris, California. Boudoir II's rapid son Your Host and one of her distinguished producing daughters, Your Hostess, were sired by Alibhai, whose early success was such that Kentucky breeders came calling with a $500,000 syndication and plucked him away from Western shores.

Your Host was Boudoir II's only stakes winner among twelve foals, eleven runners, and nine winners, but he and her daughters were of no small import. Your Host, her fourth foal, was born in 1947. As Your Host turned two, Mayer had reversed his position in the acquisition of stock and was conducting a long and glittering series of dispersals.

His son-in-law, William Goetz, was also a movie executive, and he also developed a racing stable. Goetz instructed trainer Harry L. Daniels to go as high as $15,000 for Your Host. Daniels liked the colt and recognized that his awkward way of carrying his head resulted from an neck injury and not an inherent conformation quirk.

Daniels later recounted that as the sale was unfolding, he kept his eyes glued to the floor as he bid because he was afraid if he looked across the ring to Goetz, he would receive a signal to stop. Goetz was delighted when he found he had bought the colt for a substantial raise over his intended limit, $20,000. "Thank God!," he said when Daniels admitted he had made the top bid, "I kept signaling you to keep on bidding, but you wouldn't look up!"

Your Host was a colt of breathtaking speed. He won thirteen of twenty-three races and earned $384,795. The colt won the Del Mar Futurity at two in 1949 and the next year dashed off more triumphs in the San Felipe and Santa Anita Derby. Therein, however, lay an irony, for he would become the poster boy for a syndrome that long was associated — inaccurately or not — with brilliant California-based three-year-olds.

So impressively had Your Host prepared for the Kentucky Derby that he was the post-time favorite over the Eastern star Hill Prince. Your Host flashed his early speed, but fell back to finish ninth. The so-called West Coast failure had become entrenched, but by the midway point of the decade, California-prepped Determine and Swaps had won back-to-back Derbys. When a Westerner failed, however, it tended to be with a flourish. The vaunted Silky Sullivan was a budding public hero when he fizzled in the 1958 Derby, whereas little Tomy Lee had no such heralding when he came from the West to win the Derby in 1959. Candy Spots lost in 1963 and Hill Rise was a gallant loser in 1964, but then Lucky Debonair won in 1965.

From today's perspective, when West Coast stables have won modern Derbys with such as

		Blandford, 1919	Swynford Blanche
	Blenheim II, 1927		
		Malva, 1919	Charles O'Malley Wild Arum
MAHMOUD, gr, 1933			
		Gainsborough, 1915	Bayardo Rosedrop
	Mah Mahal, 1928		
		Mumtaz Mahal, 1921	The Tetrarch Lady Josephine
BOUDOIR II, **gr m, 1938**			
		Radium, 1903	Bend Or Taia
	Clarissimus, 1913		
		Quintessence, 1900	St. Frusquin Margarine
KAMPALA, b, 1933			
		Prince Palatine, 1908	Persimmon Lady Lightfoot
	La Soupe II, 1918		
		Hermosita, 1912	Ajax Tribonyx

Boudoir II, gr, 1938-1963. Bred by C. Leigh (Eng.). Raced 2 yrs in Ire, 11 sts, 1 win, $1,648. 2nd Irish One Thousand Guineas. Dam of 12 named foals, 11 rnrs, 9 wnrs, 1 sw. Sent to USA 1942.

1943: **Charivari**, gr c, by Beau Pere. Raced 9 yrs, 95 sts, 7 wins, $23,962. 2nd California Homebred S. H; 3rd California Breeders Champion S.

1945: Succession, dk b c, by Beau Pere. Raced 3 yrs, 21 sts, 4 wins, $14,325. Sire of 186 foals, AEI 0.66.

1946: Flower Bed, dk b f, by Beau Pere. Raced 2 yrs, 9 sts, 4 wins, $9,800. Dam of 9 foals, 8 rnrs, 7 wnrs, including **FLOWER BOWL** ($174,625), **BRAMBLES** ($87,162), **FLORAL PARK** ($31,770), **Pelouse** ($43,550). Granddam of **GALLANT BLOOM, BOWL OF FLOWERS, HIS MAJESTY, GRAUSTARK, FREE HAND, BLANDFORD PARK, Istoriato.**

1947: **YOUR HOST**, ch c, by Alibhai. Raced 3 yrs, 23 sts, 13 wins, $384,795. Won Santa Anita Derby, Santa Catalina H (NTR, SA, 9 furlongs in 1:48.20), San Felipe S, California Breeders' Champion S, Thanksgiving Day H, Kent S, Golden State Breeders' H, Sheridan H, Dick Welles S, Del Mar Futurity; 2nd Premiere H, Homebred S, Salinas H, San Carlos H; 3rd American Derby, Arlington Classic.

1948: My Host, ro c, by Alibhai. Raced 4 yrs, 32 sts, 2 wins, $5,465. Sire of 172 foals, AEI 1.99. Died 1966.

1949: **Your Hostess**, ch f, by Alibhai. Raced 3 yrs, 16 sts, 3 wins, $14,575. 3rd Santa Susana H. Dam of 14 foals, 11 rnrs, 8 wnrs, including **CORAGGIOSO** ($309,281, gr. I), **T. V. COMMERCIAL** ($404,034), **ROYAL CLIPPER** ($73,234), **GALLATIA** ($41,517). Granddam of **CROWNED PRINCE, MAJESTIC PRINCE, MINSTREL GREY, MEMORABLE MITCH, PALLADIUM, LOVELY GYPSY, AUBERGE, NATIVE GUEST, MR. POMRANKY, COMMAND MODULE, RIGHT CROSS, ENCOURAGE, LOOSEN UP, RAISE YOUR SIGHTS, GALLINA, Urbana Cowboy, Unimpeachable, Protocol, Classy Twist, Betty Loraine, Runny Nose, Bugle Bow, Our Queen.** Died 1971.

1951: Miniature, br f, by Bull Lea. Raced 1 yr, 1 st, 0 wins, $0. Dam of 4 foals, 3 rnrs, 3 wnrs.

1952: Royal Hostess, ch f, by Alibhai. Raced 2 yrs, 5 sts, 1 win, $2,275. Dam of 10 foals, 6 rnrs, 4 wnrs. Granddam of **SPANISH JULIE, Paisley Square, Governor Dan.** Died 1978.

1953: Bar Le Duc, ch c, by Alibhai. Raced 1 yr, 1 st, 1 win, $1,400. Sire of 172 foals, AEI 0.97.

1954: Splendido, ch c, by Ardan. Raced 4 yrs, 39 sts, 4 wins, $9,927. Sire of 37 foals, AEI 0.25. Died 1973.

1955: Caluria, ch f, by Heliopolis. Unraced. Dam of 8 foals, 5 rnrs, 3 wnrs. Granddam of **YAMOLAI (Arg), MORISQUETA.** Died 1972.

1956: Barren.

1957: Barren.

1958: Slipped twins.

1959: Not bred.

1960: Dead foal.

1961: Bowl of Roses, ro f, by Alibhai. Raced 1 yr in Eng and NA, 6 sts, 0 wins, $200. Dam of 10 foals, 7 rnrs, 3 wnrs. Granddam of **OUI MADAME ROSE, THE NEUROLOGIST (Ire), FAHREWOHL, NICHIDO ARASHI, Nichido Raizah.** Sent to Ven 1976.

Ferdinand, Winning Colors, Sunday Silence, Silver Charm, and Real Quiet, any prejudice against a horse because he/she ran at Santa Anita instead of Gulfstream, Keeneland, or Aqueduct is ludicrous.

In addition to his association with a long buried prejudice, Your Host's name also became linked with one of the most important cases in Thoroughbred insurance. After he had softened the blow of being unplaced in the Derby with four victories in the East and Midwest, Your Host had been returned to California. There he defeated the champion filly Next Move and the accomplished On Trust in the Golden State Breeders' Handicap and beat a Kentucky Derby winner, Ponder, and Horse of the Year, Hill Prince, in the Thanksgiving Day Handicap.

At four, he carried 130 pounds in winning the one and one-eighth-mile Santa Catalina Handicap, but soon thereafter his racing career came crashing down, literally. Your Host was tripped in traffic and fell to the ground in the San Pasqual. He was not so fortunate as his dam had been in her fall years earlier; a foreleg was fractured in four places, and Your Host's survival seemed a long shot. Lloyd's of London, however, took the advice of the more optimistic veterinary analysts, and after paying off the claim of $250,000 took possession of the horse. Your Host was saved and sold to a syndicate for stud duty, being sent to Meadowview Farm in New Jersey. There he added one more phrase likely to be uttered in virtually any conversational reference to his name, and, unlike the others, it is a note of high praise: Sire of the great Kelso, racing's only five-time Horse of the Year! Those Lloyd's boys did racing quite a favor.

Your Host lived until the age of fourteen, when he was humanely destroyed because of complications from a dislocated stifle. In addition to Kelso, he was the sire of the popular West Coast sprinter Miss Todd and the major winner Social Climber.

Blooms and Majesty

Boudoir II had several owners during her broodmare career. In September of 1948, during the time of the flurry of Mayer dispersals, Boudoir II was acquired by Leslie Combs II. It was Combs, owner of Spendthrift Farm in Kentucky, who that same year engineered the syndication of Alibhai. A dozen years later, in 1960, Boudoir II was transferred to Mrs. John L. McMahan, in whose name she was entered in that year's Keeneland November sale. Boudoir II at twenty-two was purchased by Mrs. Harry Love, who with her husband operated a family farm in the horse friendly countryside of Maryland. The price was $14,700. Boudoir II was boarded by Mrs. Love at the Lexington farm of Kentucky veterinarian William R. McGee, and the mare died there at twenty-five in 1963.

The well-traveled Boudoir II had her first foal in 1943, the Beau Pere colt Charivari, who placed in a pair of California-bred stakes. Charivari won seven of ninety-five races and earned $23,962. Boudoir II had no foal in 1944, then produced another Beau Pere colt, Succession, winner of four races in twenty-one starts and earner of $14,325. Succession was given a chance at stud and sired eighteen stakes winners.

Beau Pere was a Mayer horse who died in 1947 after one of Combs' first syndications. He was also the sire of Boudoir II's third foal, and it was with that foal that the mare's importance began to unfold. The 1946 Beau Pere—Boudoir II filly was Flower Bed, who soon after officially turning two was offered in a Mayer dispersal in January of 1948. Trainer Reggie Cornell bid $20,000 to buy her on behalf of Herman B. Delman. Flower Bed won four of nine races and earned $9,800 for Delman, before he sold most of his horses at auction. In August of 1949, Your Host was a promising two-year-old, and, while Boudoir II was hardly a major name yet, Beau Pere was the sire of some two dozen New Zealand/Australian-bred stakes winners as well as such important American-bred runners as Honeymoon, Stepfather, and Judy-Rae. The varying credentials were enough to interest one of the East's most prominent stables, and Flower Bed was purchased from Delman's sale for $15,500 by Isabel Dodge Sloane's Brookmeade Stable.

Brookmeade retired Flower Bed to its broodmare band. Had none of the Mayer horses been sold, a Beau

Boudoir II

Pere—Boudoir II filly might well have been bred to Alibhai. As it was, with all the transactions, the Beau Pere—Boudoir II filly was still bred to Alibhai. The resulting Alibhai—Flower Bed foal of 1952 was named Flower Bowl. Trained by Hall of Famer Preston Burch, Flower Bowl developed late and at four in 1956 rallied from fifteen lengths behind to score the first stakes victory of her career at a most auspicious moment — in the Delaware Handicap, winning a purse of $104,875, then a record for a race for fillies and mares. Behind her was a star-studded field including champions Parlo, High Voltage, and Blue Sparkler, plus Miz Clementine, Dotted Line, and Searching. Flower Bowl ratified that performance with a victory in the one and a half-mile Ladies Handicap.

Retired to the Brookmeade broodmare band, Flower Bowl produced as her first foal the two-time champion Bowl of Flowers, by Sailor. Bowl of Flowers developed quickly enough to win the National Stallion Stakes at two in 1960, and later that year she won the Frizette and Gardenia to clinch juvenile filly honors. At three, with Burch's son Elliott training her, Bowl of Flowers added the Acorn, Coaching Club American Oaks, and Spinster Stakes to secure the championship among three-year-old fillies. Acquired by Morven Stud, Bowl of Flowers produced the stakes winner Spruce Bouquet, but a more lasting influence has been her Nijinsky II colt Whiskey Road. Sent to Australia, Whiskey Road sired Strawberry Road, a major winner around the world and sire of a brace of major American runners of the 1990s, including back-to-back filly champions and Breeders' Cup Distaff winners Ajina and Escena as well as Breeders' Cup Turf winner Fraise.

Flower Bed, daughter of Boudoir II, produced a total of nine foals, of which eight raced and seven won. Three won stakes. In addition to Flower Bowl, they were Floral Park and Brambles. Floral Park was another Alibhai filly and winner of the Bellerose

Handicap. She in turn became a tail-female ancestress of stakes winners, including Rootentootenwooten, Turn Bold, and Muckraker.

Brambles was foaled from Flower Bed in 1960, three years after the mare had been sold privately by Mrs. Sloane to Robert J. Kleberg Jr. of King Ranch. A Beau Max colt, Brambles won the $50,000 Benjamin F. Lindheimer Handicap in 1965. Among Flower Bed's foals for King Ranch was Multiflora, also by Beau Max. A non-winner from fourteen starts who earned a mere $995 by placing, Multiflora produced the wonderful King Ranch filly Gallant Bloom. A 1966 Gallant Man filly, Gallant Bloom was one of the last exceptional horses trained by Max Hirsch. Hirsch died when she was three and was succeeded by son Buddy Hirsch. At two in 1968, Gallant Bloom earned championship honors with victories in such races as the Gardenia, Matron, and National Stallion Stakes. At three, Gallant Bloom spotted Shuvee the New York Filly Triple Crown and Alabama, but still secured another championship by winning all eight of her races, including several meetings with Shuvee. The seven stakes she won at three included the Delaware Oaks, Monmouth Oaks, Gazelle, Matchmaker, and Spinster. Before retirement, Gallant Bloom added the Santa Margarita and Santa Maria the next winter and had a career record of sixteen wins in twenty-two races and earnings of $535,739.

Multiflora also became second dam of Misty Valley, Batman, and Lady's Slippers, major winners from Malaysia to Ireland to Australia.

To return now to Flower Bowl, the top stakes winner from Boudoir II's daughter Flower Bed: After the death of Mrs. Sloane of Brookmeade in 1962, Winston Guest acquired a draft of the stable's mares. Soon thereafter, many of them were resold to John W. Galbreath, whose efforts to build his Darby Dan Farm into a world-class operation had also included the acquisition of Ribot and Swaps for his stallion barn. Flower Bowl's 1963 Ribot colt was a large, liver chestnut of exceptional charisma. That he was given a name from fiction, Graustark, was appropriate, for he achieved almost legendary status despite the brevity of his career.

By the time Graustark made his first start in the summer of 1965 in Chicago, his trainer, Loyd Gentry, already had expressed amazement at the "ballyhooing" in the press about the magnificent colt. Graustark never let anyone down, for his victories were achieved with a mingling of grace and potency that lifted his status far above mere statistics. In truth, Graustark's record was so truncated that he won but a pair of stakes, the Arch Ward at two and the Bahamas at three, and he earned only $75,904. The champion of his crop, Buckpasser, had earned more than a half-million at two, and yet Graustark was seen as a serious challenger as they embarked on their routes toward the Triple Crown of 1966. Neither made it. Buckpasser had a winter injury, but came back to be Horse of the Year. Graustark took an unbeaten record of seven races into a dark and foreboding afternoon in April at Keeneland, suffered the unthinkable — defeat — and emerged with a fractured coffin bone. He was retired to a stud career at Darby Dan that ratified expectations for him. Graustark sired fifty-two stakes winners, including Key to the Mint, Proud Truth, Avatar, Caracolero, Tempest Queen, and Prove Out.

Three of Flower Bowl's four foals after Bowl of Flowers were by the unbeaten European champion Ribot. After Graustark, they included His Majesty. While lacking the brilliance of Graustark, His Majesty stayed sound enough to make twenty-two starts from two through five. He won five, including the Everglades Stakes, his only stakes win, and placed in the Widener, Seminole, and Bahamas. The younger brother joined Graustark at Darby Dan and achieved several distinctions his full brother did not. His

Majesty sired a Kentucky Derby winner, Pleasant Colony, who in turn has been one of the most significant American stallions of the 1980s and 1990s. Pleasant Colony is the sire of European classic winner St. Jovite, Belmont Stakes winner Colonial Affair, and champions Pleasant Tap and Pleasant Stage. Another son of His Majesty, Cormorant, sired Kentucky Derby winner Go for Gin. His Majesty also topped the general sire list, achieving that status in 1982. He has sired fifty-four stakes winners to date.

Other Hosts and Hostesses

The year after Boudoir II foaled Your Host, she produced another Alibhai colt, My Host, winner once from thirty-two races and earner of $5,465. My Host became a successful sire in California, where he got thirteen stakes winners. It was also in 1948 that Combs purchased Boudoir II and five other Mayer mares, and they were shipped to Spendthrift Farm in the same shipment with the new prized stallion Alibhai.

In 1949, Boudoir II foaled an Alibhai filly, which was named Your Hostess. Although bred in Combs' name, Your Hostess raced for Mayer. She was a decent sort of filly, winning three races from sixteen starts and earning $14,575, and she was third in the Santa Susana Handicap. Your Hostess produced fourteen foals, of which eleven raced and eight won. In 1958, Your Hostess was purchased from a Mayer auction for $52,000 by Millard Waldheim, owner of Bwamazon Farm in Kentucky. She was a major find. Your Hostess foaled for Bwamazon the T. V. Lark colt T. V. Commercial, who won the Arlington-Washington Futurity and Breeders' Futurity at two in 1967. All told, T. V. Commercial won fifteen races from fifty-five starts, including a total of eight stakes, and finish third in the Kentucky Derby. He earned $404,034 and had a long and successful career as a regional stallion in Maryland.

Your Hostess also foaled the tough little Gallant Man filly Coraggioso, whose nineteen wins included

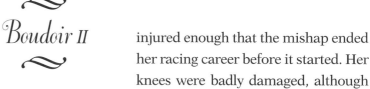

victories in the grade I Ladies Handicap and five other stakes. Coraggioso earned $309,281, and she became the first or second dam of several stakes winners. Another Gallant Man filly from Your Hostess was Gallatia, who won the Schuylerville and placed in the Spinaway. Gallatia in turn foaled the stakes winners Right Cross and Gallina.

Royal Charger was the sire of Your Hostess' 1955 foal, Royal Clipper, who won twenty-four of 159 races, including one stakes, the Salinas Stakes.

In 1963, Your Hostess at fourteen was bred to the 1959 Horse of the Year Sword Dancer and produced Dancing Hostess, a moderate winner who in turn foaled Loosen Up and Palladium. Etiquette, an early foal of Your Hostess by Bernborough, produced a pair of moderate stakes winners, and then her daughter White Lie foaled Hippodamia, the French champion two-year-old filly of 1973 and a subsequent stakes producer.

Yet another daughter of Your Hostess was Lady Ambassador, a Hill Prince mare who foaled the moderate stakes winner Minstrel Grey and also foaled the dam of Rare Treat Handicap winner With a Twist. Your Hostess was bred to Mister Gus in 1962 and, although that fine racehorse was a disappointment at stud, the result was My Guest, unraced dam of three stakes winners. In 1968, Your Hostess' foal was Votre Hostesse, by Nantallah, and she in turn produced stakes winner Auberge as well as the dam of 1990s stakes winner Danville.

The real jewel from Your Hostess, however, was Gay Hostess. Foaled in 1957, Gay Hostess was by Royal Charger, for some years regarded as a source of speed but questionable stamina, before his son Turn-to founded a staying line. Mayer had died, and Combs bought Gay Hostess from the 1958 Keeneland fall yearling sale for $6,700. She was showing high promise in training at Keeneland until a family oddity recurred: She fell. Like her dam's full brother, Your Host, Gay Hostess was injured enough that the mishap ended her racing career before it started. Her knees were badly damaged, although she was able to run with other mares and her foals in the Spendthrift fields.

Gay Hostess' first stakes winner was Lovely Gypsy, an Armageddon filly that won the Miss Chicago Stakes and Bangles and Beads Handicap. Then came the heavyweights.

Combs had added the brilliant Raise a Native to his stallion roster at Spendthrift. In 1967, Gay Hostess' colt from Raise a Native's second crop was particularly attractive. He brought a record in the Keeneland summer sale, going on a bid of $250,000 to Frank McMahon, although McMahon later was discerned to have owned half of him in the first place. Sent to retired jockey champion John Longden, who had launched his training career, the colt was given a name to match his appearance: Majestic Prince.

Like his fellow Boudoir II descendant Graustark, Majestic Prince was a colt of surpassing appearance. He was a bright chestnut of unusual luster and had an Arab look to his head, along with a physical form in which the expression of elegance was equal to that of power. In the author's experience, he was the most beautiful of all horses. Not even Secretariat created the visceral reaction from merely seeing him that Majestic Prince did, although what Secretariat did on the racetrack tilted the balance definitely his way.

Majestic Prince was late getting to the races, but he sped through his early starts in California with high style. He topped his California preparation by winning the Santa Anita Derby, prepped once at Churchill Downs, and arrived at the 1969 Kentucky Derby unbeaten in seven races. At the time, there was some question about the stamina of Raise a Native's runners, inasmuch as Affirmed, Alydar, and others were still in the future. Moreover, Majestic Prince's foes included sons of stayers Ribot (Arts and Letters) and Herbager (Dike). Nevertheless, against a high-class field also including Top Knight, Majestic Prince was favored. In a gritty battle through the long stretch, he stood off Arts and Letters to win by a neck, giving jockey Bill Hartack a record-equaling fifth win in the Derby. In the Preakness, the result was similar, and so Majestic Prince stood on the brink of a Triple Crown, a series which had not seen a winner since Citation twenty-one years before.

Longden knew Majestic Prince was getting to be a bit worn and wanted to rest him. The lure of the Triple prompted McMahon to overrule him. In the Belmont, Majestic Prince was no match for Arts and Letters and never ran again. Majestic Prince had won the first nine of his ten races and earned $414,200. He stood at Spendthrift, and, while not a great success, he did get the Belmont winner Coastal and the influential stallion Majestic Light.

The year after Majestic Prince won two-thirds of the Triple Crown, Combs and McMahon took their buy-half/keep-half routine back into the Keeneland ring in the form of another Raise a Native—Gay Hostess colt. This one brought a new record, becoming the first half-million dollar sale yearling. The final price was $510,000 in McMahon's name, and while McMahon did not actually have to pay out more than half of that, it is also true that he was turning down his share of the underbid, so the conviction of investment was hardly less than in an ordinary sale.

McMahon gave this colt another handsome name, Crowned Prince, and sent him to England. In three races, he became a champion, taking the Champagne Stakes and Dewhurst Stakes to earn top rank among English-raced two-year-olds of 1971. The following year, he was unplaced in his only start, after which it was announced he had an affliction of the soft palate and he was retired. Crowned Prince thus had a record of two wins in four starts and earnings of $37,883.

Gay Hostess also foaled the Prince John filly Betty Loraine, who placed in stakes and then produced the 1974 French Derby winner Caracolero, champion three-year-old in France. Betty Loraine also foaled the dam of the 1984 Epsom Derby winner Secreto. Even more current in classic races is Real Quiet, the 1998 Kentucky Derby and Preakness Stakes winner who is out of a daughter of Majestic Prince's full sister, Meadow Blue.

To return to Boudoir II, she had no foal in 1950, then the next year produced the Bull Lea filly who would be named Miniature. The latter was unplaced in her only start. In 1952, Boudoir II foaled the Alibhai filly Royal Hostess, who won once in five starts to earn $2,275; Royal Hostess is the third dam of stakes winner Native Goal. In 1953, Boudoir II had another Alibhai colt, who was named Bar Le Duc and who won his only start and earned $1,400. Bar Le Duc was given a chance at stud and begot eight stakes winners. In 1954, Boudoir II foaled the Ardan colt Splendido, who won four of thirty-nine races and earned $9,927. Then came Caluria, a 1955 Heliopolis filly who never raced.

Boudoir II had no live foal for five years. She was barren in 1956 and 1957, aborted twins and was not bred back in 1958, then had a foal born dead in 1960. As recounted above, she had been sold by then, and she produced her last foal for Mrs. Love in 1961. This was one more Alibhai filly, from the sire's last crop as well. It seems appropriate that Boudoir II at the end of her days would be owned by a Maryland family who had nurtured and loved its horses for many years The filly was given the lyric and evocative name Bowl of Roses, but she failed to summon the success suggested by her name and heritage, going unplaced in six starts. Bowl of Roses' foals included the Jaipur mare Flower Centre, dam of Irish Cesarewitch winner The Neurologist and German stakes winner Fahrewohl, and the Chateaugay mare Chateau Rose, dam of Japanese group winner Nichido Arashi. ❖

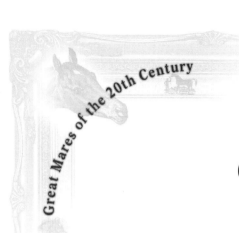

Bourtai

Bourtai, her ancestors, and close-up descendants contributed to a number of prominent stables of their times. Humphrey S. Finney, the philosophical physiognomy of the Fasig-Tipton sale firm through many a delightful season, once wrote an article for *The Blood-Horse* about the family. He dated the beginnings of its modern, American imprint to 1916, when "John Sanford had some two-year-olds returned to the United States from his French stud farm because of the virtual cessation of racing in France during World War I. Among those sent by Sanford to his Hurricana Stud in Amsterdam, N.Y., was Affection."

Affection was a daughter of Isidor out of One I Love, a crack filly of the 1890s and a half-sister to Thankful Blossom. The latter became the third dam of the great sire Bull Lea. After her evacuation from France represented the return of the family to America, Affection was acquired by John E. Madden, master of the famed Hamburg Place in Kentucky. Whether Madden preferred a good deal or a good horse is difficult to determine from his history, but is a moot point inasmuch as he had so many of both. At any rate, after Affection had foaled a pair of successful producers bred by Madden, she wound up in the ownership of Marshall Field. At the age of seventeen, Affection foaled Hug Again, dam of major winners Sun Again, Fervent, and Arrogate.

(The links of this historic female family are a pleasure to dwell upon: We have already made reference to its connection to Bull Lea, five-time leading sire, and in Sun Again we introduce the sire line that comes down in modern times to such as Damascus, Private Account, and Skip Away.)

Among Affection's four stakes winners was Escutcheon, who won the 1930 Alabama Stakes. Escutcheon was sired by the developing great stallion Sir Gallahad III, himself a son of one of the great mares of the century, i.e., the mare Plucky Liege. Born in England in 1912, Plucky Liege foaled leading American sires Sir Gallahad III and Bull Dog, plus Epsom Derby winner Bois Roussel, Grand Prix de Paris winner Admiral Drake, and two other stakes winners.

Escutcheon foaled the stakes winners Mars Shield, Strange Device, and By Far. The first two of those had come to light by the time Escutcheon's 1942 filly was entered in the Lexington tent sale which Fasig-Tipton arranged in 1943. The sale's location was in response to wartime travel restrictions, which precluded Kentucky breeders from sending their usual consignments to Saratoga.

The daughter of Escutcheon was by Stimulus, eventually the sire of thirty-nine stakes winners, including Beaugay, Clang, Risque, and Miss Dolphin. Sylvester Labrot Jr. purchased the filly for $5,500. She was named Bourtai, and she ran twelve times at two in 1944, winning twice, running third in the Pimlico Nursery Stakes, and earning a total of $3,850.

Bourtai was bred in 1945 and the following year foaled the Swing and Sway colt Ribard, winner of five races from fifty-six starts and earner of $10,610. Her second foal was Salaza, a Pilate filly who won eight of sixty-nine career starts to earn $20,495 and foaled Western Canadian stakes-placed Sir Warren among five winners.

Bourtai had no reported foal in 1948, but the next year produced her first stakes winner in Banta, a filly by Some Chance. Banta first raced for Labrot, then she was sold to Walter Edgar and later purchased by Elmendorf Farm. She was late in achieving stakes success, taking a division of the Correction Handicap at five in 1954. Banta won eleven of fifty-eight races and earned $59,000. As we shall see later, she was the first of the outstanding producers foaled from Bourtai.

In 1950 and 1951, Bourtai produced two extraordinarily durable sons of 1947 Kentucky Derby winner Jet Pilot. The first, Four to Go, won twenty-one races in 228 starts from ages three to eleven and earned $44,758. He was followed by stakes-placed Sir Boss, who won thirty-one of 233 races from two through eleven and earned $53,277.

By 1951, Labrot's health problems prompted him to begin selling his stock, and he asked Finney to shop a package. As Finney recalled it, he was asked to look for a buyer of five mares and "a couple of foals." There were numerous reasons to look to Claiborne Farm. The mares were assembled there as boarders, and Claiborne had consigned Bourtai as agent for Field at the 1943 yearling sale. The deal was struck.

Bourtai's first foal for Claiborne was Delta, who was in the first American crop of the milestone import Nasrullah. Delta was foaled in 1952, and it was with her crop that Claiborne amended a tradition of nearly seventy years, involving three generations of the Hancock family, of selling the preponderance of its homebreds as yearlings. Claiborne thus retained a major winner, and a future Broodmare of the Year. Delta raced in the Claiborne silks for three seasons, winning nearly half of her races, sixteen of thirty-three, and earning $269,215. She won a half-dozen of the better stakes in Chicago and placed in three other added-money races. At two, one of Delta's rivals was Lea Lane, who was a homebred for Charlton Clay, a kinsman and Bourbon County, Kentucky, neighbor of Claiborne owners Arthur B. Hancock, Senior and Junior. In the $50,000 Arlington Lassie of 1954, Delta edged Lea Lane in a closely inspected photo finish.

In 1953, the year after foaling Delta, Bourtai produced Levee, whose name indicated a cleverness and theme mentality which Claiborne has used in naming ever since. Levee was by the young champion Hill Prince. It was surmised by Finney that A. B. (Bull) Hancock Jr.'s willingness to deal off Levee at two in 1955 resulted from the apparent superiority of another homebred Claiborne filly, Doubledogdare. Claiborne was able to trade Levee for a promising English filly Kerkeb. Hancock was dealing with Vernon Cardy of Montreal, who thus took Levee into his stable. Levee became a star of track and paddock while Kerkeb proved disappointing, but, Doubledogdare did prevail as champion filly at both two and three, and, anyway, Claiborne still owned Bourtai.

Levee came to hand well enough at two to win the Selima Stakes. At three, she turned in a campaign that, if not for peer Doubledogdare, would have secured a championship among three-year-old fillies in many seasons. She won the longest of the major races for the division, the Coaching Club American Oaks (then run at one and three-eighth miles) over the high-class Calumet Farm filly Princess Turia. Levee added the Monmouth Oaks, and in the fall took on older fillies and mares in the Beldame and won over Amoret and Searching. (Doubledogdare capped her championship season

		Commando, 1898	**Domino** Emma C.
	Ultimus, 1906		
		Running Stream, 1898	**Domino** Dancing Water
STIMULUS, ch, 1922			
		Uncle, 1905	Star Shoot The Niece
	Hurakan, 1911		
		The Hoyden, 1899	Esher The Maid
BOURTAI, **b m, 1942**			
		Teddy, 1913	Ajax Rondeau
	Sir Gallahad III, 1920		
		Plucky Liege, 1912	Spearmint Concertina
ESCUTCHEON, b, 1927			
		Isidor, 1894	Amphion Isis
	Affection, 1914		
		One I Love, 1893	Minting The Apple

Bourtai, b, 1942-1970. Bred by Marshall Field (N.Y.). Raced 1 yr, 12 sts, 2 wins, $3,850. 3rd Pimlico Nursery S. Dam of 13 named foals, 13 rnrs, 12 wnrs, 5 sw.

1946: Ribard, dk b c, by Swing and Sway. Raced 3 yrs, 56 sts, 5 wins, $10,610.

1947: Salaza, dk b f, by Pilate. Raced 3 yrs, 69 sts, 8 wins, $20,495. Dam of 8 foals, 7 rnrs, 5 wnrs, including **Sir Warren** ($29,557). Granddam of **WANDERLURE**. Died 1962.

1949: BANTA, ch f, by Some Chance. Raced 5 yrs, 58 sts, 11 wins, $59,000. Won Correction H; 3rd Step Lightly H. Dam of 5 foals, 4 rnrs, 3 wnrs, including **MANDATE** ($45,625). Granddam of **TALKING PICTURE, SELARI, ILLUSTRIOUS, Close Attention**. Died 1971.

1950: Four to Go, ch g, by Jet Pilot. Raced 11 yrs, 228 sts, 21 wins, $44,758.

1951: **Sir Boss**, b c, by Jet Pilot. Raced 10 yrs, 233 sts, 31 wins, $53,277. 2nd Grand Union Hotel S; 3rd Saratoga Special.

1952: DELTA, b f, by Nasrullah. Raced 3 yrs, 33 sts, 16 wins, $269,215. Broodmare of the Year in 1968. Won Arlington Lassie S, Princess Pat S, Arlington Matron H, Clang H, La Salle H, Myrtlewood H; 2nd Arlington Futurity, National Stallion S; 3rd Jasmine S. Dam of 10 foals, 10 rnrs, 9 wnrs, including **OKAVANGO** ($153,802, gr. II), **DIKE** ($351,274), **CANAL** ($280,358), **CABILDO** ($267,265), **SHORE** ($62,357), **Moss** ($46,491). Granddam of **POLONIA, PEAT MOSS, NAPLES, Eleven Pelicans, Buckmaster, Chicago Bid, Alligatrix, Louboff**. Died 1973.

1953: LEVEE, ch f, by Hill Prince. Raced 3 yrs, 40 sts, 8 wins, $223,305. Broodmare of the Year in 1970. Won Coaching Club American Oaks, Beldame H, Selima S, Monmouth Oaks; 2nd Adirondack S, Delaware Oaks; 3rd Acorn S, Test S, Alabama S, Astarita S, Prioress S. Dam of 11 foals, 9 rnrs, 7 wnrs, including **SHUVEE** ($890,445, champion older female), **ROYAL GUNNER** ($334,650), **NALEE** ($141,631), **A. T'S OLIE** ($82,211). Granddam of **SHUDANZ, NORDANCE, DOC SYLVESTER, SHUKEY, NALEES FOLLY, NALEES MAN,** **MENEVAL, TOM SWIFT, BENEFICE, GOOSIE, Nalees Knight, Nalees Rialto, Bold Tradition, Lonesome Dancer, Vatza, Nalee's Fantasy, Shufleur, Take Warning, Pretty Fancy, Hypermetric**.

1954: BAYOU, ch f, by Hill Prince. Raced 3 yrs, 32 sts, 7 wins, $143,759. Champion 3yo filly. Won Delaware Oaks, Acorn S, Gazelle H, Maskette H; 2nd Coaching Club American Oaks. Dam of 11 foals, 10 rnrs, 8 wnrs, including **BATTEUR** ($198,984). Granddam of **SLEW O' GOLD, SLEW O'DYNA, COASTAL, SLEW'S EXCELLER, FLAG OFFICER, Samalex (GB)**. Died 1982.

1955: Poetic License, ch f, by Count Fleet. Raced 2 yrs, 2 sts, 0 wins, $0. Dam of 9 foals, 9 rnrs, 6 wnrs, including **Blue Medley** ($6,325). Granddam of **TELL AGAIN, WHITE FIR**. Died 1978.

1956: Barren.

1957: AMBASSADOR, b g, by Nasrullah. Raced 3 yrs, 16 sts, 3 wins, $16,726. Won Annapolis Hurdle S; 2nd Promise Hurdle S. Died 1980.

1958: Barren.

1959: Bethel, ch c, by Dedicate. Raced 2 yrs, 21 sts, 2 wins, $6,285. Sire of 34 foals, AEI 0.78.

1960: Mogul, ch c, by Bold Ruler. Raced 2 yrs, 5 sts, 1 win, $2,700. Sire of 3 foals, AEI 0.53. Sent to Ven 1964.

1961: Barren.

1962: Louisiana, ch f, by Nadir. Raced 2 yrs, 14 sts, 1 win, $1,736. Dam of 8 foals, 6 rnrs, 4 wnrs. Granddam of **RAISE A BOY, Memento Mori**.

1963: Barren.

1964: Barren.

1965: Barren.

1966: Barren.

by defeating older distaffers, in the inaugural Spinster Stakes.) Levee won eight races from forty starts in two seasons and earned $223,305.

The Hill Prince—Bourtai filly whom Claiborne traded away lost the three-year-old title in 1956 to another Claiborne filly, and then another Hill Prince—Bourtai filly, whom Claiborne kept, secured the same title in 1957. The second of the Hill Prince—Bourtai fillies was Bayou, a 1954 foal who at three won the Acorn, Delaware Oaks, Maskette, and Gazelle. In the Maskette, Bayou stepped out of her age division to defeat the accomplished older mare Rare Treat, giving her two pounds of actual weight. Bayou won seven of thirty-two races at two, three, and four and earned $143,759.

In 1955, Bourtai foaled the Count Fleet filly Poetic License, who was unplaced but foaled a half-dozen winners. In 1956, Bourtai was barren, then the following year, she had a Nasrullah foal, Ambassador. This full brother to Delta became a stakes winner via a steeplechasing career. The gelding won the Annapolis Hurdle among three wins from sixteen starts, and earned $16,726.

Bourtai foaled no further stakes winners, although she had three more foals over the next five years. Her 1959 Dedicate colt, Bethel, won twice from twenty-one starts and earned $6,285; her 1960 Bold Ruler colt, Mogul, won once in five races and earned $2,700; and her last foal, Louisiana, a Nadir filly, won once in fourteen races and earned $1,736 before foaling four winners.

Bourtai thus had a total produce record of thirteen foals. All of them got to the races, twelve won, five won stakes, and two of them, Delta and Levee, were Broodmares of the Year.

A Flow of Importance

The escutcheon of Bourtai's daughters as producers is shiny and lasting. Banta, the first major stakes winner for Bourtai, produced only five foals, and just one of those, Mandate, achieved stakes winner status, but Banta's shadow has been long. One of Banta's foals was the 1956 Ambiorix filly Golden Sari, a winner, who produced Selari. A son of Prince John, Selari won the Grey Lag Handicap and earned $196,807 before a successful career at stud. Prince John was one of Elmendorf's key assets during part of the era the historic Kentucky farm was owned by Maxwell Gluck, and Selari's full sister, Silver Sari, foaled the powerful colt Big Spruce. Sired by Herbager, Big Spruce won six major events, including the Marlboro Cup, two runnings of the Gallant Fox, and the grade I Governor Stakes and San Luis Rey Stakes. He excelled on dirt and turf, hinting at a versatility of the family which would extend also to European classics.

Silver Sari also produced stakes winners Manta and Jabot. Manta was a memorable West Coast mare, winning eleven California stakes, including the Santa Margarita, and in the East she won the Firenze.

The prestigious Greentree Stable also purchased into this family, and, from Golden Sari's unplaced Tom Fool filly Royal Folly, Greentree bred the stakes winners Majestic Folly and Prince Valiant. Royal Folly also produced the 1990s French group winner, Polski Boy.

Banta's unraced Nasrullah filly Poster Girl foaled the champion Talking Picture. Arriving during the height of Elmendorf owner Gluck's success — twice the leading owner — Talking Picture was half a remarkable double for the breeder-owner and for trainer Johnny Campo. She reigned as champion two-year-old filly of 1973, and stablemate Protagonist ruled the two-year-old colts. Talking Picture was later acquired by Walter Haefner, owner of Moyglare Stud in Ireland and of a notable international stable. Talking Picture produced five stakes winners, four of them coming from repeated bookings to the 1978 American Triple Crown winner Affirmed.

Bourtai

One of the Affirmed—Talking Picture foals was the classic winner Trusted Partner, who won the Irish One Thousand Guineas in 1988. The others by that persistent consort were Irish champion miler Easy to Copy, Irish and American stakes winner Low Key Affair, and Epicure's Garden. Among Talking Picture's ten winners from sixteen foals was another stakes winner, Guaranteed Income, sired by Saratoga Six.

In addition to champion Talking Picture, Banta's daughter Poster Girl also foaled the stakes-winning Round Table colt Illustrious, he more illustrious as the broodmare sire of Gold Beauty than for his victory in the Native Dancer Handicap. Poster Girl also foaled the stakes producer Middle Cornish. The millionaire Honor Medal was among other stakes winners from this branch of the Bourtai family.

The Tides of Delta and Levee

Claiborne Farm's Delta, Bourtai's 1952 Nasrullah filly, had ten foals; all of them reached the races, and nine won. Her five stakes winners were Dike, Canal, Cabildo, Okavango, and Shore. Dike, by Herbager, aroused A. B. (Bull) Hancock Jr.'s lifelong ambition of winning the Kentucky Derby when he won the Breeders' Futurity at two and came back in the spring of 1969 to win the Wood Memorial.

Hancock was realistic. Shown a video of early Derby favorite Majestic Prince in action, he admitted it was enough "to scare a man to death." As matters transpired, it was Majestic Prince holding on to remain unbeaten in winning the Derby by a neck from Arts and Letters. Dike turned in a gallant effort in closing to be third, beaten about a length. Dike added the Seminole Handicap at four.

Okavango was a full brother to Dike. He was not a classic contender, but won the grade II San Pasqual Handicap and the grade III Salvator Mile.

The other three stakes winners from Delta (Canal, Cabildo, and Shore) were by Round Table, a champion bred and initially raced by Claiborne and returned there for a distinguished stud career. (Round Table lived to be thirty-three. When Queen Elizabeth II toured Kentucky farms in 1984, her itinerary included Claiborne, where conversation turned to Round Table; surprised to learn he was still living, Her Majesty altered her schedule to visit his pensioner's paddock on the farm.)

Shore, winner of the Bewitch Stakes, was one of several of Delta's daughters to extend the family influence. She foaled three stakes-placed horses, one of which was Alligatrix, by two-time Prix de l'Arc de Triomphe winner Alleged. Alligatrix was bred by Shirley Taylor and Charles Wacker III, Americans with connections to Europe, and she was stakes-placed in England. Alligatrix produced the group I French winner Croco Rouge and other stakes winners Persianalli and Alidiva. In turn, Alidiva became the dam of two group I English winners — classic One Thousand Guineas winner Sleepytime and Sussex Stakes winner Ali-Royal — as well as Italian/German champion Taipan. Sleepytime also placed in two English group I races.

Yet another Round Table filly from Delta was the stakes-placed Moss, dam of Polonia, a Danzig filly who earned multiple ratings atop European sprint divisions and won the storied group I Prix de l'Abbaye de Longchamp. Moss also foaled a horse of another stripe in Peat Moss, by Herbager. Peat Moss's game was hardly sprints, and he ran a close second to John Henry in the Jockey Club Gold Cup as well as winning three stakes.

The other stakes winners descending in their bottom line from Delta include Silver Ending, Siberian Summer, and, in the Antipodes, Te Akau, Pearl, and Champagne.

Levee had one fewer stakes winner than her half-sister Delta's five, but one of them was the wonderful race mare Shuvee. Levee had eleven foals, of which nine raced and seven won. As recounted above, Levee raced for Mrs. Vernon Cardy. A later partnership arrangement brought Greif Raible in as part owner. Before Levee's second foal, Nalee, had emerged as the mare's first major winner, the partnership was broken up, and Finney of Fasig-Tipton once again became involved with the family. He was asked to find a buyer for Levee, and he approached Whitney Stone, who was in the process of retooling his approach at Morven Stud in Virginia. Stone was reducing the numbers in his broodmare band to concentrate on acquiring a few, top-quality mares. Although Levee was barren at the time, he agreed to the stout price of $150,000 for Levee. He also had acquired the champion Bowl of Flowers, and the pair of mares was to send some glossy youngsters into his Saratoga yearling consignments.

Levee's aforementioned daughter Nalee was by 1955 Horse of the Year Nashua. Although never a championship contender in the crop of Affectionately, Lamb Chop, etc., Nalee was a useful stakes winner, and she produced ten winners, a number of which have assayed a strong branch of the family. Nalee foaled a European classic winner, Irish St. Leger victor Meneval, and other stakes winners Nalees Folly and Nalees Man. Five other of her foals were stakes-placed. One which was not, Nalees Flying Flag, nevertheless produced Sacahuista, by which time this branch of the bloodline had been bought into by the family of the late George Humphrey, Secretary of the Treasury under Dwight Eisenhower and an avid Thoroughbred breeder. Sacahuista won the Breeders' Cup Distaff and was champion three-year-old filly of 1987.

Levee produced the major stakes winner Royal Gunner, by Royal Charger, and the lesser black-type filly A. T's Olie, by Mongo. In 1966, Stone had at Morven a Sailor yearling filly out of Levee, and, as

any market breeder is wont to do, figured retaining at least one filly from such a mare was a matter of wise planning for the future. The Sailor filly was set to stay home, but then a hole in the Morven consignment developed when a Never Bend yearling was hurt. Since Levee by then had foaled another filly, it was decided to send the Sailor filly on to the sale: The one Stone sold brought a record price and the one he thus kept set a record in earnings! From such circumstances do decisions enhance many a racing man's status.

The Sailor—Levee filly was purchased by a powerful tandem of Charles W. Engelhard, the leading market buyer at the time, and Paul Mellon of Rokeby Farms. She went for $177,000, then the all-time record for a filly. Named Many Happy Returns, she won only twice and, although foaling the Irish St. Leger third Hypermetric, was not a notable producer in the context of her family.

The filly who was retained to race in the name of Mrs. Whitney Stone was another by Nashua and was named Shuvee. Few fathers and daughters have as much in common as did Nashua and Shuvee: They each won the Jockey Club Gold Cup twice, and both times when it was run at two miles.

At two, Shuvee came on strongly enough to win the Frizette and Selima, but could not wrest a championship from the brilliance of Gallant Bloom and Process Shot. At three, Shuvee swept the New York Filly Triple Crown and added the Alabama for trainer Mike Freeman, but still could not dislodge Gallant Bloom as champion. At both four and five, however, Shuvee held sway as the champion older filly and mare. During those campaigns, she won two runnings of the Top Flight Handicap and Diana Handicap, as well as defeating males twice in the Jockey Club Gold Cup. She also scored in the Beldame. Shuvee won sixteen of forty-four starts and earned $890,445, then a record for fillies and mares.

Shuvee was, of course, a treasure in the making for Morven. One of her more spectacular yearlings was the Nijinsky II colt Vatza, for whom John A. Bell III bid a sale-topping $800,000 at Saratoga in 1978. Vatza was stakes-placed for Bell and partners, but was retired by injury and died early at stud.

Shuvee produced three stakes winners — Shukey, Tom Swift, and Benefice — a successful career, but hardly one of the best within her glorious family. Her full sister Sister Shu, who placed once, is dam of stakes winners Shudanz and Nordance, and second dam of Manzotti, Arbusha, and Nicholas.

Gold and Bayou

Levee's full sister Bayou went into the Claiborne Farm broodmare band. She foaled only one stakes winner among eleven foals and eight winners, but was a lasting influence. Her 1960 Bold Ruler filly, named Batteur, raced in the colors of William Haggin Perry, with whom Claiborne had a crop sharing arrangement. A sportsman and horseman of the ilk of Perry is not your usual sharecropper; he and Bull Hancock worked out a deal whereby Perry would purchase half-interest of all Claiborne-bred yearlings and would divide them into their separate stables while having joint ownership.

Batteur, like Perry's Lamb Chop, was an early indicator that one and a quarter miles would not be beyond the tether of all Bold Rulers. While this may seem obvious today, in the early crops of Bold Ruler there were enough defeats at the distance to call the matter into question. Batteur set a course record of 1:58 2/5 in the one and a quarter-mile Santa Barbara Handicap at Santa Anita. She also won five other stakes on both coasts, including the Santa Margarita.

Batteur foaled the Illinois Derby winner Flag Officer and also Flail. Flail in turn was dam of three stakes winners, including the Herbager filly Anifa, who placed in the French St. Leger and returned to America to win the Turf Classic.

A full sister to Batteur was Bayou Blue, whose daughter Harbor Flag is the dam of Louisiana Derby winner Country Light and the stakes-winning filly Packet. Another Bold Ruler—Bayou filly was Slew, dam of grade I Flower Bowl Handicap winner Slew's Exceller and the Japanese stakes winner Slew O'Dyna. Slew also foaled Youthful Lady, who produced five stakes winners.

Slew was foaled in 1972 and had only a sire-line connection to the more famous Slew (Seattle Slew), who won the Triple Crown in 1977. However, the Bayou family genes were destined to achieve some of their best work when crossed with Seattle Slew.

In 1969, Bayou foaled Alluvial, who would become one of many distinguished daughters sired by the Claiborne stallion Buckpasser. Alluvial did not get to the races, but she foaled a champion and a classic winner. The champion was Slew o' Gold, by Seattle Slew. Raced by a partnership involving Seattle Slew's owners (Jim and Sally Hill and Mickey and Karen Taylor), Slew o' Gold was champion three-year-old of 1983 and champion older horse of 1984. He won two runnings of the Jockey Club Gold Cup, earned more than $3.5 million, and was elected to the Hall of Fame. Slew o' Gold and Seattle Slew both stand at Three Chimneys Farm. While the son has not matched the eminence of the sire, Slew o' Gold has sired a number of major horses. (The year after Slew o' Gold was foaled, Claiborne had its turn with a Seattle Slew colt, having bred Swale, who won the Kentucky Derby and Belmont Stakes.)

Alluvial's son Coastal was a disappointment at stud, but he, too, had been an outstanding runner. Coastal was by the dual-classic winner Majestic Prince and raced for Perry, who anted up $20,000 to supplement the colt for the 1979 Belmont Stakes. This dig into the pocket entitled Coastal to challenge Spectacular Bid, then apparently sailing toward the Triple Crown. Coastal upset Spectacular Bid in the one and a half-mile classic and also won the Monmouth Invitational and Dwyer.

Another confluence of Bayou's family and Seattle Slew resulted in the 1995 Hollywood Oaks winner Sleep Easy. She was by Seattle Slew and out of Alluvial's unraced daughter, Dokki, by Northern Dancer.

The waters had run swift and deep. ❖

Courtly Dee

At any of several points over much of the 20th Century, one could reach into the female succession of the family of Courtly Dee and find a suitable representative for a retrospective on outstanding mares. Courtly Dee gets the call to represent the family in part because of currency and also because she and her daughters and granddaughters will surely be a link to the 21st Century.

The frame of reference for this volume is the 20th Century, but the distinction of Courtly Dee's family crosses back into the 19th. We will begin with Wanda, a foal of 1882, whose dam, Minnie Minor, was twenty-one when the filly was foaled. It is a footnote worth savoring that Minnie Minor was a daughter of none other than Lexington, the American stallion nonpareil of the 19th Century. Lexington's direct influence bridged pre- and post-Civil War eras, and he led the sire lists sixteen times, a record unmatched in any following era.

Wanda was bred and owned by Pierre Lorillard, who with his brother, George, divvied up major races of the time in a manner that any other brothers — even Mohammed and Hamdan al Maktoum — would find impressive. Running one-two-three in major stakes, while not an everyday occurrence, ceased to be a rarity for the Lorillards. Wanda, sired by the imported French stallion Mortemer, won twelve of twenty-four races at two and three,

frequently venturing out of her gender and age group. One of her most important victories was very much an in-house affair, but a fair race all the same. George Lorillard was president of Monmouth Park, the fashionable track near the Jersey Shore, and to attract most of the best three-year-olds of 1885, Monmouth put up a winning purse of $18,530 for a race at one and a half miles. Looking around for an appropriate name, management settled on the Lorillard Stakes. Wanda won in a canter, the beaten field including Belmont Stakes winner Tyrant.

In the stud, Wanda foaled two stakes winners, Urania and Glacier. Urania in turn foaled three stakes winners, including the dam of Epsom Derby winner Durbar II. Another daughter of Wanda was Countess Wanda, who in turn foaled two stakes winners and producers: Fairy Wand, dam of Hopeful winner Epithet and Dwyer winner Genie; and Planutess, dam of Tracksend, Uncle's Lassie, and Paavo.

It was Uncle's Lassie who would eventually be the fourth dam of Courtly Dee, and there was much glory between them. Uncle's Lassie was by Uncle, also sire of the popular Old Rosebud. Planutess, dam of Uncle's Lassie, was by the imported Planudes, a son of St. Simon; thus the family merged influences of one of the greatest of American sires and one of the greatest of English sires.

Uncle's Lassie won two stakes at two in 1918, the Lynbrook Selling Stakes and Mineola Selling Stakes, each with a good purse for the day, $2,000. All told, Uncle's Lassie made eighty-three starts, won fourteen times, and earned $18,254, or slightly less than her third dam took in from the Lorillard Stakes. In the stud, she produced nothing but winners — well, almost, foaling twelve winners from thirteen foals. Five won stakes.

Owner Herbert Gardner sent Uncle's Lassie to a series of the best sires of the time, and got commensurate results. In 1926, Uncle's Lassie produced a colt by Man o' War. Later gelded, he was named Clyde Van Dusen in honor of the fellow who would train him for Gardner. The Clydes Van Dusen teamed to win the Kentucky Derby in 1929, beating twenty others, including Blue Larkspur. At two, Clyde Van Dusen had won the Kentucky Jockey Club Stakes.

In 1928, Uncle's Lassie foaled a filly to the cover of another leading sire (to be), Sir Gallahad III. The filly was named Betty Derr and was foaled at the Lexington farm, called Few Acres Farm, of trainer Van Dusen. Betty Derr came out quickly at two to win the Debutante at Churchill Downs, another Debutante at Washington Park, and the Clipsetta Stakes at Latonia. At three, Betty Derr won the $10,000 Latonia Oaks.

She had become the property of Van Dusen by 1939, when all-around Kentucky horseman Dan Midkiff was representing Hollywood mogul Louis B. Mayer in his growing bloodstock operation. In negotiating with Van Dusen to take over as trainer of Mayer's horses, Midkiff offered on his boss's behalf to purchase some of the breeding stock to which Van Dusen was then devoting much of his time.

Betty Derr had a Blue Larkspur foal at foot (the moderate winner Blue Serge), and Midkiff bought the pair for Mayer for about $10,000. Earlier, Betty

Derr had foaled the Cincinnati Trophy winner Betty Sweep, by Sweep All. After Mayer bought her, she was sent to Man o' War's best son, War Admiral, in 1940, when the Triple Crown winner was standing his first season at stud. The resulting foal was named Iron Maiden, who was foaled at Glade Valley Farm in Maryland, where leading sire Challenger II was at stud. It was Iron Maiden who would link the family of Clyde Van Dusen to two additional Kentucky Derby winners.

Maryland-bred Iron Maiden would have this impact on Kentucky by way of California, where she was racing at three when Mayer sold her to fellow West Coast breeders Ellwood B. Johnston and W. W. (Tiny) Naylor. Iron Maiden was taken out of training at four, bred to Mayer's Beau Pere, and foaled a filly named Iron Reward. While it is common to assign to human beings a heightened sense of job responsibility after they have become parents, the idea generally makes no sense when applied to horses. Nevertheless, Iron Maiden, who had not been a stakes winner before, came back to the races after the foal was weaned, and at six in 1947, she won the Del Mar Handicap.

The Beau Pere—Iron Maiden filly, named Iron Reward, was sold to Rex Ellsworth and became the dam of 1955 Kentucky Derby winner Swaps; Iron Maiden herself was later sold to Calumet Farm and became the dam of 1957 Kentucky Derby winner Iron Liege, by Bull Lea. Thus, within three runnings of the classic, the stamp of Betty Derr and Iron Maiden was prominent upon two Derby winners.

Swaps was by Ellsworth's Hyperion horse Khaled, the jewel of California stallions. In addition to defeating Nashua in the 1955 Derby, Swaps defeated 1954 Derby winner Determine in the Californian. He also won the American Derby before losing to Nashua in their match race late in the summer of 1955. At four, Swaps raced through

		Nearco, 1935	Pharos / Nogara
	Nasrullah, 1940		
		Mumtaz Begum, 1932	Blenheim II / Mumtaz Mahal
NEVER BEND, dk b, 1960			
		Djeddah, 1945	Djebel / Djezima
	Lalun, 1952		
		Be Faithful, 1942	Bimelech / Bloodroot
COURTLY DEE, dkb/br m, March 8, 1968			
		Man o' War, 1917	Fair Play / Mahubah
	War Admiral, 1934		
		Brushup, 1929	Sweep / Annette K.
TULLE, dk b, 1950			
		Beau Pere, 1927	Son-in-Law / Cinna
	Judy-Rae, 1944		
		Betty Derr, 1928	Sir Gallahad III / Uncle's Lassie

Courtly Dee, dkb/br, 1968-1995. Bred by Donald Unger (Ky.). Raced 2 yrs, 33 sts, 4 wins, $19,426. Broodmare of the Year in 1983. Dam of 18 named foals, 17 rnrs, 15 wnrs, 8 sw. ($900,000, 1980 keenov, Alydar).

1974: **ALI OOP**, gr c, by Al Hattab. Raced 2 yrs, 23 sts, 7 wins, $174,020. Won Sapling S (gr. I), Dragoon S, Boardwalk S (T); 2nd Cowdin S (gr. II); 3rd Tyro S. Sire of 253 foals, AEI 0.85.

1975: **NATIVE COURIER**, ch g, by Exclusive Native. Raced 6 yrs, 51 sts, 14 wins, $522,635. Won Seneca H (gr. IIIT), Brighton Beach H (gr. IIIT), Bernard Baruch H (gr. IIIT), Laurel Turf Cup H (T); 2nd Man o' War S (gr. IT), Lawrence Realization S (gr. IIT), Bernard Baruch H (gr. IIIT), Fort Marcy H (gr. IIIT), Seneca H (gr. IIIT), Rutgers H (T); 3rd Turf Classic (gr. IT), Manhattan H (gr. IIT, three times), Bernard Baruch H (gr. III).

1976: Vireo, ch f, by True Knight. Raced 2 yrs, 15 sts, 1 win, $15,090. Dam of 7 foals, 5 rnrs, 5 wnrs, including **CHIEF TURKO** ($82,942), **Rush for Gold** ($81,130). Granddam of **MISS ANGELINA**, **PRECIOUS GLITTER**, **Sir Dancer**, **Prolific Protege**. Died 1997.

1977: Ragtime Knight, b c, by True Knight. Raced 9 yrs, 73 sts, 5 wins, $24,486.

1978: **PRINCESS OOLA**, ro f, by Al Hattab. Raced 3 yrs, 22 sts, 5 wins, $108,291. Won Whitemarsh H; 2nd Affectionately H (gr. III). Dam of 7 foals, 7 rnrs, 5 wnrs, including **AZZAAM** ($661,306), **BALWA** ($42,692). Granddam of **BET TWICE PRINCESS**, **Reel Tough Lady**. Died 1992.

1979: Foreign Courier, b f, by Sir Ivor. Unraced. Dam of 11 foals, 10 rnrs, 7 wnrs, including **GREEN DESERT** ($308,015, Eng-I), **YOUSEFIA** ($154,631). Granddam of **MYTHICAL GIRL**.

1980: Embellished, b f, by Seattle Slew. Raced 2 yrs, 9 sts, 1 win, $13,340. Dam of 11 foals, 10 rnrs, 10 wnrs, including **SEATTLE DAWN** ($276,250, gr. II), **TRUCKEE** ($221,538), **ISLAND OF SILVER** ($92,113), **Lord Charmer** ($149,208, in Eng and NA), **Alydar's Son** ($33,167, in Ger). Granddam of **GOLD SUNRISE**, **Premium Thunder**, **Te n Te**.

1981: **ALTHEA**, ch f, by Alydar. Raced 2 yrs, 15 sts, 8 wins, $1,275,255. Champion 2yo filly. Won Arkansas Derby (gr. I; ETR, OP, 9 furlongs in 1:46.80), Hollywood Starlet S (gr. I), Santa Susana S (gr. I), Del Mar Futurity (gr. II), Del Mar Debutante S (gr. II), Hollywood Juvenile Championship (gr. II), Las Virgenes S; 2nd Oak Leaf S (gr. I), Fantasy S (gr. I), Landaluce S (gr. II), Anoakia S (gr. III). Dam of 5 foals, 4 rnrs, 4 wnrs, including **YAMANIN PARADISE** ($1,457,353, champion 2yo filly in Japan), **DESTINY DANCE** ($86,596), **AURORA** ($285,236), **ALYSSUM** ($190,655). Granddam of **ARCH**. Died 1995.

1982: Barada, ch f, by Damascus. Raced 2 yrs in Eng, 3 sts, 0 wins, $0. Dam of 7 foals, 7 rnrs, 6 wnrs. Sent to Japan 1995. ($725,000 ftkjul yrlg).

1983: **KETOH**, ch c, by Exclusive Native. Raced 2 yrs, 5 sts, 3 wins, $173,550. Won Cowdin S (gr. I), Bolsa Chica S (R). Died 1986.

1984: Maidee, dkb/br f, by Roberto. Raced 3 yrs, 14 sts, 1 win, $39,910. Dam of 5 foals, 5 rnrs, 5 wnrs, including **DEFACTO** ($229,635). Sent to Japan 1994.

1985: Namaqua, b f, by Storm Bird. Raced 1 yr, 3 sts, 1 win, $9,373. Dam of 7 foals, 6 rnrs, 4 wnrs, including **NAMAQUALAND** ($165,013), **Lemon Dove** ($58,140).

1986: Karraar, ch c, by Saratoga Six. Raced 4 yrs in Eng and NA, 23 sts, 3 wins, $23,334. Died 1991. ($1,000,000 keejul yrlg).

1987: **AISHAH**, ch f, by Alydar. Raced 2 yrs, 14 sts, 6 wins, $169,340. Won Rare Perfume S (gr. II), Ocean Tide S. Dam of 5 foals, 4 rnrs, 4 wnrs, including **ALDIZA** ($496,394, gr. I), **Aunt Anne** ($99,404), **Elajjud** ($225,055).

1988: Barren.

1989: **AQUILEGIA**, ch f, by Alydar. Raced 4 yrs, 30 sts, 8 wins, $446,081. Won New York H (gr. IIT), Black Helen H (gr. IIIT); 2nd Sheepshead Bay H (gr. IIIT); 3rd New York H (gr. IIT), Boiling Springs H (gr. IIIT), Mrs. Revere S (T). Dam of 2 foals, 1 rnr, 1 wnr, **BERTOLINI** ($107,003).

1990: **Press Card**, b c, by Fappiano. Raced 3 yrs, 13 sts, 3 wins, $206,500. 2nd Pegasus H (gr. I), Pennsylvania Derby (gr. II); 3rd Champagne S (gr. I). Sire of 101 foals, AEI 0.47.

1991: **TWINING**, ch c, by Forty Niner. Raced 1 yr, 6 sts, 5 wins, $238,140. Won Peter Pan S (gr. II), Withers S (gr. II); 2nd Dwyer S (gr. II).

1992: Amizette, b f, by Forty Niner. Raced 1 yr, 8 sts, 0 wins, $6,930.

a series of world records, dominated his rivals (he and Nashua never met again), and was voted Horse of the Year. Swaps' son Chateaugay put the family on the top side of a Derby winner's pedigree, winning the Run for the Roses in 1963.

After her acquisition by Calumet Farm, Iron Maiden foaled three stakes winners: Trentonian, Iron Liege, and Aczay. In one of those Derbys which immediately settle into the race's lore, Iron Liege deputized for his injured stablemate, favored Gen. Duke, and held off Gallant Man, whose rider, Bill Shoemaker, mistook the sixteenth pole for the finish line in a millisecond that will live forever. Round Table and Bold Ruler followed. Although Iron Liege would not again defeat such high-class competition, he proved a very useful colt, adding the Jersey Stakes, Sheridan and McLennan Handicaps, and Laurance Armour Memorial.

One of the foals Betty Derr produced in California for Mayer was the Beau Pere filly Judy-Rae, who won the Anita Chiquita Stakes at two in 1946. Coldstream Stud of Kentucky later bought Judy-Rae for $45,000 from one of Mayer's spectacular dispersals. When Coldstream had its own dispersal, Millard Waldheim plucked Judy-Rae from that sale for $43,000.

In 1955, Judy-Rae's Nasrullah filly Judy Rullah romped through a spring day at Keeneland to win the Thoroughbred Club Dinner Purse by eight lengths. She was but one of many nice two-year-olds that Keeneland fans came to expect to carry Waldheim's blue and white Bwamazon Farm silks to early victories. Later that year, Judy Rullah won the Pollyanna Stakes and Arlington Lassie in Chicago.

As a broodmare, Betty Derr's granddaughter Judy Rullah added to the family collection. She foaled the Jersey Derby winner Creme dela Creme, by Olympia, and the stakes-winning Rhubarb, by Barbizon. Rhubarb in turn foaled stakes winner Bottle Top, dam of classics-placed Strodes Creek.

Other rather distant stakes-winning descendants of Judy-Rae would eventually include Appealing Missy, Wickerr, Palauli, Lets Don't Fight, Tenacious Tiffany, Fight Over, and the distaff champion Cascapedia.

Courtly Dee's Dam

It was through Judy-Rae that the family of Wanda, Uncle's Lassie, and Betty Derr led to Courtly Dee. In addition to her stakes winners, Judy-Rae's foals included the 1950 War Admiral filly Tulle. At the age of twenty, Tulle foaled stakes winner Tom Tulle, by Tom Rolfe, earlier having foaled stakes-winning Auhsan, by Nashua.

Courtly Dee was Tulle's 1968 foal. She was by Never Bend, Capt. Harry Guggenheim's 1962 juvenile champion, a son of Nasrullah and the Kentucky Oaks winner Lalun. In the same foal crop as Courtly Dee was Never Bend's son Mill Reef, who would reign as champion of Europe in 1971, generating an ongoing success for Never Bend blood abroad.

Courtly Dee was bred by Donald Unger and was knocked down for only $13,000 in the name of O. Unger when offered at the 1969 Keeneland September sale. At the start of her racing career, her pedigree was a happy talking point. At the conclusion of her racing days, her pedigree was still all there was to mention. Courtly Dee was unraced at two, then made eleven starts at three before winning a maiden race. She scored at six furlongs in September at Delaware Park, racing for Holmehill Stable and trained by Budd Lepman. She had two more wins late that year at Tropical Park.

The following year, Lepman had run her eleven times again without a victory, when he put her in for $15,000 at Atlantic City. She won, and was claimed in the name of Marty Fallon. If Fallon had the hope of moving her up, he was disappointed. Not running her for a price again, he sent her out

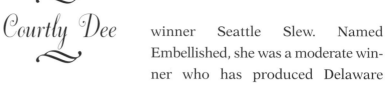

three times, during which she beat one horse, once. Courtly Dee, scion of a family of Derby winners and a future Broodmare of the Year, last raced at Liberty Bell over an off track on Dec. 21, 1972. At odds of 87-1, she finished last. The Never Bend filly left the track covered not with glory, but with mud.

Courtly Dee had won four of thirty-three races and earned $19,426. If a filly with a pedigree like hers is a dream for a trainer, it is no less enticing for an astute breeder. Lee Eaton and Leo Waldman's Red Bull Stable acquired Courtly Dee and began breeding sale yearlings from her. The black type was not dormant for long. Courtly Dee's first two foals were stakes winners: Sapling Stakes winner Ali Oop, by Al Hattab, and graded grass-course handicap winner Native Courier, by Exclusive Native.

She had two True Knights which were moderate winners, although the first, Vireo, foaled the dams of stakes winners. Returned to Al Hattab, Courtly Dee in 1978 foaled Princess Oola, who won the Whitemarsh Handicap and foaled Australian stakes winner Azzaam and English stakes winner Balwa, as well as the dam of stakes winner Bet Twice Princess.

To the cover of Sir Ivor, Courtly Dee foaled Foreign Courier, a 1979 filly who was unraced but produced the group I European sprinter Green Desert, by Danzig. Green Desert won the July Cup and other high-class races, placed in the classic Two Thousand Guineas, and has become an important international sire (ten percent stakes winners, including Sheikh Albadou, Desert Prince, Tropical, Desert Style, etc.). He is the broodmare sire of 1999 Dubai World Cup winner Almutawakel. Foreign Courier also foaled added-money winner Yousefia, a Danzig filly who in turn foaled English group III winner Mythical Girl.

Courtly Dee's 1980 filly was by Triple Crown winner Seattle Slew. Named Embellished, she was a moderate winner who has produced Delaware Handicap winner Seattle Dawn and two other stakes winners.

The King Ranch Connection

In the fall of 1980, Eaton and Red Bull consigned Courtly Dee to the Keeneland November breeding stock sale. When Helen Groves, daughter of King Ranch's master horseman Robert Kleberg Jr., heard about her, she had immediate hopes. One of her daughters, Helen Alexander, called to inquire if there was anything in the sale her mother was interested in pursuing. Mrs. Groves had been looking for a Never Bend mare, admiring the stallion as well as his dam, Lalun.

"So, Helen called again, and she was very much excited, and she said, 'I have found a mare I just love,'" Mrs. Groves later recounted for *Spur* magazine. "'We simply have to get this mare, but she's going to go for a lot of money.'"

As she often would, Helen Alexander referred the matter to Irish agent and accomplished horseman Tom Cooper, and a group was put together consisting of Mrs. Groves, Miss Alexander, and Cooper's brother-in-law, David Aykroyd. In the inflated market of the time, they had to go to $900,000 to purchase the mare, who was barely a month away from being thirteen.

Courtly Dee was in foal to Alydar from his first season at stud, and the following year foaled a dark chestnut filly who grew into a fetching yearling. Having had to pay nearly $1 million for the mare, the partners had in mind the sound business strategy of selling at least some of her foals. The Alydar filly, Althea, was headed for the Fasig-Tipton Kentucky summer yearling auction, but went lame very close to sale time and had to be withdrawn. When the problem turned out to be only a gravel and was attended to easily, the partners still realized selling might be the smart approach.

Dudley's restaurant is a friendly spot in Lexington and horsemen gather there with some frequency. The owners of Courtly Dee sat nervously around a table for lunch one day that summer of 1982 and each wrote down a figure at which they thought it would be best to sell the filly if an offer was forthcoming within a week. Whatever action took place in their lives that week, what did not happen turned out to be a blessing. With their prices not matched, the die was cast: Althea would be retained to race.

The Alydar—Courtly Dee filly was sent to trainer D. Wayne Lukas, and she developed into the strong sort of powerfully quartered racer that has been so frequently a star for the record-setting trainer. Lukas did not shrink from racing her against colts, and Althea won the Hollywood Juvenile Championship and Del Mar Futurity, as well as a pair of major juvenile filly races on the West Coast. She was voted the champion two-year-old filly, and Courtly Dee was Broodmare of the Year for 1983.

At three, Althea added the Santa Susana and Las Virgenes against other fillies, then overpowered a field of colts in the Arkansas Derby. Althea was headed not to the Kentucky Oaks, but to the Kentucky Derby.

Lukas eventually would win his first Derby with a filly, Winning Colors, and he tried with two of them in 1984. The Amazon team of Life's Magic and Althea was made the post time favorite, but neither placed. Althea came back next to last, and worse for the experience. She was later retired with eight wins in fifteen starts and earnings of $1,275,255.

Helen Alexander was managing the family's Lexington division of King Ranch and also acquired her own Middlebrook Farm nearby. Althea immediately became a mainstay in the broodmare band, producing high-priced yearlings that justified every dollar their eager buyers bid. One was Yamanin Paradise, a

Danzig filly who brought $800,000 at Keeneland. Yamanin Paradise was sent to Japan, where she was the champion two-year-old filly of 1994.

Althea also foaled Aurora, another Danzig filly, who won the Aqueduct Budweiser Breeders' Cup and has produced the 1998 Super Derby winner, Arch. To the cover of Storm Cat, Althea foaled the 1994 filly Alyssum, who won the 1997 Nassau County Stakes. A third stakes winner from Althea was Destiny Dance, sired by Nijinsky II and winner of the Sheepshead Bay Handicap. Althea's career at stud was abruptly ended in 1995 when she collided with another mare in their field and was injured too gravely to be saved.

After Althea, Courtly Dee foaled the Damascus filly Barada. She was unplaced, but foaled six winners. Next came Ketoh, a stylish chestnut colt by Exclusive Native. He won the grade I Cowdin Stakes at two, but died at three.

In 1984, Courtly Dee foaled Maidee, by Epsom Derby winner Roberto. Maidee was a winner once in fourteen starts. Before being sold to Japan in 1994, she produced the Diesis colt Defacto, who won the grade III Young America Breeders' Cup Stakes.

Courtly Dee's 1985 foal was the Storm Bird filly Namaqua, who won once from three starts. Namaqua in turn has foaled the stakes-winning Mr. Prospector colt Namaqualand. In 1986, Courtly Dee produced Karraar, a colt by Saratoga Six. Sent abroad, Karraar was a modest winner.

Then, in 1987, came another Alydar filly, Aishah. The full sister to Althea did not match the other's quality, but she did win the grade III Rare Perfume Stakes and five other races from fourteen starts and earned $169,340. Aishah has foaled Aldiza, a Storm Cat filly who edged eventual champion Escena in the grade I Go for Wand Stakes for Mrs. Groves and Miss Alexander in 1998. Aishah also has two stakes-placed foals as of early 1999.

Courtly Dee had first been bred in 1973, and she

Courtly Dee

had never missed a year producing a live foal, fourteen in succession. In 1988, at the age of twenty, she was barren for the first time, but the following year she produced another stakes-winning filly by Alydar. This was Aquilegia, who won the grade II New York and grade III Black Helen Handicaps. Aquilegia is the dam of the Danzig colt Bertolini, who at two in 1998 won the July Stakes in England and placed in two historic European juvenile events, the Middle Park and Prix Robert Papin.

At twenty-two, Courtly Dee foaled Press Card, by Fappiano. Press Card won three races and placed in a trio of important graded races, the Pegasus, Pennsylvania Derby, and Champagne, before being retired to stud.

At the age of twenty-three, Courtly Dee foaled her eighth stakes winner, Twining, by Forty Niner. After brilliant early wins, Twining gained black type by winning the Withers Stakes and Peter Pan in 1994, then was second to Holy Bull in the Dwyer. After the Dwyer, Twining went wrong and was retired to stud with five wins from six starts and earnings of $238,140.

Courtly Dee's eighteenth and last foal was Amizette, a Forty Niner filly. Amizette, a foal of 1992, placed before being retired to the broodmare band.

At the age of twenty-seven, Courtly Dee died in her King Ranch paddock in August of 1995. She had eighteen foals, of which fifteen were winners. Long forgotten was her own desultory racing career. She had truly lived up to the superb heritage she was handed. ❖

Fall Aspen

 Man o' War's impact on the Turf was great, and deep, and lasting. From the fury and grace of his athletic prowess to his evolution as a stallion into a handsome, chestnut icon of American tourism and sporting pride, Man o' War fixed his name into the consciousness of succeeding generations. His prowess as a progenitor of racehorses, and purveyor of dreams, no doubt has formed the seedling of innumerable breeding decisions by horsemen in all strata of economic and bloodline hierarchy. Few such instances can have had as long and beneficial chain of results as that which led eventually, and indirectly, to the breeding of Fall Aspen, dam of nine stakes winners.

The specifics of the sequence began in 1941, when the sportsman Walter Jeffords Sr. decided to retire, at more or less the last minute, five Man o' War fillies from the racetrack to the breeding shed. The lateness of the decision meant that he had fewer options as to which stallions they would visit than was usual for a breeder of his ilk. He settled upon the New Jersey-based Case Ace for all five. The results were so successful that the young horseman who owned Case Ace set out to imitate the bloodline pattern in reverse by breeding his Case Ace mare Carillon to Man o' War's best son, War Admiral. However simplistic this genetic analysis might have been, such was the power of the bloodlines involved that it produced a champion and

quickly set into motion the sequence that produced Fall Aspen.

Actually, the relationship of Jeffords and Man o' War blood dated to the very purchase of Man o' War himself. In 1918, Samuel D. Riddle bought the Fair Play—Mahubah colt from the Saratoga consignment of August Belmont II. Ordinarily, Belmont bred horses to replenish his vaunted racing stable, but at the time he was deeply involved in the supply elements for America's World War I Army. Major Belmont offered his entire crop of twenty-one yearlings as a package deal of singular potential, but there were no takers at his price, so three weeks before the Saratoga yearling sale they were consigned to the auction. Acting on behalf of Riddle, Ed Buhler outbid Robert Gerry at $5,000, sixth-highest price for that year's Saratoga auction, to secure Man o' War. Buhler, the uncle of present day equine artist Richard Stone Reeves, left his name on many a man-hole cover in Manhattan — his business career being more into such things than bidding on yearlings — and he thus obliquely left his stamp on the annals of the Turf. Riddle took into his own Glen Riddle Stable the best horse Belmont ever bred, and Man o' War won twenty of twenty-one races at two and three with inspirational quality and dash.

Jeffords' wife was Mrs. Riddle's niece, and the two families were associated in the operation of Faraway Farm, the Kentucky farm where Man o'

		British Empire, 1937	Colombo Rose of England
	Endeavour II, 1942	Himalaya, 1931	Hunter's Moon Partenope
PRETENSE, dkb/br, 1963		**Hyperion**, 1930	Gainsborough Selene
	Imitation, 1951	Flattery, 1938	Winalot Fickle
FALL ASPEN, **ch m,** **March 9, 1976**	Swaps, 1952	Khaled, 1943	**Hyperion** Eclair
		Iron Reward, 1946	Beau Pere Iron Maiden
CHANGE WATER, ch, 1969	Portage, 1952	War Admiral, 1934	Man o' War Brushup
		Carillon, 1939	Case Ace Sunfeathers

FALL ASPEN, ch, 1976-1998. Bred by Joseph M. Roebling (Ky.). Raced 3 yrs, 20 sts, 8 wins, $198,037. Broodmare of the Year in 1994. Won Matron S (gr. I), Astarita S (gr. III), Prioress S. Dam of 13 named foals, 12 rnrs, 11 wnrs, 9 sw. ($900,000, 1984 keejan, Raise a Native; $1,100,000, 1987 keenov, Shareef Dancer; $2,400,000, 1994 keenov, Danzig).

1982: NORTHERN ASPEN, b f, by Northern Dancer. Raced 4 yrs in Eng, Fr, and NA, 16 sts, 5 wins, $253,678. Won Gamely H (gr. IT), Prix d'Astarte (Fr-II), B. Thoughtful S (RT); 2nd Santa Barbara H (gr. IT), Santa Ana H (gr. IT), Prix Quincey (Fr-III). Dam of 6 foals, 3 rnrs, 3 wnrs. ($410,000 ftsaug yrlg).

1983: ELLE SEULE, ch f, by Exclusive Native. Raced 2 yrs in Fr and NA, 16 sts, 3 wins, $101,478. Won Prix d'Astarte (Fr-II), Prix des Tuileries; 2nd Prix de l'Opera (Fr-II), Prix du Bois (Fr-III); 3rd Prix de Royaumont (Fr-III). Dam of 8 foals, 6 rnrs, 5 wnrs, including **MEHTHAAF** ($364,497, champion 3yo filly in Ire, Ire-I), **ELNADIM** ($312,369, champion 3yo colt and older male in Eng, Eng-I), **ASHRAAKAT** ($76,110). Granddam of **OCCUPANDISTE, TOTO LE HEROS**.

1984: Native Aspen, ch c, by Raise a Native. Raced 3 yrs, 24 sts, 4 wins, $73,564. 3rd Burlington S (R). Sent to Aust 1989. ($360,000 keejul yrlg).

1985: MAZZACANO (GB), b c, by Alleged. Raced 2 yrs in Eng and Fr, 9 sts, 3 wins, $153,421. Won Goodwood Cup (Eng-III); 2nd Gold Cup (Eng-I), Insulpak Sagaro E.B.F. Stakes (Eng-III), March S; 3rd Yorkshire Cup S (Eng-II). ($70,000 ftsaug yrlg).

1986: COLORADO DANCER (Ire), dkb/br f, by Shareef Dancer. Raced 2 yrs in Fr and NA, 10 sts, 3 wins, $203,389. Won Prix de Pomone (Fr-II), Prix Minerve (Fr-III); 2nd Prix de Malleret (Fr-II); 3rd Prix Vermeille (Fr-I), Yellow Ribbon Invitational S (gr. IT). Dam of 6 foals, 3 rnrs, 3 wnrs, including **Denver County** ($56,598, in Fr and NA), **Fort Morgan** ($30,837 in Fr and Ire).

1987: Dance of Leaves (GB), b f, by Sadler's Wells. Unraced. Dam of 4 foals, 3 rnrs, 2 wnrs, including **MEDAALY** ($171,097, Eng-I), **CHARNWOOD FOREST (Ire)** ($387,162, champion older male in Eng, Eng-II). Sent to Ire 1998.

1988: Sheroog, dkb/br f, by Shareef Dancer. Raced 1 yr in Eng, 8 sts, 1 win, $9,758. Dam of 6 foals, 3 rnrs, 3 wnrs, including **KABOOL** ($114,833, Fr-II), **SHARAF KABEER** ($54,889).

1989: HAMAS (Ire), dkb/br c, by Danzig. Raced 2 yrs in Eng, 18 sts, 5 wins, $237,814. Won July Cup S (Eng-I), Duke of York S (Eng-III), Bentinck S; 2nd Hopeful S. Sire in Ire of 86 foals, AEI 1.11. ($400,000 keejul yrlg).

1990: FORT WOOD, b c, by Sadler's Wells. Raced 1 yr in Fr and Ger, 6 sts, 3 wins, $359,995. Won Grand Prix de Paris (Fr-I), Prix Noailles (Fr-II).

1991: Barren.

1992: TIMBER COUNTRY, ch c, by Woodman. ($500,000 keejul yrlg). Raced 2 yrs, 12 sts, 5 wins, $1,560,400. Champion 2yo colt. Won Preakness S (gr. I), Breeders' Cup Juvenile (gr. I), Moet Champagne S (gr. I), Balboa S (gr. III); 2nd San Felipe (gr. II); 3rd Kentucky Derby (gr. I), Del Mar Futurity (gr. II), San Rafael S (gr. II). Sent to Japan 1995.

1993: PRINCE OF THIEVES, ch c, by Hansel. Raced 2 yrs, 12 sts, 2 wins, $368,474. Won Santa Catalina S; 2nd Swaps S (gr. II), Lexington S (gr. II); 3rd Kentucky Derby (gr. I).

1994: Barren.

1995: BIANCONI, dkb/br c, by Danzig. Raced 2 yrs in Eng, Fr, and Ire, 8 sts, 3 wins, $132,807. Champion 3yo colt in Ire. Won Racal Diadem S (Eng-II); 2nd Phoenix Sprint S (Ire-III).

1996: Aspen Leaves, ch f, by Woodman. Raced 1 yr in Ire, 1 st, 0 wins, $0.

1997: Barren.

1998: Ch c, by Thunder Gulch. Sent to Ire 1998.

War served all but the first year of his stud career. This is not to say that the Riddles were always in Man o' War's rooting section. Golden Broom, whom Mrs. Jeffords had purchased for three times as much as Man o' War cost, bettered the other colt in a morning trial and on occasion at two was entered against him. When it mattered, though, Man o' War always had a handle on Golden Broom.

Riddle's management of Man o' War as a stallion often has been criticized for his unwillingness to spend enough to acquire a high-quality band of broodmares himself, and for not allowing enough outside breeders to provide a book of mares commensurate with Man o' War's status. Neither of these failures characterized the Jeffords connection. Jeffords, of course, was in a unique position insofar as access to Man o' War was concerned, while the quality of his mares was of a high order. The connection was beneficial to man and beast. Of the sixty-two stakes winners which Jeffords bred, sixteen were sired by Man o' War and sixteen others were out of Man o' War mares.

The lasting presence in pedigrees of the name Case Ace has been largely due to his having sired Raise You, the dam of Raise a Native. That, however, was far in the future in the winter of 1941 when Jeffords was hastily making arrangements for his five Man o' War fillies. The 1942 foals from that five which Jeffords retired and sent to Case Ace included Ace Card, a future Broodmare of the Year, and Pavot, unbeaten champion two-year-old of 1944 and Belmont Stakes winner of 1945.

The career of Pavot did not escape the notice of Joseph M. Roebling, who stood Case Ace at his farm in New Jersey's lovely and fashionable horse country. Case Ace (Teddy—Sweetheart, by Ultimus) had been good enough to win the 1936 Arlington Futurity and 1937 Illinois Derby. When Pavot was three, Roebling bred his six-year-old Case Ace mare Carillon to War Admiral, the 1937 Triple Crown

winner sired by Man o' War, and the following spring Carillon foaled Blue Peter, who carried Roebling's colors to championship honors among juvenile colts of 1948. Later duplications of the War Admiral—Carillon cross produced the stakes producers War Shaft and Portage.

Portage, who would become the second dam of Fall Aspen, was herself a distinguished producer. Portage produced four stakes winners: Rainy Lake, Pack Trip, Black Mountain, and Wyoming Wildcat. None of these colts was top class, and their tendencies toward sprint distances were somewhat at odds with their individual, and collective, pedigrees. Descendants of Portage's fillies include a number of significant horses, among them Cozzene, winner of the Breeders' Cup Mile and sire of Breeders' Cup winners Alphabet Soup and Tikkanen.

In 1968, Portage was bred to Swaps, the 1956 Horse of the Year who by the early 1960s had turned out such as Chateaugay, Primonetta, and Affectionately, before receding from the ranks of leading sires. The Swaps—Portage filly was named Change Water, and she was a moderate winner, after which she produced twelve foals, of which ten raced and nine won. Fall Aspen was one of them, as was the currently successful Maryland stallion Allen's Prospect.

Fall Aspen was Change Water's 1976 filly by Pretense, a standout handicap horse whose son Sham had placed behind Secretariat in the Kentucky Derby and Preakness. The mating of Pretense to Change Water created a pleasing concentration of the blood of the great English stallion Hyperion: Pretense was by the Argentine-bred Endeavour II, who went back in his bottom line to Hyperion's dam, Selene, and Pretense was out of the Hyperion mare Imitation; also, Change Water's sire, Swaps, was a son of the Hyperion stallion Khaled.

Fall Aspen was bred and owned by Roebling and was one in a pair of homebred stakes winners which cut a swath through Eastern two-year-old filly stakes in 1978. Palm Hut started early, winning three major stakes, and then Fall Aspen developed a bit later for trainer Jimmy Picou and picked up the baton to win the Astarita Stakes and the grade I Matron. In the historic Matron, Fall Aspen defeated Fair Advantage and Island Kitty.

Candy Eclair and It's in the Air came along late in the year to share the Eclipse Award for two-year-old fillies. Fall Aspen was assigned 115 pounds on the Experimental Free Handicap, four pounds below the championship pair and three pounds below the brilliant West Coast filly Terlingua. She was adjudged a pound inferior to her stablemate Palm Hut and was below several other fillies. Her 115-pound ranking was even with that of the next year's dominant filly, Davona Dale.

At three, Fall Aspen took no part in any championship skirmishes, but added one spring stakes, the Prioress, among three wins in seven races. At four, she won no further stakes, but won two of eight races and was retired with a record of eight wins from twenty starts and earnings of $198,037.

Breeder-owner Roebling died when Fall Aspen was four, and the filly was consigned to the first of several trips into the auction ring. She eventually would travel back and forth across the Atlantic as well. The Roebling estate and Fasig-Tipton presented the Roebling horses at Saratoga, where distant ancestor Man o' War had sold sixty-two years before. Fall Aspen's potential as a broodmare was widely recognized, and she topped the sale at $600,000, being purchased by Brownell Combs II and Francis Kernan.

Acorns Everywhere

Combs had emerged to follow his father, Leslie Combs II, as head of Spendthrift Farm, so he had in his barn a collection of stallions including Nashua

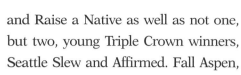

Fall Aspen

and Raise a Native as well as not one, but two, young Triple Crown winners, Seattle Slew and Affirmed. Fall Aspen, however, was dispatched to Maryland, to the court of the international star, Northern Dancer. The resulting filly was Northern Aspen, first foal and first of nine stakes winners from Fall Aspen. Northern Aspen in her turn was a $410,000 sale yearling and was sent to France, where she won the group II Prix d'Astarte. Returned to this country, she won the grade I Gamely Handicap and the B. Thoughtful Stakes.

Fall Aspen's second foal was by a Spendthrift stallion, Exclusive Native, sire of Affirmed and Genuine Risk. The resulting foal, born in 1983, was also a filly destined for Europe, Elle Seule. Following the example of her older half-sibling, Elle Seule won the Prix d'Astarte, plus one lesser stakes, and she placed in three other group races. Elle Seule has subsequently become an important producer in her own right, as the dam of Irish One Thousand Guineas winner Mehthaaf, two-time English sprint distance highweight Elnadim, and additional stakes winner Ashraakat. As these exotic names would indicate, the brood of Fall Aspen had found favor with some of the world's most important horsemen, the Maktoum family of Dubai. Elle Seule is also the grandam of European group I winner Occupandiste.

Looking back, a disappointing foal from Fall Aspen is one that does not win a stakes. The first such anomaly occurred in 1984 in the Raise a Native colt, Native Aspen. As family outcasts go, Native Aspen was not so shameful, placing in stakes before being sent to stud in Australia. By the time she foaled Native Aspen, Fall Aspen had been returned to auction, being purchased at Keeneland for $900,000 by International Thoroughbred Breeders.

Fall Aspen's next foal got her back on track, becoming her third stakes winner from four foals, although having tepid appeal in the market. This was Mazzacano, an English-foaled Alleged colt who brought only $70,000 as a yearling. While sprinting speed has been abundant in the issue, and ancestry, of Fall Aspen, the family by no means has been restricted to shorter distances. Mazzacano stretched the speed to extreme, excelling in two of England's most treasured two-mile-plus Cup events. He won the Goodwood Cup and was second in the Ascot Gold Cup. Fall Aspen was covered by Shareef Dancer and foaled her 1987 filly, Colorado Dancer, in Ireland. Colorado Dancer won the group II Prix de Pomone and group III Prix Minerve and was placed in the group I Prix Vermeille, which occupies a status on the French calendar for three-year-old fillies somewhat akin to that of the Alabama in this country. In California, Colorado Dancer placed in the grade I Yellow Ribbon.

In both 1987 and 1988, Fall Aspen foaled horses that were not even stakes-placed, but both were fillies and both became stakes producers themselves. The first, a 1987 filly by the noble Sadler's Wells, was Dance of Leaves. Although unraced, she has foaled Charnwood Forest, who was the highweight on Europe's Free Handicap for older hoses at seven to nine furlongs in 1996. Charnwood Forest won the group II Queen Anne and Challenge Stakes.

In the fall of 1987, Fall Aspen was returned to this country and sent into the Keeneland sale ring. Then eleven, she was purchased by David Jamison for $1.1 million — a nice coincidence of 1s, i.e., $100,000 for every year of her life. She was clearly getting older, but better, in the market's eyes. Fall Aspen was in foal to Shareef Dancer at that time. The resulting 1988 foal, Sheroog, was sent to England and was a modest winner. Sheroog has foaled two stakes winners, Kabool and Sharaf Kabeer.

By the spring of 1989, Fall Aspen had been sent to Ireland again, and there she foaled a Danzig colt, Hamas, who brought $400,000 as a yearling. Shouting the versatility of this family, Hamas trumped his Cup-winning half-brother by scoring in one of the most important sprints in England, the group I July Cup, as well as winning the group III Duke of York Stakes. In 1990, Fall Aspen foaled another Sadler's Wells foal, this one a colt named Fort Wood. He scored in one of France's historic events, the group I Grand Prix de Paris.

In 1991, Fall Aspen was barren. This marked the first time the "B" word had been applied to her, despite the presumed added stress of a mare travelling as often as she had. In 1992, Fall Aspen made amends by producing an American classic winner and champion. She had been bred in 1991 to the sensational young stallion Woodman, sire already at that time of Hector Protector and the developing Hansel. Her 1992 foal was a handsome chestnut who would be named Timber Country. He was purchased at Keeneland for $500,000 by trainer D. Wayne Lukas, who was confident he could find a consortium to finalize ownership. Eventually, Timber Country raced for Robert and Beverly Lewis, Overbrook Farm owner W. T. Young, and Gainesway Farm owner Graham Beck.

At two in 1994, Timber Country emerged as the champion of his crop, winning the grade I Champagne Stakes and the Breeders' Cup Juvenile. The following year, he was somewhat baffling, losing at the top level while seeming to have — but need — excuses. Then, in the Preakness, he put it all together, defeating Derby winner Thunder Gulch. Fall Aspen had added a new distinction, even by her standards, producing an American classic winner. Pavot was a distant memory, but the chain of events launched by meshing Man o' War and Case Ace bloodlines was again productive at the highest level of American racing.

On the day before the Belmont Stakes, Timber Country developed a fever. Co-owner Beck traveled from South Africa to New York City to learn that his best moments of the weekend would be dancing at

Fall Aspen

the Belmont Ball, a nice enough event, but not what he had in mind. Timber Country later was retired with five wins in twelve starts and earnings of $1,560,400. Winning three times his purchase price made him a considerable bargain, but the returns were not yet final; he was purchased by Japanese interests for $12 million and exported as a sire prospect.

In 1993, Fall Aspen had another handsome, flashy chestnut. Named Prince of Thieves, he was closely related to Timber Country, being by Woodman's Preakness-winning son Hansel. Prince of Thieves nibbled at classic status. He won the Santa Catalina Stakes, was barely beaten in the Lexington, then finished third behind Grindstone in the Kentucky Derby. He was then second in the Swaps Stakes before being injured so severely in the Pennsylvania Derby that he could not be saved for stud duty. (One avenue of future influence which the travels of life had helped deny Fall Aspen was a major-winning son at stud in North America.)

Fall Aspen was barren in the spring of 1994. By that autumn, she had been pronounced in foal to Danzig, and, despite her age of eighteen, she brought the highest price of her lengthy sale career. Two days after Timber Country won the Breeders' Cup Juvenile, Fall Aspen was back in the ring at Keeneland, where John Magnier, the key partner in Coolmore Stud of Ireland and Ashford Stud of Kentucky, bought her for $2.4 million. She was consigned by John J. Greely, agent for Jamison. Later, she was named Broodmare of the Year for 1994.

In 1995, Fall Aspen, at the age of nineteen, produced the Danzig colt to be named Bianconi. At three in 1998, Bianconi won England's group II Diadem Stakes, and he finished second in Ireland's group III Phoenix Sprint Stakes. He was adjudged the topweight on Ireland's handicap for three-year-olds at five to seven furlongs.

In 1996, at age twenty, Fall Aspen foaled a Woodman filly who was named Aspen Leaves and who was unplaced in one start so far. Fall Aspen hemorrhaged after foaling a Thunder Gulch colt in the winter of 1998 at Ashford Stud and was euthanized.

Her noble record is far from complete, but it stands as one of the beacons of the breed: From foals old enough to race as of 1998, Fall Aspen had a total of thirteen individuals, of which twelve have raced, eleven have won, and nine have won stakes.

Man o' War and Case Ace, Case Ace and Man o' War: With more than a half-century of added pedigree elements, the melody lingers. ❖

Boudoir II (above) had several owners during her brood-mare career, including Spendthrift Farm owner Leslie Combs II. Her granddaughter Flower Bowl (right) produced champion Bowl of Flowers and stakes winner and prominent sire Graustark.

Boudoir II

Boudoir II was the third dam of 1969 Kentucky Derby winner Majestic Prince (right) and champion Gallant Bloom (below).

Bourtai (bottom) had a modest race record but quickly began producing stakes winners. Her descendants included champion females Shuvee (left) and Sacahuista (below).

Courtly Dee

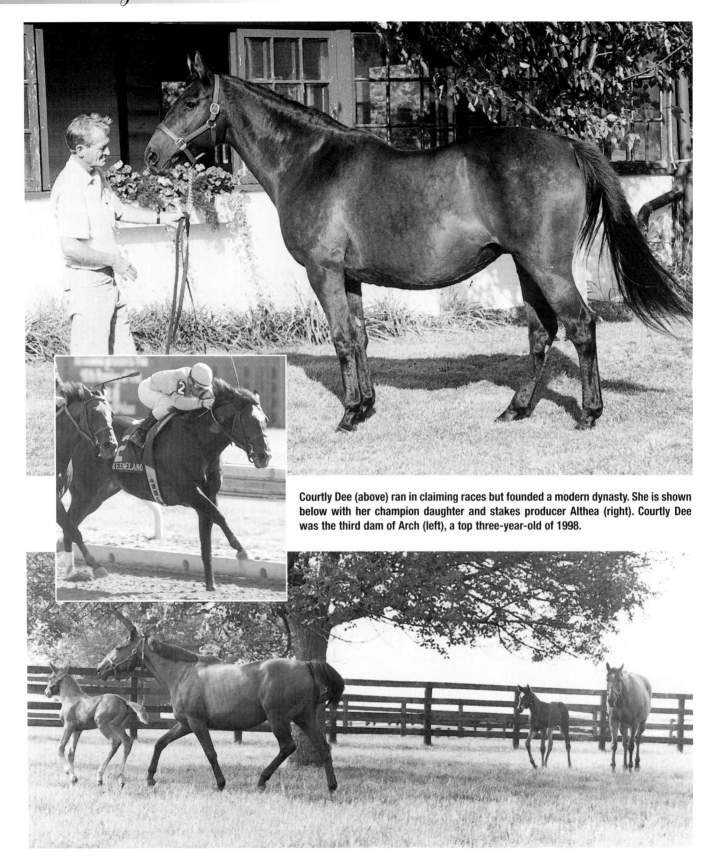

Courtly Dee (above) ran in claiming races but founded a modern dynasty. She is shown below with her champion daughter and stakes producer Althea (right). Courtly Dee was the third dam of Arch (left), a top three-year-old of 1998.

Fall Aspen (above) sold for $2.4 million at age eighteen. Her nine stakes winners included Elle Seule (above, right), the dam of two champions, and juvenile champion and Preakness winner Timber Country (right).

Grey Flight

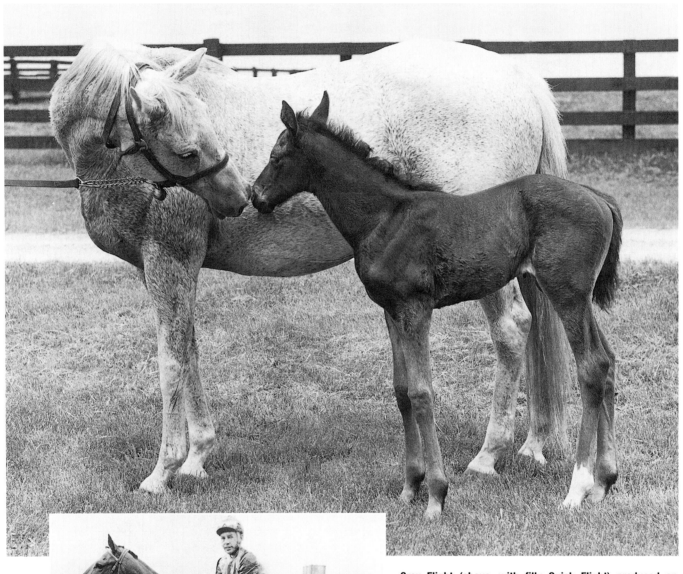

Grey Flight (above, with filly Quick Flight) produced an amazing nine stakes winners, including Bold Princess (left), herself the dam of three stakes winners.

Another daughter, Misty Morn (below), was champion three-year-old filly and handicap female and later, Broodmare of the Year. Grey Flight's great-grand-daughter, Inside Information (above), continued the championship tradition, taking honors as 1994 older female.

Hildene

Hildene (bottom) was a bargain yearling who became a rich trove for Meadow Stud. Hildene's champion son First Landing sired the champion Riva Ridge (right), and her granddaughter Cicada (above) was the best of her generation.

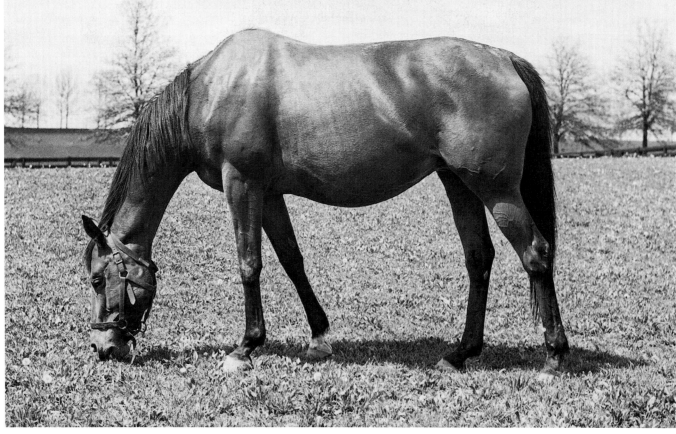

Grey Flight

rs. Henry Carnegie Phipps had been in racing for about two decades when she purchased the most expensive yearling filly at Saratoga in the immediate post-war year of 1946. Costing $35,000, that filly would carry the name of Grey Flight into a rarified air. Just how many mares have produced a specific number of stakes winners is one of those arcane statistics that no shaman of Turf lore thought of at the inception of the game. It can be stated with confidence, however, that any mare which produces nine stakes winners will not soon find her sorority over-subscribed. We are personally aware that Lady Juror, an English mare born in 1919, foaled eight major winners, and before the turn of the century, the California mare Marian had nine foals recorded as stakes winners according to the definition of the times. Then Grey Flight and Fall Aspen in modern eras of American breeding each produced nine stakes winners.

Such a mare cannot be said to have been anticipated, but Grey Flight was certainly born of elements that made some level of success no surprise. Her family had hit a high spot in 1938, when her dam's half-brother, El Chico, raced through an unbeaten season of seven races at two to earn the championship of his division. (El Chico suffered so severe a sesamoid injury in training the following year that he could not be saved.)

The sire of Grey Flight was the gray Mahmoud,

who won the 1936 English Derby for the Aga Khan in record time. Four years after his successful negotiation of such Epsom travails as Tattenham Corner and an uphill finish, Mahmoud slipped through the perils of a war-time Atlantic to survive importation, just missing placement on a ship that went down. Installed at stud at C. V. Whitney's Lexington farm, Mahmoud became one of the more influential stallions of the middle 20th Century. Many a Bluegrass tourist of the 1950s and '60s sent off post cards showing grazing gray mares among the bays, perhaps unaware that the contrast was not purely a matter of a photographer's artistry. In more prosaic terms, the gray Mahmoud led the sire list in 1946 and the broodmare sire list in 1957.

La Chica was the dam of El Chico and the second dam of the subject of this chapter, Grey Flight. There could be a strong case for La Chica herself being given pride of place in this family saga. A daughter of Sweep—La Grisette, by Roi Herode (another prolific gray), La Chica foaled four stakes winners. She was also the third dam of Native Dancer, Alfred G. Vanderbilt's great Gray Ghost of the 1950s who implanted his name in a plethora of pedigrees as the sire of Raise a Native and broodmare sire of Northern Dancer.

Be that as it may, the more immediate aspects of Grey Flight's tale begin with her dam, Planetoid, who was La Chica's 1934 foal by the speed sire Ariel.

		Blandford, 1919	Swynford / Blanche
	Blenheim II, 1927		
		Malva, 1919	Charles O'Malley / Wild Arum
MAHMOUD, gr, 1933			
		Gainsborough, 1915	Bayardo / Rosedrop
	Mah Mahal, 1928		
		Mumtaz Mahal, 1921	The Tetrarch / Lady Josephine
GREY FLIGHT, gr m, 1945			
		Eternal, 1916	**Sweep** / Hazel Burke
	Ariel, 1925		
		Adana, 1908	Adam / Mannie Himyar
PLANETOID, gr, 1934			
		Sweep, 1907	Ben Brush / Pink Domino
	La Chica, 1930		
		La Grisette, 1915	Roi Herode / Miss Fiora

GREY FLIGHT, gr, 1945-1974. Bred by J.T. Taylor (Ky.). Raced 2 yrs, 35 sts, 12 wins, $68,990. Won Autumn Day S; 2nd Astarita S, Frizette S; 3rd Astoria S, Fashion S, Rosedale S, Spinaway S. Dam of 15 named foals, 15 rnrs, 14 wnrs, 9 sw.

1950: Shamrock, ro c, by Bold Irishman. Raced 8 yrs, 124 sts, 11 wins, $48,895. Sire of 1 foal, AEI 0.37. Died 1960.

1951: **FULL FLIGHT**, b g, by Ambiorix. Raced 9 yrs, 216 sts, 15 wins, $182,732. Won Leonard Richards S, Saranac H, A.B. Letellier Memorial H, Ponce de Leon H; 2nd New Orleans H, Kent S, Bahamas H, William Penn S, Lawrence Realization; 3rd Ardsley S, Dover S, Jerome H, Camden H, Tremont S, Christmas H.

1952: **MISTY MORN**, b f, by Princequillo. Raced 3 yrs, 42 sts, 11 wins, $212,575. Champion 3yo filly and handicap female. Broodmare of the Year in 1963. Won Gallant Fox H, Monmouth Oaks, Providence S, Molly Pitcher H, Diana H; 2nd Ladies H, Saranac H; 3rd Alabama S. Dam of 10 foals, 8 rnrs, 7 wnrs, including **SUCCESSOR** ($532,254, champion 2yo colt), **BOLD LAD** ($516,465, champion 2yo colt), **SUNRISE FLIGHT** ($380,995), **BEAUTIFUL DAY** ($160,007), **BOLD CONSORT** ($38,147), **The Heir** ($18,782). Granddam of **Settlement Day**, **RESOLVER**, **QUICK TURNOVER**, **RODWELL**, **BRIGHT SUN**, **Sumter**, **Halcyon Queen**, **Club Class**, **Latest Report**, **Foreign Missile**. Died 1971.

1953: **GRAY PHANTOM**, gr c, by Ambiorix. Raced 6 yrs, 89 sts, 16 wins, $130,830. Won Robert E. Lee H, Christmas H, Coral Gables H, Ponce de Leon H; 2nd Tropical H, Shevlin S, New Year's H, Mr. Fitz H; 3rd Saratoga National Maiden Hurdle S, Governor's H, North American Stp H. Sire of 220 foals, AEI 1.30. Died 1975.

1954: Barren.

1955: **MISTY FLIGHT**, ch c, by Princequillo. Raced 4 yrs, 60 sts, 8 wins, $133,508. Won Remsen S; 2nd Futurity S, Champagne S, Sheepshead Bay H; 3rd Withers S. Sire of 284 foals, AEI 1.90. Died 1980.

1956: Barren.

1957: Daylight Flight, b c, by Princequillo. Raced 1 yr, 6 sts, 0 wins, $700.

1958: **MISTY DAY**, gr c, by Nasrullah. Raced 3 yrs, 56 sts, 9 wins, $88,801. Won Sport Page H; 2nd Vosburgh H, Excelsior H, Queens County H; 3rd Toboggan H. Sire of 370 foals, AEI 0.98.

1959: Barren.

1960: **BOLD PRINCESS**, b f, by Bold Ruler. Raced 2 yrs, 17 sts, 4 wins, $37,157. Won Schuylerville S; 2nd Polly Drummond S. Dam of 11 foals, 9 rnrs, 6 wnrs, including **INTREPID HERO** ($405,305, gr. I), **PREDICTABLE** ($191,937), **PRIMED** ($11,921), **Sovereign Dancer** ($50,487, in Fr and NA), **Brave Lady** ($23,045). Granddam of **WAITLIST**, **FORMAL DINNER**, **POPULAR HERO**, **DOUBLY ROYALE**, **Zante (Ire)**, **Dowager Empress**. Died 1981.

1961: **BOLD QUEEN**, br f, by Bold Ruler. Raced 3 yrs, 24 sts, 5 wins, $55,739. Won Black-Eyed Susan S. Dam of 13 foals, 12 rnrs, 6 wnrs. Granddam of **Pergola**. Died 1986.

1962: **SIGNORE**, gr g, by Ribot. Raced 4 yrs, 31 sts, 4 wins, $20,635. Won Saratoga National Hurdle S.

1963: Barren.

1964: **Great Era**, gr f, by Bold Ruler. Raced 2 yrs, 10 sts, 3 wins, $59,611. 2nd Matron S, Spinaway S, Prioress S; 3rd Schuylerville S. Dam of 2 foals, 1 rnr, 1 wnr. Died 1971.

1965: **WHAT A PLEASURE**, ch c, by Bold Ruler. Raced 2 yrs, 18 sts, 6 wins, $164,935. Won Hopeful S, National Stallion S; 2nd Sapling S; 3rd Gotham S. Sire of 483 foals, AEI 2.40. Died 1983.

1966: Quick Flight, b f, by Herbager. Raced 2 yrs, 14 sts, 1 win, $1,456. Dam of 4 foals, 4 rnrs, 2 wnrs, including **Night Before** ($7,989, in Eng). Granddam of **QUICK ICE**.

1967: Not bred.

1968: Clear Ceiling, b f, by Bold Ruler. Raced 3 yrs, 17 sts, 5 wins, $41,575. Dam of 14 foals, 11 rnrs, 9 wnrs, including **QUICK AS LIGHTNING** ($188,070, Eng-I), **STRATOSPHERIC** ($43,821), **INFINITE** ($122,979). Granddam of **INSIDE INFORMATION**, **EDUCATED RISK**, **POLISH TREATY**, **Hidden Reserve**, **Ultimate Goal**, **Foreign Aid**. Died 1991.

1969: Pleasant Flight, b f, by Bold Ruler. Raced 2 yrs, 15 sts, 1 win, $15,010. Dam of 13 foals, 8 rnrs, 5 wnrs, including **FLITALONG** ($209,980, gr. II), **ON A CLOUD** ($33,382). Granddam of **SOAR TO THE STARS**, **PRIVATE LIGHT**, **CASSIDY**, **LIGHT OF MINE**, **COLCONDA**, **Jetskier**, **Brighter Course**, **Jetting Along**, **Baroncourt**, **Primevere**. Died 1993.

1970: Not bred.

Planetoid was owned and trained by J. Tommy Taylor, and she won the 1936 Jeanne d'Arc Stakes and four other races from twenty-one starts, earning $7,345. Planetoid was a broodmare of remarkable consistency, producing twelve foals, all of which won. The only stakes winner among them was the Mahmoud filly who would be named Grey Flight.

Taylor sold the 1945 Mahmoud—Planetoid filly to Abram S. Hewitt, a singular figure in American historical and cultural life. Scion of a family that had produced a mayor of New York, Hewitt in a long life was a lawyer, an outspoken critic of the Russians during the Roosevelt Administration, winner and loser of more than one fortune, and a sage commentator of matters of Thoroughbred racing and breeding. Unlike many who believe they fill that final role, Hewitt had a record of achievement to back up his opinions, including his importation of the French stallion Ksar and his status as co-breeder with C. V. Whitney of the American classic winner and champion Phalanx.

In the middle 1940s, Hewitt was not disposed to keep for his own account a filly with the market potential of the Mahmoud—Planetoid filly, and he consigned the gray to the Saratoga yearling sale. At $35,000, she was the top-priced female in the auction.

Mrs. Henry Carnegie Phipps had been drawn into establishing Wheatley Stable in the late 1920s by leading owner Harry Payne Whitney. Her partner was her brother, Ogden Livingston Mills, Secretary of the Treasury under Herbert Hoover. The robust history, and economy, of America were positively reflected on both sides of the Phipps family. Henry Carnegie Phipps was the son of Henry Phipps, who had been the original bookkeeper and a minority partner of Andrew Carnegie in the establishment of Carnegie Steel Company. When J. P. Morgan bought out Carnegie, the Phipps share was said to be $50 million.

On the Western slopes of Columbia, Darius Ogden Mills became a successful merchant and banker in the aftermath of the Gold Rush, and he went back East to put his burgeoning fortune to good use on Wall Street. Mills' son, Ogden Mills, was the father of Ogden Livingston Mills and of twin daughters, Gladys and Beatrice. Their family escutcheon was enlivened by antecedents who had put their signatures to matters forever described to American school children, to wit, the Declaration of Independence and the Louisiana Purchase.

However unlikely the combination of a post-Gold Rush entrepreneur's family and the British aristocracy might have seemed, Ogden Mills later formed a partnership with England's most famous breeder of his era, Lord Derby. The partners led French owners of 1928, when their Kantar won the Prix de l'Arc de Triomphe and Cri de Guere the Grand Prix de Paris. When Mills died, daughter Beatrice — who moved abroad and became the Countess of Granard — took his place in the partnership and raced the Grand Prix de Paris winner Cappiello in 1933. Her sister Gladys' Wheatley Stable was continued after the deaths of the husband and brother. Wheatley raced a succession of important horses, including Dice, Dark Secret, High Voltage, Misty Morn, Bold Ruler, Queen Empress, and Bold Lad. The history of Mrs. Phipps' stable was not one of uninterrupted success, however. For example, at the time the aforementioned El Chico was winning a championship of 1938 for William Ziegler Jr., the Wheatley team was probably wincing a bit in observing the championship qualities of a homebred they had culled: Seabiscuit.

The lure of the Turf has never relinquished its hold on the Phipps family. By the middle 1930s, Mrs. Henry Carnegie Phipps' son, Ogden Phipps, had launched his own stable, which he still commands in the late 1990s and which has been graced by the likes of Busanda, Buckpasser, Numbered Account, Personal Ensign, and Easy Goer. Ogden

Phipps served for many years as chairman of The Jockey Club, a position held today by his son, Ogden Mills (Dinny) Phipps. Dinny Phipps and his children also were swept up in the ownership of horses, as is Ogden Phipps' daughter, Cynthia.

Lovely Flights and Mornings

Mrs. Phipps' trainer of longstanding was Sunny Jim Fitzsimmons, who took over the Mahmoud—Planetoid filly for a two-year-old campaign in 1947. Grey Flight had the sort of speed that would vault her through such fractions as :22 4/5 and :45 and six furlongs in 1:09 1/5. While such figures would not disgrace a West Coast sprinter of the 1990s, they were recorded by Grey Flight in the East in the middle 1940s. Grey Flight was not a champion filly, but she was hardy and consistent as well as speedy.

Fitzsimmons, along with such contemporaries as Hirsch Jacobs, were used to a tough breed of Thoroughbred and generally felt that they were meant to race, not stand in stalls and train for some distant, future target. At two, Grey Flight came out in mid-April and won six of fourteen races. She contested the best. The filly won only one stakes, the Autumn Day, but was second in the Astarita and Frizette and third in the Astoria, Fashion, Rosedale, and Spinaway. On the Experimental Free Handicap, she was ranked below only three other fillies, champion Bewitch leading the distaff listing.

At three, Grey Flight did not make the step in maturity that would have allowed her to improve, or resume, such form against the best in the East. She did not place in any further stakes, but continued to demonstrate a strong constitution, running no fewer than twenty-one times and winning six. She was retired with a dozen wins from thirty-five starts and earnings of $68,990.

Mrs. Phipps had established a relationship with the Hancock family's Claiborne Farm in Kentucky.

Grey Flight

After three generations in both families, the Phipps mares are still boarded at Claiborne and the two families have been associated with an ongoing roster of stallions which have stood at Claiborne.

Grey Flight's first foal, born in 1950, was Shamrock, a cleverly named son of the Wheatley horse Bold Irishman. Hindsight shows Shamrock to have had little luck, for while he was durable enough to run 124 times from two through nine and win eleven races, he was in the minority of Grey Flight's foals in that he did not win any stakes.

In 1951, Grey Flight foaled her first of nine stakes winners in Full Flight, who was also one of the early stakes winners by the future leading sire Ambiorix. Full Flight was even more rugged than Shamrock; he ran no fewer than 216 times from two through ten. A stakes winner at three, four, and six, Full Flight accounted for the Saranac, Leonard Richards, Letellier Memorial, and Ponce de Leon Handicaps. He also placed in races as important as the Jerome, Lawrence Realization, and New Orleans Handicaps, and earned a total of $182,732.

In 1952, Grey Flight foaled the only champion among her brood of high-class runners. This was Misty Morn, by Princequillo, a young stallion who had graduated from a $250 fee at the Hancocks' Virginia farm to become a budding star at Claiborne after his second crop had included Hill Prince and Prince Simon. Misty Morn was the sort of filly which Fitzsimmons must have loved. The trainer of such late-developing animals as Gallant Fox, Omaha, and Vagrancy, Fitzsimmons sent the big, rangy filly to the post forty-two times at two and three. She came on at three to earn the filly championship of 1955. The eleven races Misty Morn won included the Monmouth Oaks, Diana Handicap, Molly Pitcher Handicap, and Providence Stakes, and she punctuated her toughness by defeating older males going one and five-eighths miles in the Gallant Fox Handicap.

Misty Morn earned a total of $212,575. She beat out her Wheatley stablemate High Voltage for championship honors, although High Voltage (the crop's champion filly at two) had won the Coaching Club American Oaks. Misty Morn in turn produced two champions and three other stakes winners, as will be described in more detail later.

In 1953, the year after Misty Morn was foaled, Grey Flight produced the Ambiorix colt, Gray Phantom. Like full brother Full Flight, Gray Phantom won in nice stakes company, without any pretense to championship status. He ran eighty-nine times from two through seven and earned $130,830. Gray Phantom's stakes wins were concentrated at Tropical Park, which used to launch the South Florida winter season as a prelude to the glamorous meeting at Hialeah. He accounted for the Christmas, Coral Gables, Ponce de Leon, and Robert E. Lee Handicaps.

Grey Flight was barren in 1954, then foaled Misty Flight, a full brother to Misty Morn and a colt with near championship potential. Misty Flight won the Remsen Stakes in the fall of his two-year-old season and was second in the Champagne to that year's juvenile champion, Jewel's Reward. Misty Flight was also second to Jester in the Futurity, and he eventually completed a career of eight wins in sixty starts from two through five, earning $133,508.

Grey Flight was barren again in 1956 and the next year foaled her only non-winner, Daylight Flight, by Princequillo. In 1958, she produced Misty Day, a son of the great Claiborne stallion Nasrullah. Misty Day won one stakes, the Sport Page Handicap, at four, among nine wins from fifty-six starts at three and four. He earned $88,801.

In 1959, Grey Flight was barren for the third time in six years, hardly a sequence a mare might be expected to undergo and still rise to numerical heights of production.

Bold Ruler, a son of Nasrullah, had come along

as a Wheatley homebred of championship quality in the middle 1950s. He was Horse of the Year at three in 1957 and a brilliant and courageous stakes winner at two and four as well. He entered stud at Claiborne in 1959 and was destined to set a modern record by leading the American sire list eight times.

Grey Flight was an obvious candidate for Bold Ruler's first book of mares, and their 1960 foal was the quick filly Bold Princess. At two in 1962, Bold Princess helped introduce the Bold Ruler era — when it would become an expectation that not one, but several, of the leading juveniles in the East each year would be his get. She won the Schuylerville Stakes for juvenile fillies at Saratoga and was retired with four wins from seventeen races at two and three and earnings of $37,157 before her own rich contributions from the broodmare ranks.

Bold Princess was followed in 1961 by Bold Queen, another Bold Ruler foal from Grey Flight. Bold Queen won the Black-Eyed Susan Stakes at three in 1964, and in three seasons won five of twenty-four starts and earned $55,739. The pattern of Bold Ruler foals was broken in 1962, when Grey Flight produced a colt by the great unbeaten European star Ribot. Signore would have to be counted as a disappointment, but he added to the budding lore by winning the Saratoga National Hurdle Stakes at four in 1966. Signore won four of thirty-one races and earned $20,635.

Grey Flight was barren in 1963, then the following year foaled another Bold Ruler filly, Great Era. Although she burst onto the scene with an eighth-length win in her debut, Great Era never won a stakes. Perhaps the fates were making up for Signore's backing into black type, for Great Era was clearly a high-class filly who never quite gained that distinction, although she was second in the Matron, Spinaway, and Prioress.

In 1965, Grey Flight was twenty years old. That year, she foaled a chestnut son of Bold Ruler named

Grey Flight

What a Pleasure, who became his dam's ninth and final stakes winner. He won the Hopeful and National Stallion Stakes and was second in the Sapling. At three, What a Pleasure was third in the Gotham, and he had a career record of six wins in eighteen races and earnings of $164,935.

The French horse Herbager had been imported to Claiborne, and Grey Flight was in his book of 1965. The following year, she foaled Quick Flight, winner once from fourteen races and earner of $1,456. Grey Flight was not bred at the age of twenty-one, but was cleared for breeding at twenty-two in 1967, and the next spring foaled the Bold Ruler filly Clear Ceiling. Winner of five of seventeen races and earner of $41,575, Clear Ceiling was to gain more distinction as a broodmare.

At twenty-four, in 1969, Grey Flight foaled another Bold Ruler filly, Pleasant Flight, winner once in fifteen races at two and three and earner of $15,010. Grey Flight had no further foals, having a record of fifteen offspring, of which all fifteen raced, fourteen won, and nine won stakes. The old gray mare's death was reported in 1974, or twenty-nine years after she was foaled.

In terms of Phipps stable history, the founder, Mrs. Henry Carnegie Phipps, died in 1970, and trainer Fitzsimmons, who trained Grey Flight and her early offspring, retired in 1963 and passed away in 1966. Fitzsimmons was followed, during the years when Grey Flight's foals were still active, by trainers Bill Winfrey, Eddie Neloy, and Roger Laurin.

Distinction Down the Line

Recounting the records of Grey Flight's foals as breeding animals is also a repeating chorus of success. It began with Misty Morn, her three-year-old filly champion of 1955. First of Misty Morn's was the high-class handicap horse Sunrise Flight, who was by the accomplished Claiborne stallion Double Jay.

The Phippses sold Sunrise Flight, who later made a mark as the broodmare sire of Pleasant Colony.

Over at Calumet Farm, trainer Ben Jones years before had noted that the formula for success was to breed all the mares to Bull Lea. In the 1960s, the Phipps family might have been excused for thinking the pedigree game had been reduced to one simple rule: Keep sending its high-class broodmare band to Bold Ruler. This pattern worked in the case of Misty Morn, who produced four stakes winners by the great young Claiborne sire within five years.

The first was Bold Consort, winner of the Test Stakes and in turn the source of several other generations of stakes winners, both here and in Europe. In 1961, Misty Morn foaled Beautiful Day, winner of the New Castle, National Stallion, and Roseanna Stakes and also a stakes producer.

In both 1962 and 1964, Misty Morn foaled champion juvenile colts, each by Bold Ruler. The first of these was Bold Lad, a strikingly handsome, classy chestnut. In 1964, Bold Lad was so dominant at two in winning races such as the Hopeful, Futurity, and Champagne, that at year's end he was assigned 130 pounds on the Experimental Free Handicap, as compared to the usual topweight assignment of 126. The following spring, Bold Lad was hurt in the Kentucky Derby, but he came back at four to win the Metropolitan Handicap before a moderately successful career at stud that saw him sent to France and on to Japan.

Successor was not so impressive a juvenile champion in 1966 as Bold Lad had been, but he did win the Garden State Stakes and Champagne, defeating the streaking Dr. Fager along the way, and won the balloting for the division.

Illustrative of how much fun it must have been to own Bold Ruler, Mrs. Henry Carnegie Phipps' twin sister, the Countess of Granard, decided to honor Bold Lad by giving one of her Irish-bred colts the same name. That colt was also by Bold Ruler, and also became a champion. (It is worth noting that the Phipps operation, however, did not actually fall into the trap of depending too much on Bold Ruler. In 1965, Ogden Phipps brought out the grand Buckpasser, who was the juvenile champion sandwiched between the two Bold Rulers; Buckpasser was by outside stallion Tom Fool.)

In 1964, Misty Morn was diverted from Bold Ruler to Swaps, and the following spring, she foaled Lovely Morning. Unraced Lovely Morning produced Resolver, a stakes-winning daughter of Reviewer. Resolver foaled grade I winners Dispute, Adjudicating, and Time for a Change, plus additional stakes winner Tax Collection. Dispute won the Kentucky Oaks, Spinster, Gazelle, and Beldame; Adjudicating took the Champagne and Cowdin Stakes, and Time for a Change upset Devil's Bag in the 1984 Flamingo Stakes for Dinny Phipps.

Bold Princess, another of Grey Flight's own daughters by Bold Ruler, foaled Intrepid Hero, a Forli colt who was close to championship status as a grass specialist. Bold Princess also was the dam of the Selima Stakes winner Predictable and the Irish stakes winner Primed, and various of her daughters and granddaughters also had success in the stud internationally.

Pleasant Flight, Grey Flight's last foal, made up for her modest racing performance by producing the Pan American Handicap winner Flitalong (stakes producer), as well as the Italian stakes winner On a Cloud. Pleasant Flight's branch of the female family eventually produced the high-class European miler Priolo.

One of the richest veins in the lode of Grey Flight came through another non-stakes winner, Clear Ceiling, by Bold Ruler. Clear Ceiling's 1977 Buckpasser filly, named Quick as Lightning, gave the Phippses one of their European classic tri-umphs (they seldom have raced abroad) when she won the English One Thousand Guineas in Dinny Phipps' colors. Clear Ceiling also foaled two other stakes winners, and her daughter Pure Profit, by Key to the Mint, foaled two millionaire distaffers: Educated Risk, conditioned by the present Phipps trainer Shug McGaughey, was by Mr. Prospector and won the grade I Frizette and Top Flight as well as other stakes. Her half-sister, Inside Information, by Private Account, went her a bit better; in the fall of 1995, Inside Information added a runaway, thirteen and a half-length victory in the Breeders' Cup Distaff to a handsome collection of earlier wins and wrested an Eclipse Award from stablemate Heavenly Prize.

For the most part, this recitation of the generations of success from Grey Flight stamps it as a family of producing mares, not a sire family. Nevertheless, in the 1970s, the family was prominent otherwise, for Grey Flight's high-class Bold Ruler colt What a Pleasure twice led the sire lists, while standing at Waldemar Farm in Florida. In the tradition of his sire, What a Pleasure sired back-to-back juvenile champions in Foolish Pleasure (1974) and Honest Pleasure (1975). Both these Pleasures continued at three, Foolish winning the Kentucky Derby and Honest adding the Travers. What a Pleasure was the leading sire in American earnings in both 1975 and 1976.

More recently, stallions descending from Grey Flight's daughters in tail-female have included Sovereign Dancer. A Northern Dancer colt out of Bold Princess, Sovereign Dancer was a lightly raced winner in France, then was returned to this country. In 1984, Sovereign Dancer's son Gate Dancer won the Preakness Stakes, and in 1996 the stallion got a second Preakness winner when Louis Quatorze won the Pimlico classic.

So, the melody of the old gray mare lingers, and this one is a sweet old song. ❖

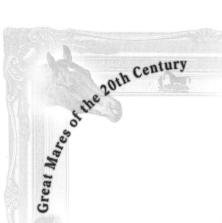

Hildene

The natural gas and public utilities industrialist Christopher T. Chenery twice reached into the pipeline of Thoroughbred genetics and found a vein of unusual importance. Their prices varied widely, but their contributions to Chenery's Meadow Stud, and to the Thoroughbred breed in general, were similar: Both produced important winners, and their daughters carried on in turn.

The first gem was difficult to discern as such. Hildene cost $750 as a yearling and, while that was a modest amount even by 1939 standards, it was several times more than she would earn as a racehorse. The second was considerably more expensive, for Chenery had to bid $30,000 to acquire Imperatrice from the W. H. LaBoyteaux dispersal of 1946. Imperatrice produced a series of stakes winners for Chenery and, more importantly, also foaled Somethingroyal, a Blue Hen in her own right and dam of the legendary Secretariat. (The exploits of Imperatrice, Somethingroyal, and others are reviewed in a separate chapter.)

Hildene came from the 1939 dispersal of Edward F. Simms. Chenery sent Norman Tallman to Kentucky for the auction, and the trainer came back with three yearling fillies. Hildene was sired by 1926 Kentucky Derby winner Bubbling Over, who got only eight stakes winners (five percent),

although Derby winner Burgoo King was among them. The dam of Hildene, Fancy Racket, by the successful sire Wrack, foaled two stakes winners, but only one of them had come forth by the time of the Simms sale. Fancy Racket's 1933 Crucifixion colt, Silas, won the $1,500 Jefferson Park Handicap in 1936; her 1934 Crucifixion gelding had the all-conquering name of Napoleon, but had not won a stakes until taking the Jolly Roger Steeplechase at the age of seven, two years after the purchase of Hildene.

Chenery's acquisition of the Simms fillies came only three years after he had begun broadening his interest in horses. Previously, he had been familiar with Thoroughbreds, but primarily for polo, which he pursued as he was building a self-made career. Born in Richmond, Virginia, in 1886, Chenery earned enough to attend Randolph-Macon and Washington and Lee by working as a surveyor's assistant for the Virginia Railway. After graduation, he worked on various engineering projects prior to World War I, during which he commanded training operations at Camp Humphries, Virginia, and emerged with the rank of major.

Chenery formed the Federal Water Service Corporation and in 1936 became chairman of Southern Natural Gas Co. Chenery held chairmanships of a half-dozen other gas and water companies. He was well established enough financially to reach back into his family's heritage and re-purchase The Meadow, an ancestral home built in 1810 at Doswell, Virginia. He used the name for the 2,600-acre farm he established there, and he raced in the name Meadow Stable. (Chenery's contributions to the Turf exceeded the breeding and racing of a number of champions: He served with Capt. Harry Guggenheim and John W. Hanes as the committee which was architect of the New York Racing Association, consolidating New York's tracks in the middle 1950s and restoring the state's status in the sport.)

Fancy Racket had failed to earn a dollar from four starts. Hildene, while technically improving on this record, also remained a maiden at the end of her own career, which consisted of eight starts. Hildene placed and earned $100. She was a bleeder. Chenery had an association with Arthur B. Hancock Sr., at whose Claiborne Farm some of the Meadow Stud mares were boarded, and he first bred Hildene to the Ascot Gold Cup winner Flares. The result was the moderate winner Sunset Bay, who made fifty-one starts and earned $7,175. In 1944, Hildene foaled her first stakes winner, Mangohick, to the cover of former leading money-earner Sun Beau. The gelding Mangohick made ninety-seven starts from two through seven and won twenty-three of them, including the Rumson and Fleetwing Handicaps. He earned $115,115. Next came Crescent City, a 1945 gelding by Pass Out who was unplaced in two starts. Hildene had no foal in 1946.

The mare had foaled a nice stakes winner when bred to a champion, but it was not until she hooked up with a former claimer that her career as a brood-mare really began to take shape. The one-time $2,500 claimer Princequillo had emerged as a worthwhile Cup horse in the hands of trainer Horatio Luro and had begun his career at stud in Virginia. He stood at Ellerslie, which the Hancock family for some years operated in addition to owning Claiborne in Kentucky.

Mangohick did not become a stakes winner until he was five in 1949, so it was not with the knowledge that he had a budding Blue Hen on his hands that Chenery sent Hildene to Princequillo in 1946. The stallion was relatively close by and stood for only $250, and such factors made him a logical match for Hildene. The first of three Princequillo—Hildene colts (all stakes winners) was foaled in 1947 and was named Hill Prince.

The marvelous qualities of Princequillo as a progenitor came to the fore quickly, and the stallion soon was transferred to Claiborne. He would eventually be a two-time leading sire. Also in the same crop as Hill Prince was Belair Stud's Prince Simon. Belair owner William Woodward Sr. did not deal with $250 stallions as a general policy, but the mare Dancing Dora had been barren three of the last four years and in 1946 was consigned to the young Princequillo. She foaled Prince Simon, who came within a head of landing Woodward his top English target, the Epsom Derby.

By the time Hill Prince came to the races, Chenery had hired as his trainer J. H. (Casey) Hayes, and the pair would remain together until late in Chenery's life. Hill Prince emerged as a high-class stakes winner early in his two-year-old season and won such races as the World's Playground, Babylon, and Cowdin. At one point that summer, Hill Prince's tail was bound too tightly, and a portion of it fell away. Thereafter, the otherwise handsome, strongly built bay was subject to reference as the "bob-tailed nag," but he also proved the sort that could "run all day."

The two-year-old picture of 1949 was inconclusive. Hill Prince suffered a cough and was unable to run in the Champagne, but he shared championship honors in the major polls with Oil Capitol. A third contender, Middleground, was the topweight on the Experimental Free Handicap.

The following spring, Hill Prince became the

		Sunstar, 1908	Sundridge Doris
	North Star III, 1914		
		Angelic, 1901	St. Angelo Fota
BUBBLING OVER, ch, 1923			
		Sweep, 1907	**Ben Brush** Pink Domino
	Beaming Beauty, 1917		
		Bellisario, 1911	Hippodrome Biturica
HILDENE, **b m, 1938**			
		Robert Le Diable, 1899	Ayrshire Rose Bay
	Wrack, 1909		
		Samphire, 1902	Isinglass Chelandry
FANCY RACKET, b, 1925			
		Ultimus, 1906	Commando Running Stream
	Ultimate Fancy, 1918		
		Idle Fancy, 1904	**Ben Brush** Fair Vision

Hildene, b, 1938-1957. Bred by Xalapa Farm (Ky.). Raced 1 yr, 8 sts, 0 wins, $100. Broodmare of the Year in 1950. Dam of 13 named foals, 12 rnrs, 9 wnrs, 5 sw.

1943: Sunset Bay, b f, by Flares. Raced 3 yrs, 51 sts, 1 win, $7,175.

1944: **MANGOHICK**, b g, by Sun Beau. Raced 7 yrs, 97 sts, 23 wins, $115,115. Won Fleetwing H, Rumson H; 2nd Oceanport H, Dade County H, Inaugural H, Governor Caldwell H; 3rd Oceanport H.

1945: Crescent City, ch g, by Pass Out. Raced 1 yr, 2 sts, 0 wins, $0.

1947: **HILL PRINCE**, b c, by Princequillo. Raced 4 yrs, 30 sts, 17 wins, $422,140. Horse of the Year, champion 2yo and 3yo colt and older male. Won Preakness S, Jockey Club Gold Cup, American Derby, Sunset H, Wood Memorial S, New York H, Withers S, Experimental Free H, Jerome H, San Marcos H, Cowdin S (NTR, Aqu, 6½ furlongs in 1:16.60), World's Playground S, Babylon H; 2nd Kentucky Derby, Dwyer S, Jockey Club Gold Cup, Sapling S, Empire City Gold Cup; 3rd Hollywood Gold Cup, Suburban H, Thankgiving Day H. Died 1970.

1948: First Flush, ch f, by Flushing II. Raced 1 yr, 3 sts, 0 wins, $0. Dam of 17 foals, 15 rnrs, 10 wnrs, including **BOLD EXPE-RIENCE** ($91,477), **VIRGINIA DELEGATE** ($75,320), **COPPER CANYON** ($66,462), **Ross Sea** ($48,641). Granddam of **UPPER CASE**, **LE BAG LADY**, **BRILLIANT ROSE**, **MS. ROSS**, **Copernica**, **New Look**, **Sharif**, **Cylinder**, **Joans Bo**, **Orchid Miss**, **Minmognovich**, **Air General**, **Quachita**, **Commanding Boss**. Died 1974.

1949: Satsuma, b f, by Bossuet. Raced 3 yrs, 8 sts, 1 win, $2,800. Dam of 6 foals, 6 rnrs, 3 wnrs, including **CICADA** ($783,674, champion 2yo and 3yo filly and older female).

Granddam of **CICADA'S PRIDE**, **Petticoat**, **Stet**, **Java Rajah**, **Targhee Pass**, **Earl Cardigan**, **Will Hail**, **Cloudy Summer**, **Cabana**. Died 1966.

1950: Chillon, ch g, by Hunters Moon IV. Unraced.

1951: **PRINCE HILL**, b g, by Princequillo. Raced 4 yrs, 57 sts, 8 wins, $98,300. Won American Bred S, Longfellow H; 3rd John B. Campbell Memorial H, San Pasqual H. Died 1956.

1952: Hildrix, b c, by Ambiorix. Raced 3 yrs, 31 sts, 1 win, $5,075. Died 1957.

1953: **THIRD BROTHER**, b c, by Princequillo. Raced 4 yrs, 69 sts, 9 wins, $310,787. Won Roamer H, Camden H, Bowie H, Long Island H; 2nd Monmouth H, John B. Campbell Memorial H, Jockey Club Gold Cup, Excelsior H, Edgemere H, Lawrence Realization, Camden H, Brooklyn H, Washington, D.C., International; 3rd Suburban H, Jockey Club Gold Cup, Pimlico Special, Choice S, Idlewild H, Mclennan H, Manhattan H, Atlantic City H. Sire of 94 foals, AEI 2.46. Died 1963.

1954: Refiner, ch g, by Count Fleet. Raced 3 yrs, 12 sts, 0 wins, $185. Died 1958.

1956: **FIRST LANDING**, b c, by Turn-to. Raced 3 yrs, 37 sts, 19 wins, $779,577. Champion 2yo colt. Won Garden State S, Monmouth H, Santa Anita Maturity, Champagne S, Laurel Maturity H (NTR, Lrl, 9 furlongs in 1:49.40), Hopeful S, Juvenile S, Great American S, Everglades S, Derby Trial, Saratoga Special; 2nd Metropolitan H, Futurity S, Suburban H, Wood Memorial S, Grey Lag H, Roamer H, San Antonio H, San Fernando S; 3rd Kentucky Derby, Flamingo S. Sire of 429 foals, AEI 2.28. Died 1987.

1957: Goodspeed, dkb/br g, by Tom Fool. Raced 3 yrs, 22 sts, 3 wins, $9,790.

first of a series of distinguished Kentucky Derby candidates for Chenery. Having won the Wood Memorial, the colt went to the post on Derby Day at 5-2, best among the Eastern colts and second choice to the fleet West Coast contender Your Host. Under Eddie Arcaro, Hill Prince got into a couple of tight spots and was unable to catch King Ranch's resolute Middleground. It was the first of the Derby disappointments for Meadow. In 1959, the returning champion First Landing (also from Hildene) finished third as post-time favorite; then, in 1962, Sir Gaylord shaped up as favorite for the race only to be injured and scratched at the eleventh hour. By the time Riva Ridge broke through as a Meadow Stable Derby winner in 1972, Chenery was confined to a nursing home, and the breeder had passed away before Secretariat's 1973 Triple Crown symphony.

Hill Prince rebounded to defeat Middleground in the one-mile Withers Stakes, and he held sway over the King Ranch colt again in the Preakness Stakes, achieving the first classic laurels both for Hildene and for Meadow. The Belmont, however, found the order reversed, as Middleground took two-thirds of the Triple Crown.

Thereafter, however, Middleground made only two more starts, one of them bringing another loss to Hill Prince, in the Jerome. Hill Prince also won the American Derby and defeated older champion Noor in the two-mile Jockey Club Gold Cup. He was Horse of the Year as well as three-year-old champion, and Hildene was Broodmare of the Year. Hill Prince repeated as a champion or co-champion for the third time, sharing handicap honors at four with Citation after a brief campaign. Hill Prince won a career total of seventeen of thirty races and earned $422,140. He later joined his sire at Claiborne, and his solid career at stud was distinguished by his getting the outstanding fillies Levee and Bayou. Hill Prince, who died in 1970, was elected to the National Museum of Racing's Hall of Fame in 1991.

More Princes, And Other Stars

Hildene's next foals after Hill Prince were the Flushing II filly First Flush and the Bossuet filly Satsuma, whose own careers as important producers we will address later in this chapter. By the spring of 1949, Hill Prince's distinction had not yet been earned, and the mare was still being sent to second-level or third-level stallions. In 1949, the dam of the up-and-coming juvenile champion was bred to Hunters Moon IV, primarily known as a sire of steeplechasers, such as the great Neji. The resulting foal, Chillon, never raced.

The emergence of Hill Prince sent Hildene back to Princequillo, sire of her 1951 foal. Hill Prince had been a success, and his full brother was named Prince Hill. He was a useful kind of horse, without classic or championship pretensions. Prince Hill won eight of fifty-seven races, including the Longfellow Handicap and American Bred Stakes, and earned $98,300. Hildene then foaled Hildrix, by Claiborne-based French star Ambiorix, and that colt was a modest winner.

In 1953 came another Princequillo colt and another stakes winner. This one was named, tellingly, Third Brother. He won four high-class Eastern handicaps, the Roamer, Camden, Bowie, and Long Island, at three and four. Third Brother was second in a handful of races that would have been grade I under today's system, among them the Washington, D.C., International, Jockey Club Gold Cup, John B. Campbell, Brooklyn, and Monmouth Handicaps. He was also third behind Nashua in another running of the Jockey Club Gold Cup. Third Brother won a total of nine races from sixty-nine starts for Chenery and Hayes and earned $310,787. Before his early death at ten, he had gotten a half-dozen stakes winners, most notable of which was Harbor View Farm's Horse of the Year Roman Brother.

Hildene was bred to Triple Crown winner Count Fleet in 1953, but the resulting produce, the gelded Refiner, failed to place in a dozen races. Hildene had a 1955 Nasrullah colt which died as a yearling, and, nearing twenty, may have seemed unlikely to improve markedly on an already estimable record. There had never been a noticeable pattern of Hildene adhering to high-percentage results, however, and in 1956 she produced a colt that was even better at two than Hill Prince. This "Prince" by another name was First Landing, a big, lengthy colt by the young stallion Turn-to.

A son of Royal Charger, Turn-to had won the newly minted richest race in the world, the Garden State Stakes, in 1953, then had been the Kentucky Derby favorite off a streaking Flamingo Stakes victory, prior to bowing a tendon, in 1954. Turn-to raced for Chenery's fellow NYRA designer, Capt. Guggenheim.

The Turn-to—Hildene colt, First Landing, tore through the juvenile division with unusual ferocity in 1958. He was unbeaten into the autumn, when Intentionally upset him in the Futurity. By that time, First Landing already had won the Juvenile, Great American, Saratoga Special, and Hopeful. He concluded his campaign with two courageous duels in which he defeated Tomy Lee at a mile in the Champagne and at one and one-sixteenth miles in the Garden State. First Landing won ten of eleven races and set a record for juvenile earnings, collecting $396,460. He was the clear choice as juvenile champion and went to Florida the next winter with the full panoply of a Kentucky Derby favorite.

First Landing did not continue to dominate his age group and had suffered several setbacks by Derby time, although he was the slight choice over Tomy Lee. The latter emerged as the winner, with First Landing third. The Meadow colt did come back later to prove a very good handicap horse in 1960, however. Despite facing a strong division also including Bald Eagle, Sword Dancer, and On-and-On, First Landing got in some more big Saturdays, winning the Santa Anita Maturity, Laurel Maturity, and Monmouth Handicap.

First Landing took to stud a career record of nineteen wins in thirty-seven races and earnings of $779,577. He rose to as high as fourth on the sire list. His outstanding contribution was the brilliant Riva Ridge, champion at two and winner of the 1972 Kentucky Derby and Belmont for Meadow Stable, by then managed by one of Chenery's daughters, Penny.

At the age of nineteen, Hildene produced her final foal. Sired by the champion handicapper and noted sire Tom Fool, the foal of 1957 was named Goodspeed. This concept was more in name than fact, however, and Goodspeed won only three of twenty-two races and earned $9,790.

Daughters of Distinction

The influence of Hildene in pedigrees was cemented to some extent by a few of Hill Prince's and First Landing's offspring. The mare's status along the bottom lines of important horses stemmed primarily from two daughters whose sires reflected the lack of fashion status Hildene had in the 1940s.

As mentioned above, Hildene in 1948 foaled First Flush, a filly whose sire, Flushing II, had moderate sire statistics, but got a champion mare in Lavender Hill. First Flush was unplaced in three starts, but by that time was known to be a half-sister to the champion Hill Prince, and so was a logical candidate for Chenery's broodmare band. She did not produce a stakes winner until she was fourteen, in 1962, but wound up the dam of three stakes winners: Bold Experience, Copper Canyon, and Virginia Delegate. Two were moderate, but Bold Experience was another matter.

Sired early in the career of the reigning stallion of the 1960s, Bold Ruler, First Flush's Bold Experience matured quickly. She dashed through victories in the Sorority Stakes and Rancocas in 1964 and won a total of five races in ten starts. Bold Experience produced Upper Case, a Round Table colt who won the Florida Derby and Wood Memorial for Meadow Stable the same year Riva Ridge won the Kentucky Derby and Belmont. Another foal of Bold Experience was the stakes winner Ms. Ross. Aces Full, another Round Table—Bold Experience foal, later produced Petite Ile, a filly who won the Irish St. Leger and then scored a pair of graded stakes wins against males on turf in California.

The aforementioned Copper Canyon won only one stakes, the Pan Zareta, but placed in the Schuylerville and Black-Eyed Susan. Copper Canyon's 1972 Nijinsky II filly, Copernica, appeared a budding superstar with her first victory in the spring of 1974, but was quickly eclipsed by Ruffian. Copernica never won a stakes, but was second in the Frizette and Matron. She produced the Hopeful Stakes winner Crusader Sword and French stakes winner Copper Butterfly. Other recent stakes winners descending from Copper Canyon include Cherokee Colony, Risen Colony, Silken Doll, and Turk Passer.

In 1964, First Flush produced another Bold Ruler filly, unraced Bold Matron. The latter became second dam of major winners Ring of Light, Dr. Blum, Spirit Level, Gilgit, and others.

Of all the treasures Hildene and her issue brought to Meadow Stable, one of the most beloved was Cicada. The dam of Cicada was Satsuma, Hildene's 1949 filly, who was a modest winner at two and earned $2,800. Satsuma was sired by Bossuet, a stallion whose stud career did nothing to add to, or detract from, his unique distinction in Turf history as having joined Brownie and Wait a Bit at the finish of the 1944 Carter Handicap — still the most famous triple dead heat in Turf lore. Satsuma had six foals. All of them raced, three of them won, and one of them was Cicada.

Cicada was Satsuma's lithe bay Bryan G. filly foaled in 1959. Bryan G. was a hard-hitting handicap horse of the early 1950s for Chenery. At stud, he

got only a half-dozen stakes winners, but two of them were Copper Canyon and Cicada.

"Hickory" was the word jockey Willie Shoemaker chose to describe Cicada. It was a fitting appellation. Casey Hayes brought out Cicada early in the winter of her two-year-old season. She started in February, hurtling down the Hialeah stretch in one of the three-furlong races by which that Florida track used to introduce many a youngster to the concept that speed matters. By year's end, Cicada had run sixteen times and had won eleven races, of which eight were stakes events. Her triumphs ranged from sprints to one and one-sixteenth miles, and the names of her most important races won included Gardenia, Frizette, Spinaway, and Matron. She also won the Blue Hen Stakes, a Delaware Park event which evoked that track's veneration of the female and its recognition of that arcane phrase as one to honor exceptional producers, such as, for example, Cicada's granddam, Hildene.

Cicada was the overwhelming choice as champion two-year-old filly of 1961, and the following winter Hayes made her assignments even more challenging. She was asked to face older fillies and mares that winter, which proved only a tune-up for such challenges as facing the powerful three-year-old colt Ridan at one and one-eighth miles in the Florida Derby. Cicada went under only by the scantiest of margins.

In the spring, Hayes prepped Cicada for the Kentucky Oaks. Why would he not? After all, Meadow Stable had Sir Gaylord, the expected favorite for the Kentucky Derby. Ironically, a man who did not cower before the thought of racing a filly against colts did not know until the eve of the Derby that Sir Gaylord would not be sound enough to compete. It was too late to change course. Cicada romped in the Oaks; Meadow had no entrant in the Derby. Cicada continued through her three-year-old season, winning eight of seventeen races, including the

Hildene

Acorn, Mother Goose, and Beldame, and she was champion again.

Voting for championships had begun in this country in 1936, and no filly ever had been champion at two, three, and four. Cicada, who at four won four of eight starts, including the Vagrancy Handicap, erased that footnote to Turf history, replacing it with her own name as the first to achieve that distinction. She was retired, came back for one race, and was retired again, reigning as the all-time leading distaff earner with $783,674. She had won twenty-three of forty-two races.

Cicada and Sir Gaylord had been unknowing co-stars of a Derby Week drama when they were three.

In 1966, Sir Gaylord was registered as the sire of Cicada's first foal, a colt born that spring and named Cicada's Pride. The gelding won the Juvenile Stakes early in his two-year-old season. Sadly, Cicada then was beset by a series of reproductive problems. She eventually had a total of six foals before her death at twenty-two, but Cicada's Pride was her only stakes winner.

Meadow Stable was to become linked forever in the hearts of horsemen and horse lovers with the startling supremacy of Secretariat. Long before, the family of Hildene had created cherished and lasting distinctions of its own. ❖

"Bring Ilsa!" Orville Brown shouted from the end of the barn. It was a steamy morning in early spring at Ocala Stud and the wiry little broodmare manager was relenting to the alteration the boys on the mare crew habitually gave the name of perhaps their most distinguished ward. "Ilsa," being called off Orville Brown's morning teasing chart, was really Iltis, and in those heady days when Ocala, Florida, was muscling onto the national scene of top-class Thoroughbred output, she was already a queen.

Two years before, Iltis' daughter, My Dear Girl, had emerged as the national champion two-year-old filly of 1959. My Dear Girl was a Florida-bred, by the Ocala Stud stallion Rough'n Tumble, and when her dam was led out to the teaser, the member of the crew on her shank was keenly aware this was not just another mare.

Iltis was a large bay mare, her nose notched noticeably, perhaps as a result of some early contretemps with her halter. She had been bred by the Brookfield Farm of Harry Isaacs, an enduring sportsman who was pleased enough with his own surname that he habitually gave his horses names beginning with the same letter. When common words were not available, he waxed creative: Hence Intent and Intentionally, but also Isasmoothie, Ifabody, Inyureye, etc.

Iltis was by War Relic, one of Man o' War's best

sons, and was produced from We Hail, a Balladier mare. The next dam, Col. E. R. Bradley's Clonaslee, produced sixteen winners from eighteen foals, including three moderate stakes winners.

Iltis was foaled in 1947 and made her first start at Garden State Park on May 14, 1949. She broke her maiden in her third try, skipping up in conditions to face male non-winners of two. This emboldened trainer D. W. Kerns to throw Iltis into stakes company, but she was seventh of eight behind star-to-be Hill Prince in the World's Playground Stakes. Apparently, however, Iltis' maiden win had been in a race which more than one horseman viewed as above average in indication of potential, for A. S. Hewitt's Cornwall, who had been fourth behind her, ran well enough to be third in the World's Playground.

Iltis had no further stakes forays, or victories, at two, but Kerns and Isaacs apparently remained ready to believe she was of high potential whenever she gave them any encouragement. She was, after all, a half-sister to the high-class stakes winner Is Proud. Kern also continued to run her against males. After she defeated County Delight in a one-and-one-sixteenth mile allowance race at Delaware Park, he put her into the Delaware Oaks. She was eighth of ten fillies in a race won by Next Move over Busanda, names which would ring down through history. Although it was hardly a discernible moral

		Fair Play, 1905	Hastings **Fairy Gold**
	Man o' War, 1917		
WAR RELIC, ch, 1938		Mahubah, 1910	**Rock Sand** Merry Token
		Friar Rock, 1913	**Rock Sand** **Fairy Gold**
	Friar's Carse, 1923		
ILTIS, b m, 1947		Problem, 1914	Superman Query
		Black Toney, 1911	Peter Pan Belgravia
	Balladier, 1932		
WE HAIL, br, 1942		Blue Warbler, 1922	North Star III May Bird
		Orpiment, 1907	Ayrshire Orphrey
	Clonaslee, 1922		
		Bullet Proof, 1914	Wax Bullet Solirena

Iltis, b, 1947-1969. Bred by Brookfield Farms (Md.). Raced 4 yrs, 53 sts, 5 wins, $19,425. Dam of 8 named foals, 6 rnrs, 6 wnrs, 3 sw.

1954: **Tiswar**, b g, by Prince Quest. Raced 5 yrs, 81 sts, 15 wins, $44,140. 3rd Gulfstream Park Dinner S.

1955: Iltis Prince, b c, by Prince Quest. Unraced.

1956: Slipped twins.

1957: **MY DEAR GIRL**, ch f, by Rough'n Tumble. Raced 3 yrs, 20 sts, 8 wins, $209,739. Champion 2yo filly. Won Frizette S, Gardenia S, Florida Breeders' S; 2nd Arlington Lassie S, Interborough H, Las Flores H; 3rd Gallorette S. Dam of 15 foals, 14 rnrs, 13 wnrs, including **SUPERBITY** ($297,992, gr. I), **RETURN TO REALITY** ($150,412), **IN REALITY** ($795,824), **MY DEAR LADY** ($52,500), **WATCHFULNESS** ($45,581), **REALLY AND TRULY** ($99,404), **GENTLE TOUCH** ($36,912), **Star of the North** ($49,750). Granddam of **DR. CARTER, KETTLE RIVER, CLOSE TO ME, NISSWA, MY DEAR FRANCES, CHEERS MARION,** Love You Dearly, **Kettle Kin,** Proud of You. Died 1988.

1958: **MY OLD FLAME**, ch f, by Count Flame. Raced 1 yr, 9 sts, 3 wins, $30,072. Won Florida Breeders' S, Florida Breeders' Futurity; 2nd Rancocas S.

1959: **Sutton Place Gal**, b f, by Needles. Raced 3 yrs, 23 sts, 1 win, $3,518. 3rd Florida Breeders' Championship. Dam of 2 foals, 2 rnrs, 1 wnr, **Rough Place** ($96,752). Granddam of **King's Honour.** Died 1968.

1960: Me Next, b f, by Rough'n Tumble. Unraced. Dam of 13 foals, 11 rnrs, 9 wnrs, including **LUCKY OLE ME** ($59,336), **MIDNIGHT PUMPKIN** ($44,587), **Leave Me Alone** ($179,810), **Show Me How** ($71,188), **After Me** ($77,412). Granddam of **TANK'S PROSPECT, REACH THE GOLD, LUCKY NORTH, SWALK, KUDZ, Roseabelle Believe, Private Player, Long Walk, Just Oneof Theboys, Winning Spurs.** Died 1988.

1961: Group Leader, br c, by Rough'n Tumble. Raced 2 yrs, 8 sts, 3 wins, $11,450. Died 1964.

1962: **TREASURE CHEST**, b f, by Rough'n Tumble. Raced 4 yrs, 49 sts, 10 wins, $75,872. Won Modesty H (T; NCR, AP, 8 furlongs in 1:37.20), Lottie Wolf Memorial S; 3rd Beverly H (T), Sweet Patootie S, Four Winds H, Blue Hen S. Dam of 13 foals, 12 rnrs, 10 wnrs, including **DIOMEDIA** ($101,678), **KANZ** ($54,193), **GOLD TREASURE** ($108,787), **Crown Treasure** ($19,776), **Pelf** ($25,162, in Eng and Italy). Granddam of **GLINT OF GOLD, DIAMOND SHOAL (GB), ENSCONSE,** Treasure Leaf, **CRYSTAL SPIRIT (GB), MEDIA STARGUEST (Ire), JETTA J., I WANT TO BE, CROWN SILVER, DIRECT ANSWER, FLYING TROVE,** Golden Guinea, **Treasurer (GB),** Diorama, **Dynamic Leader (Ire),** Majestic Treasure.

1963: Barren.

1965: Barren.

1966: Barren.

victory at the time, a footnote to the race was that Iltis did finish ahead of a filly named Almahmoud (also included in this volume).

At four, Kerns and Isaacs let Iltis slide into claiming company, and she had had several owners by the end of the year. Her only victory came under at a $6,000 tag during the Saratoga-at-Jamaica meeting. At five, Iltis won once more from thirteen starts, that score coming in a $4,000 claiming event at Gulfstream Park for Dan Chappell's Sunshine Stable. Her final start was on Sept. 12, 1952, at Aqueduct, when she finished last of twelve for $3,500. Coincidentally, the colt Cornwall also had slipped from the apparent potential of his two-year-old days and was entered in the same race, although scratched.

Iltis had won five of fifty-three starts over four campaigns and had earned $19,425. Chappell was among the early advocates of the Ocala area for breeding and placed her in the stud at his Sunshine Farm. Iltis' first foal was by Prince Quest, who stood at a farm named for him (Prince Quest Farm) farther south in Florida, in the little village of Davie. Tiswar was not a stakes winner, but he won fifteen races and placed in the Gulfstream Park Dinner Stakes, this at a time when any good stakes effort by a Florida-bred was noteworthy. After foaling another Prince Quest foal (unraced) for Chappell, Iltis produced her next foal, My Dear Girl, for Ocala Stud. She had slipped twins in between.

The establishment of Ocala Stud ranked with the classic success of Florida-bred Needles among the most significant voltage in the jump start of the Florida Thoroughbred industry. James Bright in 1936 had registered the first Florida foals, and there had been a few high points for Florida-breds in the interim, such as Liberty Rab's victory over Battlefield in the Juvenile Stakes of 1950.

When Needles won the Flamingo and Florida Derby of 1956, however, the state's breeders were still hearing comments about breeding alligators in the swamp, and Florida-breds still got a five-pound allowance in state races. (One can hardly imagine later state-breds such as Dr. Fager, Affirmed, Holy Bull, and Skip Away needing any administrative edge.)

That Iltis was already in Florida early in her breeding career was thanks to Chappell. The remainder of her rise to lasting importance to the state, however, was a story combining Kentucky, Maryland, and a couple from Minnesota.

Rough'n Tumble and a Propitious Birthday

The Minneapolis electrical equipment manufacturer Harold C. Genter bought his first Keeneland yearlings in 1948. One of them was an $8,600 colt consigned by Dr. Charles Hagyard. As would be true of most of the Genter horses, this colt was raced in the name of the Mrs. Genter, i.e., Frances Genter Stable. He was named Unbridled and won his first stakes early the next summer. (Many years after Genter's death, Mrs. Genter circled back to the same name for a colt who would bring her victory in the 1990 Kentucky Derby.)

In 1949, the Genters did not find anything they could, or wanted, to buy at the Keeneland summer sale, but Unbridled the Elder had encouraged them about the Kentucky market. Visiting Dr. Hagyard's farm, they bought a Free For All yearling from the distinguished veterinarian. The colt was somewhat scrawny at the time, but he was named Rough'n Tumble, perhaps as a subliminal boost to his self-esteem.

With Sunshine Calvert training him, Rough'n Tumble won the Primer Stakes at two and gave the Genters and their family a first glimpse at the golden halo around the Kentucky Derby. In the winter of 1951, he won the Santa Anita Derby, but classic possibilities were soon scuttled by soundness problems. Rough'n Tumble earned $126,980 even though Calvert's efforts to get him back to the races at four and five were to no avail.

By the autumn of 1953, Dr. Hagyard agreed to stand Rough'n Tumble at his farm for the Genters the following spring. Then entered the Marylanders.

Joe and Tom O'Farrell owned Windy Hills Farm in Westminster, Maryland, and were looking for a stallion prospect. They contacted the Cromwell Bloodstock Agency of John A. Bell III and Alex Bower, who called Calvert. The trainer in turned contacted the Genters, and Rough'n Tumble entered stud at Windy Hill instead of in Kentucky, with the Genters retaining ownership.

The young stallion covered seventeen mares in 1954 and thirteen the following year. It was also in 1955 that Joe O'Farrell was asked to look over a farm in Florida and became smitten by Ocala.

"I saw all those live oaks trees and hills and all that grass and I was sold," he told *The Blood-Horse* years later. "The big thing was being able to keep stock out in the sunshine."

O'Farrell was recalling his having inspected William Leach's Dickey Stable, after fellow Marylander Bruce Campbell had heard of Leach's interest in selling. The deal was quickly consummated by Campbell and several associates, and the name of the farm was changed to Ocala Stud, with O'Farrell in charge. (The farm remains a leader in the industry at the end of the century under Joe O'Farrell's son Mike.)

Although Tom O'Farrell stayed on in Maryland, it was agreed by the various parties that Rough'n Tumble would be moved to Ocala Stud, where he first stood in 1956. Early the next year, Genter sold Rough'n Tumble to Ocala Stud, the dealing involving cash and his pick among farm-owned Rough'n Tumble weanlings of 1957, as of that September. After Genter chose the filly out of Iltis, he conceded that the shrewd horsemanship decision had been abetted by the filly having been foaled on Feb. 17 — Mrs. Genter's birthday.

Calvert remained the Genter trainer as long as he was in the game, and he took over the chestnut daughter of Rough'n Tumble—Iltis, who had been named My Dear Girl, an expression frequently employed conversationally by Genter.

One of the complexities of racing in the last forty years is that, while early competition for two-year-olds fell under suspicion after research refined the ability to discern "open" and "closed" knees, there are countless examples of successful runners having been tuned to racing fettle early in their two-year-old season. Two days after My Dear Girl's, and Mrs. Genter's, actual birthday of 1959, the filly made her debut in a field of thirteen for a three-furlong dash down the front chute at Hialeah. She finished tenth of thirteen. The next week, however, apparently having caught on to the game, she led a charge of twenty-five juveniles, which finished all over the track, to win the Florida Breeders' Stakes, also at three furlongs.

She was not seen under colors again until June, when she raced five and a half furlongs in 1:03 1/5 to set a track record at Chicago's Washington Park, in an allowance race. She then was beaten a neck by Round Table's sister, Monarchy, in the Arlington Lassie, with Cain Hoy Stable's classy pair of Heavenly Body and Make Sail next in line.

Rested from July until October, My Dear Girl then won by five lengths over seven furlongs at Aqueduct. The Gardenia Stakes, distaff counterpart to the richest race in the world, the Garden State Stakes, had emerged as one of the leading races for two-year-old fillies since its inception in 1955. Champions Idun and Quill had won it in the years immediately preceding My Dear Girl. Relishing a sloppy track for the second consecutive start, My Dear Girl toured in front throughout, winning the Gardenia by five lengths, with other division contenders such as Heavenly Body and Irish Jay well beaten.

Although a championship was presumably secure with no further testing, Calvert sent her to the post once more. Yet again catching a sloppy track, My Dear Girl fought gamely from behind to edge Irish Jay to win the one-mile Frizette. My Dear Girl followed Needles as the second champion among Florida-breds, taking honors among juvenile fillies on both the *Daily Racing Form* and Thoroughbred Racing Associations polls.

My Dear Girl, who had won five of seven races at two, made thirteen additional starts at three and four. She won three more races, but no additional stakes, although she was second in the Interborough Handicap in New York and Las Flores Handicap in California and third in the Gallorette Stakes in Maryland. She was retired with a career record of eight wins from twenty races and earnings of $209,739.

By the early stages of My Dear Girl's breeding career, another Minnesota connection had become a force in Florida racing and breeding. William McKnight, head of Minnesota Mining and Manufacturing, hence known as 3-M (Scotch tape, AstroTurf), developed Tartan Farms not far from Ocala Stud. He also became owner of Calder Race Course, the new South Florida track which extended the area's racing season from a traditional late-autumn-to-early-spring schedule to year around.

Among the important purchases brought to Florida by Tartan and its management team of John Nerud and John Hartigan was the fine miler Intentionally. He had been bred and raced by Harry Isaacs, breeder of Iltis.

The Genters became clients of the McKnight farm, and in 1964, My Dear Girl produced as her second foal a bay son of Intentionally. It was a milestone crop at Tartan. Ev Clay, the genial publicist for Hialeah Race Track during some of the brightest years of its gilded time, was doing work for 3-M by the late 1960s, and he managed considerable mileage out of a color photo of three Tartan-bred yearlings of 1964 having early training lessons among the Spanish-moss draped live oaks. The three were Dr. Fager, In Reality, and Minnesota Mac, each destined for fame at the races. Dr. Fager and Minnesota Mac were Rough'n

Tumble colts bred by Tartan; In Reality was My Dear Girl's foal.

Pleasurable as that scene might have been to a publicist, it had its negative side from the standpoint of the Genters. They needed little reminder that, throughout the horses' careers, Dr. Fager was the great horse; In Reality, a cut below. Moreover, the Kentucky foal crop of 1964 included another nemesis, the vaunted Damascus.

Nevertheless, Sunshine Calvert guided In Reality to a career of remarkable consistency and durability. At two, he came along well enough to take the one and one-sixteenth-mile Pimlico Futurity late in the year, defeating that year's juvenile champion colt, Successor, by a neck. The following winter in Florida, In Reality trod a typical path for a Kentucky Derby contender, winning the Hibiscus Stakes, Fountain of Youth, and Florida Derby, but Calvert was not keen on the Kentucky Derby, so In Reality was pointed instead for the Preakness. There he got a dose of Damascus, but ran well to be second.

In the Jersey Derby, Dr. Fager ran off from In Reality, but he also was judged to have run him off (his path) early in the event, and the Genter horse was named the official winner. Later, in the New Hampshire Sweepstakes, In Reality ran a game second to Dr. Fager, giving him six pounds and losing by barely more than a length. A further example of the futility of being a three-year-old named neither Damascus nor Dr. Fager that year was the American Derby. Damascus beat In Reality by seven lengths. It could have been worse: Damascus also won the Travers by twenty-two and the Woodward Stakes by ten.

Damascus was Horse of the Year at three, and Dr. Fager was Horse of the Year at four. In Reality continued in the latter year to add to his own distinction, however, winning three of the top handicaps of the East, the seven-furlong Carter, one-mile Metropolitan, and one and one-sixteenth-mile John B. Campbell. He went to stud at Tartan with a career record of fourteen wins in twenty-seven races and earnings of $795,824.

In Reality was closely inbred to Iltis' sire, War Relic, who was his great-grandsire on the top side as well as on the bottom. His own career at stud was instrumental in the continuing success of the male line of War Relic's heroic sire, Man o' War, and the latter's progenitor, Fair Play, harking back to the early days of the century. In Reality ranked as high as second on both the general sire list and the broodmare sire list, and his male offspring included several which in more recent times have carried on the line successfully, to wit, Relaunch, Believe It, Known Fact, and Valid Appeal. In Reality's daughters included the champion Desert Vixen.

In Reality was also a part of a later confluence of the salubrious Tartan-Genter relationship. He sired the second dam of a colt Mrs. Genter bought out of the Tartan dispersal and gave the familiar old name of Unbridled.

More Dear Girls, and Boys

None of My Dear Girl's later foals were of the quality of In Reality, but some did not miss it by too far. The mare continued to turn out successful runners until she had foaled the remarkable total of seven stakes winners before her death in 1988. For consistency of production My Dear Girl was similar in numbers to her third dam, the aforementioned factory Clonaslee, and even the latter could not match her in quality. All told, My Dear Girl produced fifteen foals, of which fourteen raced and thirteen won.

Of My Dear Girl's six stakes winners which followed In Reality, Superbity also excited Triple Crown whispers when he won the Tropical Park Derby and the grade I Flamingo Stakes. The other stakes winners were Return to Reality, Really and Truly, My Dear Lady, Watchfulness, and Gentle Touch. Several of her daughters in turn became stakes producers,

Iltis

including Gentle Touch, dam of the high-class Caro colt Dr. Carter.

The only unraced foal among My Dear Girl's offspring was her first, Endearing, whose sire, Triple Crown winner Count Fleet, indicates the Genters' determination to give My Dear Girl every chance from the beginning. Endearing foaled two stakes winners, Kettle River and Cheers Marion.

More From Iltis

As would be expected, the emergence of My Dear Girl provided some significant marketing opportunities for Ocala Stud. In the spring of 1960, Iltis produced another Rough'n Tumble filly, who was purchased privately by Mrs. Richard C. du Pont for a reported $40,000. She was named Me Next and, while she never raced, she foaled the Jersey Bell Handicap winner Lucky Ole Me, who in turn produced a pair of stakes winners. More importantly, Me Next also foaled Midnight Pumpkin, who became the dam of 1985 Preakness winner Tank's Prospect.

In between My Dear Girl and Me Next, Iltis had produced two other fillies, My Old Flame (by Count Flame), winner of the Florida Breeders' Stakes and Florida Breeders' Futurity, and Sutton Place Gal (by Needles), who was stakes-placed.

The Florida-bred two-year-old sales, which had been pushed along by O'Farrell, had begun with the gimmick of offering horses ready to race — or even with a three-furlong race under their belts — and a brace of young horses had furthered the cause by seeming to outrun their pedigrees. In the offspring of Iltis, O'Farrell now had proven class of pedigree as well, and Group Leader, My Dear Girl's full brother, topped the 1963 Hialeah auction at $48,000, a record for the sale at the time. Group Leader, purchased by Louis Wolfson, proved a moderate winner. (Wolfson had pleasant memories of that sale, however, for he got future Horse of the Year Roman Brother from the Ocala Stud consignment for $23,500.)

The following year, Ocala Stud offered another Rough'n Tumble two-year-old from Iltis. This was a filly, and by then there was a clear pattern of her fillies being better than her colts. Named Treasure Chest, this filly went for another sale record, $70,000, being purchased by David Shaer.

Treasure Chest became Iltis' third stakes winner and the vehicle of yet additional multi-generational continuation of the mare's influence. Iltis had no further foals and died in 1969 at the age of twenty-two.

Treasure Chest won the Modesty Handicap and Lottie Wolf Memorial, placed in four other stakes, and earned $75,872. As a producer, Treasure Chest exhibited the same hardiness of her ancestry, producing thirteen foals, of which twelve raced and ten won. They included the stakes winners, Gold Treasure, Diomedia, and Kanz.

In the fall of 1968, Shaer sold Treasure Chest back to Ocala Stud, reportedly for $225,000, and Ocala Stud soon sold her on to Keswick Stable of Virginia, which began selling her yearlings at Saratoga.

Treasure Chest and a combination of her foals and their daughters brought the Iltis brood into the sphere of influence of Northern Dancer blood. Treasure Chest's stakes-winning son Gold Treasure was by the great Canadian-bred himself. Diomedia, by Sea-Bird II, foaled Media Starguest to the cover of Be My Guest. Media Starguest was one of a growing number of individuals who carried the blood of Iltis to success on foreign soil, winning three stakes in England. Also, Treasure Chest's daughter Kanz (by The Minstrel) won the 1984 Princess Elizabeth Stakes and placed in that year's Yorkshire Oaks, both in England.

Earlier, In Reality's son Known Fact had won the English Two Thousand Guineas on the disqualification of Nureyev and subsequently sired such European winners as category champions Warning and Markofdistinction.

Additional European distinction for the family came in the 1980s in the form of two full brothers by Paul Mellon's great champion Mill Reef. These were Glint of Gold and Diamond Shoal. The full siblings were foaled from Treasure Chest's stakes-placed Graustark filly, Crown Treasure. Bred by Keswick, Crown Treasure was the fourth-highest-price filly at the 1974 Saratoga sale, where Mellon bought her for $98,000.

The first Mill Reef—Crown Treasure winner, Glint of Gold, was runner-up for Mellon in two classics in England, the Derby and the St. Leger, as well as winning the Great Voltigeur Stakes. Glint of Gold also won the Italian Derby, a fact Mellon modestly pointed out as an addenda to the fame he received in 1993 as the only man to have won the Kentucky Derby (Sea Hero), Epsom Derby (Mill Reef), and Prix de l'Arc de Triomphe (Mill Reef). Glint of Gold also won the historic Grand Prix de Paris and Grand Prix de Saint-Cloud in France as well as Germany's group I Preis von Europa. He was rated a champion in both Italy and Germany.

Glint of Gold's full brother, Diamond Shoal, also was taken on many a voyage by Mellon's English trainer, Ian Balding. At home, he won in group company and placed in the St. Leger, and his travels included victory in the Grand Prix de Saint-Cloud, plus group I wins in Italy and Germany.

So, Europeans have seen Mellon, the master of Rokeby Farm, winning classics and other historic races with such bloodlines. The victory stands of Europe seemed far, indeed, from the claiming mare who started turning out "alligator-breds" in the 1950s. ❖

Imperatrice

A s the dam of Secretariat and Sir Gaylord, the mare Somethingroyal may seem the representative of her family most likely to lend her name to a chapter. Somethingroyal, however, was herself a daughter of a remarkable producer in Imperatrice, dam of six stakes winners, and so we backtrack one generation.

Imperatrice, foaled in 1938, was bred by William H. LaBoyteaux, a member of The Jockey Club who had assembled a stallion and broodmare operation at his Hop Creek Farm in Holmdel, New Jersey. At the time, Imperatrice could not be said to have been bred at the very height of fashion — a cliché which would apply to later generations — but her pedigree did have considerable support from the better elements of the Stud Book. Her sire, Caruso, was by Polymelian, he a paternal half-brother to the pivotal sire Phalaris. Polymelian sired twenty-one American stakes winners and distinguished himself further as the broodmare sire of Polynesian.

Caruso (whose dam was Sweet Music) was among 1929s better two-year-olds in this country for LaBoyteaux, winning the United States Hotel Stakes and three other stakes. He made no impression on the three-year-olds of 1930, the Triple Crown season of Gallant Fox, but Caruso's curtain had not yet descended, for he won the Toboggan, George Washington, and California Handicaps at four. He then was put to stud at Hop Creek, where he had modest results, four stakes winners from a total of only seventy-nine foals.

Imperatrice, best of his runners, was from unraced Cinquepace, she in turn a daughter of another unraced mare, Assignation. Cinquepace was by Brown Bud, who won the 1927 Travers Stakes and was disqualified from victory in the Jockey Club Gold Cup for bearing in; Brown Bud was the sire of only two stakes winners. Assignation was by the influential sire Teddy. Justification for successive generations of non-runners to be included in high-class broodmare bands stemmed in part from Imperatrice's third dam, Cinq a Sept, a Roi Herode filly who won the Irish Oaks and a series of good races in England for American Marshall Field during the late 1920s.

Imperatrice was turned over by LaBoyteaux to George Odom, who was a Hall of Fame jockey and later a successful trainer. Odom sent the filly to the post thirty-one times at two, three, and four, and she won eleven races, earning $37,255. She first won a stakes in the summer of 1941, when she scored in the seven-furlong Test Stakes at Saratoga. She added the New England Oaks and New Rochelle Handicap later that year, then won the Fall Highweight Handicap at four. In facing males in the Highweight, Imperatrice got in with 119 pounds compared to the 140 carried by third-placed favorite Doublrab. (The world of racing is filled

102

with coincidences. Among them is that the runner-up in Imperatrice's Fall Highweight Handicap was Tola Rose, a half-sister to Imperatrice's broodmare sire, Brown Bud. Another is that when Brown Bud won the Travers, his runner-up was Nimba, who was owned by Marshall Field; it was the same year that Imperatrice's third dam, Cinq a Sept, won the Irish Oaks for Field.)

Thus, Imperatrice had been a winner of one of New York's top sprints and was sired by the winner of another (Toboggan Handicap). Imperatrice's first foal was Imperieuse, by Jack High. She placed and earned $850, then foaled the stakes winner Hi-Sag and four other winners.

Imperatrice's second foal was the first of her six stakes winners. This was the filly Scattered, a 1945 foal by Triple Crown winner Whirlaway. Scattered was not foaled at Hop Creek, but at Charles Williams' Stradacona Farm in Maryland. Mrs. Williams sat in a stall with the filly's head in her lap when the young Scattered suffered through a baffling rectal hemorrhage. Whatever the internal cause, it seemed to have no lasting effects, and, in light of what the family later achieved, it is tempting to assign some genetically forwarded spunk to the very fact that she survived. At any rate, when Scattered appeared in the ring at the 1946 Saratoga yearling sale, she was attractive enough that the head of King Ranch, Robert J. Kleberg Jr., and his trainer, Max Hirsch, were willing to spend $23,000 for her. This made her one of the top seven fillies at the sale, which was topped by Grey Flight at $35,000.

Whatever caprice of genetics it is that, with some repetition, produces early success for stallions destined ultimately to be moderate, the assignment fell to Scatttered to be among those who teased about the prowess of Whirlaway. As would be true of many a King Ranch candidate, Scattered did not cut much of a figure at two, instead being given plenty of time to develop. At

three, she came into full bloom, winning the Pimlico Oaks and Coaching Club American Oaks under jockey Warren Mehrtens, who two years before had guided King Ranch's Assault through a sweep of the Triple Crown. Scattered was third in the Delaware Oaks to the season's three-year-old filly champion, Miss Request.

Scattered won four of twenty-six races and earned $80,275. For King Ranch, she foaled two important winners: Disperse, by Middleground, who won the Hempstead Handicap and placed in Celtic Ash's 1960 Belmont Stakes; and Here and There, a Middleground filly, who won the 1957 Alabama Stakes, then, incredibly, died in a stable fire later that evening.

Imperatrice foaled Imperium in 1946. Imperium, by another Hop Creek sire, Piping Rock, won eleven of twenty-eight races at three and four, including the Bing Crosby Handicap at Del Mar, and, to remind of the speed in the family, matched the six-furlong track record of 1:09 2/5 at Santa Anita. Imperium earned $34,125. He sired three stakes winners.

In 1947, Imperatrice foaled another Piping Rock colt. Named Squared Away, he was gelded and raced from three through ten, winning thirty-one of 103 starts to earn $255,145. Squared Away won eight stakes, including the New Rochelle, Paumonok, Roseben, and Interborough, and he placed in fourteen other added-money races. He also set or equaled sprint distance records for Aqueduct and Pimlico.

LaBoyteaux's death in 1947 meant that Imperatrice and other Hop Creek stock were sent up for auction. Imperatrice was purchased for $30,000 by Christopher T. Chenery, the utilities executive who had established a broodmare band at his ancestral home, The Meadow, in Doswell, Virginia. (see chapter on Hildene)

Imperatrice was to prove priceless for The Meadow, but that eventuality was not immediately discernible. She had no foal in 1948, and then in

		Polymelus, 1902	Cyllene / Maid Marian
	Polymelian, 1914		
		Pasquita, 1907	Sundridge / Pasquil
CARUSO, b, 1927			
		Harmonicon, 1910	Disguise / Harpsichord
	Sweet Music, 1917		
		Isette, 1910	Isinglass / Brielle
IMPERATRICE, dk b m, 1938			
		Brown Prince II, 1914	Dark Ronald / Excellenza
	Brown Bud, 1924		
		June Rose, 1916	Myram / Pietra
CINQUEPACE, b, 1934			
		Teddy, 1913	Ajax / Rondeau
	Assignation, 1930		
		Cinq a Sept, 1924	Roi Herode / Rackety Coo

IMPERATRICE, dk b, 1938-1972. Bred by W.H. LaBoyteaux (N.J.). Raced 3 yrs, 31 sts, 11 wins, $37,255. Won New England Oaks, Fall Highweight H, New Rochelle H, Test S; 2nd Beldame H; 3rd Scarsdale H. Dam of 16 named foals, 13 rnrs, 10 wnrs, 6 sw.

1944: Imperieuse, b f, by Jack High. Raced 3 yrs, 11 sts, 0 wins, $850. Dam of 6 foals, 6 rnrs, 5 wnrs, including **HI-SAG** ($71,752). Granddam of **Intrepid Way**.

1945: **SCATTERED**, ch f, by Whirlaway. Raced 3 yrs, 26 sts, 4 wins, $80,275. Won Coaching Club American Oaks, Pimlico Oaks; 2nd Gazelle S; 3rd Autumn Day S, Marguerite S, Delaware Oaks. Dam of 7 foals, 6 rnrs, 5 wnrs, including **DIS-PERSE** ($76,824), **HERE AND THERE** ($39,102), **Distray** ($81,560). Granddam of **SLY GRIN**. Died 1979.

1946: **IMPERIUM**, dk b c, by Piping Rock. Raced 4 yrs, 28 sts, 11 wins, $34,125. Won Bing Crosby H; 2nd Solana Beach H. Sire of 57 foals, AEI 0.99. Died 1971.

1947: **SQUARED AWAY**, b g, by Piping Rock. Raced 8 yrs, 103 sts, 31 wins, $255,145. Won Paumonok H, Sport Page H, Autumn Day H, Interborogh H, Roseben H, Bay Shore H, New Rochelle H, Armed H; 2nd Fall Highweight H, Fleetwing H, Paumonok H, Carter H, Princeton H; 3rd Bay Shore H (twice), Roseben H, Fleetwing H, Oceanport H, Camden H, Interborough H, Wilson H (twice).

1949: North River, dk b f, by By Jimminy. Unraced. Dam of 11 foals, 8 rnrs, 4 wnrs. Granddam of **Cape Fame**.

1950: Queens Moon, b f, by Hunters Moon IV. Raced 2 yrs, 26 sts, 3 wins, $13,900. Dam of 13 foals, 10 rnrs, 10 wnrs, including **QUEEN'S DOUBLE** ($105,981), **LAKE CHELAN** ($38,340), **Rio Branca** ($25,590), **Glencara** ($20,197), **Bianca Mano** ($14,899). Granddam of **A GRAY GHOST**, **Prince Tobin**, **Piece of the Moon**, **Bold Chelan**.

1951: Bel Esprit, br g, by Bossuet. Raced 3 yrs, 38 sts, 4 wins, $16,330.

1952: Somethingroyal, b f, by Princequillo. Raced 1 yr, 1 st, 0 wins, $0. Dam of 18 foals, 15 rnrs, 11 wnrs, including **SECRETARIAT** ($1,316,808, Horse of the Year, twice, champion 2 and 3yo colt and turf male, gr. I), **SIR GAYLORD** ($237,404), **FIRST FAMILY** ($188,040), **SYRIAN SEA** ($178,245), **Somethingfabulous** ($54,045), **Grand Coulee** ($52,445), **Mostar** ($44,065), **Capital Asset** ($30,184), **Cherryville** ($24,515). Granddam of **ALADA, AT EASE, HEAVENLY MATCH, Fabulous Fraud, Shee Clachan, Lost in Iowa, Spring to Life, Inchmarlo**.

1953: Morning Watch, ch g, by Discovery. Raced 7 yrs, 115 sts, 7 wins, $26,069.

1954: Black Amber, ch f, by Hill Prince. Raced 2 yrs, 14 sts, 1 win, $2,075. Dam of 6 foals, 4 rnrs, 2 wnrs.

1955: **YEMEN**, ch c, by Bryan G. Raced 4 yrs, 49 sts, 8 wins, $39,172. Won Hutcheson S; 3rd Churchill Downs H. Sire of 27 foals, AEI 0.79.

1956: **IMPERIAL HILL**, b f, by Hill Prince. Raced 2 yrs, 11 sts, 2 wins, $13,695. Won Polly Drummond S. Dam of 16 foals, 13 rnrs, 9 wnrs, including **Hula Girl** ($26,452), **Happy Boy** ($13,935, in Fr, Ger, and Ire). Granddam of **SOMETHING GORGEOUS, NO JOKE, HULA CHIEF, DON'T JOKE, LUMINEUX, MAIKAI, BRAVE DANCE, Native Uproar, Donna Chere, Mubhedj, Lean To, Sir Ivorson, Bequa, Maimiti**.

1957: Rare Jade, b f, by Hill Prince. Unraced. Dam of 4 foals, 3 rnrs, 2 wnrs. Died 1965.

1958: Rock Imp, b f, by Piping Rock. Unraced. Dam of 8 foals, 7 rnrs, 5 wnrs. Died 1977.

1959: Barren.

1960: **SPEEDWELL**, b f, by Bold Ruler. Raced 2 yrs, 33 sts, 6 wins, $56,000. Won Prioress S, Debutante S; 3rd Jasmine S. Dam of 8 foals, 6 rnrs, 5 wnrs, including **LULUBO** ($135,388), **SI SI YOU** ($101,813), **Quick Cure** ($27,935). Granddam of **EVANGELICAL, CURE THE BLUES, Mermaid Cove**. Died 1989.

1961: Egremont, ch c, by Third Brother. Raced 1 yr, 2 sts, 0 wins, $0.

1962: Barren.

1967: Not bred.

1968: Not bred.

1969: Not bred.

Key Bridge (bottom) produced champion Key to the Mint (below), a leading broodmare sire. His daughter Kamar (right) produced stakes winners such as Seaside Attraction, dam of champion Golden Attraction (below, right).

La Troienne

La Troienne (below) is perhaps the most influential broodmare of the 20th Century, founding a still-active dynasty through daughters such as Big Hurry (bottom, left), and sons such as champion Bimelech (bottom, right).

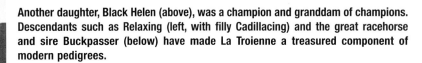

Another daughter, Black Helen (above), was a champion and granddam of champions. Descendants such as Relaxing (left, with filly Cadillacing) and the great racehorse and sire Buckpasser (below) have made La Troienne a treasured component of modern pedigrees.

Marguerite

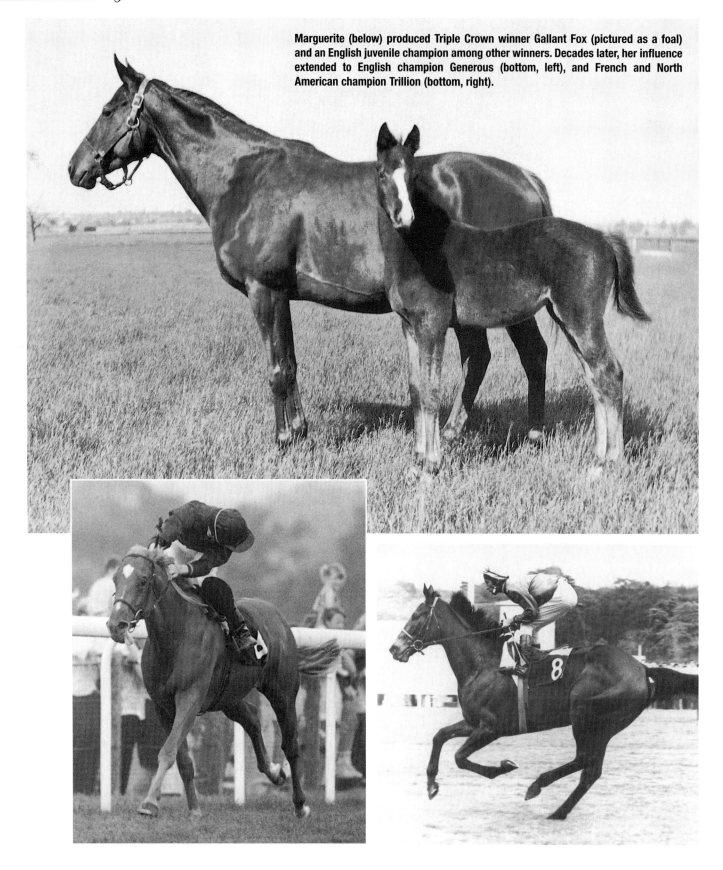

Marguerite (below) produced Triple Crown winner Gallant Fox (pictured as a foal) and an English juvenile champion among other winners. Decades later, her influence extended to English champion Generous (bottom, left), and French and North American champion Trillion (bottom, right).

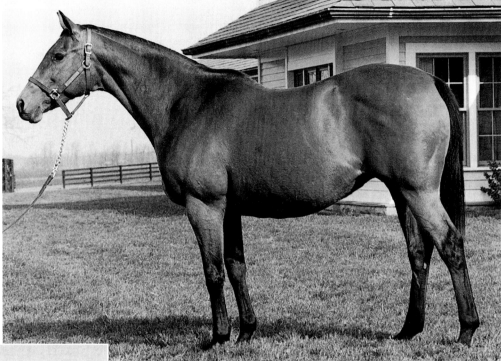

Missy Baba's daughter Toll Booth (right) produced eleven winners and was named Broodmare of the Year. Lassie Dear (below), a granddaughter of Missy Baba, was the dam of Weekend Surprise as well as two European stakes winners. Missy Baba's dam, Uvira II (bottom, right) won the Irish Oaks before her importation to America.

Missy Baba

Missy Baba is active in the pedigrees of modern-day American classic winners through descendants such as Weekend Surprise (above), the dam of Belmont Stakes winner A.P. Indy (left) and Preakness winner Summer Squall, sire of 1999 Kentucky Derby winner Charismatic.

1949 foaled a filly by By Jimminy. (By Jimminy is the answer to an obscure cocktail party question, i.e., "Who was the champion three-year-old of 1944?") He sired only three stakes winners, but one of them was 1951 Preakness winner Bold. Imperatrice's By Jimminy filly, North River, was unraced, and only four of her eleven foals were winners.

In 1950, Imperatrice foaled the filly Queens Moon, by the steeplechase sire Hunters Moon IV. Queens Moon won three of twenty-six races and earned $13,900, then foaled two high-class stakes winners. Queens Moon's 1966 Double Jay filly, Queen's Double, won two of the more important New York juvenile filly stakes, the Spinaway and the Demoiselle. Queens Moon also foaled Lake Chelan, a 1964 Bryan G. filly who won the Fashion Stakes and has several stakes-class descendants.

Imperatrice's 1951 foal, Bel Esprit, a Bossuet gelding, won four of thirty-eight races and earned $16,330. Then, in 1952, Imperatrice foaled Somethingroyal, a filly by Princequillo. Looking back at Princequillo as a leading sire and brood-mare sire, having fathered the likes of Round Table, Hill Prince, Prince John, Misty Morn, and Quill, it is easy to assign him high standing among international sires. In 1951, when Imperatrice was sent to him, however, Princequillo had just graduated from status as a $250 Virginia stallion via the performances of Chenery's champion Hill Prince and Belair Stud's classics-placed English runner, Prince Simon. Princequillo became a mainstay at Claiborne Farm in Kentucky. Still, one cannot help but conjecture that, when the Princequillo—Imperatrice filly, Somethingroyal, was unplaced once and then did not train on to run again, Chenery must have begun to despair of the $30,000 paid for Imperatrice ever coming back.

Imperatrice's desultory results for Chenery continued with the 1953 Discovery gelding Morning Watch, winner of seven of 115 starts to earn $26,069, and the 1954 Hill Prince filly Black Amber, who won once in fourteen efforts to earn $2,075, then became a moderate producer.

In 1955, Imperatrice foaled the colt Yemen, by Chenery's high-class handicapper Bryan G. Yemen was not a top horse, but set the six-furlong record at Belmont Park at 1:09 3/5 and won the Hutcheson Stakes at Gulfstream. By then, eleven years had passed since Chenery's purchase of Imperatrice, and the Hutcheson was the first stakes race any of her issue had won for him.

In 1956, Imperatrice continued her reliable foal production record for Chenery's Meadow Stud and Stable operation. She foaled the Hill Prince filly Imperial Hill, who won the Polly Drummond Stakes at two in 1958 and earned $13,695 at two and three. Imperial Hill was to bear sixteen foals, of which thirteen raced and nine won. One of them was the stakes-placed Hula Girl, by Native Dancer, and she in turn produced stakes winners Hula Chief and Maikai. Various other stakes winners descend from Imperial Hill's branch of the family.

In 1957, Imperatrice foaled Rare Jade, an unraced Hill Prince filly who proved a moderate producer, and then came Rock Imp, an unraced Piping Rock filly who also failed to distinguish herself. In 1959, Imperatrice was barren for only the second time in the last sixteen years. She was twenty-one that year, but was accepted in the first book of mares sent to the new Claiborne Farm stallion Bold Ruler, Horse of the Year of 1957 and a distinguished two-year-old and handicapper in the years immediate preceding and following. Imperatrice in 1960 produced the Bold Ruler filly Speedwell, who helped launch the sire that would spend eight years atop the general sire list. Speedwell won six of thirty-three races at two and three and earned $56,000. She became Imperatrice's sixth stakes winner, taking the 1962 Debutante Stakes at two and defeating Fashion Verdict in the Prioress Stakes at three.

Speedwell foaled the grade III winner Lulubo and additional stakes winner Si Si You.

Speedwell also became the dam of the Dr. Fager filly Quick Cure, who foaled the spectacular juvenile winner Cure the Blues. A 1978 foal by Stop the Music, Cure the Blues subsequently proved a stallion of international influence, as sire of sixty stakes winners, including Gaily Gaily, American Chance, Le Glorieux, Stop Traffic, and Rock and Roll.

Imperatrice had one foal after Speedwell, that being the 1961 Third Brother colt Egremont, who failed to place. She was barren in 1962 and later was pensioned, living on another decade until the effects of age prompted her euthanasia at the advanced age of thirty-four in 1972. Imperatrice had sixteen foals, of which thirteen raced, ten won, and a half-dozen were stakes winners.

Royal in Name and Production

Imperatrice's major status as a shaper of the modern breed lies in the produce of one of her foals which did not win. Somethingroyal, her 1952 Princequillo filly, got to the races but once, finishing sixth of ten in a Saratoga maiden sprint on Aug. 2, 1954. The winner was Misty, she also an indifferent racer from a distinguished producer, Silver Fog.

Somethingroyal was taken into Chenery's broodmare band at three in 1955, and her first foal was unraced, he a Bryan G. gelding named Havildar. Somethingroyal then foaled stakes-placed Cherryville, by Correspondent, and then came Sir Gaylord. A 1959 son of the top young sire Turn-to, Sir Gaylord blossomed for Chenery and trainer Casey Hayes in the summer of his two-year-old season, when he whipped through wins in the National Stallion, Great American, Tyro, and Sapling to achieve brief leadership among Eastern two-year-olds of 1961. He was unable to carry on mastery of his crop, but the following winter, he handed Ridan

Imperatrice

his first defeat in winning the Bahamas and then claimed Kentucky Derby favoritism by winning the Everglades Stakes.

Sir Gaylord had a setback, then won his return prep and was still regarded as the Derby choice as the big week unfolded. On Friday, however, Sir Gaylord was lame when he returned to his barn from morning training, and X-rays revealed a hairline fracture of a sesamoid. Had the injury occurred the day before, Hayes and Chenery might have opted to run their champion filly, Cicada, in the Derby. As it was, Cicada won the Kentucky Oaks to help brighten a sad Friday, and Meadow Stable had to sit out the Derby.

Sir Gaylord was retired with ten wins in eighteen starts and earnings of $237,404. He stood at Claiborne Farm for most of his career, although he had some seasons in France. He sired sixty stakes winners, and one of his non-stakes-winning sons, Drone, was also an important stallion. Sir Gaylord made a lasting contribution to both the genetic and economic direction of modern Thoroughbred racing and breeding by siring the colt Sir Ivor. It was Sir Ivor's victory in the 1968 Epsom Derby that helped eliminate a stamina prejudice against the line of Turn-to and, more importantly, launched an era of unprecedented achievement by American-breds in the best races of Europe. The attendant influence on the economics of the American stallion and yearling markets was significant, as Sir Ivor was followed by the brigade of Northern Dancer runners abroad as well as other successful American pedigrees. Sir Gaylord also sired the successful European runner and sire Habitat.

In 1962, Somethingroyal foaled a colt by the Meadow champion First Landing, another son of Turn-to. Named First Family, this colt was not of top class, but he did get the Meadow silks into the frame of a classic race again when he was third behind Hail to All and Tom Rolfe in the 1965 Belmont Stakes. First Family also won the Gulfstream Park Handicap, Palm Beach Handicap, Leonard Richards Stakes, and Dade Metropolitan Handicap. He earned $188,040.

In 1965, Somethingroyal produced the first of her foals sired by Bold Ruler, then emerging as an extraordinary sire with Lamb Chop, Bold Lad, and Queen Empress, among others, to his credit. The filly was named Syrian Sea, and at two she won the Selima, Colleen, and Astarita Stakes. The half-dozen other stakes in which she placed included the Coaching Club American Oaks. Syrian Sea won six of twenty-six career starts and earned $178,245. As the history of Chenery and his estate was played out, Syrian Sea was sold at auction at Keeneland in 1979 and set a record for the time, selling for $1.6 million. Before that, however, she had foaled the Riva Ridge filly Alada, who won four stakes for one of Chenery's daughters, Ms. Helen (Penny) Tweedy.

By 1968, Bold Ruler had achieved such status that Claiborne Farm owner A. B. (Bull) Hancock Jr. and the Phipps family developed an enlightened way of using the stallion. An accepted mare would be bred to the horse twice, with the mare owner to receive one foal and the Phippses (Bold Ruler's owners) to receive the other. A coin toss would decide who would own which foal. Somethingroyal's earlier Bold Ruler filly, Syrian Sea, had already emerged as an important winner, and the Chenery mare was booked to Bold Ruler under the new arrangement. In 1969, Somethingroyal foaled a Bold Ruler filly who went to Ogden Phipps via the formula. Named The Bride, she was unplaced, but produced stakes winners At Ease and Heavenly Match. Short of winning the Derby or rescuing children from a burning building, there was little The Bride could have done to avoid being known in history as the one-who-was-not-Secretariat. Most horses are not

Secretariat, but the matter doesn't come up. In the case of The Bride, however, she was the first Bold Ruler—Somethingroyal foal under the two-year deal, and Secretariat was the second.

Foaled at The Meadow in Virginia, Secretariat followed by one year the Chenery homebred Riva Ridge, who was champion at two and won the Kentucky Derby and Belmont at three. Chenery was confined to a nursing home, and the affairs of Meadow Stud and Stable were being run by his daughter Helen. Secretariat was so dominant at two that he emerged as Horse of the Year. He won seven of nine at two, sweeping such races as the Hopeful, Futurity, Laurel Futurity, and Garden State Stakes. Horsemen often say of a remarkable animal that "it isn't what he did; it was the way he did it." In Secretariat's case, the way was with surpassing finality, and his vaulting stride would often demolish his field on the turn, even while he spotted ground by taking the overland route.

Chenery passed away early in 1973, and estate matters prompted syndication of the colt. Bull Hancock had died the previous autumn, and young Seth Hancock — in one of the first major achievements of his own watch at Claiborne — syndicated Secretariat for a record $6 million. It was preordained under the arrangement that the horse would retire at the end of his three-year-old season. Thus, like Man o' War among horses which commonly are regarded as among the best of all time, Secretariat could not be tested as a handicapper at four.

Anyone fortunate enough to have witnessed even one moment of Secretariat's three-year-old spring undoubtedly has private, treasured memories. Having not seen the colt at two, and noting how bulky he appeared in certain photos, we personally entertained some skepticism as encomiums were poured upon his victories in the Bay Shore and Gotham. Therefore, we chewed the lower lip in serious thought after Hall of Fame trainer Syl Veitch

remarked without hesitation when asked one morning at Keeneland his impression of Secretariat: "I think he'll be the next Man o' War." (Oh, I guess you like him, then.) Another masterful horseman, Horatio Luro, agreed with the observation that the colt's powerful frame and heavy muscling did not create the beau ideal for a classic horse or stayer, but the Senor assured us that this one would get any distance put before him.

Chick Lang, then the virtual impresario of the Preakness Stakes, had uttered the most succinct explanation of the response so many had to Secretariat: "It was as if God had decided to create the perfect horse."

Our first glimpse at the horse, in the squint-worthy morning light of a Churchill Downs spring, washed away most doubts: Oh, that's what they're talking about. While racing is no beauty contest, beauty is nothing to disdain. Secretariat was wonderful to behold, a large-framed, large-boned, muscular chestnut with a fine air of masculine fire melding with artistry of motion.

Although he had been third in the Wood Memorial, Secretariat was favored for the Kentucky Derby, and he looped the field to assume command, winning in record time of 1:59 2/5. It is axiomatic in Thoroughbred racing that final time does not alone define the quality of its author, but there is something nice about a horse winning the fastest Kentucky Derby of all time (a record still standing as of 1999).

In the Preakness Stakes, jockey Ron Turcotte found himself near the rear again as he approached the turn, and when he let Secretariat go, he zoomed around the entire field to be in front straightening away. The turn in question, though, was the first, and Secretariat toured in front from the top of the backstretch to the wire. His official time was placed at 1:54 2/5, although it was widely believed that a

teletimer malfunction denied him official credit for bettering Canonero II's mark of 1:54. The denial ultimately would rob Secretariat of the unique standing of having set the record for each Triple Crown event.

From the standpoint of history, Secretariat's reach forward into the hearts of generations is difficult to fathom. In 1998, the twenty-fifth anniversary of his appellation spring seemed almost to summon memories in members of the public who had not been born in 1973. The magnitude of a few individuals apparently is passed down from one generation to the next, and in that context Secretariat seems to be in the league of a Babe Ruth or Jack Dempsey or Jim Thorpe.

Nonetheless, since a thirty-year-old today was an infant when being thirty or more was widely seen as sinister, perhaps it is worth a few lines to put Secretariat's Triple Crown into context. Insofar as racing was concerned, no horse since Citation in 1948 had swept the Derby, Preakness, and Belmont. An achievement attained four times between 1941 and 1948, the year Citation won, had then gone unmatched for a quarter-century. As more horses came to the last race only to fail, and as years passed, an aura grew around the series which had been missing back when it was frequently won. As a negative to this glamour, however, despair over ever seeing another Triple Crown winner even created some thought that the series should be made easier.

From the standpoint of America in general, Secretariat was a streak of gold in a time of rusty iron. The Watergate scandal and the Vietnam War created a turmoil of guilt, fear, hatred, and even confusion over what it meant to be patriotic. The attendant excusing of undisciplined behavior created enormous public awareness of drug use and other living habits which were profoundly disturbing to many while being hailed as enlightened by others. When the war dead were crowded from headlines, it was all too frequently because of riots in American cities.

That Secretariat's photo adorned the covers of *Newsweek* and *Time*, even in this tumult, is an indication of the hold he had on a portion of America's collective longing. Individuals who had not known what racing's Triple Crown meant now fervently wanted Secretariat to win it.

Finally, Belmont Day arrived. The stylish and gracious Penny Chenery Tweedy was the queen of sport. Trainer Lucien Laurin and jockey Turcotte were cementing Hall of Fame status. But would disappointment and disillusion come again?

Secretariat made the Belmont a personal monument. Running the second half faster than the first, Secretariat tore up the early challenges and proceeded in splendid, and disdainful, loneliness. Five lengths, ten lengths, twenty-five lengths: The margin increased, and doubled, and doubled again, as his audience cheered and wept in rapture. He won officially by thirty-one lengths, in record time of 2:24. For a moment, sport had soothed heavy hearts of a beleaguered public. Forever, Secretariat had provided racing men with a beacon of achievement.

Secretariat shocked us in two later losses almost as much as he thrilled in victory, but these reality checks were overshadowed by four more wonderful triumphs. He was Horse of the Year and also champion three-year-old and champion grass horse. Secretariat took to stud the positives of a record of sixteen wins in twenty-one starts and earnings of $1,316,808; he also took to stud the negatives of unrealistic expectations.

Over the one and a half decades he was at stud at Claiborne, Secretariat gradually took on the aroma of a whispered disappointment, however illogical this might have been as he sired fifty-seven stakes winners. In the latter 1980s, however, he was represented by Horse of the Year Lady's Secret and Preakness-Belmont winner Risen Star. Secretariat died in 1989, three years before ascent to the top of an area long anticipated to be his foil, i.e., leading the broodmare sire list.

In modern pedigrees, nothing could seem more glamorous than a foal by Northern Dancer and out of the dam of Secretariat. This materialized in the form of Somethingroyal's 1972 colt, who was named Somethingfabulous. He was one of eighteen foals, fifteen runners, and eleven winners from Somethingroyal. Somethingfabulous won four of twenty races and placed in the grade I Flamingo Stakes, and thereafter established himself as a useful stallion in California. His best runner was the $700,000-earner Fabulous Notion, dam of Test Stakes winner Fabulously Fast. Fabulous Notion and her half-brother, the Epsom Derby-placed Cacoethes, were bred by Ray Stark, masterful movie producer with credits such as "Annie" and "Steel Magnolias." What better as an oblique footnote to the wonders of the family of Secretariat than an international winner with roots in Hollywood? ❖

Great Mares of the 20th Century

Key Bridge

Unlike many other mares in this volume, Key Bridge did not launch an abundance of female descendants which spread influence along the bottom lines of prominent pedigrees. She did, however, produce two champions among four stakes winners, one of which is a prominent sire in modern pedigrees. Also, there are some tail-female representatives flourishing today, one of them having accounted for the 1997 classic-winning English colt Silver Patriarch.

Key Bridge's champions were Fort Marcy, who burst upon the scene as grass champion in 1967, co-champion grass horse in 1968, and champion grass horse again three years later, while also sharing champion older male and Horse of the Year distinction; and Key to the Mint, champion three-year-old of 1972. Key to the Mint became an important sire and is, posthumously, a prominent broodmare sire at the end of the 20th Century.

Key Bridge came from a family which represented a key development in the history of Paul Mellon's Rokeby Stable. Mellon bought into the family at the generation of her dam, buying Blue Banner from a breeder who had already developed the sort of broodmare band Mellon wanted to build. The breeder was Mrs. John D. Hertz.

While both Mellon and John Hertz would be known at the end of their lives as wealthy sportsmen, their routes to that status began poles apart.

Hertz was an Austrian immigrant who started in business as a Chicago lad selling papers, worked his way through the newspaper and fight games, and eventually launched the Yellow Cab taxi company as well as the innovative rental car agency that still bears his name. When life's struggles allowed them to, Mr. and Mrs. Hertz built a racing and breeding operation. They established Stoner Creek Stud, won the 1928 Kentucky Derby with Reigh Count, and bred and raced Reigh Count's son, Count Fleet, winner of the 1943 Triple Crown.

Mellon, on the other hand, was born of such circumstances to justify the name of his personal memoir, *Reflections in a Silver Spoon*. The old up-by-your-own-bootstraps scenario had been taken care of a couple of generations earlier in the Mellon ancestry. His father, Andrew Mellon, was Secretary of the Treasury and bequeathed to America the National Gallery of Art, but he bristled at the aesthetic tendencies of his son. The young Mellon made a valiant attempt to engross himself in the banking and boardroom world of his father, but it did not last long. He, too, had an affinity for situations where fellows good and true sit in rows with wood coming into play in the surroundings; instead of luxurious boardroom paneling, however, Paul preferred that the key wood be tightly grasped oars with which to row across calm waters, as when he had crewed for Clare College, Cambridge.

110

Mellon became the archetypal sportsman/gentleman/philanthropist. His tenure in his father's comfortable milieu was short; his career was long, and enduring, in the worlds of art and literature collection, bequests thereof, and financial support of other worthwhile social causes.

Mellon, who died at ninety-one early in 1999, had become involved with steeplechase racing in the 1930s. Cambridge pal James Cox Brady encouraged him to branch out into flat racing and breeding, and Mellon eventually did so, headquartered at his rambling, rolling Rokeby Farm in Virginia. He collected masterpieces for the paddocks of Rokeby, just as he did for the private art gallery on the farm, known affectionately as The Brick House.

During Rokeby's last four decades, its stable was home to the likes of Quadrangle, Arts and Letters, Mill Reef, Fort Marcy, Key to the Mint, and Sea Hero. There had been lean years earlier, however. Some degree of success was enjoyed early in the 1950s with County Delight, but not even the breeding of a good horse always turned out correctly; Pardala, for example, had been sold before emerging to win the Diana, Matriarch, and Black Helen in the mid-1950s. (When Quadrangle won the Wood Memorial in 1964, Mellon noted that he had never had a Derby colt before, then appended whimsically, that it would not be going too far to say he had "never had a three-year-old before.")

The foundations, however, had been established. Mellon's 1948 yearling buy Tap Day would become the dam of English sprint champion Secret Step as well as Belmont Stakes winner Quadrangle; the 1949 purchase of Red Ray would bring to Rokeby the female family that produced the great Mill Reef. Similarly, purchase of Key Bridge's dam laid down another element of foundation for lasting success.

The broodmare band of the Hertzes of Stoner Creek had undergone a similar development. As has been true of so many successful breeders of the 20th Century, Hertz benefited from the advice, and bloodstock, of the Hancock family's Claiborne Farm. Hertz had an edge in this regard, for Stoner Creek the Farm lay just across Stoner Creek the Creek from Claiborne.

Hertz would later recall the day he was dickering about purchasing some fillies from A. B. Hancock Sr., who urged him to add to the group the filly Risque, asserting that she "will pay the way for the others."

That Claiborne had the filly in its possession resulted from a keen sense of irony — as well as horse sense and business sense. During the early 1920s, Hancock had purchased Risque's second dam, Venturesome II, for about $1,600 in England. The modesty of her price owed in no large part to the early 20th Century proclamation on behalf of the English Stud Book that many American strains would no longer be accepted for inclusion, since there were questions about the purity of their ancestry. (This policy, known as the Jersey Act, was not rescinded until 1949.)

In the case of Venturesome II, the culprit was none other than the great American runner and sire Hanover. Part of the problem was that Hanover's fourth dam was by Wild Medley, a stallion whose ancestry traced to a horse imported not from the birthplace of the breed, England, but instead from Spain of all places. (Get that Armada out of here!)

While history has tended to emphasize the unfairness of the Jersey Act to American horses, and horsemen, the case of Venturesome II showed the other side, i.e., that English breeders who had purchased American-related strains in good faith suddenly found themselves with some breeding stock of diminished value. Hancock knew the main chance when he saw it.

Venturesome II was carrying Risky when imported, and she foaled that filly at Claiborne in 1924. Risky was unraced, but foaled stakes winners Risque and Riskulus as well as other producing

		Rose Prince, 1919	Prince Palatine Eglantine
	Prince Rose, 1928		
PRINCEQUILLO, b, 1940		Indolence, 1920	Gay Crusader Barrier
		Papyrus, 1920	Tracery Miss Matty
	Cosquilla, 1933		
KEY BRIDGE, b m, April 10, 1959		Quick Thought, 1918	White Eagle Mindful
		Man o' War, 1917	Fair Play Mahubah
	War Admiral, 1934		
		Brushup, 1929	Sweep Annette K.
BLUE BANNER, b, 1952		Blue Larkspur, 1926	Black Servant Blossom Time
	Risque Blue, 1941		
		Risque, 1928	Stimulus Risky

Key Bridge, b, 1959-1979. Bred by Paul Mellon (Va.). Unraced. Dam of 11 named foals, 8 rnrs, 7 wnrs, 4 sw.Broodmare of the Year in 1980.

1963: Tabitha, b f, by County Delight. Raced 3 yrs, 35 sts, 5 wins, $15,775. Dam of 8 foals, 7 rnrs, 4 wnrs, including **What a Delight** ($6,470). Granddam of **ARTIC EXPLOSION, PLEASURE ME MORE, MRS LYON, Capricorn Son (Ire)**.

1964: **FORT MARCY**, b g, by Amerigo. Raced 6 yrs, 75 sts, 21 wins, $1,109,791. Horse of the Year, champion turf male (three times) and older male. Won Washington, D.C., International S (twice), United Nations H (T), Man o' War S (T), Hollywood Park Invitational Turf H (T), Sunset H (T; NCR, Hol, 12 furlongs in 2:26.60), Nashua H (T), Tidal H (T, twice), Bougainvillea H (T), Dixie H (T; NCR, Pim, 12 furlongs in 2:27.40), Bowling Green H (T), Stars and Stripes H (T), Kelly-Olympic H (T), Bernard Baruch H (T), Long Branch S; 2nd Man o' War S (T, twice), Grey Lag H, Kelly-Olympic H (T, twice), Nassau County S, San Juan Capistrano Invitational H (T), Hollywood Park Invitational Turf H (T), Century H (T), Ford Pinto Invitational Turf H (T), Bowling Green H (T), Bougainvillea H (T); 3rd United Nations H (T, three times), Washington, D.C., International S (T), Man o' War S (T), Edgemere H (T), San Juan Capisrano Invitational H (T), Hialeah Turf Cup H (T), Kelly-Olympic H (T). Died 1991.

1965: Barren.

1966: **National Park**, b g, by Nashua. Raced 6 yrs in Eng and NA, 37 sts, 7 wins, $19,255. 3rd Peter Hastings S, Newbury Spring Cup.

1967: Barren.

1968: Seven Locks, b f, by Jacinto. Unraced. Dam of 10 foals, 7 rnrs, 6 wnrs. Granddam of **LYKATILL HIL, CLASSIC ACCOUNT, PAT COPELAN, HE'S A SQUALLING, INDOMITABLE, Art of Dawn, Cameroon, Ginny Dare, Wood Key, Slew of Fury**.

1969: **KEY TO THE MINT**, b c, by Graustark. Raced 3 yrs, 29 sts, 14 wins, $576,015. Champion 3yo colt. Won Suburban H (gr. I), Excelsior H (gr. II), Brooklyn H (ETR, Aqu, 9½ furlongs in 1:54.80), Woodward S, Travers S, Withers S, Whitney S, Remsen S, Derby Trial; 2nd Metropolitan H (gr. I), Jockey Club Gold Cup, Cowdin S; 3rd Preakness S, Garden State S. Sire of 622 foals, AEI 2.28.

1970: **KEY TO THE KINGDOM**, dkb/br c, by Bold Ruler. Raced 4 yrs, 38 sts, 7 wins, $109,590. Won Stymie H (gr. III). Sire of 567 foals, AEI 1.36.

1971: Key Link, dkb/br f, by Bold Ruler. Raced 1 yr, 2 sts, 0 wins, $0. Dam of 16 foals, 11 rnrs, 10 wnrs. Granddam of **MENSAGEIRO ALADO, Link to Pleasure, Puppet Show**. Died 1992.

1972: Key to the Heart, b f, by Arts and Letters. Unraced. Dam of 12 foals, 10 rnrs, 7 wnrs, including **Stage Door Key** ($135,525), **Key Deputy** ($93,407). Granddam of **Mari's Key, Energy Square**.

1973: Dumbarton Oaks, b f, by Arts and Letters. Unraced. Dam of 9 foals, 7 rnrs, 6 wnrs, including **Iron Bridge** ($16,883). Granddam of **IT'S SUZIE**.

1974: B c, by Graustark. Died 1975.

1975: Gliding By, b f, by Tom Rolfe. Raced 1 yr, 1 st, 1 win, $6,000. Dam of 12 foals, 10 rnrs, 7 wnrs, including **CLARE BRIDGE** ($29,755), **SONG OF SIXPENCE** ($212,930). Granddam of **SILVER PATRIARCH, WESSAM PRINCE, MY PATRIARCH**.

1976: Barren.

1977: **KEY TO CONTENT**, b c, by Forli. Raced 3 yrs, 22 sts, 7 wins, $354,772. Won United Nations H (gr. IT; NCR, Atl, 9½ furlongs in 1:52.80), Saranac S (gr. IIT), Fort Marcy H (gr. IIIT), Choice H (T); 2nd Bowling Green H (gr. IIT), Japan Racing Association H (T). Sire in Italy of 275 foals, AEI 0.66. Sent to Italy 1988.

1978: Barren.

112

daughters. Risque, the Stimulus filly whom Hancock pressed upon Hertz, won the 1930 Spinaway and Lassie Stakes and the 1931 Alabama Stakes and Arlington Matron. (Winning at Arlington was particularly gratifying to Hertz, for he had been among the Chicago businessmen who stepped forward to purchase control of the track when Al Capone seemed on the brink of taking it over; Hertz had prevailed upon the Wright family to join his cause, and Warren Wright also enjoyed many an Arlington triumph under the name Calumet Farm.)

In 1941, Risque foaled the Blue Larkspur filly Risque Blue, who was unraced but produced stakes winners Risque Rouge and Blue Banner. Sent to Keeneland's 1953 yearling sale, Blue Banner, by Triple Crown winner War Admiral, was purchased for Mellon by one of his early flat trainers, J. T. Skinner. The price was $14,500, well above that summer sale's average of $9,746.

Blue Banner was a high-class filly. At two, she finished second to champion High Voltage in the Matron, and at three she won the Test Stakes at Saratoga and was second to Rico Reto in the Alabama, with champion Misty Morn third. At four, Blue Banner added the Distaff and Firenze Handicaps. In the Firenze, at one and one-eighth miles, she defeated Happy Princess, Manotick, Rare Treat, Flower Bowl, and Dotted Line. Soon thereafter, Blue Banner finished second in the Gallorette, and Mellon sent her home to Rokeby with a career record of fifteen wins in forty-six starts and earnings of $121,175. Blue Banner had eleven foals, of which seven were winners and one, Branford Court, was a moderate stakes winner.

Forts and Mints

Blue Banner's 1959 foal was a filly by the champion sire Princequillo, whose get was blessed with both speed and staying power. Mellon named the filly Key Bridge, a name familiar to many who have addressed Washington, D.C., traffic at key hours. Although ruggedness and soundness would be the hallmark of her first champion, Key Bridge herself did not stand training to make it to the races. Her unraced status duplicated that of her second dam, Risque Blue, and her fourth dam, Risky.

At four, Key Bridge produced her first foal, Tabitha, by County Delight. Tabitha won five of thirty-five races and earned $15,775. Her What a Pleasure filly, What a Delight, was stakes-placed, and a trickle of stakes winners came from her other daughters.

Key Bridge's second foal was the 1964 colt Fort Marcy, who was gelded. Fort Marcy was sired by the Virginia-based stallion Amerigo, who, but for an early death, arguably could have been one of the mid-century's more significant stallions. Amerigo was a son of the great Nearco. In England, Amerigo gained the reputation for roguish behavior, but he proved a high-class racehorse, endowed with considerable stamina. Amerigo won England's Coventry Stakes at two, then won a half-dozen stakes over three years in the United States, including the San Juan Capistrano.

Nothing about Mellon's breeding or training program was geared toward pushing for early two-year-old success. Fort Marcy, who was trained by one of Rokeby's two Hall of Fame horsemen, Elliott Burch (he was succeeded by Mack Miller), benefited from that patient approach. Even Rokeby patience wore thin, however, and he was entered in a sale of horses of racing age at three in 1967. Bidding reached $76,000, which was not quite enough to induce Burch and Mellon to bid him adieu. They bid him in, instead, at $77,000.

Soon thereafter, Fort Marcy blossomed into a stakes winner. Having been converted to grass courses, he swept four stakes in succession, but as the level of competition grew higher, he then lost four in a row. In Fort Marcy's eighteenth and final start at three, he stared down the challenge of the magnificent three-year-old Damascus to win by a nose over one and a half miles in the Washington, D.C., International, then America's most important international event. Damascus was coming off routes of his fields in the Woodward and Jockey Club Gold Cup and was unimpeded in his Horse of the Year bid, but the International gained Fort Marcy championship status in the grass division.

For the next four years, Fort Marcy and Burch toured the nation, taking on the best of the East, Midwest, and California. The gelding won eleven more stakes, including another Washington, D.C., International, as well as the United Nations, Man o' War, and Sunset. In 1970, Fort Marcy was again the grass course champion, and shared Horse of the Year honors with Personality. Fort Marcy won twenty-one of seventy-five races and earned $1,109,791. As Mellon was wont to do for his best horses, he had the gelding depicted in bronze, by John Skeaping.

Fort Marcy lived a long life as a pensioner at Rokeby, where he died at twenty-seven in 1991. He was elected to the National Museum of Racing's Hall of Fame in Saratoga Springs, New York, in 1998.

The year after Fort Marcy was foaled, Key Bridge was barren, then she had the Nashua colt National Park in 1966. Sent with one of Rokeby's drafts to England, National Park, who was gelded, was stakes-placed and won seven of thirty-seven starts, earning $19,255. Barren again in 1967, Key Bridge next foaled Seven Locks, an unraced Jacinto filly. Seven Locks is the second dam of several stakes winners, including Classic Account, Lykatill Hil, and Pat Copelan.

In 1969, Key Bridge foaled Key to the Mint. He was sired by Ribot's brilliant son Graustark, whose dam, Flower Bowl, had been beaten by Key Bridge's dam, Blue Banner, years before. A huge and impres-

Key Bridge

sive colt, Key to the Mint was given all the usual patience, but he was of such quality that he came to hand early enough that Burch had him at Churchill Downs in the spring of 1972. He had won the Remsen the previous fall at two.

Burch and Mellon had seen Quadrangle and Arts and Letters run well in the Kentucky Derby and Preakness and then win the Belmont. In the case of Key to the Mint, they won the last prep, the Derby Trial, but demurred on the Derby itself. The Preakness that year turned up muddy and Key to the Mint was third behind Bee Bee Bee, as the Kentucky Derby winner and defending two-year-old champion, Riva Ridge, finished unplaced. Key to the Mint won the Withers Stakes at a mile, but Riva Ridge bounced back to win the Belmont Stakes and seemed to have the three-year-old division locked up when he then went West to win the Hollywood Derby.

Key to the Mint took an unorthodox route to his eventual conquest in championship balloting. Having won none of the biggest spring or summer races for three-year-olds, he ventured out of the division to defeat older Autobiography while getting ten pounds in the Brooklyn Handicap. With the wind in his sails, Key to the Mint then swept the Travers and defeated older horses again in the Whitney and Woodward Stakes. In the Woodward, he beat older champion Autobiography again, this time at scale weights. Riva Ridge had faltered, and the latter-season heroics of Key to the Mint landed him the three-year-old title.

At four, Key to the Mint carried 126 pounds and gave True Knight eight pounds in winning the Suburban. He also won the Excelsior. He was retired with fourteen wins in twenty-nine starts and earnings of $576,015. Key to the Mint sired forty-five stakes winners, including the Rokeby standout Java Gold as well as champions Jewel Princess and Plugged Nickle. Key to the Mint's important producing daughters include the full sisters Kamar (dam of Seaside Attraction, Gorgeous, etc.) and Love Smitten (dam of Swain).

Bold Ruler was the star sire of the 1960s, and in 1969 Mellon sent Key Bridge to the great Phipps family stallion. The result was Key to the Kingdom, who won the Stymie Handicap among seven wins from thirty-eight starts and earned $109,590. Key to the Kingdom's stakes winners included 1988 Breeders' Cup Turf winner Great Communicator.

In 1971, Key Bridge had another Bold Ruler foal, the filly Key Link. She failed to place in two starts, then produced sixteen foals, of which eleven raced and ten won. One of Key Link's daughters foaled a Brazilian champion, Mensageiro Alado.

Key Bridge was bred to Rokeby's 1969 Horse of the Year Arts and Letters in 1971 and the next year foaled the filly Key to the Heart. It was obviously a sentimental name to Mellon, but the filly was unraced. She foaled two stakes-placed runners. In 1973 came another Arts and Letters filly, Dumbarton Oaks, also unraced. She had one stakes-placed runner. Returned to Key to the Mint's sire, Graustark, Key Bridge foaled a colt in 1974, but it died as a yearling.

In 1975, Key Bridge foaled Gliding By, a filly by champion Tom Rolfe. She broke the unraced string of the mare's foals, winning her only race. Gliding By produced the English stakes winner Song of Sixpence (by The Minstrel) and Irish stakes winner Clare Bridge (by Little Current). Clare Bridge in turn foaled Wessam Prince, a Soviet Star colt who won stakes in France and was highweight older sprinter in Germany.

The greatest impact from the produce of Key Bridge's daughter Gliding By has come from Early Rising. A 1980 Grey Dawn II filly, Early Rising was a winner and foaled the high-class Saddlers Hall colt Silver Patriarch. In 1997, Silver Patriarch was edged by Benny the Dip in the Epsom Derby and won the classic St. Leger Stakes. He was the high-weight staying three-year-old in England, where he added the group I Coronation Cup at four. Silver Patriarch also ventured to Italy, where he won the Gran Premio del Jockey Club and was a division highweight, and he was classic-placed in Ireland. Silver Patriarch's half-sister, My Patriarch, by Be My Guest, was a group III winner in England.

Key Bridge was barren in 1976, then in 1977 produced her last foal, Key to Content, a colt by Forli. Key to Content developed for trainer Mack Miller into a major grass runner, although not of the stripe of half-brother Fort Marcy. Key to Content won the United Nations Handicap in record time as well as the Saranac, Choice, and, appropriately enough, the Fort Marcy Handicap. He won seven of twenty-two races and earned $354,772. He was promising enough to go to stud at Claiborne Farm, but was disappointing and was exported to Italy.

Key Bridge died in March of 1979 at the age of twenty. She was in foal at the time to Riva Ridge, her son Key to the Mint's rival of earlier in the decade. Key Bridge had produced twelve foals, of which eight started, seven won, and four were stakes winners.

A year after her death, she was named Broodmare of the Year. ❖

La Troienne

The practice of giving a gift to one's host or hostess after a stay as a house guest is well and properly established. Such tokens can range from flowers or chocolates to more exalted fare, depending upon the social and economic order of the parties involved — or perhaps on some occasions flavored as well by the guest's future ambitions. Be that as it may, return thanks for hospitality rarely reach the tone of Ogden Phipps' thanks to John Hay (Jock) Whitney for providing a roof and clean sheets at Saratoga in the summer of 1946. Phipps stayed with Whitney for awhile, and then gave him La Troienne. (Well, sort of.) Here is what happened:

The great breeder and owner Col. E. R. Bradley had died that year and, as Ogden Phipps told the author in an interview for *The Blood-Horse* some forty years later, "John Bradley, the brother, just didn't want to have anything to do with racehorses. He was the executor, and he wanted to get this thing over with. Bob Kleberg spoke to me about the Bradley horses. He thought we could buy them as a bunch. I said I would like to go in, but I'd rather like to have Jock have a chance at it, too, since I was staying with him. Bob said that was fine, so we proceeded."

At issue was the Thoroughbred stock which had been developed by Col. Bradley and nurtured at his Idle Hour Stock Farm with the help of manager Olin Gentry. Bradley was famed for several things, one being testifying before Congress that he was a gambler, with horizons virtually unlimited insofar as potential events on which to invest. Another was winning the Kentucky Derby, which, before Calumet Farm got the full wind in its sails, Bradley was more efficient at doing than any other owner. He had won four. The Bradley breeding stock included such distinguished stallions as Black Toney and Blue Larkspur and a broodmare band including a number of jewels of contemporary American breeding, none more glistening than the aged La Troienne.

If Bradley harbored ambitions that his horses would continue to influence racing and breeding after his own transference beyond earthly bounds, he could hardly have contrived a more positive scenario than that which developed. All three who would direct the management of the Bradley horses for the next generations were established and proven as sportsmen and successful horsemen. Phipps is the son of Wheatley Stable's founder, Mrs. Henry Carnegie Phipps, and had been racing and breeding on his own for more than a decade; now, with the war over, the Navy man could get back to giving serious attention to developing his stable. Robert Kleberg Jr. was the head man at King Ranch, and he had added Thoroughbreds to the activities of the massive cattle, oil, and ranch-horse operation; at the time of the Bradley business,

Kleberg was riding high as breeder-owner of the year's Triple Crown winner, Assault. The third member of the group, Whitney, had, like Phipps, developed his own racing and breeding operation at the same time his mother had one of the nation's best. Whitney and his sister, Joan Payson, had then merged their own stables into the Greentree Stud and Stable of Mrs. Payne Whitney, when she died in 1944. Whitney was a publisher, who for a time owned the New York *Herald-Tribune*, and he had come back from the war after leaping from a POW train — a decision made no less harrowing in execution by the impeccable logic of its purpose.

There were eighty-eight horses in the Bradley estate for John Bradley to liquidate. Phipps, Kleberg, and Whitney formed a syndicate which purchased a large majority of them and then sold off sizable drafts to Edward S. Moore and Charles S. Howard. Bimelech, the 1939 juvenile champion and 1940 three-year-old champion, was retained by the syndicate and sent to stand at Greentree Stud near Lexington.

The stock retained by the three tenders was put into groups labeled A, B, C, and, then, in one of Thoroughbred racing's more consequential lunches, Phipps, Kleberg, and Whitney divvied them up by drawing matches. It was a luncheon at which each received his just desserts. La Troienne was drawn into the Greentree fold, but various individuals among her issue were beneficial to all three of the members, and subsequent generations have spread her exceptional qualities to many other breeders.

La Troienne had been bred by Marcel Boussac, a French textiles magnate who led the French owners' list nineteen times and who raced the winners of a dozen French Derbys, as well as six Prix de l'Arc de Triomphes. England came to shudder at the thought of another arrival of Boussac horses from across the Channel, and his many invasive triumphs in the birth country of the Thoroughbred included the Epsom Derby of Galcador, the Epsom Oaks of Asmena, a pair of St. Leger victories, and an Ascot Gold Cup. It is easy to give a mental identity to La Troienne as the product of a long and successful stint from the Boussac breeding genius. In fact, she came along relatively early in his career and came from a family associated with the foundation bloodstock of the Joel family's Childwickbury Stud in England.

La Troienne was sired by the renowned stallion Teddy, whose son, Sir Gallahad III, was a rising star in America. La Troienne's dam, Helen de Troie, by Helicon, had won one race on the flat and three over jumps before being purchased by Boussac. The broodmare sire, Helicon, was a moderate winner in England who was standing in France. Boussac had entered breeding in 1914 on a cautious note, as partner with Count Gaston de Castelbajac, owner of eight mares. Five years later, Boussac purchased the bucolic Haras de Fresnay-le-Buffard, which still graces international breeding, today in the ownership of the Niarchos family.

La Troienne was foaled in 1926. Her racecourse management differed dramatically from that which a promising prospect might anticipate today. There apparently was no sense of taking her through her conditions or trying to make sure she was a winner for purposes of later catalogue pages. She made her debut in September, 1928, in the Prix de Sablonville, for which she was held at 4-1. La Troienne was unplaced, as she was in her only other race at two, the Prix d'Arenberg. Boussac had won his first French Derby seven years earlier with the Castelbajac-bred Ramus, so he presumably had some grasp of what a classic three-year-old was all about. Nonetheless, the management of La Troienne in the spring of her three-year-old season invites the question of whether her owner was still enamored of simply seeing his colors go to the post in the best races. She reappeared for the Prix Chloe, for which she was on offer at 38-1, and again was

		Flying Fox, 1896	Orme Vampire
	Ajax, 1901		
		Amie, 1893	Clamart Alice
TEDDY, b, 1913			
		Bay Ronald, 1893	Hampton Black Duchess
	Rondeau, 1900		
		Doremi, 1894	Bend Or Lady Emily
LA TROIENNE, **b m, 1926**			
		Cyllene, 1895	Bona Vista Arcadia
	Helicon, 1908		
		Vain Duchess, 1897	Isinglass Sweet Duchess
HELENE DE TROIE, b, 1916			
		St. Denis, 1901	St. Simon Brooch
	Lady of Pedigree, 1910		
		Doxa, 1901	Melton Paradoxical

La Troienne, b, 1926-1954. Bred by Marcel Boussac (Fr.). Raced 2 yrs in Eng and Fr, 7 sts, 0 wins, $146. Dam of 14 named foals, 12 rnrs, 10 wnrs, 5 sw.

1932: **BLACK HELEN**, b f, by Black Toney. Raced 2 yrs, 22 sts, 15 wins, $61,800. Champion 3yo filly. Won American Derby, Florida Derby, Maryland H, Coaching Club American Oaks. Dam of 12 foals, 12 rnrs, 8 wnrs. Granddam of **BUT WHY NOT**, **OEDIPUS**, **RENEW**, **THE IBEX**, **IMAGEM**, **OPEN SHOW**, **ROUND PEARL**, **HULA BEND**, Never Hula, Captain's Cross, Itsaberry, Damascene, Connecticut II.

1934: **BIOLOGIST**, ch g, by Bubbling Over. Raced 4 yrs, 41 sts, 3 wins, $4,680. Won Albany H.

1935: Baby League, b f, by Bubbling Over. Raced 2 yrs, 11 sts, 1 win, $1,800. Dam of 13 foals, 10 rnrs, 9 wnrs, including **BUSHER** ($334,035 Horse of the Year, champion 2 and 3yo filly and older female), **HARMONIZING** ($262,088), **MR. BUSHER** ($83,875), **STRIKING** ($32,625, Broodmare of the Year in 1961). Granddam of **HITTING AWAY**, **JET ACTION**, **BATTER UP**, **JUNGLE ROAD**, **SHAVETAIL**, **MY BOSS LADY**, **GLAMOUR**, **CAROLOS**, **GUILLAUME TELL**, **BASES FULL**, **Buck's Nashua**, **Turn Penny**.

1936: **BIG HURRY**, br f, by Black Toney. Raced 2 yrs, 12 sts, 4 wins, $29,860. Won Selima S. Dam of 14 foals, 13 rnrs, 12 wnrs, including **SEARCHING** ($327,381), **BRIDAL FLOWER** ($222,055, champion 3yo filly), **BE FEARLESS** ($89,543), **GREAT CAPTAIN** ($74,415), **THE ADMIRAL** ($37,225), Ambulance ($21,100). Granddam of **STRAIGHT DEAL**, **AFFECTIONATELY**, **PRICELESS GEM**, **KING OF THE CASTLE**, **ADMIRING**, **ISASMOOTHIE**, **BEYLERBEY**, **MARKING TIME**, Tropical Breeze, Search Tradition, Swingster, Stealaway.

1937: **BIMELECH**, b c, by Black Toney. Raced 3 yrs, 15 sts, 11 wins, $248,745. Champion 2 and 3yo colt. Won Preakness S, Belmont S, Futurity S, Pimlico Futurity, Saratoga Special, Hopeful S, Blue Grass S, Derby Trial S; 2nd Kentucky Derby, Withers S; 3rd Classic S. Died 1966.

1938: **Big Event**, b f, by Blue Larkspur. Raced 2 yrs, 9 sts, 2 wins, $4,200. 2nd Selima S. Dam of 8 foals, 7 rnrs, 6 wnrs, including **HALL OF FAME** ($234,430), **Audience** ($115,046), **Queen Caroline** ($10,050). Granddam of **THE AXE II**, **MALICIOUS**, **FRANCIS S.**, Nasomo.

1939: Businesslike, br f, by Blue Larkspur. Raced 1 yr, 2 sts, 0 wins, $0. Dam of 8 foals, 8 rnrs, 8 wnrs, including **BUSANDA** ($182,460), **AUDITING** ($80,265), **Bradentown** ($22,880), **His Duchess** ($21,375). Granddam of **BUCKPASSER**, **BUPERS**, **BUREAUCRACY**, **COMIC**, **Mexican Music**, **Controlling**, **Management**.

1940: Besieged, br f, by Balladier. Raced 2 yrs, 4 sts, 1 win, $1,300. Dam of 12 foals, 9 rnrs, 5 wnrs, including **HOOK MONEY** ($19,847), **Make Tracks** ($10,336, in Eng). Granddam of **PERTSHIRE**, **LISTEN TO REASON**, **THINK QUICK**, In Rhythm. Died 1962.

1941: **Broke Even**, b c, by Blue Larkspur. Raced 4 yrs, 44 sts, 11 wins, $28,065. 3rd Bunker Hill H. Sire of 69 foals, AEI 0.76.

1942: Back Yard, ch g, by Balladier. Unraced.

1944: **BEE ANN MAC**, b f, by Blue Larkspur. Raced 2 yrs, 13 sts, 2 wins, $46,480. Won Selima S; 3rd Alabama S. Dam of 10 foals, 8 rnrs, 3 wnrs. Granddam of **OUT THE WINDOW**.

1945: Belle Histoire, b f, by Blue Larkspur. Raced 1 yr, 3 sts, 0 wins, $0. Dam of 10 foals, 10 rnrs, 8 wnrs, including **ROYAL RECORD** ($139,848), **Counter Spy** ($62,880), **Sea Tale** ($49,250). Granddam of **NO TURNING**, **VUELO**, **BRAVE PILOT**, **CATULLUS**, **KING'S STORY**, **PIERPONTELLA**, Eastern Pageant.

1947: Belle of Troy, br f, by Blue Larkspur. Unraced. Dam of 7 named foals, 6 rnrs, 5 wnrs, including **COHOES** ($210,850). Granddam of **INTERVENE**, **BEST GO**. Died 1970.

1948: Trojan War, ch g, by Shut Out. Raced 5 yrs, 66 sts, 2 wins, $6,340.

unplaced. With a clean slate of never placing in three races, she then was sent to the post for the French spring's first filly classic, the one-mile Poule d'Essai des Pouliches (One Thousand Guineas equivalent), and, at 31-1, again finished unplaced.

That there had been some hint of class in La Troienne's training was supported to a degree by subsequent outings that year. Sent across the English Channel, La Troienne finished third in the five-furlong Snailwell Stakes at Newmarket, for which she was held at about 12-1. This performance sent her to the post the odds-on choice for the seven-furlong Freckenham Stakes nearly a month later, but she was beaten by one and a half lengths by Arguide. Her second-place finish was the highlight of her racing days, for in her only remaining start, about a week later, the Boussac filly was unplaced in a six-furlong Welter Handicap at Windsor. A non-winner of all her seven starts, she was, nonetheless, bred the following spring to Gainsborough, who had won an English Triple Crown during World War I. Even though the great Hyperion was still in the future of Gainsborough's stud record, the stallion already had established himself as a sire of high-class runners ranging from English two-year-old leaders to Ascot Gold Cup winners. Solario was one of his best.

In an article first published in *The Blood-Horse* in 1977 under the name "The Running Tide," Abram S. Hewitt remarked of Boussac that his "initial policy was to cull what did not suit him, so… there were only three mares owned by Boussac in 1920 which he still owned in 1925."

Apparently adhering to that plan, Boussac included La Troienne in a consignment of six mares to Newmarket's December sale of 1930. The four-year-old La Troienne, in foal to Gainsborough, topped that group at 1,250 guineas, the equivalent at the time of $6,250. This was far from the top of the market, but also far from the bottom. National

economies around the world were slipping into depression, and England, in particular, had seen a depressed market at yearling sales through the season. Moreover, the economic news as the December sales approached was clouded by a strike of thousands of Scottish miners. All things considered, the December sale that year was stronger than could have been expected. Still, the average for mares and four-year-old fillies, which included La Troienne, dropped from 507 guineas in 1929 to 404 guineas in 1930. Only six mares sold for 3,000 guineas or more, down from twenty-five as recently as two years before, so at 1,250 La Troienne was a well-sought mare. Her price was no doubt abetted by the fact that her full brother Leonidis had won the historic Lincolnshire Handicap at the launch of the English racing season of 1930.

La Troienne was purchased by American horseman Dick Thompson for the account of Col. Bradley of Idle Hour. Col. Bradley, like Boussac, had strong notions about broodmare prospects. Manager Gentry used to recall that "Mr. Bradley would buy any mare that could run three furlongs in :34 or better," even if proof of this ability was assayed in the morning rather than in actual races. Another strategy with Bradley was the importing of European mares to cross with his American stallions representing such lines as Domino and Ben Brush. Given the vast differences in training philosophies, it is unlikely that either Bradley, Gentry, or Thompson could ascertain whether La Troienne was capable of running three furlongs in :34, morning, afternoon, or evening.

Neither did she quite qualify for another Bradley strategy implied in a comment Gentry recalled, which was, "I can't afford an English Oaks winner, so get me mares that are from good families."

La Troienne was to become the half-sister to an Oaks winner, French Oaks winner Adargatis, but that was four years after Bradley had purchased

La Troienne

her. (Adargatis became a notable broodmare in her own right, as the dam of Ardan, Pardal, Adaris, and others. While there was no such gusher of class as emanated from La Troienne, the blood of Adargatis was powerful in a classic context. Ardan sired Hard Sauce, he in turn the sire of Epsom Derby winner Hard Ridden, and Pardal sired another Epsom Derby winner in Psidium.)

For a mare destined for sustained glory, little La Troienne had a poor start as a Bluegrass matron. The Gainsborough foal she was carrying at the time of her sale "had something wrong with her back," Gentry recalled years later, and no solution could be found. Astounding as it seems from the vantage point of today, Bradley took the tack that a useless filly from La Troienne should not be allowed into the Idle Hour breeding program or foisted off on some other breeder, so he instructed Gentry to do away with the unfortunate youngster.

Thereafter, the breeding record of La Troienne was peerless, both from the standpoint of racing class in her direct offspring and the bounty of genes apparently consigned over and over to more than six decades of descendants. We shall address them in the order by which they were foaled, although in several cases, the individual tale vaults us all the way back to the present.

Black Helen, 1932

After the misfortune of La Troienne's first foal, the tiny size at birth of her second foal, Black Helen, must have created some pessimism about the mare. However, the small filly by Black Toney was to become widely regarded as the best three-year-old filly of 1935. (Such matters were not certified by polls until the following year.) Black Helen defeated colts in the Florida Derby, American Derby, and Maryland Handicap and also won the Coaching Club American Oaks over Bloodroot and Good

Gamble. Black Helen won fifteen of twenty-two races and earned $61,800. She was elected to the National Museum of Racing's Hall of Fame in 1991.

Black Helen had twelve foals, all of which raced, including eight winners. None won stakes, but her 1937 daughter Be Like Mom (by Sickle) foaled King Ranch's champion three-year-old and handicap filly of 1947. This was But Why Not, a daughter of Blue Larkspur.

But Why Not won twelve of forty-six races from two through six and earned $295,155. Her eight major triumphs included a brace of the traditionally important distaff races, such as the Acorn, Beldame, and Alabama, and she defeated colts in the Arlington Classic. But Why Not foaled the high-class West Coast handicap horse How Now.

Black Helen's daughter Be Like Mom also foaled the steeplechase champion Oedipus and the Firenze and Top Flight Handicaps winner Renew. Other stakes winners tracing to Black Helen included granddaughter Hula Bend, in turn the dam of Australian stakes winners Hula Chief and Hula Drum; also Ladies Handicap winner Destro, The Ibex, among others.

Biologist, 1934

La Troienne was barren in 1933, then foaled Biologist, by Kentucky Derby winner Bubbling Over, in 1934. The gelded Biologist won three of forty-one starts, including the Albany Handicap, and earned $4,680.

Baby League, 1935

Also sired by Bubbling Over, the filly Baby League was a modest runner, winning once from eleven starts to earn $1,800. She thereupon launched into her own broodmare career of great and lasting fame. Baby League had thirteen foals, of which ten raced and nine won. Four were stakes winners.

During the last years of Idle Hour, Bradley and

Gentry were successful in crossing a number of the mares with the outside sire War Admiral. Baby League went to that son of Man o' War in 1941 and the result was Busher, who was purchased by Louis B. Mayer. Busher was a great enough three-year-old filly to defeat the emerging older champion male Armed in the one and a quarter-mile Washington Park Handicap. Busher had been champion filly at two, and at three she not only was champion of her division, but was voted Horse of the Year. She won fifteen of twenty-one races and earned $334,035. She entered the Hall of Fame in 1964. Purchased by Elizabeth Arden Graham for $150,000, Busher foaled the high-class colt Jet Action and Popularity, dam of three stakes winners.

Baby League foaled a full brother to Busher in 1946. Given the imaginative name Mr. Busher, he won the Arlington Futurity and National Stallion Stakes and was of some success at stud. Bred to the staying Belmont and Jockey Club Gold Cup winner Counterpoint, Baby League in 1954 foaled Harmonizing. Gelded, Harmonizing developed quickly enough to win the Sanford at two, later showed a knack for turf racing, and won the Man o' War and three other stakes.

Most prolific of the branches from Baby League, however, was from the Phipps filly Striking. Another by Triple Crown winner War Admiral, Striking was a foal of 1947 who won the Schuylerville at two and placed in the Selima, Pimlico Futurity, and three other juvenile stakes. Striking produced five stakes winners: Hitting Away and the fillies Glamour, Bases Full, Batter Up, and My Boss Lady. Each of those stakes-winning daughters in turn had something to add to the legacy.

Glamour herself foaled four stakes winners: the 1972 English St. Leger winner Boucher, the Round Table colt Poker, Royal Ascot, and Jaunty. Poker played an unusual role in the history of Ogden Phipps' stable: In 1967, Phipps' great colt Buckpasser

was rolling along on a fifteen-race winning streak. Tried on grass with the view of an adventure to France, Buckpasser failed in the Bowling Green, and stablemate Poker came along to win it, although scarcely assuaging the owner's disappointment. Poker also became the broodmare sire of 1977 Triple Crown winner Seattle Slew and the 1997 Kentucky Derby/Preakness winner Silver Charm.

Glamour's foals besides her stakes winners included the stakes-placed Swaps mare Intriguing, who in turned foaled Numbered Account. Numbered Account was Phipps' dominant two-year-old filly champion of 1971, when she was so brilliant that trainer Roger Laurin was emboldened to try her against the champion colt, Riva Ridge, in the Garden States Stakes. That did not produce victory, but Numbered Account came back to win the Spinster Stakes and other important races. Numbered Account represented sufficient separation in generations from ancestress La Troienne that inbreeding to the mare was workable; Numbered Account's sire was Phipps' vaunted Buckpasser, whose dam, Busanda, was out of La Troienne's daughter Businesslike.

Numbered Account foaled two stakes winners, one of which was the successful stallion Private Account, sire of Phipps' unbeaten champion Personal Ensign. The current Maryland stallion Polish Numbers is also out of Numbered Account, as was the stakes winner Dance Number, dam of champion Rhythm (the 1989 juvenile colt Eclipse Award winner repatriated from Japan). The sire power from this line of the family also extends to Woodman.

Woodman, a son of Mr. Prospector out of Numbered Account's full sister, Playmate, is among the prominent international stallions of the 1990s, represented by champions of America and Europe — Timber Country, Hansel, Bosra Sham, Hector Protector.

Other stakes winners descending from Glamour in tail female include Lady Shirl, Assatis, Warrshan,

La Troienne

Razeen, Cunning Trick, Anguilla, Tresoriere, Weldnaas, and Absurde.

To return to Striking, daughter of Baby League, one of her stakes winners, Batter Up, foaled Daring Young Man. Another, My Boss Lady, foaled Landscaper. Illustrating the far flung nature of this tale, those limbs of the family also accounted for Australian Oaks winner Bravery and Norwegian champion River Scape.

Bases Full, another stakes winner from Striking, produced Bold and Brave, a Bold Ruler colt who won the Jerome Handicap and later sired the Hall of Fame filly Bold 'n Determined. Bases Full also produced Stolen Base, in turn the dam of grade I Delaware Handicap winner Basie and three other stakes winners. Frances Genter Stable's Basie foaled Thoroughbred Club of America Stakes winner Jeano. Typically, a smattering of additional stakes winners around the world traces to Bases Full.

The naming of So Chic, a 1954 Nasrullah filly from Striking, put a non-baseball spin on the family, although "diamonds" are forever in many spheres of life. So Chic produced the well-named Beau Brummel, winner of the Garden State Stakes (for years the world's richest race); Fashion Verdict, winner of the Adirondack; French stakes winner Pas de Deux, and also Dapper Dan, a Ribot colt whose stretch kicks carried him to within a half-length of victories in the Kentucky Derby and Preakness of 1965. With Fashion Verdict comes another burst of success in the story, for that Court Martial—So Chic filly produced three stakes winners and also foaled The Garden Club. The Garden Club produced stakes winners Nostalgia and Up the Flagpole. A Hoist the Flag filly who won the Delaware Oaks for William S. Farish, Up the Flagpole produced no fewer than seven stakes winners, including English and Irish classification highweight Flagbird, Alabama Stakes winners Runup the Colors, and Acorn/Ashland winner Prospectors Delite, dam of 1998 grade I winner Tomisue's Delight.

The group III French winner and grade I American winner Louis le Grand is but one of many other stakes winners tracing to So Chic.

Yet another daughter of Striking was Sparkling, a Bold Ruler who foaled the major winner Effervescing and the stakes-winning filly Bubbling.

Another chapter to the legacy of Baby League was her daughter La Dauphine, a 1957 foal by Princequillo. La Dauphine set a world record for a broodmare sold at auction when she attracted a bid of $177,000 from Charles Wacker in the consignment of Leslie Combs II and John W. Hanes at Keeneland in 1964. La Dauphine was in foal to Bold Ruler at the time; her subsequent foal, Bold Discovery, was unplaced, but La Dauphine did produce a pair of stakes winners in Jungle Road and Guillaume Tell. Moreover, her Nashua filly Azeez produced the international winner Obraztsovy and two other stakes winners.

Big Hurry, 1936

A Black Toney filly, Big Hurry won the 1938 Selima Stakes over Inscoelda. Her record was four wins in twelve starts and earnings of $29,860.

Several years before Col. Bradley's death, Ogden Phipps, recognizing the successful patterns developing with the La Troienne blood, had made a private acquisition of Big Hurry from Idle Hour. He, too, set about crossing her with War Admiral, a pursuit which some might have expected would be impeded by the way Samuel D. Riddle managed his stallions. Phipps once quipped that "nobody who ever had a decent mare" had been allowed to breed to Riddle's first great stallion, Man o' War, a comment reflecting Riddle's reputation in that matter. However, Phipps was able to secure the use of War Admiral, which "was the stallion I wanted most."

Big Hurry produced fourteen foals, of which thirteen ran, twelve won, and five won stakes. Two of the major winners were foaled before Phipps' purchase of the mare, and one was the champion three-year-old filly of 1946, Bridal Flower, by the leading sire Challenger II. Typical of the brood, and perhaps the era, Bridal Flower defeated colts, notably Triple Crown winner Assault in the Roamer Handicap. Her distaff triumphs included the Beldame and Gazelle. Within the context of other issue of La Troienne, Bridal Flower was not an outstanding broodmare, although she foaled one moderate stakes winner Beylerbey and the dam of another, Full Regalia.

Another of Big Hurry's earlier foals was Be Fearless, who won a stakes at Del Mar and five in Mexico during an adventurous career of thirty-three wins in ninety-six starts. Be Fearless was a son of Kentucky Derby winner Burgoo King.

The first of Big Hurry's foals bred in Phipps' name was the moderate 1944 Sickle filly Early Harvest. Phipps did not get Big Hurry to War Admiral until 1945, and the next year she foaled The Admiral, who at two won the Tremont Stakes and United States Hotel Stakes.

Two other War Admiral—Big Hurry foals also won stakes. The first, Great Captain, developed late, winning the Saratoga Cup at five and the San Marcos Handicap at six. The other, the filly Searching, was also slow to come to hand. Phipps, like any breeder, was unable to keep all his prospects, and, with the acquisition of a share of the Idle Hour stock, had to take care to avoid too much concentration of similar bloodlines. Hirsch Jacobs, on the other hand, had no glut of La Troienne blood, although he had claimed Big Hurry's daughter No Fiddling from Phipps for $7,500. Mr. and Mrs. Jacobs and partner Isidor Bieber had pulled their own racing operation up from claiming horses to a champion with Stymie, and also were delving into quality bloodstock by that time. The ever-astute Jacobs bought Searching at two from Phipps for $16,000, after which she came on to be one of the strongest distaffers of the mid-1950s. Although Searching never was the champion of any year, she later was elected to the Hall of Fame with an even dozen stakes wins amid a career mark of twenty-five victories from eighty-nine starts, and $327,381.

From Searching sprang one of the richest of all founts emanating from La Troienne. To the cover of Swaps, Searching foaled Affectionately, so swift that she was a champion two-year-old filly of 1962, so gritty that she won under 137 pounds and was champion sprinter and champion older mare at five. Affectionately's first foal was Personality, by the Bieber-Jacobs star Hail to Reason. A few months after Hirsch Jacobs' death in 1970, son John Jacobs saddled Personality to win the Preakness. At year's end, Personality was voted co-champion as Horse of the Year, along with Fort Marcy. (Oddly, with such credentials, Personality failed as a sire.)

Bred to Hail to Reason, Searching foaled the filly Admiring, who became the first stakes winner for her sire when she won the Arlington-Washington Lassie Stakes of 1964. Admiring was another messenger of the richness of La Troienne into the folds of other breeders and owners. Charles Engelhard and Paul Mellon created a formidable financial duo and bid a record amount at the time, $310,000, to purchase Admiring from Hirsch Jacobs' reduction sale at Saratoga in the summer of 1966. It was the top price for a horse in training.

Admiring foaled Mellon's Glowing Tribute, who was a graded stakes winner by Graustark and became Broodmare of the Year in 1993. Glowing Tribute foaled no fewer than seven stakes winners, one of whom, Sea Hero, carried Mellon's silks to a glorious triumph late in the old sportsman's life in the 1993 Kentucky Derby. Trained by Mack Miller, Sea Hero was an inconsistent winner, but picked his spots with sagacity, also taking the Champagne and Travers Stakes. Sea Hero was by Polish Navy, who also descended from La Troienne. Mellon donated a statue of Sea Hero, which now adorns the walking ring at Saratoga.

La Troienne

Another of Glowing Tribute's stakes winners was Mellon's Northern Dancer filly Wild Applause, herself dam of three stakes winners. One of these put the famous Claiborne Farm silks on a descendant of La Troienne: The Forty Niner colt Roar won the 1996 Jim Beam Stakes for the Hancock family and was owned in partnership with Adele Dilschneider.

Admiring's brood is also the family that produced the spectacular Lite Light, who won the Kentucky Oaks and Coaching Club American Oaks of 1991 for the family of the rap singer and dancer M. C. Hammer. The star ripped off his shirt and stood up and waved it from a front-row box at Belmont the day Lite Light won the CCA Oaks. Neither Messrs. Mellon, Phipps, Whitney, nor Kleberg is thought to have responded similarly to any of his own successes with this bloodline, but their elation was no doubt up to Hammer standards.

To return to Searching, the mare produced a full sister to Admiring the following year. Named Priceless Gem, she defeated distant kinsman Buckpasser in the 1965 Futurity Stakes and then foaled the marvelous Sea-Bird II filly Allez France. Sold by the Jacobses as a weanling, Allez France carried the colors of Daniel Wildenstein to a glorious career in France, culminating in a Prix de l'Arc de Triomphe victory. She was a champion in France at two, three, and four, a classic winner, and an adoptive heroine. Years after La Troienne was banished by one sterling French owner, her descendant covered another in continuous glory.

Many of the females in the La Troienne heritage sent to ground those proponents of the theory that good race mares do not make good broodmares. Allez France was looking like a beacon on the other side, as she had no stakes winners until she was fifteen. Impishly, Allez France then produced one European stakes winner: Action Francaise, who in turn produced stakes winners Android and Astorg.

In addition to Allez France, Priceless Gem also foaled the stakes-placed Secretariat filly Lady Winborne, from whom came four stakes winners, including Al Mamoon and La Gueriere, the latter being dam of 1990s stakes winner Lasting Approval. Another of Priceless Gem's foals was Priceless Countess, dam of the 1996 Champagne Stakes winner, Ordway.

A nice touch attended the Big Hurry portion of the dynasty in the form of the filly Dashing By, her 1948 daughter by Menow. Following Col. Bradley's death, Olin Gentry landed back as manager of much of the old Idle Hour Property outside Lexington, after it was purchased by John W. Galbreath and became known as Darby Dan Farm. Galbreath bought into the family and wound up breeding True Knight from Dashing By's daughter Stealaway. True Knight was by Chateaugay, and Gentry said the smallish, dark colt was much more in the mold of many of the La Troiennes than he was of the sire. True Knight won the Suburban, Haskell, Campbell, and other handicaps in the 1970s, so Gentry got a whiff of some of the success to which he had been connected some years before.

Searching was not the first daughter of Big Hurry whom Hirsch Jacobs had mined from the Phipps' reserves. Earlier, he had claimed No Fiddling, Big Hurry's 1945 filly by King Cole, for $7,500. No Fiddling failed to win in eighteen starts and she was late paying important dividends in the Bieber-Jacobs breeding operation, but eventually she became an extraordinary benefit. No Fiddling's 1953 filly, Miz Carol, was by the Jacobses' beloved Stymie, a $1,500 claim that earned more than $900,000 and helped boost them into the breeding business. Stymie was not an outstanding stallion, but in Miz Carol had sired the dam of a future champion. In 1964, after the related Searching family had risen to stardom, Miz Carol foaled a Hail to Reason filly. Named Regal Gleam, she became the champion two-year-old filly of 1966 for Bieber-Jacobs, winning the Frizette, Selima, and Blue Hen. Regal Gleam later was sold to Claiborne Farm, for which she foaled Foreseer, dam of the French classic winner and leading European sire Caerleon. Foreseer also foaled three other stakes winners.

When she was seventeen, No Fiddling had another Hail to Reason filly, who was named Straight Deal. One of the toughest of modern mares, Straight Deal won twenty-one of ninety-nine races, earned $733,020, and was named champion older mare of 1967. Jacobs campaigned her from coast to coast, and she won the Delaware Handicap, Spinster, and Santa Margarita among thirteen stakes triumphs. Straight Deal, too, countered any notions about tough racing sapping a mare's reproductive potential. She produced three stakes winners: Desiree, Reminiscing, and Belonging. Each also has made her mark. Reminiscing foaled stakes winners Commemorate, Persevered, and Premiership; Belonging foaled the stakes-winning Danzig colt Belong to Me, a rising young stallion of the late 1990s and sire of Jersey Girl; Desiree foaled the Santa Margarita winner Adored, in turn the dam of Compassionate. The Jacobses' daughter, Patrice, had married Louis Wolfson, owner of Harbor View Farm, and some of these mares became part of that operation. This was not the first instance of Harbor View benefiting from the legacy of La Troienne.

Mais Oui, Imperfect World, Qualify are other stakes winners from this branch of the family.

Ogden Phipps needed no sympathy, for he still was reaping benefits from Big Hurry, too. In 1954, he sent Big Hurry to Counterpoint. The result was Allemande, an unraced filly. But Allemande, to the cover of To Market, foaled the 1966 Acorn Stakes winner Marking Time. Again crossing different branches of the La Troienne tail-female family, Phipps sent Marking Time to Buckpasser in 1975 and thus bred Relaxing. Exported to England because of fears for her soundness if raced over dirt tracks, Relaxing was good enough to win four of nine races. Returned to this country, she proved capable on the dirt as well and at five in 1981 became champion older mare for Phipps and trainer Angel Penna Sr. The rangy bay mare won an album of the old standards such as Phipps had been taking in for many years — the Ruffian, Delaware, Firenze — and she did not duck colts. Relaxing defeated males in the John B. Campbell and Gallant Fox and was third in the Jockey Club Gold Cup. She loved distance and set a track record at one and five-eighths miles.

In 1985, Relaxing was bred to Calumet Farm's grand stallion Alydar, and the result was magic: In Easy Goer, Phipps bred and raced a colt that perhaps rivaled Buckpasser as his most spectacular. Trained by Shug McGaughey, Easy Goer won fourteen of twenty races and earned $4,873,770. He was a burnished chestnut with an emotionally satisfying grace of stride, this despite shortish pasterns.

At two, he won the Cowdin and Champagne and was voted champion two-year-old colt. The following year, he was smashing in the Gotham and Wood Memorial, and cruised through a series of races similar to that of his sire: the Whitney, Travers, Woodward, and Jockey Club Gold Cup. Easy Goer was bedeviled by Sunday Silence, the 1989 Horse of the Year who won three of four meetings, but the Phipps colt got in one major score when he handed his owner his first Belmont Stakes in a runaway at the rival's expense.

At four, Easy Goer added the Suburban Handicap before an injury sent him to stud at Claiborne Farm. He died young, but got Phipps' My Flag, winner of the Breeders' Cup Juvenile Fillies and Coaching Club American Oaks.

La Troienne

In addition to Easy Goer, 1989 Broodmare of the Year Relaxing foaled two grade I-winning daughters, Easy Now and Cadillacing, the latter dam of Futurity winner Strolling Along.

Bimelech, 1937

Bimelech was sired by Black Toney when the old Idle Hour stallion was twenty-five. Although never particularly popular with outside breeders, Black Toney had been a consistent resource for Bradley, and his sons begot the likes of Blue Larkspur, Double Jay, and Spy Song. In Bimelech, the combination of Black Toney and La Troienne produced a colt of heroic stature. Such was the aura surrounding him after he strode undefeated through his two-year-old season that Bradley, a very horse-wise fellow by then, but always the bold gambler, spoke freely about his thought that this would be his fifth Kentucky Derby winner. Bimelech reigned as champion at two in 1939 with six wins in six starts. Only once was he pressed, as he dashed through the Saratoga Special, Hopeful, Futurity, and Pimlico Futurity. Bradley grandly offered to match him against anyone's horse of any age, at a mile, for money, a trophy, or just the glory of the thing. There were no takers to this grandiose offer, although other owners' collective good judgment was no doubt more responsible than timidity.

At three, Bimelech returned to thrill his hometown crowd by taking Keeneland's Blue Grass Stakes in Lexington, then tuned up further by winning the Derby Trial. His legion of admirers, then, were stunned to despair when he failed at 2-5 in the Kentucky Derby. Bimelech led into the stretch, but was passed by Milky Way Farms' 35-1 Gallahadion. The Bradley colt put things as near right as he could afterward by winning the Preakness and the Belmont, but he lost twice more during the year. Repeating as voted champion, he was retired with eleven wins in fif-teen starts and earnings of $248,745. He was elected to the Hall of Fame in 1990.

Bimelech proved an adequately successful sire, getting thirty stakes winners, including the important broodmare Be Faithful, dam of Lalun, who in turn was the dam of Never Bend.

Big Event, 1938

A filly by Blue Larkspur, Big Event failed to win a stakes, but was second in the 1940 Selima. She won two of nine races, earning $4,200. She had eight foals, of which seven raced, and six were winners. For Greentree, she produced the 1948 gelding Hall of Fame, by Shut Out. Hall of Fame won the 1951 Arlington Classic and five other stakes and earned $234,430. Big Event also foaled Blue Eyed Momo, a War Admiral filly whose son Francis S. won the Wood Memorial and Dwyer for Harbor View Farm, then a newly established stable.

In 1950, Big Event foaled a full sister to Hall of Fame named Blackball. She was unraced, but produced for Greentree the superb turf horse The Axe II, by Mahmoud. The Axe II was a stakes winner in England before being returned to North America, where he won thirteen of twenty-nine races, including the Man o' War, San Luis Rey, and Canadian Championship among nine stakes victories. Blackball also foaled Malicious, who for Greentree won seven stakes, including the Aqueduct, Stymie, Nassau County, Hollywood Juvenile Championship, and Jim Dandy. In a memorable Whitney Stakes, Malicious tested the great Kelso before conceding.

The other immediate stakes winners from Big Event were not of similar class, among them three from Blackball's marvelously named Hester Prynne. National Football League Hall of Famer Sam Huff raced one of the better distant descendants, Bursting Forth, in 1998 and 1999.

Businesslike, 1939

A filly by Col. Bradley's grand Blue Larkspur, Businesslike was unplaced in both her races at two. As a broodmare, however, she was another gem, foaling eight winners among eight foals, of which Busanda and Auditing were stakes winners.

Busanda, a foal of 1947, was a product of the War Admiral cross which had been so successful for Idle Hour. She was unpredictable and inconsistent, winning ten of sixty-five races from two through five. When Busanda had a good day, however, so did owner Ogden Phipps. She won seven stakes, including the Alabama and a few others against her own gender, plus the coveted Suburban and consecutive Saratoga Cups again males.

Busanda foaled three stakes winners, two of them good, the other one Buckpasser. The first was Bureaucracy, who won the Dwyer, National Stallion, and Providence and ran Gallant Man to a half-length in the Travers. Next came Bupers, winner of the 1963 Futurity Stakes.

Busanda's great son Buckpasser was by Tom Fool and was dropped in by fate — and a heritage of class — among a swirling collection of high-class Bold Ruler colts and fillies which the Phipps family was breeding in the 1960s. Trained initially by Bill Winfrey, who had conditioned the great Native Dancer, Buckpasser was a majestic and lovely bay who prominent artist Richard Stone Reeves found the most nearly perfect subject of his many years. At two, Buckpasser won the National Stallion, Tremont, Sapling, Hopeful, Arlington-Washington Futurity, and Champagne. Only the uppity Priceless Gem's victory in the Futurity marred his march through his historic objectives. He was champion at two, and the following year, although a quarter crack eliminated his participation in any Triple Crown race, he was three-year-old champion and Horse of the Year. At three, Buckpasser, then trained by Eddie Neloy, took on

older horses as well as three-year-olds and came close to perfection, winning thirteen of fourteen. He reduced the world record for a mile to 1:32 3/5 in the Arlington Classic, excelled at twice that distance in the Jockey Club Gold Cup, and also won such events as the Flamingo, American Derby, Brooklyn, Travers, and Woodward. The following year, Buckpasser's winning streak reached fifteen races as he added the Metropolitan under 130 pounds and the Suburban under 133 before defeat. He was voted champion older horse, his third year as a champion, and had a career record of twenty-five wins in thirty-one starts and earnings of $1,462,014. He was elected to the Hall of Fame in 1970. Buckpasser sired thirty-six stakes winners, and produce of his daughters has made him the leading broodmare sire four times.

In addition to her stakes winners, Buckpasser's dam Busanda also foaled Navsup, by the South American import Tatan. Navsup produced Polish Navy, a Danzig colt who won the Woodward and Champagne and sired the Kentucky Derby winner Sea Hero. Busanda also foaled Oak Cluster, who produced three stakes winners. Harbor View Farm's Outstandingly, champion two-year-old filly of 1984, was out of a granddaughter of Busanda. Other stakes winners descending in tail female from Busanda include Lovelier, Caress, Country Cat, Outdoors, Splendid Spruce, and South African champion Splendid Ann.

Businesslike, daughter of La Troienne, also foaled the Selima runner-up His Duchess, by Blenheim II. His Duchess foaled Discovery Handicap winner Comic, by Tom Fool, and the winner So Social, by Tom Fool's son Tim Tam. So Social was another gusher than would spring up in this line: She produced five stakes winners — Banner Gala, Social Business, Ward McAllister, Hasty Reply, and Snobishness.

Snobishness foaled two stakes winners and the dams of several others, including My Big Boy. A stakes-placed filly from So Social, the 1972 Bold Ruler filly Queen's Gambit, foaled Whiffling, dam of Loblolly Stable's Preakness winner Prairie Bayou, champion three-year-old male of 1993.

Besieged, 1940

Sired by Black Toney's son, Balladier, Besieged won once from four starts and earned $1,300. She had twelve foals, of which nine raced and five won. One of them was the 1951 Bernborough colt Hook Money, who won several moderate stakes in England; another was the stakes-placed Eight Thirty colt Make Tracks, who spread the family influence as a prominent sire and multiple leading broodmare sire in Argentina.

From Besieged's 1950 Brookfield filly Twitter came Atwitter, by Battlefield. Atwitter's influence is current in the Jonabell Farm broodmare band of John A. Bell III and his family. Atwitter foaled the graded stakes winner Aglimmer, who in turn produced stakes winners Dudley Wood and Aflicker. The latter foaled Forest Glow, winner of the Laurel Dash and Hollywood Park Breeders' Cup in the early 1990s. Atwitter also foaled College Boards, whose daughter College Bold is the dam of four stakes winners, including the speedy young Hermitage Farm stallion Pembroke and the Brooklyn Handicap winner Nasty and Bold.

Broke Even, Back Yard, 1941-43

A son of Blue Larkspur, Broke Even won eleven of forty-four races and placed in the Bunker Hill Stakes, earning a total of $28,065. Among La Troienne's foals, he was followed in 1942 by the unraced Balladier gelding Back Yard. La Troienne was barren in 1943.

Bee Ann Mac, 1944

A filly by Blue Larkspur, Bee Ann Mac won one of her female family's frequent targets, the Selima Stakes, and finished third in the Alabama. She won two of thirteen races and earned $46,480, then foaled ten foals, of which eight raced and three won. None was a stakes winner. The smattering of stakes winners in the immediate generations from Bee Ann Mac included Out the Window, Taipo, and Guards Up.

Belle Histoire, 1945

Another Blue Larkspur filly, Belle Histoire was unplaced in three starts. She had ten foals, all of which raced and eight won. Belle Histoire's one stakes winner was Royal Record, a 1958 Nasrullah colt who won the Bowling Green, Seneca, and Longfellow. Several of Belle Histoire's daughters foaled stakes winners, the second generation including Catullus and Pierpontella. Another rich vein came through a daughter, Narrative, who produced the stakes winners Brave Pilot and King's Story.

A 1960 filly by Bold Ruler, King's Story won the Miss Woodford Stakes, and she foaled Autobiography, a Sky High II colt who was bred by Wheatley Stable and sold to Sigmund Sommer. Autobiography won the Jockey Club Gold Cup to clinch handicap championship honors for 1972. A number of other stakes winners descended from Narrative, among them Promise, winner of the Carter, Equipoise Mile, Jennings, and Cherry Hill Handicaps.

Belle of Troy, 1947

The year after the division of former Idle Hour stock, La Troienne foaled a Blue Larkspur filly whom Greentree Stable gave the evocative name Belle of Troy. La Troienne had been barren in 1946. Belle of Troy was unraced, but produced the high-class Mahmoud colt Cohoes. The only stakes winner among Belle of Troy's eight foals (six raced, five won), Greentree's Cohoes won the Brooklyn, Sysonby, and Saranac Handicaps, plus the Whitney and Grand Union Hotel Stakes. In the stud, he got Paul Mellon's Quadrangle, winner of the 1964 Belmont Stakes.

Other stakes winners descending up close from Belle of Troy included Intervene and Best Go.

Trojan War, 1948

Not the most gratifying aspect of the incredible career of La Troienne was that her final foal had little to commend him. A gelded son of Shut Out, Trojan War was durable, but that was about it. He made sixty-six starts, won only twice, and earned $6,340.

La Troienne had no further foals. On Jan. 30, 1954, at the age of twenty-eight, she was euthanized at Greentree as her condition warranted, and was buried near the stallion paddock of her son Bimelech.

If we take into account only officially elected U.S. champions (plus Black Helen), the foregoing tale of La Troienne mentions seventeen such distinguished animals produced along the tail female descent. Ten of them were fillies. At least one of the seventeen graced each decade starting with the 1930s.

In a sport which properly honors tradition, and the building upon it, La Troienne seems as comforting as a proverb, but as fresh as a sunrise. ❖

Marguerite

 During her lifetime, Marguerite was revered as the dam of an American Triple Crown winner, a champion English two-year-old, and two other major stakes winners. More than a half-century later, various female descendants along her genetic highway still were emerging occasionally as important runners or producers, notably Margarethen and the internationalists Trillion, Triptych, and Generous.

Marguerite was instrumental in helping the Belair Stud saga of William Woodward Sr. attain virtually legendary status. Also benefiting was the career and lasting veneration of one James Fitzsimmons, the beloved "Sunny Jim" who trained the most distinguished of Marguerite's brood.

Woodward, born in 1876, recalled having been taken to the races occasionally by his father and specifically remembered Sir Dixon's victory in the 1888 Belmont Stakes. That longest of American classic races was to be an event of concentrated interest to Woodward later in life.

Woodward was scion of a family whose initial wealth had been derived from selling cotton to the Confederate government, according to the research of Sarah Braudy, whose 1992 volume *This Crazy Thing Called Love* centered on the life and death of Woodward's son but also included details on all the family.

The Woodwards were keen to move up both in business and Society, and Woodward achieved a great deal in this regard. Indeed, he may be said to have raised his family's status to the same classic strata that his horses achieved on his behalf. He was graduated from Groton, Harvard, and Harvard Law School. In *The Great Ones*, Kent Hollingsworth attributes to Woodward the conclusion that he was "too wise to engage in the practice of law." Instead, he took a post as secretary to Joseph Choate, American ambassador to England. The experience solidified a comfort with England and things English — including racing at Newmarket and Ascot — and Woodward often was looked upon as a Victorian and patrician, in manner, dress, and outlook.

Returning to New York in 1903, he joined Hanover Bank, of which an uncle was president, and that year at Saratoga he made the acquaintance of Elsie Cryder. This winsome young lady was also of a family with upward-mobility ambitions. More than a little of the Cryders' opportunity in this regard came from the fact that Elsie and her two sisters had all been born together. The Cryder Triplets thus had a measure of fame because of their birth (and Mrs. Cryder had license to take the attitude that she had certainly gone beyond any reasonable call of duty on behalf of her family's notoriety).

Woodward and Elsie Cryder were married the year after they met, and, to be fair, their subsequent lives were exemplary not merely in rising to acceptance at the highest social levels but in genuine belief in living useful lives.

Their approach to life perhaps carried a hint of condescension with regards to the so-called upper classes having a patriarchal responsibility toward others, but it was productive.

William Woodward Sr. had about as good a run in the Rich Uncle Sweepstakes as a fellow could possibly expect. He inherited Belair Stud from his Uncle James, and he also succeeded his uncle as president of the family's Hanover National Bank in 1910. Years later, when the bank was merged in 1929 with Central Union Trust, the mature Woodward became chairman of the resulting Central Hanover Bank and Trust.

Belair was a rambling Maryland estate with a history compatible with Woodward's leanings toward England and the gentry. Past owners had included a collection of Ogles, Taskers, and Bowies, who had served sundry terms as governors of Maryland — some of them in a day when the title carried an aura of nobility which would not survive the rough and tumble game of modern politics. In Thoroughbred annals, Belair was glorified in lore as having for some time been the home of the foundation matron Selima.

Belair had fallen into disrepair, and to retrieve and rebuild it to past grandeur was a gratifying project for Woodward. The young squire's interest in horse racing already had been translated into action. In 1903, the year he met his bride and seven years before he inherited Belair, Woodward had made his first bloodstock purchases. They consisted of three mares said to cost an average of $50, and the $300 stallion Capt. Hancock. These first purchases, modest though they were in fashion, did result in some early success. The Capt. Hancock filly Aile d'Or became his first winner and then produced his first stakes winner in 1920 Toboggan Handicap victor Lion d'Or.

Coincidentally, Woodward's later emergence on the Turf was abetted by his lasting business connection to the family of another Capt. Hancock. Wounded Civil War Confederate Capt. Richard Hancock had begun Ellerslie Stud in Virginia and was the father of Arthur B. Hancock Sr., who re-directed the family's operations to Claiborne Farm in Kentucky. Woodward developed the pattern of boarding his mares at Claiborne, where they foaled, and sending his foal crops to Belair as weanlings. His top stallion prospects also went to Claiborne.

Near the end of World War I, Woodward noted an advertisement for a sale of Thoroughbreds in France. He cabled an associate and purchased five daughters of Ajax for about $5,000. These fillies were to help establish the foundation of his broodmare band, being joined also by Filante, whom he bought as a yearling at Saratoga. For some years, Woodward also sold at Saratoga, but eventually gave up the practice and concentrated almost exclusively on breeding to race homebreds in his selected silks of white with red polka dots and red cap — an imitation of Lord Zetland's English colors.

Looking Toward Europe

Woodward set about establishing his breeding operation at a time when casting one's eyes to European bloodlines was common among many American horsemen and not solely the strategy of Anglophiles. In 1916, the British Bloodstock Agency's acquisitions included three mares from the estate of Sir Robert Jardine. American buyers then purchased two of the three, Henry Oxnard of Virginia taking Autumn and Frederick Johnson of New York buying Fairy Ray.

Two years later, Fairy Ray was purchased by Hancock. She was bred the following spring to Celt, a son of Commando standing at Claiborne. The filly foal she produced in 1920 thus combined the vaunt-

		Domino, 1891	Himyar Mannie Gray
	Commando, 1898		
		Emma C., 1892	Darebin Guenn
CELT, ch, 1905			
		Amphion, 1886	Rosebery Suicide
	Maid of Erin, 1895		
		Mavourneen, 1888	Barcaldine Gaydene
MARGUERITE, **ch m, 1920**			
		Bend Or, 1877	Doncaster Rouge Rose
	Radium, 1903		
		Taia, 1892	Donovan Eira
FAIRY RAY, ch, 1911			
		St. Frusquin, 1893	St. Simon Isabel
	Seraph, 1906		
		St. Marina, 1895	Janissary St. Marguerite

Marguerite, ch, 1920-1945. Bred by Claiborne Farm (Ky.). Raced 1 yr, 1 st, 0 wins, $0. Dam of 9 named foals, 7 rnrs, 5 wnrs, 4 sw.

1925: PETEE-WRACK, b c, by Wrack. Raced 4 yrs, 48 sts, 12 wins, $98,990. Won Suburban H, Philadelphia H, Metropolitan H, Merchants and Citizens H, Travers Midsummer Derby, Baltimore H, Twin City H; 2nd Pimlico Futurity, Carter H, Suburban H, Arlington Cup, Manhattan H, Walden H; 3rd Manhattan H, Maryland H,

1926: Anastasia, br f, by Wrack. Raced 1 yr, 8 sts, 0 wins, $100. Dam of 7 foals, 6 rnrs, 5 wnrs, including **Sirasia** ($9,775), **Happy Go** ($6,075). Granddam of **Option**.

1927: GALLANT FOX, b c, by Sir Gallahad III. Raced 2 yrs, 17 sts, 11 wins, $328,165. Horse of the Year, champion 3yo colt. Won Kentucky Derby, Preakness S, Belmont S, Dwyer S, Jockey Club Gold Cup, Wood Memorial S, Lawrence Realization S, Saratoga Cup, Flash S, Junior Champion S; 2nd Travers S, United States Hotel S; 3rd Futurity S (twice). Sire of 322 foals, AEI 0.89.

1932: Marigal, dk b f, by Sir Gallahad III. Raced 1 yr, 5 sts, 0 wins, $0. Dam of 9 foals, 7 rnrs, 7 wnrs, including **LONE EAGLE** ($160,245), **MY EMMA** ($39,695), **UNCLE SEA-WEED** ($8,700). Granddam of **SIR RULER**.

1934: Lucky Pledge, dk b f, by Sir Gallahad III. Raced 2 yrs, 11 sts, 1 win, $1,925. 2nd Pimlico Oaks. Dam of 7 foals, 7 rnrs, 6 wnrs, including **Word of Honor** ($15,655). Granddam of **Magic Maiden**.

1935: FIGHTING FOX, b c, by Sir Gallahad III. Raced 4 yrs, 35 sts, 9 wins, $122,000. Won Massachusetts H, Wood Memorial S, Paumonok H, Grand Union Hotel H, Carter H, Fleetwing H, Jamaica H, Wilmington H; 2nd Kenner S, Wilson S, Harford H, Toboggan H, Excelsior H, Empire City H, Junior Champion S; 3rd Hopeful S, Travers S, Whitney S, Futurity S, Aqueduct H, Champagne S, Bay Shore H, Queens County H. Sire of 305 foals, AEI 1.91.

1936: FOXBROUGH, b c, by Sir Gallahad III. Raced 4 yrs in Eng and NA, 22 sts, 5 wins, $48,850. Champion 2yo colt in Eng. Won Butler H, Yonkers H, Hopeful S, Middle Park S; 2nd Aqueduct H, Scarsdale H, Westchester H, Massachusetts H; 3rd Edgemere H, Continental H. Sire of 14 foals, AEI 0.29. Died 1950.

1938: Marguery, b f, by Sir Gallahad III. Unraced. Dam of 11 foals, 11 rnrs, 9 wnrs, including **MARULLAH** ($58,125), **WHIRLING FOX** ($50,855), **Alarullah** ($52,010), **Twirler** ($5,827 in Eng). Granddam of **HANDSOME BOY**, **BLESSING ANGELICA**, **MR. BROGANN**, **MARGARETHEN**, **Handsome Kid**, **Steven Would**, **Ramflow**, **Margalo**, **Fleet Runner**.

1939: Maraschino, b f, by Sir Gallahad III. Unraced. Dam of 12 foals, 8 rnrs, 5 wnrs, including **REINZI** ($133,208), **THE SENATOR** ($6,325). Granddam of **AMBER DIVER**, **BRUCE SOUTH**, **BALLET ROSE**, **AMBER STONE**, Lake Huron, **Shallow Diplomat**.

ed American sire line of Himyar-Domino-Commando with some of the more productive bloodlines in the English Stud Book. Fairy Ray was sired by Radium, he in turn having been sired by the great 19th Century stallion Bend Or when the latter was twenty-five. The female family of Fairy Ray was also the family of English Triple Crown winner Rock Sand (broodmare sire of Man o' War),

Oaks-St. Leger winner Seabreeze, and One Thousand Guineas-Oaks winner Thebais.

Seraph, dam of Fairy Ray, was a granddaughter of the noted mare St. Marguerite, and the similar name of Marguerite was given the Celt—Fairy Ray filly foaled in 1920. Woodward had purchased the filly from Hancock's 1921 Saratoga consignment for $4,100. Marguerite trained like a good prospect, but wrenched her back making her first start and finished last. She did not get back to the races.

In 1925, Marguerite produced her first foal, to the cover of Claiborne's Wrack. Woodward was still selling some of his yearlings at Saratoga, where this colt was purchased by John R. Macomber. Given the name Petee-Wrack, he established Marguerite as a prominent producer. Petee-Wrack defeated Preakness winner Victorian in the historic Travers in 1928, and his career total of seven stakes victories also included such important handicaps as the Metropolitan, Suburban, and Philadelphia. He was tough as well, winning a total of twelve races from forty-eight starts at three through five, and earned $98,990 at a time when $100,000-earners were rare. Marguerite's second foal, a filly, was also by Wrack. Named Anastasia, she made it exactly to the $100 earnings mark, but without comma or further zeros. A placed, non-winner from eight tries, she did foal a pair of stakes-placed horses in Sirasia and Happy Go.

The third foal from Marguerite was her first by Sir Gallahad III. In 1925, Woodward had joined in a partnership with Hancock, Marshall Field, and R. A. Fairbairn in purchasing Sir Gallahad III for $125,000. This proved one of the more important imports of the century. Ensconced at Claiborne, Sir Gallahad III was to lead the sire list four times and the broodmare sire list a dozen times. Moreover, his success led to importation of his full brother Bull Dog (Teddy—Plucky Liege, by Spearmint) and eventually their sire. Bull Dog also led both sire lists, and he got the great stallion and broodmare sire Bull Lea.

Marguerite's 1927 foal grew into a lengthy sixteen-hand bay colt with a blaze and an overall handsomeness. By the time this foal was a yearling, Petee-Wrack had begun to show his ability, and the Sir Gallahad III—Marguerite colt was retained by Woodward, who gave the handsome youngster the equally handsome name of Gallant Fox.

Woodward had set his sights on the classics, both in this country and with the drafts of Belair prospects he soon began sending to England. Sunny Jim Fitzsimmons had taken over the Belair runners in 1923, and he duly took charge of Gallant Fox. Although there was no pressure to rush the colt at two, Gallant Fox's quality encouraged his placement against top competition and carried him to a pair of victories from seven starts, including a win in the one-mile Junior Champion Stakes. He also placed in the Futurity and several other stakes and was recognized as a promising sort for the following year, 1930.

In fact, Woodward had such hopes for Gallant Fox that he prevailed on the great jockey Earl Sande to come out of retirement with the special (for the time) stipulation of ten percent of everything the colt earned at three. An extraordinary year began to take shape in late April, when Gallant Fox reappeared under colors for the Wood Memorial. By the end of 1930, Woodward had had his first tour through the American classic races and had also been elected chairman of The Jockey Club, not only a social plum but a recognition of his wisdom and strengths of leadership.

Gallant Fox won the Wood Memorial easily from Crack Brigade, despite having not had a prep, then moved on to Pimlico for the Preakness, which in those days was sometimes run before the Kentucky Derby. Again, he disposed of Crack Brigade.

The Kentucky Derby was run on a dark, rainy

day. Lord Derby attended and watched the event with Adm. Cary Grayson, formerly the personal physician to President Woodrow Wilson.

The Derby was only slightly more than a half-century old at the time, and only fifteen years had elapsed since Regret's big boost to it as a national event rather than largely a regional affair, so Lord Derby's presence was not without importance from a prestige standpoint. It was one of his ancestors, after all, whose name had been affixed first to the Epsom Derby and thence to important horse races throughout the world. (Lord Derby and Adm. Grayson had attended the races together at least once before, when the horseman/Admiral had prevailed on his chief to take a break from negotiations of the Versailles Treaty and motor from Paris out to Longchamp. As a great breeder and owner, Lord Derby, representing England in the world-shaping goings-on, presumably needed no convincing that such a side trip was a capital idea.)

The Kentucky Derby found Sande working Gallant Fox through the early traffic of a fifteen-horse field to move outside and win by two lengths from the similarly named Gallant Knight. The race inspired Damon Runyon's quickly composed lead for the next morning's paper, a poetic tribute to having seen once more that "Handy Guy named Sande bootin' a winner in." (Sande had won the Derby only five years before, so Runyon's wonderment that the pages somehow had been turned "back to the racin' ages" might be seen as a bit of hyperbole, but it was highly effective.)

What happened next invites the guess that, however impressive he seems in retrospect, Gallant Fox at the time must have been one of those colts that are met by grumblings that they either are not very impressive or are meeting indifferent competition. Despite having two spring classics to his credit, Gallant Fox was not even the favorite for the con-

Marguerite

cluding classic of his year, the Belmont Stakes. Instead that honor fell to Harry Payne Whitney's Whichone. At two, Whichone and Boojum had carved up several of the top prizes between then, and Whichone had reappeared at three with a dashing victory at a mile in the Withers Stakes.

Unconcerned, Sande put Gallant Fox on the lead, and he won his Belmont the way the race has been won with some frequency over the years, controlling the proceedings with a rapid galloper's pace and turning back any challenge. Whichone and Questionnaire closed to within a length turning for home, but The Fox of Belair opened up again to win by three.

He thus had followed Sir Barton, who in 1919 became the first to win the Derby, Preakness, and Belmont, the series which became known as America's Triple Crown. Many today ascribe to Charlie Hatton the honor of having first written of the three races in that context, although a case also could be made for Brian Field having begun using the term Triple Crown at about the same time, or before, Hatton.

Gallant Fox continued his tour through the division, taking the Dwyer and the newly minted Midwestern event, the Arlington Classic. He and Whichone then gave their names, and their speed, to an event which would live in the lore of Saratoga. Dueling on the front in the Travers, they weakened themselves and created an opening for the 100-1 shot Jim Dandy to dash through in the mud. The Jim Dandy Travers ranks with Upset's 1919 Sanford Stakes win over Man o' War among the most compelling events which earned for Saratoga a nickname less sinister in intent than in actual wording, to wit, the "Graveyard of Champions."

The race finished Whichone, but Gallant Fox bounced back two weeks later to win the one and three-quarter-mile Saratoga Cup against older horses. He had a close call against Questionnaire in the Lawrence Realization, then closed his career with a handy tour through the two miles of the Jockey Club Gold Cup. He had won nine of ten starts at three, had one second, and earned a record for one year at that time, $308,275.

Gallant Fox went to stud the next year and in his first crop attained a standing that he alone still enjoys: A Triple Crown winner who sired a Triple Crown winner. That crop included Omaha, who swept the series for Fitzsimmons and Woodward in 1935 and was a foil for the width and depth of Woodward's sporting instincts when he was sent to England. Omaha lost a storied race with Quashed for the time-honored Ascot Gold Cup, but Gallant Fox set matters right by siring another colt, Flares, who landed that noble prize for Woodward. Moreover, in his second crop, Gallant Fox begot another Belmont winner, Granville, who at the end of 1936 became the first to gain the official laureate of Horse of the Year, as formalized voting for year-end championships was inaugurated in 1936.

Oddly, despite such a powerful beginning to his breeding career, Gallant Fox was unable to maintain momentum, and his reputation soon languished. He ranked fourth on the sire list in Omaha's Triple Crown season, as well as in Granville's championship year, and tenth in 1937, but never cracked the top twenty again. He sired a total of nineteen stakes winners. Neither Omaha nor Granville made successful sires, although Omaha's name nudged into some prominent pedigrees as the broodmare sire of Summer Tan and Doubledogdare and as sire of Nijinsky II's third dam.

A Dismal Streak, Then Renewed Success

After Marguerite foaled Gallant Fox in 1927, the mare's fortunes as a producer tested Woodward's and Hancock's ability to accept things as they come in animal husbandry. The mare had no registered foal again until 1932. Her 1928 foal broke its neck,

and her 1929 full brother to Gallant Fox died at three days. Then Marguerite was barren in 1930 and slipped twins in 1931. The birth, and survival, of her 1932 Sir Gallahad III filly was undoubtedly greeted with relief and enthusiasm. This filly, named Marigal, failed to place, but produced the goodish Isolater colt Lone Eagle. As would be the case with a number of Woodward horses, Lone Eagle campaigned on both sides of the Atlantic. In England, he won the Gold Vase (as distinguished from the more important Gold Cup), Queen Elizabeth Stakes, and Burwell, and placed in the 1949 St. Leger. In five subsequent campaigns in North America, he won the Saratoga and Manhattan Handicaps and placed in several other important route races.

Marigal also foaled the moderate stakes winner My Emma (by Isolater) and My Emma in turn foaled the 1950s stakes-winning Nasrullah colt Sir Ruler.

In 1933, Marguerite slipped again, and then in 1934, still being bred to Sir Gallahad III, she produced the filly Lucky Pledge (apparently a play on words of Sir Gallahad III's internationally acclaimed dam, Plucky Liege). Lucky Pledge placed in the Pimlico Oaks.

Marguerite's 1935 colt by Sir Gallahad III was Fighting Fox, who brought memories of Gallant Fox early in his career. Fighting Fox came to hand quickly enough at two to win the Grand Union Hotel Stakes, and he placed in the Junior Champion. The following spring, Fighting Fox won the Wood Memorial, and he went to the post the betting favorite for the 1938 Kentucky Derby, but finished sixth behind Lawrin.

Although Fighting Fox did not live up to the hopes for classic success, he continued as a useful runner. He showed a versatility typical of his pedigree. His nine victories among thirty-five races from two through five included sprint races such as the Carter and Paumonok Handicaps, but also the

Massachusetts Handicap at one and one-eighth miles. Fighting Fox earned $122,000. His eighteen stakes winners included the crack handicapper Crafty Admiral, broodmare sire of 1978 Triple Crown winner Affirmed.

A Champion Abroad

In 1936, Marguerite foaled yet another Sir Gallahad III colt, and this one was selected by Woodward to be sent abroad. He was named Foxbrough and grew into an impressive, sixteen-hand-plus colt of good length and scope similar to Gallant Fox. The youngster was trained by Capt. (later Sir) Cecil Boyd-Rochfort, who had many successes for Woodward and later trained for Capt. Harry Guggenheim and others among the Americans who ventured to send horses to England. Willie Stephenson, himself later a successful trainer and Newmarket stud farm owner, recalled galloping Foxbrough when he was a lad weighing "six stone" (eighty-four pounds).

Foxbrough made only two starts at two in 1938, and he won both times, first in the Hopeful Stakes and then in the important Middle Park Stakes. He was ranked atop the official Free Handicap for two-year-olds in England that year, at 133 pounds, four pounds above Blue Peter, whom he had defeated by one and a half lengths in the Middle Park.

Foxbrough went into the winter as the strong favorite for Woodward's greatest English target, the Epsom Derby. When reappearing, however, he left the impression of a colt which had been well grown at two and did not progress in the right way, and after he was unplaced in his debut his Derby status quickly evaporated. He made only one further start at three and was again unplaced.

Blue Peter, conversely, developed into a dual classic winner for Lord Rosebery, taking both the Two Thousand Guineas and Derby. His chance at a Triple Crown was eliminated when prevailing international affairs caused cancellation of the St. Leger, in which he would have met his French counterpart, Pharis. Given that the international situation brewing at the time turned out to be World War II, one might look wryly on the lament in the *Bloodstock Breeders' Review* of 1939: "This was particularly unfortunate, as the St. Leger, before the war intervened, had promised to be one of the most interesting for many years."

For Foxbrough, dreams of classic victory eventually gave way to concern for just getting him out of England safely. A report in *The Blood-Horse* of 1940 noted that the fall of France had ended hopes for any more Thoroughbreds to be rescued from that country, but that two boats from England carrying thirty-five horses had been reported to arrive safely in New York Harbor. Although initial reports could not identify all the horses, it was known that Foxbrough was among the five Woodward horses — four runners and the mare Flying Gal — included in the shipment.

Foxbrough's career resumed under the tutelage of Fitzsimmons. Boyd-Rochfort had a great many successes in his career and was revered in part for the victories he achieved for Queen Elizabeth II with Aureole and others, but over the years he must have grown tired of learning about the later triumphs of some of the horses sent from his yard in various degrees of disgrace. In 1958, he banished Capt. Guggenheim's obstreperous Nasrullah colt Bald Eagle only to seem him mature and settle down under trainer Woody Stephens and win two Washington, D.C., Internationals and a handicap championship back home in the United States. Then Stephens beat Kelso in the Suburban Handicap with Iron Peg, who for Boyd-Rochfort had faded badly in the Epsom Derby after rounding Tattenham Corner with the leaders.

In the case of Foxbrough many years before, it seemed for a number of months that there would be no restoring of a reputation under Fitzsimmons. During his four-year-old season, Foxbrough had made ten starts in America and was without a win. Fitzsimmons had a lifetime of success in directing campaigns with a high percentage of wins from starts — Gallant Fox, Omaha, Johnstown, Nashua, Bold Ruler, and other top horses. At times, however, he seemed content to keep running horses through long losing streaks, perhaps feeling they needed to be raced into effective form. He started Seabiscuit thirty-five times at two and gave returning champion High Voltage a four-year-old campaign of seventeen races, which netted a single allowance victory.

Whatever the reasons behind the strategy, Foxbrough eventually came back to winning form. He broke through as a winner in his eleventh start in this country, came back five later to run second in a handicap, then won one of the better handicaps of the time, the $25,000 Butler. The accomplished Fenelon had been scheduled to be his Belair entry-mate in the one and three-sixteenths-mile Butler, but Fitzsimmons elected to run only Foxbrough over the drying-out track, and he came on to take command in the stretch and won by five lengths. Foxbrough had a later win, in the Yonkers Handicap, and placed in six additional stakes, including the Aqueduct and Massachusetts Handicaps. He had an American record of three wins in twenty starts and earnings of $48,850. (Of course, in today's environment, an English champion two-year-old who was a full brother to a Triple Crown winner would more likely have been retired immediately after his first gaff at three, the trainer lamenting that some injury or another had cut short the career of perhaps the best colt he had ever laid hands upon.) Foxbrough made no mark at stud.

Ironically, it was the last two foals of Marguerite which projected the blood of the mare farthest into future generations insofar as tail female descent is concerned.

Following Foxbrough's birth in 1936, Woodward continued to breed Marguerite to Sir Gallahad III as he had done since 1926, the year Gallant Fox was conceived. The mare was barren in 1937, but then in 1938 and again in 1939 foaled Sir Gallahad III fillies, Marguery and Maraschino, respectively. Both were unraced, but both produced stakes winners.

Marguery foaled two stakes winners. First was the 1945 Whirlaway colt Whirling Fox, who was second in the Futurity, Hopeful, and Grand Union Hotel at two, but eventually won only one stakes, the Long Branch Handicap. Marguery's second stakes winner was Marullah, a 1954 Nasrullah filly who won the Sorority Stakes and placed in three other nice stakes at two.

Maraschino, the last foal of Marguerite, produced the useful handicapper Reinzi (by Some Chance) and moderate English stakes winner The Senator (by Isolater), who was later converted to jump racing. Maraschino's daughter Rosy Finch, by Woodward's English classic-placed Prince Simon, produced the stakes-winning Native Dancer filly Ballet Rose, who in turn foaled the Ribot colt Riboronde, a useful competitor in Europe and the United States. The champion American steeple-chaser Amber Diver (by Ambiorix) was also among the smattering of stakes winners produced from female descendants of Maraschino.

Marguerite's penultimate foal, the aforementioned Marguery, was considerably more influential. She produced a pair of Nasrullah fillies, Marullah and Russ-Marie, in the 1950s, and they most successfully extended Marguerite's legacy.

Many things had changed by that time. Woodward died in 1953, having won many classics in the United States and England, but without having won his cherished Epsom Derby. (More details on his English winners appear in the chapter on the brood of Vagrancy.) At the time of his death, perhaps the greatest horse he bred, Nashua, was a yearling and was scheduled to be sent to Boyd-Rochfort. Son William Woodward Jr. felt that taking over an American breeding and racing enterprise was enough responsibility, so Nashua remained to demonstrate his championship qualities in America.

Arthur Hancock Sr. was still living at the time of Woodward's death, but was in ill health and his son, Arthur B. (Bull) Hancock Jr. had long since taken over management of Claiborne. It was Bull Hancock who overcame various obstacles to purchase and import Nasrullah, a decision at least equalling the importance of his father's acquisition of Sir Gallahad III.

Ironically, the Woodward family after years of reputation for social propriety was thrust into headlines, and in a tragic mode. William Jr. was fatally shot by his wife in their home on Long Island in the autumn of 1955. Months of controversy led to a legal decision that Ann Woodward had mistaken her husband for a prowler, but many individuals thought otherwise. Years later, the prominent writer Dominick Dunne used the Woodward history and tragedy for his book *The Two Mrs. Grenvilles*, which later was made into a television movie.

In real life, the death of William Woodward Jr. presaged the end of the Belair Stud and Stable. The horses were sold in several packages. Nashua, as Horse of the Year for 1955, commanded a separate sale by sealed bid. A syndicate organized by Leslie Combs II placed the winning offer at $1,251,200, so the champion was the first horse sold for as much as $1 million. Nashua became a major tourist attraction during his stallion career at Combs' Spendthrift Farm in Kentucky, where he lived until the age of thirty.

An irony to the Woodward family saga was that one of William Woodward Sr.'s daughters, Edith,

Marguerite

was far more enthralled by racing and breeding than was her brother William Jr. A parental attitude less fettered by a lingering devotion to primogeniture might have enabled William Sr. to devise a will that allowed the daughter to continue what had been so dear to his own life. As it were, Edith, who married textile magnate Thomas Bancroft, did manage to return her father's colors to prominence. She was the owner and breeder of the 1967 Horse of the Year Damascus, although, sadly, she was virtually comatose during that colt's championship campaign. One of the Bancrofts' sons, Thomas, became chairman of the New York Racing Association, which Edith Woodward Bancroft's father undoubtedly would have lauded, and Thomas and his brother, William, used the old Belair colors for their Pen-Y-Bryn Stable.

Recalling that Marguerite's later foals included Marguery, the story picks up again here with the latter's daughter Marullah, the Sorority winner. Marullah's foals included two of the most successful runners bred and raced by the Hobeau Farm of Jack Dreyfus. The Dreyfus Fund (with an ambulatory lion in TV commercials) constituted a major business for Dreyfus, but he also established a major farm in Florida and was for a time head of the New York Racing Association.

Marullah foaled Handsome Boy, who carried Dreyfus' colors to an upset of champion Buckpasser in the 1967 Brooklyn Handicap. Marullah also foaled Blessing Angelica, who won consecutive runnings of the Delaware Handicap, long one of America's most important races for fillies and mares.

Russ-Marie, Marullah's 1956 Nasrullah filly, was a moderate winner. Her descendants included Harbor View Farm's $845,863-earner and grade I winner Life's Hope, as well as Partez, who finished third as trainer D. Wayne Lukas' first entrant in the Kentucky Derby in 1981.

One of Russ-Marie's daughters was Margarethen, who was sired by Tulyar, yet another major European runner imported to stand at Claiborne. Margarethen won five important distaff stakes in the Midwest and foaled two European stakes winners, Trillion and Margravine, both by Hail to Reason. Trillion was the more accomplished of the two. Racing for Nelson Bunker Hunt and Edward Stephenson, she was a champion twice in France and achieved an unusual distinction in this country. In 1979, Trillion failed to win a race on these shores, but placed admirably in such a series of major grass events against the best male competition that she was voted an Eclipse Award as champion female on grass in 1979. (A champion that did not win a race! It would have been a difficult concept to explain to William Woodward Sr.) Trillion's foals included Triptych (by Riverman), who was purchased by Peter Brant for $3.4 million from the Alan Clore dispersal in the midst of an impressive career during which she was four times a distaff champion in France, twice a champion older mare in England, and a classic winner and champion in Ireland.

Margarethen's other stakes winner, Margravine, also still is appearing in pedigrees of important winners as the century nears conclusion. One of them is Juvenia, winner of the group I Prix Marcel Boussac at Longchamp in 1998.

Other daughters of Margarethen who contributed to the continuation included Hail Maggie, dam of Sabona. Lastly, there was Doff the Derby, a 1981 foal from Margarethen and sired by Preakness winner Master Derby. One cannot make much in the way of a genetic cause-and-effect equation about Marguerite's five-generation and seven-decade connection to a chestnut Caerleon—Doff the Derby colt named Generous. Still, it is appealing to consider that what William Woodward Sr. wished for so many of his Belair chargers, Generous achieved in 1991: Triumph in the Derby over the elegant and testing contours of Epsom Downs. ❖

Missy Baba

Uvira II was twenty when she foaled Missy Baba in 1958. It might be presumed that this daughter who created the most lasting influence in the family was Uvira II's swan song as a broodmare, but such is not the case. Uvira II already had produced four stakes winners, and she had one more to foal, at age twenty-five giving birth to the Donn and Ben Ali Handicaps winner Francis U. Moreover, she was twenty-one when she foaled the unraced Tulyar filly Blarney Bess. Such was the longevity of this branch of the family that an international group/grade winner of the 1990s, Dernier Empereur, still could claim Uvira II as his third dam — this a half-century since she put her own name on classic winner lists by capturing the Irish Oaks. Finally, at twenty-six, Uvira II foaled the Sword Dancer filly Oonagh, who produced the 1975 English Derby-placed Hunza Dancer.

What we have in the career and family of Missy Baba, clearly, is one of those prolific female lines which have spanned eras, and the Atlantic, and still are renewing themselves.

Uvira II was bred by the Aga Khan, the present Aga Khan's grandfather. She was by his Champion Stakes winner Umidwar. The filly was consigned to the Newmarket December Sales of 1939 as a yearling. She was purchased for 510 guineas by Gerald Wellesley, who was acting on behalf of Vicomte de Fontarce. Uvira II disappointed in her two outings at two. Vicomte de Fontarce was in declining health and sold her back to Wellesley, who was acting on behalf of Sir Thomas Dixon in that second sale.

(Vicomte de Fontarce was rudely treated by the muses of the sale ring, breeding farm, and racecourse. In the last year of his life, he not only had his hands on Uvira II, soon to be a classic winner and later a superb broodmare, but also sold the Mahmoud filly Boudoir II, from whence descended another coterie of major horses, including Graustark and Majestic Prince in tail female. Given those fillies and a few more years of good health, the Vicomte might well have found his name placed higher among 20th Century breeders revered for their acuity.)

Uvira II discarded her immature ways and handily won all five of her races at three, among them the Irish Oaks. Mr. and Mrs. Emerson Woodward had established Valdina Farms in Texas and late in 1941 purchased Uvira II. The filly was destined for continual turnover. After the Woodwards' deaths, their racing and breeding stock were purchased by Kentucky market breeder Henry S. Knight, owner of Almahurst Farm. Knight bred one foal from Uvira II, then sold her to C. C. Tanner, who in turn sold the mare to Crispin Oglebay in 1944. Uvira II already had had seven owners, which were either wheeler-dealers or in bad health, or both. Uvira II had several foals for Oglebay, who then died in October of 1949. The next month, his estate sent her into the Keeneland sale ring. Uvira II's revolving door of ownership, of course, had not reflected her having failed as either a racing filly or a broodmare. By the autumn of 1949, she had emerged as the dam of two nice stakes winners and another winner from her first three foals. A. B. (Bull) Hancock Jr. of Claiborne Farm bid a record figure for her at the Oglebay sale, going to $61,000. Hancock also paid the second-highest price of the Oglebay dispersal, bidding $57,500 for the 1941 Coaching Club American Oaks winner Level Best, then age eleven.

Both Uvira II and Level Best were thus acquired for the broodmare band of John S. Phipps. Level Best foaled for Phipps the homebred 1953 Jockey Club Gold Cup winner Level Lea. Compared with the previous owners of Uvira II, Phipps had an unusually long tenure, about nine years, before his death in 1958. He bred only one stakes winner, Parnassus, from her.

Uvira II then passed to Phipps' son, Michael Phipps, her ninth owner, and her first foal bred in his name was Missy Baba.

Earlier, Uvira II also had produced Colonel O'F, winner of the Hyde Park, George Woolf Memorial, and Lafayette Stakes at two in 1946; Noble Impulse, winner of a half-dozen stakes including four as a two-year-old and the Salvator Mile at four; and General Staff, purchased for $25,000 by Larry MacPhail from the Oglebay dispersal and winner of a half-dozen stakes at four in 1952, including the Pimlico Special and Narragansett Special. A non-stakes winner from Uvira II was the fine broodmare Obedient, who foaled stakes winners Iron Ruler and Don't Alibi, stakes-placed Obey and Blazing Count, and several other stakes producers. Obedient's 1960 Swaps colt, Swapson, was the first American yearling to bring as much as $100,000 at auction. Uvira II produced a total of thirteen foals, of which eleven ran, ten won, and five won stakes.

Missy Baba, Uvira II's 1958 filly, was sired by the English Two Thousand Guineas winner My Babu,

who had been imported to Spendthrift Farm in Kentucky. Michael Phipps sent the filly to trainer T. J. Kelly, who sent her out for the first time at three at Monmouth Park on July 10, 1961. Missy Baba led throughout and won by two and a quarter lengths. The promise of this start was not to be fulfilled. In each of her six subsequent races, one of which was on grass, Missy Baba showed enough speed early to set or contest the pace, but began to fall back soon and was never again better than fifth at the finish. "Stopped badly after a quarter" was *Daily Racing Form*'s chart comment after her last race, on Oct. 11, at Garden State Park, and more or less was a profile of her brief racing career. Bill Hartack, not known for gentle evaluation of poorly performing mounts, rode her that day. Missy Baba raced no more, but, of course, her pedigree was such as to ensure her a place in the Phipps broodmare band. She had won once in seven starts, earning $2,275.

Sires and Dams

The issue of Missy Baba did not constitute either a sire family, or a broodmare family. There would be plenty of success among both genders, both at the races and in the stud.

Her first foal, Master Piper, a 1963 Sword Dancer colt, won twelve of 104 races, but no stakes, and earned $107,077. While six furlongs had been too far for his dam, Master Piper went to the other extreme, setting a course record at Belmont Park for two and one-eighth miles. Missy Baba then foaled the cleverly named Kindegartn Dropout, by Dunce, an unraced dam of only two winners from eleven foals. Missy Baba broke through as the dam of a stakes winner with her third foal, a 1965 colt by the rising force named Bold Ruler. This colt was Master Bold, who won the Dade Metropolitan Handicap and placed in nine other stakes. He had nine wins in forty-nine races and earned $106,721. Michael Phipps was an avid polo man and had

			Tourbillon, 1928	Ksar Durban
	Djebel, 1937			
MY BABU, b, 1945			Loika, 1926	Gay Crusader Coeur a Coeur
			Badruddin, 1931	**Blandford** Mumtaz Mahal
	Perfume II, 1938			
MISSY BABA, **b m,** **May 13, 1958**			Lavendula, 1930	Pharos Sweet Lavender
			Blandford, 1919	Swynford Blanche
	Umidwar, 1931			
UVIRA II, dk b, 1938			Uganda, 1921	Bridaine Hush
			Son-in-Law, 1911	Dark Ronald Mother-in-Law
	Lady Lawless, 1923			
			Entanglement, 1915	Spearmint Rambling Rose

Missy Baba, b, 1958-1980. Bred by Michael G. Phipps (Ky.). Raced 1 yr, 7 sts, 1 win, $2,275. Dam of 13 named foals, 12 rnrs, 12 wnrs, 6 sw.

1963: Master Piper, ch c, by Sword Dancer. Raced 9 yrs, 104 sts, 12 wins, $107,077. Died 1974.

1964: Kindegartn Dropout, b f, by Dunce. Unraced. Dam of 9 foals, 3 rnrs, 2 wnrs. Died 1981.

1965: **MASTER BOLD**, b c, by Bold Ruler. Raced 3 yrs, 49 sts, 9 wins, $106,721. Won Dade Metropolitan H; 2nd Cherry Hill H, Sheridan S, Fountain of Youth S, City of Miami Beach H; 3rd Assault H (T), Everglades S, Midwest H, Ventnor H (T), Oil Capitol H (T). Sire of 73 foals, AEI 1.38. Sent to Arg 1970.

1966: **CHOKRI**, ch f, by Herbager. Raced 3 yrs, 27 sts, 4 wins, $32,165. Won Durazna S.

1967: **GAY MISSILE**, b f, by Sir Gaylord. Raced 4 yrs, 40 sts, 10 wins, $94,006. Won Ashland S; 2nd La Troienne S; 3rd Vagrancy H, Louis S. Meen Memorial H, Yo Tambien H. Dam of 9 foals, 9 rnrs, 7 wnrs, including **GAY MECENE** ($361,389, champion older male in Fr, Fr-I), **LASSIE DEAR** ($80,549), **GALLAPIAT** ($130,688), **GALLANTA (Fr)** ($66,966), **Brave Shot (GB)** ($47,016, in Fr, Italy, and NA), **Harlem Shuffle** ($50,471, in Fr and NA). Granddam of **WOLFHOUND, WEEKEND SURPRISE, FOTITIENG, GAY GALLANTA, SPECTACULAR SPY, SPORTSWORLD, FOX-HOUND, Lassie's Lady, Al Mufti**. Died 1985.

1968: **RAJA BABA**, b c, by Bold Ruler. Raced 4 yrs, 41 sts, 7 wins, $123,287. Won Francis Scott Key S, Delaware Valley H, Alligator H; 2nd Phoenix H, Japan Racing Association H, Garrison H; 3rd Breeders' Futurity, Hutcheson S, Hibiscus S, Firecracker H, Hannibal H. Sire of 572 foals, AEI 2.48.

1969: Ch c, by Buckpasser. Died 1970.

1970: Sooni, b f, by Buckpasser. Raced 2 yrs, 17 sts, 3 wins, $27,418. 3rd Seashore H (gr. III). Dam of 16 foals, 14 rnrs,

7 wnrs, including **BLACK CASH** ($175,800), **MY MARCH-ESA** ($132,996), **C. Sharp** ($28,967, in Fr and NA), **Super Sam** ($65,991, in Ger). Granddam of **Ayers Rock, Learious, Chanticlair**.

1971: Toll Booth, b f, by Buckpasser. Raced 2 yrs, 22 sts, 3 wins, $32,330. Broodmare of the Year in 1991. Dam of 12 named foals, 12 rnrs, 11 wnrs, including **CHRISTIECAT** ($799,745, gr. I), **PLUGGED NICKLE** ($647,206, champion sprinter, gr. I), **KEY TO THE BRIDGE** ($289,747), **TOLL FEE** ($333,917), **TOLL KEY** ($290,218), **IDLE GOSSIP** ($101,721), **TOKENS ONLY** ($50,455), **Chicago Bound** ($46,105, in NA and PR), **Banker's Favorite** ($70,470). Granddam of **TOKEN DANCE, IDLE SON, PETROSKI, ISLE-FAXYOU, LIBOR, The Bink, Token Gift, J P Hamer, Token of Youth**. Died 1993.

1973: Babas Fables, b c, by Le Fabuleux. Raced 6 yrs, 44 sts, 7 wins, $134,314. 3rd Leonard Richards S (gr. IIIT), Brighton Beach H (gr. IIIT). Sire in Arg of 44 foals.

1974: **DROMBA**, b c, by Droll Role. Raced 4 yrs in Arg and NA. Complete statistics unavailable. 31 known sts, 4 wins, $28,929. Won Clasico Omnium.

1975: **SAUCE BOAT**, ch c, by Key to the Mint. Raced 1 yr, 5 sts, 3 wins, $144,465. Won Arlington-Washington Futurity (gr. I). Sire of 568 foals, AEI 1.40. Died 1998.

1976: Barren.

1977: Barren.

1978: Vast Empire, b c, by Empery. Raced 3 yrs, 17 sts, 1 win, $27,570. Sire of 53 foals, AEI 0.37.

1979: Pennyworth, ch f, by Key to the Mint. Raced 2 yrs, 14 sts, 4 wins, $74,120. Dam of 8 foals, 3 rnrs, 2 wnrs, including **WORTHEROATSINGOLD** ($328,645, gr. II). Granddam of **DAYLIGHT SAVINGS**.

many business deals with Argentina, both with racing and polo stock, and Master Bold eventually was exported there to stud.

In 1966, Missy Baba had her fourth foal by four different sires. This was the filly Chokri, whose sire, Herbager, had been imported from France. Chokri won the Durazna Stakes, among four wins from twenty-seven starts, and earned $32,165. She produced only one foal, Bold Missy, in turn only the dam of a pair of winners.

The different sire per year continued, and Missy Baba in 1967 foaled the filly Gay Missile, by Sir Gaylord. Gay Missile was Missy Baba's third consecutive stakes winner and launched a prolific branch of the family which has seen two American classic winners of the 1990s. At the racetrack, Gay Missile won the 1970 Ashland Stakes at Keeneland and placed in four other stakes. She ran for four years, winning ten of forty starts, and earned $94,006.

Michael Phipps died early in 1973, and that fall Claiborne Farm consigned Gay Missile and others from the estate to the Keeneland breeding stock sale. Vic Heerman paid $300,000 for her on behalf of Jacqueline Getty Phillips, for whom she foaled the Buckpasser filly Lassie Dear the following year. In 1975, Gay Missile produced the group I-winning French colt, Gay Mecene, by Vaguely Noble. Gay Mecene won the Grand Prix de Saint-Cloud and three other group races and was ranked as a champion older horse in France. Gay Missile had another European runner in Gallapiat, by Buckpasser. Gallapiat won in France and placed in the group I Observer Gold Cup in England before returning to the United States, where he won the Oakland Handicap.

Later, more European success came from the Gay Missile branch. Gallanta was her stakes-winning Nureyev filly who in turn produced the English group I winner Gay Gallanta and Irish group II winner Sportsworld.

William S. Farish had been a friend and sort of protégé of Michael Phipps. Also an avid rider and polo player, Farish hailed from a Texas family of the old Standard Oil regime, but found the lure of racing and breeding took him to Kentucky, where he has developed Lane's End Farm into one of the world's premier operations. The year before Phipps' death, Farish had bought into the Missy Baba family; two years later, when Gay Missile's yearling filly by Buckpasser was consigned by Mrs. Phillips to the Keeneland summer sale, she was purchased for $76,000 in the name of W. S. Kilroy, with whom Farish has bred a number of major horses.

The Buckpasser filly was the aforementioned Lassie Dear, and in Kilroy's colors she won the grade III Villager Stakes and Marica Handicap and placed in two other stakes. Lassie Dear won five of twenty-six races and earned $80,549.

The granddaughter of Missy Baba then was retired to be bred, and Farish swapped a partial interest in another mare, Bold Bikini, for an interest in Lassie Dear. (This was a win-win situation: From Bold Bikini, Kilroy and Farish bred the European classic winner Law Society.)

Lassie Dear was a gem in her own right. She produced fourteen foals, of which eleven raced and all won. Among them were four stakes winners: Wolfhound, by Nureyev, was a group I winner in France and a highweight sprinter in Europe; Spectacular Spy, by Spectacular Bid, won a pair of stakes in this country; Foxhound, by Danzig, won the Prix la Fleche; and Weekend Surprise won two graded stakes and has foaled two classic winners.

The Lassie Dear foals which were not stakes winners were not all disappointments, for they included stakes-placed Al Mufti and Lassie's Lady (dam of stakes winners Bite the Bullet and Shuailaan), and the winners Deerhound (sire of 1997 champion juvenile filly Countess Diana) and Charming Lassie (dam of 1999 Belmont Stakes winner Lemon Drop Kid).

It was Weekend Surprise who has been the most

accomplished of Lassie Dear's produce. She was sired by the brilliant Secretariat.

"I told Mr. Kilroy I thought Weekend Surprise might be the best mare we'd ever have, because of the talent she had, the pedigree, the whole works," Farish later told *The Blood-Horse*. "There were a number of reasons why I liked the mating of Secretariat and Lassie Dear, and I liked it physically, a fact that we strongly emphasize." Secretariat was of stout build, the mare delicate and feminine.

Farish added that the result, Weekend Surprise, the Secretariat—Lassie Dear filly, "was not a typical Secretariat. She's quite feminine, very, very attractive, but no resemblance to him. To see her progeny is interesting, because there's a strong female side pull coming through this whole family. I guess it has to go back to Missy Baba or Uvira II."

Weekend Surprise gave Farish a memorable victory when she came from behind to win the grade III Schuylerville Stakes at Saratoga so swiftly that he had been hoping merely for a place as late as the sixteenth pole. She also won the Golden Rod Stakes, also grade III, and Pocahontas Stakes that year and placed in the grade I Frizette and Matron. She raced on at three and four, placing in additional grade I races, including the Delaware Handicap and La Canada, for a record of seven wins in thirty-one starts and earnings of $402,892.

Her first foal was a tidy little son of Storm Bird, a son of Northern Dancer, which thus introduced another prominent modern bloodline to the already impressive mixture. Named Summer Squall, the Weekend Surprise colt raced for Cot Campbell's Dogwood Stable and was trained by Neil Howard. He was unbeaten at two, when he won the grade I Hopeful and three other stakes. The following spring, he was second to Unbridled in the Kentucky Derby, but reversed that result in winning the Preakness. Summer Squall also won the Blue Grass, Jim Beam, and Pennsylvania Derby, and the following year at four he added the Fayette. Retired to Lane's End with thirteen wins from twenty starts and earnings of $1,844,282, Summer Squall has sired 1996 juvenile filly champion Storm Song and 1999 Kentucky Derby and Preakness winner Charismatic.

Two months after Summer Squall's 1990 Preakness Stakes, his half-brother entered the ring at Keeneland. He was a large, handsome son of Seattle Slew, which meant he was inbred to Bold Ruler — Seattle Slew's great-grandsire and Weekend Surprise's maternal grandsire. The colt topped all yearlings sold at auction that year, at $2.9 million. Named A.P. Indy, he began racing for Japanese investor Tomonori Tsurumaki and, after an undescended testicle was removed, the colt blossomed into a grade I winner late in his juvenile season. He won the Hollywood Futurity and early the next year added the Santa Anita Derby.

Thereafter, a sequence of physical problems hampered trainer Neil Drysdale in his management of A.P. Indy, but he had the colt sound to win the Belmont Stakes and Breeders' Cup Classic, securing the three-year-old championship and Horse-of-the-Year crown for 1992. Weekend Surprise was named Broodmare of the Year. She was the seventh mare to have produced two winners of American Triple Crown races, but none of the others had done so since the late 1920s; insofar as the eras when the Triple Crown races have had the stature they have today, the feat was unprecedented.

A.P. Indy, who won eight of eleven races and earned $2,979,815, joined Summer Squall at Lane's End, and his fast start at stud has already produced Pulpit, Tomisue's Delight, and Old Trieste.

Weekend Surprise has also foaled the stakes-placed Honor Grades and Weekend in Seattle.

More From Missy Baba

Returning to Missy Baba — dam of Gay Missile and great-granddam of Weekend Surprise — it will be recalled that Michael Phipps had been breeding her to a different stallion each year through the early and middle 1960s. In 1967, he sent her a second time to Bold Ruler, and the result was Raja Baba. A moderate stakes winner, Raja Baba won the Francis Scott Key, Delaware Valley, and Alligator Handicaps. He had a record of seven wins in forty-one starts and earnings of $123,287. He was one of the horses which Farish bought prior to Phipps' death. Farish did not have his own major Kentucky operation yet, and when an injury prompted him to retire Raja Baba, he sold a half-interest to Warner L. Jones Jr., at whose Hermitage Farm the stallion had a long and successful stud career.

A runner of Raja Baba's credentials would hardly have seemed likely to lead a modern sire list, but he ascended to the top in 1980. Raja Baba sired sixty-two stakes winners.

In 1969, Missy Baba's foal by Buckpasser died, and then in 1970 she foaled the stakes-placed Buckpasser filly Sooni, who was third in the grade III Seashore Handicap and won three of seventeen races to earn $27,418. Sooni foaled a pair of stakes winners of the 1990s in Black Cash and My Marchesa.

Despite Missy Baba's success, Phipps sold her. She was twelve years old in 1970 and, Farish recalled, "Mike Phipps always sold mares — no matter how good they were — at age twelve to fourteen."

Just as her dam, Uvira II, had rewarded various owners, Missy Baba the next year produced a successful mare for John Schiff, who had purchased her from Phipps. (Schiff deserved a bit of luck in timing, for a couple of years before he had found himself in a "tax year" and so parted with a yearling later to be named Hoist the Flag.)

The first Missy Baba foal of Schiff's was another Buckpasser, the filly Toll Booth. She won three of twenty-two races and earned $32,330, and went on to be named Broodmare of the Year in 1991. She had eleven winners among thirteen foals. They included the versatile Eclipse Award sprinter Plugged Nickle and six other stakes winners: Christiecat, Toll Fee, Toll Key, Key to the Bridge, Idle Gossip, and Tokens Only. Toll Booth's branch of the family also remains active in the late 1990s.

Missy Baba had no foal in 1972, then in 1973 produced the stakes-placed Le Fabuleux colt, Babas Fables, who won seven of forty-four races, placed in two graded stakes, and earned $134,314. Bred next to Schiff's exceptional grass horse Droll Role, Missy Baba in 1974 foaled Dromba, who became a stakes winner at six by taking Argentina's Clasico Omnium. Before export, Dromba had won three of thirty-one races in North America, earning $28,929.

At age seventeen in 1975, Missy Baba produced another high-class stakes winner and significant sire. Bred to Key to the Mint, she foaled Sauce Boat, who won three of five starts at two, including the grade I Arlington-Washington Futurity, and earned $144,465 before retiring to Hermitage Farm. He sired fifty-six stakes winners and is the maternal grandsire of the 1994 Preakness/Belmont Stakes winner Tabasco Cat.

Missy Baba was barren in 1976 and 1977, then foaled Vast Empire, a colt whose sire, Epsom Derby winner Empery, was a major disappointment at stud. Vast Empire won once in seventeen races and earned $27,570. At twenty-one, Missy Baba produced one last foal for Schiff in the Key to the Mint filly Pennyworth. The filly won four of fourteen races and earned $74,120. Pennyworth is the dam of Ladies Handicap winner Wortheroatsingold, by Naskra, and Wortheroatsingold is the dam of Daylight Savings, a late-1990s stakes winner by Sky Classic.

Missy Baba, who died in 1980, had produced fourteen foals, of which a dozen raced and all won. Six won stakes, and two of her descendants were Broodmares of the Year. ❖

Myrtlewood

The racing public is admirable in its willingness to expend emotion. On occasion, something about a particular racehorse excites strong popular sentiment that exceeds those directed toward horses of similar merit. The written word, and observation, convinces us that Whirlaway and Alydar among Kentucky heroes, for example, were accorded in the hearts of the public a secure place even before their racing performances completely justified it. In the West, state pride embraced Swaps, while Silky Sullivan's garish running style was its own catnip. Among Florida-breds, Carry Back seemed more beloved than other horses of similar or greater achievement.

In the annals of the Bluegrass, Myrtlewood, since her early days at the races, was another who the public took to its heart. This connection had much to do with sheer speed, of course, but beyond that there was a magnetism that mankind recognized, and savored. John Hervey waxed eloquent in his description of the filly in *American Race Horses* of 1936: "She stands full sixteen hands tall, has a bloodlike, hawky head, a long, elegant neck." She was not the typical sprinter in type, he went on, possessing a body "robust and powerful, but of fine lines and proportions, and legs of good bone. In appearance she was regal upon the course, having the high carriage and queenly ways, though her deportment was at all times quiet and controlled."

Myrtlewood left the track in the autumn of 1936, winning a match race against Miss Merriment at the newly minted Keeneland Racecourse. Her owner, Brownell Combs, and Miss Merriment's owner, John Hay Whitney, had agreed to run the match for no purse, only a trophy, and Keeneland — even in its infancy possessed of a fine sense of history — produced a gold number originally made for the 1815 Lincoln Cup in England. At the time, Myrtlewood held the American record for females at both six furlongs and one mile, had track records at five Midwestern tracks, and had been beaten a nose when Clang established the prevailing world record for six furlongs; it had been Clang's only victory over her in five meetings.

Myrtlewood's heritage combined some of the best of contemporary American stock with classic English connections. She was in the first crop of Col. E. R. Bradley's popular Domino-line champion Blue Larkspur, and she was out of Frizeur, a daughter of Sweeper and the historic Frizette. Sweeper had been conceived in Kentucky, but foaled in England, where he won the Two Thousand Guineas. He was by Harry Payne Whitney's great stallion Broomstick, while Frizette was by another of America's most important stallions, Hamburg, son of Hanover.

On the bottom, Frizette, herself a noble winner and taproot producer, traced to great English sires St. Simon and Bend Or. Frizette's female family was also that of the Duke of Westminster's Shotover, one of only six fillies to win the English Derby.

Myrtlewood was bred and raced by Combs. She was foaled in 1932, at which time her dam, Frizeur, was sixteen and had foaled three earlier stakes winners in Black Curl, Pairbypair, and Crowning Glory. Brownell Combs was from a racing family. His grandfather, Gen. Leslie Combs, had been president of the Lexington Association track. Brownell Combs' father had been a career diplomat, with postings in Central America, but had found time to breed the 1938 juvenile champion, El Chico; he was married to the daughter of Daniel Swigert, founder of Elmendorf Farm.

Brownell Combs turned Myrtlewood over to trainer R. A. Kindred, and after a brief two-year-old campaign, she launched into her series with Clang and other crack horses of what was then called racing's "West," i.e., Kentucky and Chicago. At one point at three, she held the American record for six furlongs, regardless of gender, at 1:09 3/5. Although she thrilled her fans with front-running flash, she at times could take back, and she won at a mile and one and one-sixteenth miles. In one incredible assignment, Myrtlewood was beaten only about two lengths at one and one-eighth miles in the Stars and Stripes Handicap, in a field led home by Stand Pat, but also including Discovery, Azucar, Roman Soldier, and Whopper. Myrtlewood won fifteen of twenty-two races and earned $40,620.

Observing her retirement, Hervey mused: "Mr. Combs has announced that she will be mated next spring with Equipoise. It will be a unique alliance, as he holds the American mile record and she the mare's record; hence the foal will inherit from sire and dam average mile speed (which will be) difficult to live up to."

Yearlings, Sales, and Champions

That first Myrtlewood chick, foaled in 1938, was Crepe Myrtle. The filly did nothing so startling as her miler genes might have promised, winning once in four starts to earn $950. In the stud, however, Crepe Myrtle hastily set about establishing the influence of Myrtlewood as a broodmare. The name of Myrtlewood became associated with the Spendthrift Farm of Combs' nephew, Leslie Combs II, who eagerly worked his way in as co-breeder of some of her issue. Myrtlewood's descendants over several generations were to be bulwarks of Spendthrift consignments which topped the Keeneland July sale sixteen consecutive times (1949-64).

That first foal, Crepe Myrtle, produced Myrtle Charm, an Alsab filly. Myrtle Charm was purchased by Leslie Combs II for Elizabeth Arden Graham, who was establishing a stable after the success of her cosmetics corporation. If ever "Cousin Leslie" Combs II encountered someone who could recognize skin-deep charm it was Elizabeth Arden, but their connection was positive for both. Myrtle Charm won the Matron and Spinaway and placed in the Futurity for Mrs. Graham's Maine Chance Farm and was voted champion two-year-old filly. Myrtle Charm in turn foaled the Frizette and Alcibiades Stakes winner Myrtle's Jet, by Kentucky Derby winner Jet Pilot (also selected for Maine Chance by Combs).

Myrtle Charm's segue to champions of the latter quarter of the 20th Century came through her 1959 filly Fair Charmer. Fair Charmer was sired by Jet Action, who as a racehorse came close to living up to the high hopes fostered by his pedigree: He was by Kentucky Derby winner Jet Pilot and out of Horse of the Year Busher. Jet Action was an indifferent sire, but, no matter, his daughter Fair Charmer in due course produced the filly My Charmer, by Round Table's stakes-winning son Poker. My Charmer, great-great-granddaughter of Myrtlewood, was foaled in 1969. She was bred by Ben Castleman, a Kentucky Racing Commissioner whose White Horse Acres was across the road from Maine Chance and was named for his tavern in the

		Black Toney, 1911	Peter Pan / Belgravia
	Black Servant, 1918		
		Padula, 1906	Laveno / Padua
BLUE LARKSPUR, b, 1926			
		North Star III, 1914	Sunstar / Angelic
	Blossom Time, 1920		
		Vaila, 1911	Fariman / Padilla
MYRTLEWOOD, b m, 1932			
		Broomstick, 1901	Ben Brush / Elf
	Sweeper, 1909		
		Ravello II, 1896	Sir Hugo / Unco Guio
FRIZEUR, ch, 1916			
		Hamburg, 1895	Hanover / Lady Reel
	Frizette, 1905		
		Ondulee, 1898	St. Simon / Ornis

MYRTLEWOOD, b, 1932-1950. Bred by Brownell Combs (Ky.). Raced 3 yrs, 22 sts, 15 wins, $40,620. Champion sprinter and older female. Won Francis S. Peabody Memorial H, Hawthorne Sprint H (twice), Quickstep H, Lakeside H, Motor City H, Cadillac H, Ashland S, Keen H; 2nd Lincoln H; 3rd Crete H, Kentucky Jockey Club S. Dam of 11 named foals, 8 rnrs, 5 wnrs, 2 sw.

1938: Crepe Myrtle, b f, by Equipoise. Raced 1 yr, 4 sts, 1 win, $950. Dam of 7 foals, 6 rnrs, 3 wnrs, including **MYRTLE CHARM** ($81,830, champion 2yo filly). Granddam of **MYRTLE'S JET**, **MASKED LADY**, **Never Give In**, **My Captain**, **Jet's Charm**.

1939: **MISS DOGWOOD**, dk b f, by Bull Dog. Raced 3 yrs, 21 sts, 14 wins, $31,712. Won Kentucky Oaks, Steger H, Keeneland Special Event, Phoenix H; 2nd Prairie State S, Breeders' Futurity; 3rd Autumn H, Hawthorne Speed H. Dam of 9 foals, 9 rnrs, 7 wnrs, including **BERNWOOD** ($91,410), **BELLA FIGURA** ($56,970), **SEQUENCE** ($54,850), **Amiga** ($8,095). Granddam of **TUMIGA**, **GOLD DIGGER**, **DEDIMOUD**, **NOORSAGA**, **ALERT PRINCESS**, **PENINSULA PRINCESS**, **HERMOD**, **CARRIER X.**, **Ribchester**, **Royal Consort**.

1940: Sicklewood, b c, by Sickle. Raced 1 yr, 1 st, 0 wins, $0.

1941: **DURAZNA**, b f, by Bull Lea. Raced 3 yrs, 19 sts, 9 wins, $70,201. Champion 2yo filly. Won Beverly H, Sheridan H, Clang H, Prairie State S, Hawthorne Juvenile H, Breeders' Futurity; 2nd Match Race; 3rd Arlington Matron H, Washington Park Juvenile S, Modesty H. Dam of 5 foals, 5 rnrs, 4 wnrs, including **Myrtlemoud** ($50,775). Granddam of **QUEEN JANINE**, **MR. HINGLE**, **JOURNALETTE**, **Tuzana**.

1943: Gallawood, b f, by Sir Gallahad III. Unraced. Dam of 9 foals, 6 rnrs, 6 wnrs. Granddam of **MR. BRICK**, **JERONIA**.

1944: Spring Beauty, b f, by Sir Gallahad III. Raced 1 yr, 3 sts, 2 wins, $5,150. Dam of 8 foals, 8 rnrs, 7 wnrs, including **YOUNG MAN'S FANCY II** ($6,470), **Spring Tune** ($8,390), **Sonata II** ($535, in Eng). Granddam of **LADY WAYWARD**, **LYFORD CAY**, **Village Beauty**.

1945: Moonflower, b f, by Bull Dog. Raced 1 yr, 7 sts, 0 wins, $900. Dam of 4 foals, 3 rnrs, 2 wnrs, including **MOON GLORY** ($70,078). Granddam of **AQUA VITE**, **MOON SHOT**, **FINAL RETREAT**, **Gun Boat**.

1946: Bull Run, b c, by Bull Lea. Unraced. Sire of 101 foals, AEI 1.02.

1947: Bullfighter, b c, by Bull Dog. Raced 4 yrs, 37 sts, 9 wins, $29,385. Sire of 103 foals, AEI 0.86.

1949: Dragona, b f, by Bull Lea. Unraced. Dam of 7 foals, 7 rnrs, 6 wnrs, including **ROYAL ATTACK** ($168,952), **Slaipner** ($53,210). Granddam of **Shoo Fly**. Died 1972.

1950: Civic Virtue, b c, by War Admiral. Raced 1 yr, 4 sts, 0 wins, $1,300. Sire of 76 foals, AEI 0.70.

Cincinnati area. My Charmer was good enough to win the Fair Grounds Oaks at three in 1972. When it was time to retire her and pick a stallion, Castleman turned to young Seth Hancock, successor to his father Bull Hancock in management of Claiborne Farm. Given Castleman's price range, Hancock suggested Bold Reasoning.

The resulting Bold Reasoning—My Charmer foal was a burly, dark colt whom Castleman offered as a yearling at the Fasig-Tipton Kentucky sale of 1975.

148

The colt was purchased for $17,500 and was owned thereafter by a partnership of Dr. Jim Hill and his wife, Sally, and Mickey and Karen Taylor. They named the colt Seattle Slew, and he took them to the moon. Seattle Slew was the only horse in history to win the Triple Crown while undefeated, and he was a champion at two, three, and four. A near-fatal illness was overcome early in his four-year-old season, and he came back to win racing's first meeting of Triple Crown winners, outrunning the three-year-old Affirmed to win the Marlboro Cup of 1978. Seattle Slew won fourteen of seventeen races and earned $1,208,726. He was retired to Spendthrift Farm, by then under direction of another Brownell Combs, son of Leslie Combs II and great-nephew of the Brownell Combs who had raced the fifth dam, Myrtlewood.

Seattle Slew was subsequently moved to Robert N. Clay's Three Chimneys Farm in Kentucky and has added to the legend of Myrtlewood. He was America's leading sire in 1984, when his son Swale won the Kentucky Derby and Belmont Stakes. Seattle Slew's other champions include A.P. Indy, Slew o' Gold, Capote, and Landaluce, and he is the broodmare sire of the two-time Horse of the Year Cigar, plus Escena, Golden Attraction, among others.

The success of Seattle Slew brought buyers to the doorstep of My Charmer's owner, Castleman, and the mare was purchased by Warner L. Jones Jr. and William S. Farish. She subsequently foaled the English Two Thousand Guineas winner Lomond, by Northern Dancer, and other stakes winners Argosy and Seattle Dancer. A son of Nijinsky II, Seattle Dancer was sold for the all-time record price of $13.1 million for a yearling at the 1985 Keeneland summer sale. Even Leslie Combs II himself could hardly have dreamt of a descendant of Myrtlewood, or anyone else, bringing such a price when he first began to show off members of the family at Spendthrift cocktail parties.

At the time Warner Jones dispersed his Hermitage Farm stock, in 1987, My Charmer's Nijinsky II weanling filly brought $2.3 million, and My Charmer herself, at eighteen, was purchased by Allen Paulson for $2.6 million. My Charmer foaled unraced Allen's Charmer in 1989 and unraced Charmer's Gift in 1993, the same year of her death.

The reader will no doubt appreciate that the link between Myrtlewood's first foal and the modern Triple Crown winner and champion sire Seattle Slew illustrates the depth and breadth of the female family before us. There is no thought here to mention every important winner descending from Myrtlewood, close up or long term. However, it is interesting to note that the potency of the family was such that even some horses of no racing distinction overcame the attendant mediocrity of breeding opportunities. A case in point was Jet Jewel, a Jet Pilot colt from Myrtlewood's first daughter, Crepe Myrtle. Jet Jewel failed to place in six starts, but sired Mrs. Graham's 1957 juvenile co-champion, Jewel's Reward.

Moreover, it is from Crepe Myrtle that descend a number of other horses whose names are familiar in the 1980s and 1990s. Crepe Myrtle's granddaughter Masked Lady, for example, foaled the stakes winner Who's To Know, who in turn foaled graded stakes winner Angel Island, by Cougar II. Angel Island kept the pattern intact and foaled the international stakes horse Sharrood as well as Island Escape and Our Reverie. (Our Reverie won the My Charmer Handicap, keeping it all in the family.) It is also this branch of the family that produced the Sir Ivor mare Jolie Jolie, whose four stakes winners include the millionaire Jolie's Halo.

Mr. Prospector, et al

Myrtlewood's first foal, then, became ancestress in tail female of a Triple Crown winner and one of the great stallions of the final decades of the century. Myrtlewood's second daughter, Miss Dogwood, can claim a related distinction, for she is the third dam of Mr. Prospector. While he cannot claim any racing distinction comparable to Seattle Slew's Triple Crown, Mr. Prospector has pride of place among all stallions in total number of stakes winners, with 165. The stallion died at Claiborne Farm on June 1, 1999, at the age of twenty-nine.

Sired by Bull Dog, Miss Dogwood was foaled in 1939. Fitting nicely into her Kentucky heritage, Miss Dogwood won the Kentucky Oaks of 1942, as well as the Phoenix Handicap, which Keeneland rescued from the defunct Kentucky Association track. Miss Dogwood won two other stakes and placed in four more, including Devil Diver's Breeders' Futurity at Keeneland. Miss Dogwood nearly equaled her dam's racing mark, with fourteen wins in twenty-one starts, and she earned $31,712.

She became the dam of three stakes winners: Bernwood, Bella Figura, and Sequence. The Count Fleet filly Sequence matched that mark, producing Noorsaga, Hermod, and Gold Digger. A 1962 filly by the champion Nashua, Gold Digger was retained to race for Leslie Combs II and won the Gallorette Stakes twice, plus runnings of the Columbiana, Yo Tambien, and Marigold Stakes. Gold Digger was runner-up to Amerivan in the 1965 Kentucky Oaks.

Gold Digger followed the pattern of her immediate female ancestors in foaling three stakes winners herself: Gold Standard, Lillian Russell, and Mr. Prospector. Sired by the rapidly rising stallion Raise a Native, Mr. Prospector was consigned by Spendthrift to the 1971 Keeneland July yearling sale. Among those interested was trainer Jimmy Croll, who was searching on behalf of A. I. (Butch) Savin. Savin had been in the game long enough to conclude that a Florida farm owner, such as himself, had little chance of landing a top-class sire prospect unless he raced the colt in his own stable and therefore could keep him in the state if he so

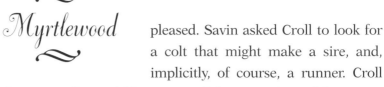

Myrtlewood

pleased. Savin asked Croll to look for a colt that might make a sire, and, implicitly, of course, a runner. Croll directed him to one of the great sires of the century, and Savin bought Mr. Prospector for $220,000 to top the Keeneland sale.

Mr. Prospector excited the crowd with his six furlongs in 1:07 4/5 at Gulfstream Park in the winter of 1973, just as Myrtlewood had startled her audiences with times a few seconds slower in the 1930s. Mr. Prospector's career was shortened by physical problems, and he entered stud with the image of a sprinter, having won the Gravesend and Whirlaway Handicaps. Croll's watchfulness led to the colt missing his two-year-old season, but might have saved Mr. Prospector from a breakdown so early that his initial opportunity at stud would have been seriously diminished. Initial X-rays did not reveal anything in the summer of 1972, when Croll was about to get the colt to the races, but the trainer, heeding the comments of his exercise rider and his own instincts, kept looking for the source of "a couple of bad steps." More X-rays from different angles turned up a minute spot, and Croll backed off. He did not have a two-year-old contender, but he still had a racehorse.

Although speed perhaps remained the hallmark of Mr. Prospector, both before and after he had become so successful that he was moved from Florida to Claiborne Farm in Kentucky, his offspring includes the Belmont Stakes winner and Horse of the Year Conquistador Cielo. Mr. Prospector also sired the versatile Gulch, who got Kentucky Derby and Belmont winner Thunder Gulch, while the Mr. Prospector colt Forty Niner won the Travers Stakes at one and a quarter miles. This was not a one dimensional phenomenon.

Mr. Prospector's runners also include such other important sires as Woodman, Fappiano, Gone West, and Miswaki, as well as champion fillies such as Ravinella, Golden Attraction, and Queena. Mr. Prospector led the American sire list and the broodmare sire list, each twice.

Gold Digger is also the second or third dam of numerous stakes winners, including Chief Bearhart, the North American champion turf horse and Breeders' Cup Turf winner in 1997.

More From Myrtlewood

Picking up the thread of Myrtlewood's own produce record, the Combs mare foaled a Sickle colt in 1940. Given the rather obvious combination name Sicklewood, he failed to place in his only start. The next year, in 1941, came Durazna, Myrtlewood's foal from the first crop of Calumet Farm's young sire Bull Lea. Durazna was the champion two-year-old filly of 1943, and she went out of her sex division to become so. She won the Breeders' Futurity and Prairie States Stakes over co-champion juvenile colt Occupy and also beat colts in the Hawthorne Juvenile. Durazna raced through four, winning nine of nineteen races and earning $70,201. She added stakes wins in the Beverly and Sheridan Handicaps, as well as the handicap named for her dam's old adversary, Clang.

Durazna made no immediate mark as a producer, but, over time, her brood did its share for the Myrtlewood dynasty. For example, Durazna's daughter Manzana foaled the stakes winner Journalette, in turn the dam of 1972 champion older mare Typecast. Durazna also foaled Querida, second dam of 1969 juvenile filly champion Tudor Queen, plus Irish champion juvenile filly Highest Trump and California stakes winner April Dawn. The name Highest Trump, in turn, is current today as the second dam of 1995 English champion Bahri, as well as being second dam of Ajina, champion three-year-old filly and Breeders' Cup Distaff winner of 1997.

Myrtlewood had no foal in 1942, then foaled Gallawood, an unraced filly by Sir Gallahad III,

the following year. The 1963 Sapling Stakes winner Mr. Brick and 1976 Hawthorne Derby winner Wardlaw were among the stakes winners descending from Gallawood in the first three generations.

In 1944, Myrtlewood bore another Sir Gallahad III foal, Spring Beauty. The filly won two of three starts and earned $5,150. Spring Beauty had an international career. As a broodmare, she spent several years in England, where she conceived her only stakes winner, a daughter of the distinguished stayer and sire Alycidon. This was Young Man's Fancy II, who was foaled after Spring Beauty's return to the United States. Young Man's Fancy II was sent back to England, where she won the Fifinella and Pretty Polly Stakes. A number of other stakes winners in North America, South America, and Europe trace to Spring Beauty.

Most prolific branch from Spring Beauty came through her stakes-placed Spy Song filly of 1954, Spring Tune. Spring Tune's foals included Village Beauty, a My Babu filly foal of 1960. Village Beauty produced four stakes winners, and one of them, Silent Beauty (by Creme dela Creme), added another Kentucky Oaks for the Myrtlewood family, in 1971, while flying the Spendthrift colors. (The Combses sold a lot of good fillies from the family, but occasionally had good luck in deciding which ones to keep.)

In 1945, Myrtlewood foaled the Bull Dog filly Moonflower, who made seven starts, placed, and earned $900. Moonflower produced the Norseman filly Moon Glory, who, in a nice touch, won the Durazna Stakes. She also won the Alcibiades Stakes and placed in the Spinster. Moon Glory later foaled multiple stakes winner Aqua Vite. Timepiece, a 1952 Eight Thirty filly from Moonflower, produced Frequently, who in turn foaled the international runner Jumping Hill, winner of the Royal Hunt Cup in England and the grade I Widener Handicap in the United States.

Myrtlewood

Myrtlewood's 1946 foal was another by Bull Lea, son of Bull Dog. The foal was named Bull Run and while never raced, he got the major winner Manassas and one other stakes winner at stud. Myrtlewood's mating then skipped back to the previous generation, and she foaled a 1947 colt by Bull Dog. He was Bullfighter, who won nine of thirty-seven races and earned $29,385, but garnered no stakes credentials. Like Bull Run, Bullfighter got two stakes winners, one of them a major winner, Vapor Whirl.

Myrtlewood had no foal in 1948, then produced her final filly in 1949. The last daughter was the Bull Lea filly Dragona, another who was unraced. Dragona foaled 1962 Santa Anita Derby winner Royal Attack, by Royal Charger. Myrtlewood's last foal was the War Admiral colt Civic Virtue, foaled in 1950. Civic Virtue placed and earned $1,300. Typically, he was given a chance at stud because of his pedigree, and he sired one stakes winner, Civic Pride.

At the time of Myrtlewood's retirement, historian Hervey had concluded that, as a racing filly, "under all tests she qualified for permanent remembrance. It now remains for Myrtlewood to do so in the final one, that of the breeding paddock." Myrtlewood produced eleven foals of which only five won and two won stakes, but the wellspring of quality would not be capped. She obliged history in her own way as seven of her foals were fillies. All seven left their mark at least to some extent through succeeding generations. Being an ancestress of Mr. Prospector and Seattle Slew surely qualifies Myrtlewood the broodmare for as much "permanent remembrance" as Myrtlewood the racing filly, and, of course, they are only part of the comfortable, lasting presence of her name. Hervey would have been pleased. ❖

152

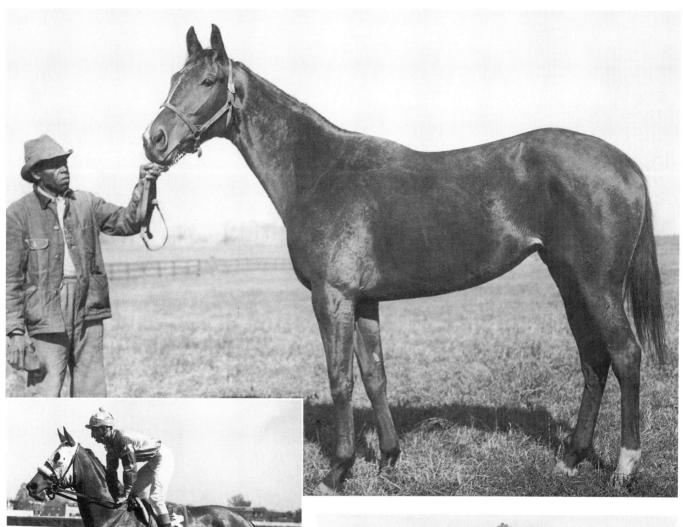

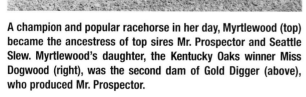

A champion and popular racehorse in her day, Myrtlewood (top) became the ancestress of top sires Mr. Prospector and Seattle Slew. Myrtlewood's daughter, the Kentucky Oaks winner Miss Dogwood (right), was the second dam of Gold Digger (above), who produced Mr. Prospector.

Myrtlewood

My Charmer (below), dam of Seattle Slew, is shown in 1987 with a full sister to world-record $13.1 million yearling Seattle Dancer, by Nijinsky II. Triple Crown winner Seattle Slew (right) has sired classic winners Swale and A.P. Indy, while Mr. Prospector (bottom) leads all stallions in total number of stakes winners.

No Class (bottom) defied her name by producing six stakes winners, including Eclipse Award winner Sky Classic and Canadian champion filly Classy 'n Smart (right). In turn, Classy 'n Smart produced the brilliant champion race mare Dance Smartly (below).

Rose Leaves

Rose Leaves (below, with her final foal, Dogpatch) made her contribution to the Thoroughbred breed through her influential son, Bull Lea (bottom, right). Bull Lea, who stood at Calumet Farm, was a five-time leading sire. Among his top progeny were Calumet's champion fillies Bewitch (top, right) and Twilight Tear (bottom, left).

Imported to the U.S. by Bull Hancock, Rough Shod II (below) established a dynasty at Claiborne and extended her influence back overseas, through her descendant, European leading sire Sadler's Wells (right).

Rough Shod II

Rough Shod II's daughter, Moccasin (left), is the only two-year-old filly to earn Horse of the Year honors. She later earned distinction as a broodmare with seven stakes winners, including Indian (pictured as a foal). Gamely (below, left), out of Rough Shod II's daughter Gambetta, was a champion filly for longtime Claiborne partner, William Haggin Perry. Leading sire Nureyev (below) descends from Rough Shod II through his dam, Special, a granddaughter of the subject mare.

Two Bob (below), who won the 1936 Kentucky Oaks, became the fifth dam of 1988 Kentucky Derby winner Winning Colors (right), one of only three fillies to win the vaunted classic. Two Bob's best runner was her daughter, Two Lea (bottom, right), who was a two-time champion and later produced 1958 Derby winner Tim Tam. Two Bob was the fourth dam of champion Chris Evert (bottom, left, foreground). Chris Evert is pictured with her 1976 filly Six Crowns, who became a stakes winner and the dam of champion Chief's Crown.

Vagrancy

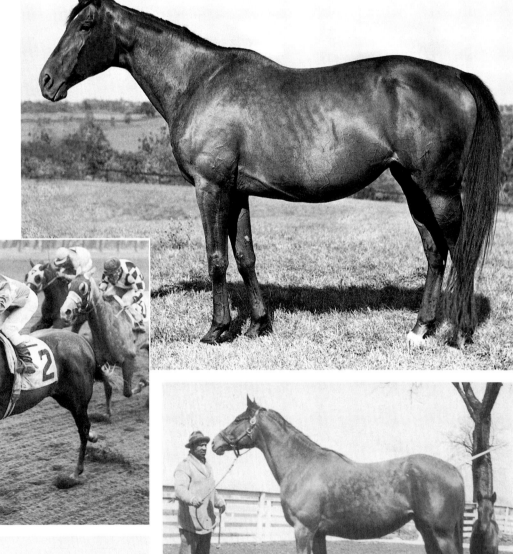

Vagrancy (top) was a champion race mare and top producer for William Woodward Sr.'s Belair Stud. Her dam, Valkyr (above), produced three other stakes winners, including Vicar (pictured as a foal). Vagrancy was the dam of three stakes winners, including English champion Black Tarquin (bottom, left), plus stakes producer Natasha, whose daughter Natashka (top, left) was a high-class racehorse and later Broodmare of the Year.

No Class

The career of No Class as a broodmare embodied the ongoing, repetitive theme of refuting her name. She produced six stakes winners, of which four were champions. Lest the fact that she and her produce were operating often in the cozy confines of the relatively small racing country of Canada tend to dampen this achievement, it should be noted that one of her champions, Sky Classic, won an Eclipse Award; another one produced the Eclipse Award winner and one-time leading distaff money-earner Dance Smartly.

The status of Canada as a fount of world-class horses took a dramatic upswing with the advent of Northern Dancer, winner of the Kentucky Derby and Preakness of 1964. Subsequently, Northern Dancer's sons, such as Nijinsky II, chipped more deeply into any lingering prejudice — a prejudice which had some relevance in earlier times when the sparsely populated country with the short racing season and short growing season had seemed unlikely to compete successfully at the top echelons of Thoroughbred racing and breeding.

Today, the Canadians have the best of both worlds: The records of such Dominion-breds as Northern Dancer, Nijinsky II, Fanfreluche, Deputy Minister, Sunny's Halo, and Glorious Song have long since rendered any prejudice obsolete; on the other hand, Canadians, when they so choose, still can see themselves as the underdog compared to the behe-moth geographically just below them, and so can muster extra pleasure in the international accomplishments of their equine sons and daughters.

The history of No Class is tied to such longing, and achievement, on two sides of the equine scene. Three decades ago, Ernie Samuel was reveling in his decision not to sell the show jumper Canadian Club when his partners felt the pressure to cash in on a good thing. Samuel thus preserved for himself the unsullied pleasures of watching Canadian Club and young rider Jim Day soaring over obstacles in Mexico City as they contributed to the Canadian equestrian team's show jumping gold medal in the 1968 Olympics.

The following year, another Canadian, jolly Jack Hood — owner of a school supply business — watched with similar enthusiasm as master trainer Horatio Luro orchestrated the owner's Sharp-Eyed Quillo toward victories in the classic Prince of Wales Stakes and the Quebec Derby.

These two strains of Canadian equine lore merged in 1975, when Samuel purchased a filly Hood had bred from the family of Sharp-Eyed Quillo. The filly was consigned in the name of the Gateway Farm of Roy Kennedy, who in time moved from Toronto to establish a farm and spearhead the advent of the Ocala Breeders' Sales Company in Florida. The filly in question was by Nodouble, and she cost Samuel $25,000 at the Canadian

		Star Kingdom, 1946	Stardust / Impromptu
	Noholme II, 1956		
		Oceana, 1947	Colombo / Orama
NODOUBLE, ch, 1965			
		Double Jay, 1944	Balladier / Broomshot
	Abla-Jay, 1955		
NO CLASS, b m, March 30, 1974		Ablamucha, 1947	Don Bingo / Sweet Betty
		Nasrullah, 1940	Nearco / Mumtaz Begum
	Outing Class, 1960		
		Track Medal, 1950	Khaled / Iron Reward
CLASSY QUILLO, dkb/br, 1969			
		Princequillo, 1940	Prince Rose / Cosquilla
	Quillopoly, 1958		
		Tonga, 1949	Polynesian / Tirl

No Class, b, 1974-1993. Bred by Jack Hood Farms (Ont.). Raced 3 yrs, 29 sts, 3 wins, $37,543. 2nd Yearling Sales S (R); 3rd Princess Elizabeth S (R). Dam of 8 named foals, 7 rnrs, 7 wnrs, 6 sw.

1980: Classy Cannonade, dkb/br g, by Cannonade. Raced 3 yrs, 20 sts, 1 win, $10,205.

1981: **CLASSY 'N SMART**, b f, by Smarten. Raced 1 yr, 9 sts, 5 wins, $303,222. Champion 3yo filly in Can. Won Canadian Oaks (R), Fury S (R), Bison City S (R), Ontario Colleen H (RT). 2nd Selene S, Duchess S, Canadian S (T). Dam of 8 foals, 3 rnrs, 3 wnrs, including **DANCE SMARTLY** ($3,263,835, Horse of the Year and champion 2 and 3yo filly in Can, champion 3yo filly, gr. I), **SMART STRIKE** ($337,376, gr. I), **Secret 'n Classy** ($183,104). Granddam of **Dance Brightly**, **Go Classic**.

1982: Barren.

1983: **GREY CLASSIC**, gr c, by Grey Dawn (Fr). Raced 4 yrs, 28 sts, 7 wins, $602,039. Champion 2yo colt in Can. Won Summer S (gr. IIIT), Laurel Turf Cup H (gr. IIIT), Connaught Cup S (RT), Coronation Futurity (R), Cup and Saucer S (RT); 3rd Arlington H (gr. IT), Mutual Savings Life Gold Cup (T), Fair Grounds Budweiser Breeders' Cup H (T). Died 1989.

1984: Barren.

1985: **REGAL CLASSIC**, ch c, by Vice Regent. Raced 3 yrs, 27 sts, 8 wins, $1,456,584. Champion 2yo colt in Can. Won Grey S (gr. III), Summer S (gr. IIIT), Eclipse S (gr. III), Marine S, Coronation Futurity (R), Prince of Wales S (R), Cup and Saucer S (RT), Plate Trial S (R); 2nd Breeders' Cup Juvenile S (gr. I), Ben Ali H (gr. III), Molson Export Challenge, Queen's Plate (R), Bull Page S (R); 3rd Hollywood Futurity (gr. I), Blue Grass S (gr. I). Sire of 292 foals, AEI 1.97.

1986: Barren.

1987: **SKY CLASSIC**, ch c, by Nijinsky II. Raced 4 yrs, 29 sts, 15 wins, $3,320,398. Champion 2yo colt, turf male, and older male in Can, champion turf male. Won Rothmans Ltd. International S (gr. IT; NCR, WO, 12 furlongs in 2:27.80), Turf Classic Invitational S (gr. IT; NCR, Bel, 12 furlongs in 2:24.50), Caesars International H (gr. IIT), Early Times Manhattan H (gr. IIT), Arlington H (gr. IIT), Grey S (gr. III), Summer S (gr. IIIT), Early Times Dixie H (gr. IIIT), King Edward Gold Cup H (gr. IIIT), Cup and Saucer S (RT), Canadian Maturity S (RT), Connaught Cup S (RT), Seagram Cup H (RT); 2nd Breeders' Cup Turf (gr. IT), Rothmans International H (gr. IT), Arlington Million (gr. IT), Early Times Turf Classic S (gr. IIIT), Clarendon S (R), Vandal S (R). Sire of 204 foals, AEI 1.56.

1988: Classic Slew, dkb/br f, by Seattle Slew. Unraced. Dam of 3 foals, 2 rnrs, 1 wnr, **Comet Kris** ($61,280).

1989: **CLASSIC REIGN**, ch f, by Vice Regent. Raced 2 yrs, 22 sts, 7 wins, $327,645. Won Mint Julep H (T), Canadian Maturity S (RT); 2nd Breeders' S (T), Dowager S (T), Wonder Where S (RT). NCR, CD, 8 furlongs in 1:34.68.

1990: Barren.

1991: Slipped.

1992: Foal died.

1993: **ALWAYS A CLASSIC**, ch c, by Deputy Minister. Raced 2 yrs, 8 sts, 6 wins, $388,648. Won Early Times Turf Classic S (gr. IT), Explosive Bid H (gr. IIIT), Mardi Gras H (T); 3rd Manhattan H (gr. IT). Sent to Tur 1998.

Thoroughbred Horse Society yearling sale at Woodbine. Samuel named her No Class.

At the time of the Olympic gold medal, and for a few years afterward, Samuel was operating on the thought of remaining in the show jumping world in a commercial capacity. He developed Sam-Son

Farm in the Toronto suburb of Milton, Ontario. Samuel was born in London, England, the son of a surgeon, but he was raised and educated in Toronto, where he took over and expanded the family steel business founded by a great-grandfather in 1855.

"We want to encourage and train promising young riders and horses," Samuel told the *Canadian Horse* magazine in 1968. "It's a fallacy to think that you have to pay a lot to end up with an Olympic standard horse. Young horses can be bought and schooled by their riders. We bought Canadian Club solely for Jim Day to ride in the last Olympics. Jim did all the schooling himself and produced a winner."

Samuel used to say that it was a "semi-coincidence" that he was dealing in part with Thoroughbreds in that endeavor. As the economics of major sports changed in response to the growing influence of television and commercialism, the realities of 1968 would not remain as applicable in later years, and Sam-Son gradually developed a relationship with Thoroughbred racehorse trainers, first Art Warner and then Glenn Magnusson.

By the latter 1970s, his commercial show jumping operation had been closed down, and Sam-Son was drawn into racing on the fashionable, but somewhat secluded, Ontario circuit that then included Woodbine, Greenwood, and Fort Erie. Day made the change, as well, and became Sam-Son's private trainer in some of Samuel's brightest days of success as a breeder and owner of racehorses.

Class Behind No Class

Jack Hood had bred No Class from Classy Quillo, a half-sister to Sharp-Eyed Quillo. There was an abundance of sire power, and more than a bit of distaff prowess, to the family. Sharp-Eyed Quillo's dam, Quillopoly, was sired by Princequillo, whom Luro had developed from a claimer into a major Cup winner in the 1940s and who quickly had ascended the fashion scale among American stallions.

Quillopoly was foaled from Tonga, she a daughter of 1945 Preakness winner Polynesian. Tonga had won the Del Mar Debutante of 1951 and the Sea Breeze Stakes at three in 1952. Her dam, Tiri, by Tick On, was out of the Gallant Fox mare Glamour-Girl.

Quillopoly foaled the stakes winners Allquillo and Baccalaureate, in addition to Sharp-Eyed Quillo. Following one of the more important patterns of the day, Hood sought the cross of Nasrullah and Princequilllo. Sharp-Eyed Quillo was by the Nasrullah stallion One-Eyed King, and Baccalaureate was by another Nasrullah stallion, Greentree Stable's Hopeful and Dwyer Stakes winner Outing Class.

The year before Quillopoly foaled Baccalaureate, and the same year Hood was applauding Sharp-Eyed Quillo's success, the mare foaled another Outing Class foal, the filly to be named Classy Quillo. She won two of fourteen races and earned $5,040. In the stud, Classy Quillo foaled the stakes winners Money By Orleans and Baraquillo. Earlier, she had produced No Class.

No Class, a foal of 1974, was sired by Nodouble, a hardy son of the Australian Horse of the Year Noholme II. Nodouble won nine major stakes in this country and was voted champion older horse of 1969 and 1970. He sired ninety-one stakes winners and led the North American sire list in 1981.

After Samuel purchased the Nodouble—Classy Quillo filly in 1975, she was sent to trainer Magnusson. Indicative of the quality of the Ontario Jockey Club circuit, she hooked up in her first start with the Northern Dancer filly Northernette, subsequently the winner of the Apple Blossom and Top Flight Handicaps and a full sister to Storm Bird. Northernette won, with No Class third. Nevertheless, No Class was tried next in stakes company and was fourth behind Nurso in the My Dear Stakes. She broke her maiden in her fourth start and later that year won once more. She was second in the Yearling Sales Stakes and third at one and one-sixteenth miles in the Princess Elizabeth Stakes. The latter found her beaten seventeen lengths, as her Sam-Son stablemate Loudrangle won by six lengths from Northernette, with No Class eleven lengths behind the runner-up.

No Class raced again at three and four, but managed only one win in nineteen combined starts during those seasons. She was retired with a record of three wins from twenty-nine starts and earnings of $37,543.

A Succession of Champions

The first foal of No Class was Classy Cannonade, a gelding by Kentucky Derby winner Cannonade and a moderate winner. Next came Classy 'n Smart, her first champion. That filly was sired by Smarten, whom trainer Woody Stephens had sent around the country to win a brace of graded three-year-old stakes just below the top rung. Classy 'n Smart was the champion three-year-old filly in her native Canada in 1984, when she won the Canadian Oaks, Fury Stakes, Bison City Stakes, and Ontario Colleen Handicap. She won five of her nine races and earned $303,222 in her only year of racing.

As a broodmare, Classy 'n Smart has been even better. Like her own dam, No Class, she eventually earned a Sovereign Award as her country's Broodmare of the Year. Most brilliant of her foals has been Dance Smartly, who came to the races under trainer Day in 1990. By then, Sam-Son had begun using the top echelon of stallions in Kentucky, while also supporting a number of the best Canadian-based stallions. Dance Smartly was by the leading sire Danzig, one of Northern Dancer's battalion of internationally important sons.

At two, Dance Smartly was Canada's champion two-year-old filly and showed the promise of her abilities to compete on the world stage when she was third behind Meadow Star in the Breeders' Cup

No Class

Juvenile Fillies. At three, Dance Smartly swept all before her. Over a range of distances up to one and a half miles, against colts and older fillies and mares, she won eight of eight and reigned as Horse of the Year in Canada and as North America's Eclipse Award winner among three-year-old fillies.

Dance Smartly prepped for Canada's Triple Crown by winning the country's one classic race designated solely for fillies, the Canadian Oaks. She then plunged onto the Triple Crown trail, becoming the only filly to sweep the Canadian version. She was dominant in the Queen's Plate, Prince of Wales Stakes, and Breeders' Stakes. The last-named race, which she won by eight lengths, tests Canadian three-year-olds at one and a half miles and concludes the Triple on turf.

Only a few weeks later, the $1-million Molson Export Million loomed ahead of Day, and right at home, at Woodbine. The temptation was great, and with Samuel's having become a leader within the Ontario Jockey Club, adding his glamorous filly to the field was definitely a positive. Against the previous year's North American juvenile colt champion, Fly So Free, Dance Smartly was not shaken, winning by two lengths over Shudanz.

One challenge remained, and it was exceptionally testing. Against a sterling collection of fillies and mares at Churchill Downs for the $1-million Breeders' Cup Distaff, Dance Smartly and her Sam-Son entrymate, Spinster Stakes winner Wilderness Song, went off at 1-2. Bettor confidence in the validity of the Canadian form was ratified as jockey Pat Day brought the bay filly up from fourth to assume control in the upper stretch, then held off the fine three-year-old Versailles Treaty to win by one and a half lengths. The beaten field included the year's champion older filly, Queena.

Dance Smartly led a record-setting year for Sam-Son, as Samuel established a new North

156

American one-year earnings mark of $6,881,902. Another Canadian outfit, Kinghaven Farm, had topped the list for North American owners the previous year.

Dance Smartly's four-year-old season was short and anti-climactic, as she did not come exactly right after a lengthy layoff, although she did add the Canadian Maturity. Her career earnings of $3,263,835 set a record for her gender.

After Dance Smartly, Classy 'n Smart foaled the Mr. Prospector colt Smart Strike, who emerged briefly as a contender for the highest honors among three-year-olds. In the summer of 1995, Smart Strike, with Mark Frostad by then training most of Sam-Son's horses, dropped below the border for dashing triumphs at Monmouth Park in the Salvator Mile and the Philip H. Iselin Handicap. In the latter, he defeated Eltish and Serena's Song. Smart Strike went wrong soon thereafter and was highly prized by the Kentucky stallion establishments, being acquired to stand at William S. Farish's Lane's End Farm.

No Class for much of a decade followed a pattern of being barren in alternate years. Such a mare is frustrating to farm manager and breeder alike, but when she produces champions regularly on her good years, she is not likely to be culled.

For No Class the sequence was just that: 1981, champion Classy 'n Smart; 1982, barren; 1983, champion Grey Classic; 1984, barren; 1985, champion Regal Classic; 1986, barren; 1987, champion Sky Classic. Tammy Balaz, one of Samuel's daughters, said the mare never had a health problem, but tended to foal late. "We used to joke that it was her way of self-regulating, to build up so she could foal a champion the next year." She then had two more foals in successive years, but only one was a stakes winner.

Grey Classic was a colt by Grey Dawn II and collected a Sovereign Award as Canada's champion two-year-old of 1985, when he won Woodbine's major autumn tests, the Coronation Futurity and Cup and Saucer Stakes. He raced on through five and won the Laurel Turf Cup and Connaught Stakes, eventually earning $602,039 with seven wins in twenty-eight starts.

Regal Classic was by the top Canadian sire Vice Regent, a son of Northern Dancer. A few years before Dance Smartly, Regal Classic came close to competing with similar success in both the United States and Canada. By late autumn of 1987, the glistening chestnut had clinched Canadian juvenile honors, also winning the Cup and Saucer and Coronation Futurity double. At Hollywood Park, he was good enough to be second to Success Express in the Breeders' Cup Juvenile.

The following spring, Regal Classic contested the Kentucky Derby and Preakness, but, while he was not outclassed, he was unable to break into the top ranks. At home, he did win the classic Prince of Wales Stakes, and the following year he added the Eclipse Handicap. Regal Classic won eight of twenty-seven races and earned $1,456,584 and now stands at Prestonwood Farm in Kentucky. He is the sire of a Queen's Plate winner, Regal Discovery, as well as Prince of Wales winner Stephanotis.

In the summer of 1989, Samuel and his family were wont to gravitate to the stall of a big, leggy chestnut two-year-old whenever showing visitors their stable at Woodbine. The colt was sired by Nijinsky II, the heroic Canadian who had won England's Triple Crown and then returned to North America to follow in the gaudy stud success of his sire, Northern Dancer.

Named Sky Classic, the Nijinsky II colt was destined to be the most accomplished of the champion runners foaled from No Class. His size and scope were not best geared specifically for early sprints, but Sky Classic thrived on the later fall races at Woodbine and he earned yet another juvenile

No Class

Sovereign, winning the Grey Stakes, Summer Stakes, and the Cup and Saucer. The following year, however, instead of improving on the experience of Regal Classic, Sky Classic won nothing. In five starts, he managed two placings, but one augured well for his maturity: He was second in the Rothmans International.

At four, Sky Classic was kept on grass, and he earned recognition as best older horse in Canada overall, as well as best on grass. That year, he won the Rothmans, as well as four other stakes. At five, Sky Classic reached full bloom, and he was the champion turf horse of North America.

Sky Classic won five major races from spring into autumn, and they came at four tracks. Reveling in opportunities for middle-distance runners and one and a half-mile horses on grass, Sky Classic won Pimlico's Early Times Dixie and Belmont's Early Times Manhattan. In Chicago, he took the Arlington Handicap. At Atlantic City, he won the Caesars International, and back at Belmont he capped the year by winning the Turf Classic. A narrow loss to Fraise in the Breeders' Cup Turf at Gulfstream Park did not tip the voting scales, and he was voted the Eclipse Award for males on grass.

Sky Classic won fifteen races in twenty-nine starts and earned $3,320,398. Again, the fashion of the family had been recognized, and Josephine Abercrombie had bought an interest in Sky Classic during his racing career. Upon retirement, he was sent to her Pin Oak Stud in Kentucky, where as a young sire he has been represented early by stakes winners both in North America and Europe.

In 1988, No Class foaled Classic Slew, an unraced filly by Triple Crown winner Seattle Slew. The next year came Classic Reign, a Vice Regent filly who won the Mint Julep Handicap and Canadian Maturity and was second in the Breeders' Stakes.

As she neared twenty, No Class was barren in 1990 and aborted in 1991, and then her Seattle Slew foal of 1992 died. Nevertheless, her success was not yet complete. In 1993, at the age of nineteen, No Class foaled the Deputy Minister colt who would be named Always a Classic. Developing late, Always a Classic showed the quality to contend for an Eclipse in the turf division. At four, he won the 1997 Mardi Gras and Explosive Bid Handicaps in New Orleans, then scored in the Early Times Turf Classic at Churchill Downs before an injury stopped him. Always a Classic won six of eight races and earned $388,648. He has been sent to stand in the burgeoning breeding industry of Turkey.

No Class died in 1993. The irony of her name only became more pronounced as her career unfolded. ❖

Rose Leaves

mong enduring themes in which American Thoroughbred racing can take pride over much of the 20th Century was the history of Calumet Farm. For the most part, it was a sweet ride, although it had to endure the death of its founder and, at one point, a prolonged slump. Sadly, Calumet was driven into bankruptcy by an heir and in-law in a matter still resonating in courts. Fortunately, a white knight appeared in the person of Henryk de Kwiatkowski to purchase the farm and return to pristine condition the fields beloved by Lexington, Kentucky citizens in and out of the horse business.

The early history of Calumet, as developed by Warren Wright Sr., is reviewed in the chapter on Blue Delight. Like Blue Delight, Rose Leaves was a key benefactress to Wright's developing of a vaunted stable, although she was never owned by Calumet. She was instead the dam of the most important yearling sale purchase of Wright's career. Indeed, insofar as what Bull Lea did for his buyer over a prolonged period, he might be regarded as ranking with Man o' War as the most historic sale yearling of the century. Without Bull Lea, Calumet undoubtedly would have succeeded; with Bull Lea in the stallion barn, it achieved a unique glory.

Rose Leaves was nineteen when she produced Bull Lea. As a foal of 1916 and the granddam of Kentucky Derby winners as late as 1957, she repre-

sented various eras. Rose Leaves was sired by Ballot, who had won more than a dozen stakes including the 1908 Suburban Handicap, in which he carried 127 pounds and defeated the three-year-olds King James (ninety-eight pounds) and Fair Play (111). Ballot raced in England at five, winning the Select Stakes. He was among the leading American sires annually from 1917 through 1924. Ballot lived to be thirty-three years old and his last birthday was occasion for a party at Keeneland.

Rose Leaves's dam was the Trenton mare Colonial, who was imported by James Ben Ali Haggin. Colonial was owned briefly by W. O. Parmer, who is identified as breeder of Rose Leaves. Colonial then became the property of Hal Price Headley and William Baldwin Miller at Beaumont Farm near Lexington. Colonial was a noteworthy producer of winners and was also the third dam of Calumet Farm's first champion, the filly Nellie Flag.

Rose Leaves raced for J. W. McClelland. She failed to place in six starts at two at Saratoga and Jamaica. Her first foal was bred by E. F. Simms, owner of Xalapa Farm, and her subsequent foals were bred by Coldstream Stud. She had ten foals, all of which raced, and she numbered six stakes winners among a total of seven winners. The first was Ruddy, a 1920 McGee gelding who won a dozen races from 174 starts from two through nine and earned $11,413. Ruddy got his black type by

		Friar's Balsam, 1885	**Hermit** / Flower of Dorset
	Voter, 1894		
		Mavoureen, 1888	Barcaldine / Gaydene
BALLOT, ch, 1904			
		Lowland Chief, 1878	Lowlander / Bathilde
	Cerito, 1888		
		Merry Dance, 1879	Doncaster / Highland Fling
ROSE LEAVES, br m, 1916			
		Musket, 1867	Toxophilite / Mare by West Australian
	Trenton, 1881		
		Frailty, 1877	Goldsbrough / Flora McIvor
COLONIAL, b, 1897			
		Paradox, 1882	Sterling / Casuistry
	Thankful Blossom, 1891		
		The Apple, 1886	**Hermit** / Black Star

Rose Leaves, br, 1916-1939. Bred by W.O. Parmer (Ky.). Unraced. Dam of 10 named foals, 10 rnrs, 7 wnrs, 6 sw.

1920: RUDDY, b c, by McGee. Raced 8 yrs, 174 sts, 12 wins, $11,413. Won Rainbow Selling S.

1923: ESPINO, br c, by Negofol. Raced 3 yrs, 37 sts, 9 wins, $56,310. Won Lawrence Realization S, Saratoga Cup; 2nd Belmont S, Champagne S, Huron H, Jockey Club Gold Cup; 3rd Walden H, Oceanus H, Wood S, Dwyer S, Withers S, Brookdale H, Saratoga Cup. Sire of 96 foals, AEI 2.07.

1924: BOIS DE ROSE, b/br c, by Negofol. Raced 3 yrs, 31 sts, 3 wins, $20,450. Won Empire City Derby; 2nd Belmont S, Junior Champion S; 3rd Dwyer S, Withers S. Sire of 40 foals, AEI 0.60.

1925: Barren.

1926: Ch f, by My Play.

1927: Pan of Roses, b f, by Peter Pan. Raced 1 yr, 10 sts, 0 wins, $0. Dam of 9 foals, 9 rnrs, 8 wnrs.

1928: B c, by Pot au Feu.

1929: Slipped.

1930: Dead foal.

1931: Ch c, by Pot au Feu. Died 1932.

1932: NECTARINE, dk b f, by Bull Dog. Raced 3 yrs, 26 sts, 11 wins, $10,265. Won Miami Beach H; 3rd Joseph Mclennan Memorial H. Dam of 8 foals, 7 rnrs, 7 wnrs, including

APPLEKNOCKER ($55,475), **Pindus** ($31,200). Granddam of **YING AND YANG**, **PASSADO**, **Cavort**, **Fresh Meadow**, **Sweet Woman**.

1933: Swift Rose, ch f, by Lord Swift. Raced 1 yr, 2 sts, 0 wins, $0. Dam of 7 foals, 7 rnrs, 3 wnrs. Granddam of **Hesarocket**.

1935: BULL LEA, br c, by Bull Dog. Raced 3 yrs, 27 sts, 10 wins, $94,825. Won Widener H, James C. Thorton Memorial H, Autumn H, Blue Grass S, Kenner S, Pimlico H; 2nd Champagne S, Hopeful S, Classic S, Continental S, Narragansett Special, Potomac H, McLennan Memorial H; 3rd Aquidneck H, Saratoga Special. Sire of 376 foals, AEI 4.33. Died 1964.

1936: Ten Carat, ch c, by Jean Valjean. Raced 1 yr, 2 sts, 0 wins, $0. Sire of 50 foals, AEI 0.27.

1937: Summer Time, br f, by Bull Dog. Raced 3 yrs, 15 sts, 1 win, $1,480. Dam of 9 foals, 8 rnrs, 8 wnrs, including **Unification** ($24,015). Granddam of **ROYAL LIVING**, **RILEY**, **STEVE'S LARK**, **BLUE BALLAD**, **Hail Navy**.

1938: Barren

1939: DOGPATCH, br c, by Bull Dog. Raced 5 yrs, 62 sts, 13 wins, $38,828. Won Shevlin S; 2nd Babylon H, Del Mar H, Walter Connolly H; 3rd Speed H, Breeders' Futurity. Sire of 115 foals, AEI 1.15. Died 1954.

winning the Rainbow Selling Stakes at two.

Rose Leaves had no live foal for three of the next six years, but the two colts she produced during those seasons were both good-class stakes winners and pronounced stayers. Both were sired by Negofol, sire of the 1928 Belmont Stakes winner Vito. The first Negofol—Rose Leaves colt was Espino, foaled in 1923. He had enough early maturity to place in the Champagne Stakes and the next spring placed as well in the Wood Memorial and Withers Stakes before running second to Crusader in the Belmont Stakes. The longer the distance, the more Espino thrived. In the Saratoga Cup at one and three-fourths miles, he defeated fellow three-year-old Display, with the hardy mare Princess Doreen third, and in the one and five-eighths-mile Lawrence Realization, he turned the tables on Crusader, with Mars third. Crusader defeated him again, however, in the Jockey Club Gold Cup, perhaps costing Espino recognition as the top staying three-year-old of his year. Espino won a total of nine races from thirty-seven starts from two through four and earned $56,310. Although not in the class of Bull Lea, Espino was Rose Leaves' first significant son at stud. His ten stakes winners included 1944 Belmont Stakes winner Bounding Home and 1937 older distaff champion Esposa.

The second Negofol—Rose Leaves colt was of a similar stripe, although not as successful as Espino. Named Bois de Rose, the 1924 model also placed in stakes at two and in the Withers the following spring. In the Belmont Stakes, Bois de Rose finished second to Chance Shot. He got his one stakes triumph in the Empire City Derby and won a total of three races from thirty-one starts, earning $20,450.

For C. B. Shaffer's Coldstream Farm, Rose Leaves had the unplaced Peter Pan filly Pan of Roses in 1927. Then came three more years without a registered foal. A 1931 colt, by Pot au Feu, died the following year. Rose Leaves foaled a filly in 1932 by Coldstream's new stallion Bull Dog, who had been imported from France by Shaffer at about the time his full brother Sir Gallahad III was beginning to ascend the American sire ranks. The first of Rose Leaves' Bull Dog foals was named Nectarine, and she won the 1936 Miami Beach Handicap for Mrs. Emil Denemark, defeating the male Whopper. Nectarine won eleven of twenty-six races and

earned $10,265. In the stud, she foaled the Dick Welles Handicap winner Appleknocker, but Nectarine's lasting importance stemmed more from an unraced Display filly she foaled in 1939.

The Display filly was named Bramble Bug and she became the dam of stakes winner Passado and two stakes-placed runners, Cavort and Sweet Woman. A Roman filly, Sweet Woman in turn foaled the 1952 juvenile filly champion, Sweet Patootie, by Alquest. Sweet Woman also foaled the speedy two-year-old stakes winner I'm For More, by Olympia, and at nineteen produced another stakes winner in Lady Swaps, by Swaps. Stakes winners Macedonia, Gold Box, and Wild Note also descended from Bramble Bug.

In 1933, Rose Leaves had an unplaced Lord Swift filly named Swift Rose, then missed another year before being returned to Bull Dog. The result of that second mating with Bull Dog was Bull Lea. Before addressing the wonders of that colt, let us complete the review of Rose Leaves. The mare foaled the unplaced Ten Carat, by Jean Valjean, in 1936, and the winner Summer Time, by Bull Dog, in 1937. Summer Time foaled Easy Living, who in due course became the dam of two good runners, San Juan Capistrano Handicap winner Royal Living and Dwyer and Lawrence Realization winner Riley. Easy Living also foaled Save Time, a War Admiral mare who produced a pair of Canadian stakes winners, Dorothy Glynn and Captain Vancouver. Dorothy Glynn was in the first crop of Northern Dancer, and so a full sister (Summer Time) to the great sire Bull Lea became the third dam of a daughter of a great sire from another segment of the century.

Rose Leaves' daughter Summer Time also foaled Big Harvest, the second dam of Oil Royalty, one of the first major winners raced by John R. Gaines of Gainesway Farm.

Rose Leaves had no foal in 1938, and then in 1939, at the age of twenty-three, had her final foal before her death that same year. The last foal was another Bull Dog colt. Named Dogpatch, he gave the old mare a sixth stakes winner on her record when he won the Shevlin Stakes. He placed in five other stakes, including the Breeders' Futurity and Del Mar Handicap, and won a total of thirteen races from sixty-two starts to earn $38,828. Such was the sire power of the family, and the opportunity afforded many of its males, that even with such modest credentials to take into stud, Dogpatch — brother to Bull Lea — sired fourteen stakes winners, or twelve percent from foals.

A Bull Like No Other

We return now to Bull Lea. Without him, Rose Leaves would have been a significant mare, dam of five stakes winners and with two colts that placed in the Belmont as well as being the tail-female ancestress of a champion filly. As the dam of Bull Lea, Rose Leaves became revered as the mare that foaled a five-time leading sire and four-time leading broodmare sire.

Entered in the Coldstream consignment to the Saratoga yearling sale in 1936, the Bull Dog—Rose Leaves colt attracted considerable attention. Calumet owner Wright went to $14,000, topping by $400 the immediate underbid, entered by Ethel Mars' Milky Way Stable. Brandywine Stable owner Donald Ross also had taken part in the bidding action. The price was $4,000 lower than the top price paid for Saratoga yearlings that year; Milky Way got both of the $18,000 lots. Only one additional yearling sold for more than Bull Lea's price.

Ben A. Jones and his son, Jimmy, were to be the trainers most associated with Calumet's great years, but they had not joined Calumet at the time Bull Lea came to the races. He was trained by F. J. Kearns. Although a half-brother to a pair of late developing Belmont Stakes-type colts, Bull Lea, son

of Bull Dog, came to hand quickly enough to win a maiden event in his second start in the summer of his two-year-old season. He was competitive in the Arlington Futurity and placed in the Saratoga Special and Hopeful. The Belmont Futurity was the premier race for two-year-olds in those days, and Bull Lea was progressing toward it when he finished second in the Champagne, but a minor lameness caused him to miss the key target.

The following spring, Bull Lea defeated two-year-old champion Menow in the Blue Grass Stakes and, like Nellie Flag before — and a battalion afterward — took Calumet's devil red and blue silks to the post of the Kentucky Derby with the status of a top contender. He was second choice to Fighting Fox, but both finished unplaced. Ironically, it was Ben A. Jones who sent out his first Derby winner, saddling Lawrin for Woolford Farm. Bull Lea also ran unplaced in the Preakness Stakes.

In addition to the Blue Grass, Bull Lea won the Kenner Stakes, Pimlico Handicap, Autumn Stakes, and James C. Thornton Memorial Handicap, but it was his victory in the 1939 Widener Handicap at four which ranked with the Blue Grass as his best achievements as a racehorse. The Widener found him getting one and a quarter miles, which perhaps had seemed beyond his scope as the speediness attributed to Bull Dog may have obliterated the memory of half-brother Espino. In the Widener, Bull Lea received seven pounds from Stagehand and dominated through the closing stages under jockey Irving Anderson. The Widener was, at that time, the most important race yet won by Calumet and it seemed to presage a fine handicap season for Bull Lea, but ankle trouble soon sent him off to stud. Bull Lea had won ten races from twenty-seven starts and earned $94,825.

His first crop, foaled in 1941, established him as a young sire of exceptional merit, for it included both two-year-old fillies who shared championship honors in that division in 1943, namely Durazna and Twilight Tear. At three, Twilight Tear proved one of the great fillies when she won fourteen of seventeen races, ended her campaign with a defeat of older male champion Devil Diver, and was named Horse of the Year. A later developing member of Bull Lea's first crop was the 1947 Horse of the Year, the gelding Armed.

By then, the Jones boys were under the Calumet shed. Calumet had broken through with a first Kentucky Derby winner and Triple Crown winner in Whirlaway, by Blenheim II, in 1941, and now with Bull Lea they had a seemingly innumerable caravan of high-caliber contenders, not just for the Derby, but for every division. In 1947, the year Armed was Horse of the Year, two Calumet two-year-olds by Bull Lea swept juvenile honors: Bewitch among fillies and Citation among colts. Citation was pronounced by the elder Jones as the best horse of all time, and the great jockey Eddie Arcaro spent a good deal of his career placing Citation as the best of all the great horses he rode. At three in 1948, Citation made the grind of the Triple Crown appear nothing more than three Saturdays of controlled exercise. That year, he won nineteen of twenty races, and it mattered not where he ran, what the distance was, or how closely his races were spaced.

He defeated older horses in the winter at three, threw in a victory in the Jersey Stakes amidst the three classics in the Triple series, and won in Florida, New Jersey, Kentucky, Maryland, New York, Illinois, and California, from February through December. On Sept. 29, Citation won the Sysonby at one mile; three days later, he won the Jockey Club Gold Cup at two miles!

Ankle trouble cost Citation his four-year-old year and worried the Joneses for the next two years, but since Wright wanted the horse to become the first million-dollar earner, they continued with him. He achieved the goal at six, winning the Hollywood Gold Cup, after Wright's death. Wright's widow continued the farm and later married Adm. Gene Markey.

Bull Lea had emerged as America's leading sire for the first time in 1947, and he repeated as the leader in 1948 and again in 1949. It was in 1949 that his son Coaltown deputized for Citation, sharing Horse of the Year honors with Capot. Citation had been Bull Lea's first Derby winner, and in 1952, Calumet's Hill Gail became his second. Five years later, Calumet's Bull Lea colt Iron Liege filled in for Calumet's favored Bull Lea colt, Gen. Duke, when the latter was injured, and became the sire's third Derby winner. The next year, Bull Lea became the broodmare sire of a Derby winner, in Tim Tam.

Bull Lea also led the sire list in 1952 and 1953, for a total of five times, and he led the broodmare sire list four consecutive years beginning in 1958. In addition to Citation, Durazna, Armed, Bewitch, Twilight Tear, and Coaltown, Bull Lea sired other year-end champions Real Delight, Next Move, and Two Lea — nine champions in all. His total of fifty-seven stakes winners (fifteen percent from foals) also included Bubbley, Beau Prince, Faultless, Good Blood, Level Lea, Mark-Ye-Well, Twosy, and Yorky. Bull Lea died in 1964 and was buried in the Calumet cemetery, where a statue of him had already been given a place of honor.

Despite its prolonged triumphs, the saga of Bull Lea was not without its strange twist: His sons, so accomplished at the racetrack, were individually and collectively disappointing at stud. Citation began with the Preakness winner Fabius in his first crop, and followed up with champion Silver Spoon, but he was a letdown at only four percent stakes winners (twelve). Coaltown never got a stakes winner, while Hill Gail surprised by getting the English Two Thousand Guineas winner Martial among little else. Gen. Duke died without being able to enter stud, Iron Liege was soon sold to Japan, while Yorky and Beau Prince got one stakes winner each.

Faultless was a moderate success at five percent stakes winners, and one of Bull Lea's lesser sons, Bull Page, sired the Canadian Triple Crown winner New Providence and the Queen's Plate winner Flaming Page, thus becoming the broodmare sire of Nijinsky II. However, Bull Page was not a consistent success and had been sent to Western Canada before his grandson's fame was achieved.

The Bull Lea mares created a more melodic chorus. They produced more than 100 stakes winners, including classic winners Tim Tam, Quadrangle, and Gate Dancer, plus such other distinguished individuals as Idun, Leallah, A Gleam, Bramalea, Bardstown, Barbizon, Restless Wind, Advocator, Pucker Up, and Lady Golconda (dam of Forego).

Both the renaissance and decline of Calumet through the 1970s and into the early 1990s were wrapped around the glamorous homebred racehorse and sire Alydar. Bull Lea's name was present in two lines of descent to Alydar's dam, Sweet Tooth. Thus, the Calumet monarchy of long ago has its echoes even today. ❖

Rough Shod II

 or nearly three centuries, Americans have looked to England specifically, and Europe in general, as the sources of bloodstock importations. The varying economics of the times, and of individuals, have been such that the former colonists often have had to scrap for the less-distinguished half-siblings to this or that classic winner, while, in other eras, American breeders were raiding the motherland for the very best.

The Hancock family, owner of Claiborne Farm for three generations, has played both roles. A. B. Hancock Sr. looked a bit below the classic fashion to import Sir Gallahad III, but was shopping at the top of the pyramid when he brought home Blenheim II. Similarly, his son, A. B. (Bull) Hancock Jr., went bargain hunting when he bought Rough Shod II, whereas there were other days when he plucked the likes of Nasrullah, Nijinsky II, Tulyar, and Sir Ivor. The present master of Claiborne, Seth Hancock, has been acutely successful in turning out individuals that the Europeans breeders and owners have coveted.

The heritage, career, and subsequent influence of Rough Shod II embody each of these patterns. When Bull Hancock bought her in England in 1951, Rough Shod II was typical of one scenario: representing a classic family, but individually of such mediocrity that the price was not spectacular (although she ranked in the top twenty mares by

price at the Newmarket December sale of 1951). Two decades later, descendants of her daughters were eagerly embraced by Continental buyers. In the 1990s, the name Rough Shod II smiles at us from behind the pages of history, showing up in the tail-female pedigrees of such internationally renowned stallions as Sadler's Wells and Nureyev.

The brood of Rough Shod II is as English as apple pie, and as American as shepherd's pie — and vice versa.

The names "rough shod" and "bogside" do not immediately sound like equations for the heights of fashion. Nevertheless, the little course of Bogside was the site of the only racing triumph from seven starts of Rough Shod II.

The filly was foaled in 1944. She was bred by Maj. H. S. Cayzer. At three, she was sent up for auction and brought 1,600 guineas. Four years later, she was returned to the Tattersalls sale ring in Newmarket, consigned by another fellow with a military title, Lt. Col. E. Shirley, and Hancock bought her for slightly more than twice the earlier figure, 3,500 guineas. At the time, she had produced one foal, Sollander (by Solferino), a colt of no distinction.

The diamond-in-rough aspect of Rough Shod II lay in her female family. Rough Shod II was by the speed sire Gold Bridge, but from the Yorkshire Oaks winner, Dalmary. The latter was by the great stallion Blandford, himself sire of Epsom Derby

		The Boss, 1910	**Orby** Southern Cross II
	Golden Boss, 1920		
GOLD BRIDGE, ch, 1929		Golden Hen, 1901	Chevele d'Or Hazlehen
		Diadumenos, 1910	**Orby** Donnetta
	Flying Diadem, 1923		
ROUGH SHOD II, **b m, 1944**		Flying Bridge, 1911	Bridge of Canny Gadfly
		Swynford, 1907	John o' Gaunt Canterbury Pilgrim
	Blandford, 1919		
DALMARY, br, 1931		Blanche, 1912	White Eagle Black Cherry
		Simon Square, 1904	St. Simon Sweet Marjorie
	Simon's Shoes, 1914		
		Goody Two Shoes, 1899	Isinglass Sandal

Rough Shod II, b, 1944-1965. Bred by Harold S. Cayzer (Eng.). Raced 1 yr in Eng, 7 sts, 1 win. Dam of 11 named foals, 8 rnrs, 7 wnrs, 4 sw. Sent to USA 1952.

1951: Sollander, br c, by Solferino. Raced 3 yrs in Eng, 10 sts, 0 wins, $0.

1952: **GAMBETTA**, b f, by My Babu. Raced 2 yrs, 12 sts, 6 wins, $28,738. Won Susan S, Debutante S; 3rd Pollyanna S. Dam of 7 foals, 6 rnrs, 6 wnrs, including **GAMELY** ($574,961, champion 3yo filly and older female), **STARETTA** ($145,297), **Terminator** ($94,062), **Gambrosia** ($13,710), **Zonah** ($10,955). Granddam of **CELLINI, TAKE YOUR PLACE, DRUMTOP, SITZMARK, GEORGE SPELVIN, LADY BRILLIANCE, MESSINA, Birthday List, Super Charge, Zonely, Flinging Star**. Died 1965.

1954: Rough Morning, b f, by Arise. Unraced. Dam of 4 foals, 4 rnrs, 3 wnrs, including **Froid** ($14,087). Granddam of **Attention Getter**.

1955: Ruffrullah, ch f, by Nasrullah. Raced 3 yrs, 24 sts, 3 wins, $10,750. Dam of 2 foals, 2 rnrs, 1 wnr, **Riot** ($55,540).

1956: Dark Fate, dk b c, by Dark Star. Raced 4 yrs, 67 sts, 6 wins, $17,060.

1957: Foal died.

1958: Barren.

1959: **RIDAN**, b c, by Nantallah. Raced 3 yrs, 23 sts, 13 wins, $635,074. Champion 2yo colt. Won Florida Derby, Arlington Futurity, Washington Park Futurity, Arlington Classic, Bluegrass S, Palm Beach H, Hibiscus S, Hyde Park S, Prairie State S; 2nd Preakness S, Travers S, Bahamas S, American Derby, Flamingo S; Seminole H; 3rd Kentucky Derby, Aqueduct S. Sire of 323 foals, AEI 1.84. Sent to Aust 1976.

1960: Barren.

1961: **LT. STEVENS**, b c, by Nantallah. Raced 2 yrs, 26 sts, 9 wins, $240,949. Won John B. Campbell H, Palm Beach H, Saranac H; 2nd Valley Forge H, Fayette H, Choice S, Jerome H, Discovery H, American Derby, Lamplighter H, Arlington Classic; 3rd Grey Lag H, Donn H, Princeton H, Benjamin Franklin H. Sire of 408 foals, AEI 2.09. Died 1985.

1962: Gay Shoes, dk b f, by Double Jay. Unraced. Died 1964.

1963: **MOCCASIN**, ch f, by Nantallah. Raced 3 yrs, 21 sts, 11 wins, $388,075. Horse of the Year and champion 2yo filly. Won Gardenia S, Matron S, Selima S, Spinaway S, Test S, Phoenix H, Alcibiades S; 2nd Barbara Fritchie H, Columbiana H; 3rd Acorn S, Ben Ali H, Four Winds H. Dam of 9 foals, 8 rnrs, 7 wnrs, including **APALACHEE** ($94,834, champion 2yo colt in Eng and Ire, Eng-I), **NANTEQUOS** ($64,391), **BELTED EARL** ($34,129, champion sprinter and older male in Ire), **BRAHMS** ($4,534), **FLIPPERS** ($247,739), **SCUFF** ($110,723), **INDIAN** ($67,272). Granddam of **EBROS, HAIL ATLANTIS, TOLTEC, Syrdario, Explosive, Mexican Honey**. Died 1986.

1964: **Thong**, b f, by Nantallah. Raced 3 yrs, 22 sts, 5 wins, $50,036. 2nd Alcibiades S; 3rd Selima S, Golden Rod S. Dam of 13 foals, 13 rnrs, 10 wnrs, including **KING PELLINORE** ($631,605, gr. I), **THATCH** ($89,791, champion 2yo colt in Ire, champion miler in Eng, Eng-I), **LISADELL** ($30,267, Eng-II), **ESPADRILLE** ($63,228), **Marinsky** ($17,372, in Eng and Ire), **Dusty Boots** ($65,747), **Stratford** ($3,960, in Eng and Ire). Granddam of **NUREYEV, YEATS, Fairy Bridge, BOUND, FATHERLAND (Ire), NUMBER, FESTIVAL HALL, GOLDEN DOME, Lisaleen, Rosa Mundi**. Died 1986.

1965: Cleat, b c, by Sir Gaylord. Unraced. Died 1968.

winner and leading American sire Blenheim II. Dalmary was out of Simon's Shoes, who also had foaled Carpet Slipper, dam of two classic winners in three years. Carpet Slipper's 1937 filly, Godiva, won a wartime One Thousand Guineas and Oaks in England in 1940; Carpet Slipper's 1939 foal, Windsor Slipper, swept Ireland's Triple Crown of 1942. (From later generations, the influential French stallion Val de Loir and additional English Guineas/Oaks winner Valoris were foaled from close representatives of the family.)

The classic antecedents of Rough Shod II were perhaps responsible for her having been accepted into the 1951 book of Two Thousand Guineas winner My Babu, to whom she was in foal when purchased for America that year. Her ownership was ultimately assigned to Thomas Girdler, retired president of Republic Steel.

The annual volume *American Race Horses* of 1961 described Girdler as a "singer of lusty songs and teller of ten thousand salty yarns." Had fate granted him good health for another decade or so, Girdler would have had a supply of true tales to tell via the exploits of his acquisition from England. The My Babu foal which Rough Shod II was carrying when purchased at Newmarket was foaled at Claiborne the next spring. Given the name Gambetta, she was bred in Girdler's name and carried his colors to victory in the Susan Stakes and Churchill Downs' Debutante Stakes of 1954. Gambetta became the first of Rough Shod II's remarkable string of major producing daughters, as will be described in due time.

The Nadir Reversed

In 1953, Rough Shod II was barren, then in 1954, she produced Rough Morning, an unraced filly by Arise; the stallion was a Travers winner, but an indifferent sire. Rough Shod II was bred in 1954 to Claiborne's new star, Nasrullah, but the resulting filly, Ruffrullah, was not much of an improvement on Arise's results. In 1956 came Dark Fate, by Kentucky Derby winner Dark Star, and he, too, was a moderate racehorse.

Things got worse before they got great. In 1957, Rough Shod II's foal died, and in 1958, she was barren. In the spring of 1958, she was bred to Nantallah, a young Nasrullah stallion who had flashed impressive speed in winning four of seven races and placing in a pair of two-year-old stakes. Claiborne Farm does not ordinarily have a place for non-stakes winners in its stud barn, but Nantallah was a worthwhile exception (as, in later years, Seth Hancock would find Danzig to be).

At the time the Nantallah—Rough Shod II foal was a yearling, Girdler's poor health was prompting him to sell his bloodstock, and the colt was purchased to race for a partnership of Mrs. Moody Jolley, Ernest Woods, and John L. Greer. The price was $11,000. Mrs. Jolley's husband, Moody Jolley, had trained the Nasrullah colt Nadir to win the Garden State Stakes for Claiborne, and he found the big, rakish, blaze-faced Rough Shod II colt so similar in appearance that he crafted the name Ridan — Nadir spelled backwards.

Trained by the Jolleys' young son, future Hall of Famer LeRoy Jolley, Ridan was one of the most charismatic colts of his era. At two, he burst onto the scene early, winning over three furlongs at Hialeah in the winter. By season's end, he remained unbeaten in seven races, including the Arlington Futurity, Washington Park Futurity, and two lesser stakes. So dominant were most of his performances that he shared juvenile championship honors with Crimson Satan, although a splint stopped him before he could face off with such crack colts as Sir Gaylord, Jaipur, Donut King, and the co-champion.

At three, Ridan won the Florida Derby, Arlington Classic, Blue Grass, and Hibiscus Stakes. The 1962 season included duels of unusual dramatics; Ridan

was involved in three, and won only once. In the winter, he out fought the gritty filly Cicada to plant his white face on the wire of the Florida Derby just in time. In the spring, he and Greek Money sparred to the wire of the Preakness Stakes. Ridan's jockey invoked his impromptu Marquess of Manny Ycaza Rules and aimed his left elbow toward his rival, and then had the nerve to claim foul, but nothing could get Ridan's nose to the wire in time. Then, in August, Ridan dueled with Jaipur for the length and depth of the one and a quarter-mile Travers Stakes, again taking the worst of a photo-determined difference.

Ridan added one additional stakes at four and was retired with thirteen wins in twenty-three starts and earnings of $635,074.

Rough Shod II was barren in 1960, then foaled another Nantallah colt in 1961. Also a handsome, white-faced fellow, this colt was named Lt. Stevens. He lacked the brilliance of Ridan, but had plenty of class and won the John B. Campbell, Palm Beach, and Saranac Handicaps. He won nine of twenty-six races and earned $240,949. Ridan and Lt. Stevens were both successful stallions, without being leaders. Lt. Stevens carved an additional notch for himself as the broodmare sire of Kentucky Derby winner and Horse of the Year Alysheba.

Girdler had passed away, and Hancock moved to maintain Rough Shod II at his Claiborne Farm and was the breeder of Lt. Stevens and Rough Shod II's subsequent foals. By then, he had formed a lasting partnership with the Virginia sportsman William Haggin Perry whereby half of the Claiborne-bred foals each year were owned jointly, and over more than three decades, this arrangement thrived at the racetrack, breeding shed, and sale ring.

As a young man, Hancock had fallen for the racehorse Double Jay and contrived to bring him to Claiborne, where the horse became a notable stallion. Hancock sent Rough Shod II to Double Jay in

1961, but the result, Gay Shoes, a filly, never raced and died at two. By the time Rough Shod II was to be mated again, in the spring of 1961, Ridan had suggested that the cross with Nantallah was workable, and Hancock responded accordingly.

Rough Shod II's next Nantallah foal was another, large, lengthy, white-faced number, but this one was a filly. Raced in the Claiborne colors and trained by future Hall of Famer Harry Trotsek, Moccasin was something not seen before or since: Balloting for championships had begun in 1936, and distaffers Twilight Tear, Busher, All Along, and Lady's Secret have been Horse of the Year; two-year-olds Native Dancer, Secretariat, and Favorite Trick also have won, or shared the title. Combining those characters, however, only one two-year-old filly has been named Horse of the Year, and that was Moccasin. She was voted Horse of the Year by the Thoroughbred Racing Associations, one of the major polls then operating separately before Eclipse Award balloting unified American championships as of 1971.

Moccasin was a dazzling, 16.2-hand chestnut with three white socks. At two, she won eight of eight, including five of the most important tests for the division: the Gardenia, Matron, Selima, Spinaway, and Alcibiades. Her margins were as gaudy as her appearance, i.e., the Matron by six lengths, the Alcibiades by fifteen. Remarkably, there was another filly in her crop who seemed a valid challenge as the year wound down. This was Priceless Gem, who defeated the shining colt champion Buckpasser in the Futurity and also won the one-mile Frizette. Hancock had planned to stop on Moccasin after the Alcibiades in Kentucky, but recognized the validity of a champion pro-tem taking on all comers. He sent her back East for the one and one-sixteenth-mile Selima. The meeting never came off, for Priceless Gem bucked shins and was finished for the year. Moccasin and jockey Larry

Adams won the Selima by five, and, since it was there, added the Gardenia by two and a half lengths. (The two fillies were both priceless as broodmares: Priceless Gem foaled the French icon Allez France; Moccasin's produce record is reviewed later in this chapter.)

As distinguished a horseman as horse-worldly Kentucky ever produced, A. B. (Bull) Hancock Jr. never had many days as frustrating as the afternoon of Moccasin's return at three in the spring of 1966. The booming voice and grinding jaw told it all. The filly had lost, and at the hometown track of Keeneland. Hancock found no fault with trainer or jockey, but resolved never again to turn out such a filly between her two-year-old and three-year-old seasons. (Hancock died of cancer only a half-dozen years later.)

Although Moccasin never again was dominant, she remained a high-class winner at three and four, winning the Test against fillies and the Phoenix against males. She was retired with eleven wins in twenty-one starts and earnings of $388,075.

In 1964, Rough Shod II foaled her third Nantallah foal, and, while she did not win a stakes, the filly Thong proved more than able to add to the family's modern distinction. Thong placed in the Alcibiades, Selima, and Golden Rod, and won five of twenty-two starts from two through four to earn $50,036. Her descendants bring this matter up to date into the late 1990s, among them Nureyev and Sadler's Wells.

Rough Shod II had one remaining foal, Cleat, a 1965 foal by Sir Gaylord, but he was unraced and died at three. Rough Shod II herself died in 1965 at the age of twenty-one. She had had eleven foals, of which eight raced, seven won, and four won stakes.

A Dynasty Knowing No End

Backtracking to the first American-bred foal of Rough Shod II, we revisit Gambetta, the My Babu filly who was also the first of her major producing daughters. Also absorbed into the Claiborne fold, Gambetta produced the 1964 Bold Ruler filly Gamely. Raced in the Perry colors, Gamely was a champion distaffer at three, four, and five. She won sixteen races from forty-one starts and earned $574,961. Her grit and class carried her to wins in a succession of America's top distaff races East and West, including two runnings of the Beldame, plus the Santa Margarita, Alabama, Vanity, and Diana. She also scored over males.

Gamely had only two foals, but one of them was Cellini. A 1971 colt by Claiborne champion Round Table, Cellini was the top-priced yearling in the dispersal prompted by the death of Bull Hancock. He was bought for $240,000 by Jonathan Irwin of BBA (Ireland). Sent aboard, Cellini won the group I Dewhurst Stakes and ranked third among English-raced two-year-olds of 1973. (It was a remarkable year in England for the family of one-time Bogside winner Rough Shod II. Topping the two-year-old list was Moccasin's colt Apalachee, while Thong's son Thatch was the year's champion miler.)

Gambetta, Rough Shod II's first stakes winner, also foaled dual stakes winner Staretta, a Dark Star filly who in turn produced the National Stallion Stakes winner Lady Brilliance, by Globemaster. Others representing this branch of the Rough Shod II family also include multiple English group winner Asteroid Field, by Forli.

In 1958, Gambetta foaled the Nasrullah filly Zonah, who placed in the Mermaid Stakes. Bred to Round Table, Zonah foaled the distinguished grass distaffer Drumtop, who defeated males consistently, winning such races as the Canadian International, Hialeah Turf Cup, Bowling Green, Camden, and Edgemere. Although distance was Drumtop's game, her three stakes winners included the high-class sprinter and major stallion Topsider, by Northern Dancer. A full brother to Drumtop, Take Your Place won the group I Observer Gold Cup in England in 1975, and a full sister, stakes-placed Zonely, foaled Hollywood Derby winner Victory Zone. Sitzmark, Regal Rumor, Table the Rumor, Grand Jewel, and others also descend from Gambetta.

Rough Shod II's most distinguished runner, Moccasin, was also a superb producer. She had nine foals, of which eight raced, and seven won: All seven were stakes winners.

As mentioned above, one of them was Apalachee. A Round Table colt foaled in 1971, Apalachee went into the Irish racing stable of John A. Mulcahy, with whom Bull Hancock had been developing a business connection at the time of his death. Apalachee was the top-ranked two-year-old raced in England in 1973, following his victory in the Observer Gold Cup. He placed in the Two Thousand Guineas at three, and later was a successful sire back in America.

A second champion from Moccasin was Belted Earl, by Damascus, a 1978 foal who was sent abroad and ranked as Ireland's champion sprinter of 1982. Moccasin's sons Nantequos, by Tom Rolfe, and Brahms, by Round Table, also won stakes in Ireland, and Nantequos returned to win the Chula Vista Handicap in California. Another son, Indian, by Round Table, was a stakes winner in this country.

In 1980, Moccasin at seventeen was bred to Perry's 1979 Belmont Stakes winner Coastal. By and large, Coastal was not a particularly successful sire by Claiborne standards, but Moccasin's filly, Flippers, won the Golden Rod, Pocahontas, and Pleasant Hill Stakes, and placed in grade II company. Flippers in turn foaled 1990 Santa Anita Oaks winner Hail Atlantis, by Seattle Slew, and Hail Atlantis to date is the dam of stakes winner Stormy Atlantic.

Yet another stakes winner from Moccasin was Scuff, a 1979 filly by the Argentine superstar Forli, sire of Forego and Thatch. Scuff won the Kilijaro, Bally-Park Place, and Ocean City Stakes.

She then foaled Ebros, winner of the grade II Round Table Handicap.

Thus Moccasin the grand race mare and Gambetta the more modest race mare founded branches of the family which have accounted for the major winners named here as well as a continuing tide of influence. Nevertheless, as matters stand in early 1999, it is Thong who, among Rough Shod II's daughters, takes pride of place as a producer of ongoing international influence. This is the case even though Thong was some distance below Moccasin as a runner and foaled four stakes winners to her older sister's seven.

Thong's first was the aforementioned Thatch, a 1970 Forli colt who was champion two-year-old in Ireland and champion miler in England. Then came the Round Table colt King Pellinore, who was a classics-placed stakes winner in Ireland, before returning to the United States to win the Oak Tree Invitational, Champions Invitational, and other top races, earning more than a half-million dollars in the 1970s.

Thong also foaled Espadrille, a Damascus filly who won the Busanda Stakes and is the antecedent of major winners. Thong's 1971 Forli filly, Lisadell, won group races in England and Ireland and is the dam of Irish stakes winners Fatherland, Golden Dome, and Yeats.

Sword Dance, the 1988 Del Mar Handicap winner, who is the sire of Marlin and other 1990s stakes winners, is out of Lisadell's Secretariat filly Rosa Mundi, as is steeplechase champion Corregio.

Among Thong's foals, however, it is Special who has been the most extraordinary. A 1969 filly by Forli—Thong, Special was unplaced in her only start. It is just as well, for hanging around the racetrack any longer would only have delayed her entry into stud; this observation admittedly is a perversion of the entire exercise of breeding to race, but Special is, indeed, a special case.

Bull Hancock had preferred to breed to race

rather than sell, but his will recognized an economic reality favoring the market insofar as a succession was concerned. Seth Hancock shares his father's feeling that he was better equipped as a breeder and owner than a hawker of wares, and he brought the Claiborne approach back to some racing of homebreds as soon as was feasible. Claiborne has continued to market some of its stock, however, and in the summer of 1978, its Keeneland summer yearling consignment included a flashy Northern Dancer colt from Thong's daughter Special. The colt topped the sale at $1.3 million. Purchased by Stavros Niarchos, he was given the light-on-his-feet name of Nureyev, and he did the great ballet dancer of that name proud. He was first across the wire in each of his races, although disqualified from his most important one, England's Two Thousand Guineas.

Nureyev's importance at stud has been in the same league as his sire, Northern Dancer, and the latter's other sons such as Nijinsky II, Lyphard, Danzig, and Sadler's Wells. Nureyev twice has been the leading sire in France, where his runners include the spectacular 1997 Prix de l'Arc de Triomphe winner, Peintre Celebre. Theatrical, Miesque, Spinning World, Zilzal, and Soviet Star are but a few other of his 100-plus stakes winners.

In 1975, Rough Shod II's daughter Thong foaled Fairy Bridge, by the Travers Stakes winner Bold Reason, a half-brother to Never Bend. Fairy Bridge was sold to Ireland. Her four stakes winners include a sire to rank with, or perhaps above, Nureyev. In the 1981 Northern Dancer colt Sadler's Wells, Fairy Bridge produced an Irish two-year-old champion and Two Thousand Guineas winner. At stud, Sadler's Wells rapidly rose to the top in Europe. He quickly passed the 100 stakes winners mark and has been leading sire in England, France, and Ireland a composite of eleven times. His string of distinguished winners includes Salsabil, Old Vic, Northern Spur, Carnegie, In the Wings, Barathea, and Opera House.

Special's daughter Fairy Bridge was also the dam of three other stakes winners besides Sadler's Wells. They are Tate Gallery, Fairy Gold, and Puppet Dance. Fairy Bridge's lesser runners include Fairy King, who failed to place but who has joined full brother Sadler's Wells as an important sire; Arc winner Helissio is one of Fairy King's major winners.

To return to Special, she also foaled the 1984 Nijinsky II filly Bound, who won the Churchill Downs Budweiser Breeders' Cup Handicap and placed in the grade I Acorn and various other stakes. Bound later foaled the stakes winner Limit. Yet another daughter of Special was Number, also by Nijinsky II. Number won three graded stakes in this country and is the dam of three major winners: Numerous, Jade Robbery, and Chequer.

So, as the purchase of Rough Shod II approaches the half-century mark, oceans have been crossed, and crossed again. The distinction between what is "European" and what is "American" in bloodstock grows more vague, but the continuing impact of the family seems secure. ❖

Two Bob

The tale of Two Bob is one of those which bridges centuries. In more-or-less modern generations, it was built partially on a sire line regarded as American for many years, involved the re-blending with European strains, and it has produced hard-hitting fillies (including a Kentucky Derby heroine) as well as classic colts on both sides of the Atlantic. Chief's Crown and Winning Colors have been among the more recent representatives.

In more distant stanzas, the female ancestry of Two Bob traced directly back to the 1840s, to the famed mare Reel, who was a celebrated racer of the pre-Civil War South. Reel then produced Lecomte, the only horse to defeat the vaunted Lexington, and Prioress, who won the 1857 Cesarewitch to become the first American-bred ever to win an important English race. Reel was the eighth dam of Two Bob.

Two Bob was a foal of 1933 and was sired by The Porter, whose tail-male grandsire was the late-19th-Century star Ben Brush. The Porter was a tough little colt who was said to need the courtesy of mathematically rounding upward to be described as standing fifteen hands high. He was a foal of 1915 and was raced by Cmdr. J. K. L. Ross and then E. B. McLean. He scrimmaged with the likes of Exterminator, Sir Barton, Omar Khayyam, Sun Briar, and Cudgel. The Porter acquitted himself nobly in that company, winning twenty-six of fifty-four races. He went to stud first at McLean's place in Virginia and then was transferred to Mare's Nest Stud, the Kentucky farm which John Hay Whitney established before assuming co-ownership of Greentree Stud on the death of his mother. The Porter sired thirty-three stakes winners and led the sire list of 1937.

Two Bob, by The Porter—Blessings, by the imported Chicle, was bred by Whitney's cousin, C. V. Whitney, and was foaled in 1933. This was only some three years after C. V. Whitney had been handed his family's racing miter and mantle in the third generation, following the death of his father, Harry Payne Whitney. Two Bob bobbed and weaved amidst various ranks of American racing early, competing in $3,500 claiming company at times as a two-year-old. This figure was far more respectable than it would be in more recent years, and it was not the only occasion when the Whitney stable was willing to run a filly where she seemed to belong at a given time. A quarter-century later, C. V. Whitney's Silver Spoon ran in $8,000 claiming company before climbing the steps to championship status.

Two Bob had the hardiness of her sire, and toughness was a quality she passed along. She had already raced twenty-five times before she ran in the Kentucky Oaks in the spring of 1936. She had won four races and in her last start before the Oaks had finished second to Jean Bart in a handicap at

Pimlico. There were no cell phones, fax machines, or Web sites available at the time, but racing has always gotten its news distributed with dispatch. Prior to the running of the Oaks, the announcer at Churchill Downs reported the results of the Preakness: Jean Bart had finished third behind Bold Venture and Granville. Churchill fans, knowing their past performances, suddenly saw Two Bob in a different light. The Whitney filly, who had opened at 4-1, went off at 6-5, and home she strolled. She thus became the first of four Kentucky Oaks winners raced by C. V. Whitney. Two Bob raced on for a total of five years, making ninety-four starts, winning twelve races, placing in thirty others, and earning $22,170. She did not win any other stakes, but kept good company, often competing against males. She placed in a half-dozen stakes, and in overnight races had victories over Whopper, White Cockade, and Sparta.

The young Whitney had many business interests, as well as political ambitions, and he did not in his first decade as an owner pursue as constant and deep a bloodstock program as he soon would. After Two Bob was retired at six in 1939, she was sold to Emil Denemark, who the next year resold her to Calumet Farm. Thus, Two Bob won a Kentucky Oaks for one of America's most prominent outfits of the century and would produce winners for another.

The development of Warren Wright Sr.'s Calumet Farm is described in chapters on Rose Leaves and Blue Delight. By the time Two Bob began producing, Calumet already had in place its budding young stallion Bull Lea. All three of Two Bob's stakes winners were by that great sire.

Derbys and Crowns Abound

From the standpoint of bridges to the present, Two Bob's first foal, Twosy, is her most prominent, although as a racemare she was eclipsed by full sisters Two Lea and Miz Clementine. A foal of 1942, Twosy, by Bull Lea, was originally named Two. She

was a solid racemare, although the company of Twilight Tear and other mid-1940s Bull Lea fillies left her somewhat in the shadows. She won three stakes among an impressive twenty-one victories from fifty-two starts from two through five, earning $101,375. In addition to taking the Sagamore Stakes, Carroll Handicap, and Colonial Handicap, Twosy finished second in several of the top juvenile filly races, including the Matron and Arlington Lassie. The Matron marked one of several runner-up finishes to the extraordinary filly Busher.

Twosy had six foals, of which five raced, and four won. None won stakes, but her daughter Twice Over was to become the dam of stakes winners Two Relics and Miss Carmie. Twice Over was by the Kentucky Derby winner Ponder and was acquired by Preston Madden of Hamburg Place, thus assigning some of the Two Bob treasure to yet another of the great old Kentucky farms. (This was not the first time a Madden had bought into the family; Preston's grandfather, master horseman John E. Madden, once purchased Two Bob's third dam, Sanctuary, from C. V. Whitney's father.) Miss Carmie, Twice Over's 1966 filly, was sired by T. V. Lark, a colt acquired at the races by Preston Madden and later to emerge as America's leading sire. Donald Sucher, owner of Echo Valley Farm in Kentucky, bought Twice Over with Miss Carmie at her side. Miss Carmie won the Clipsetta Stakes, giving her black type to boost the market breeding operation of Echo Valley. To the cover of the superb racehorse, but moderate sire, Swoon's Son, Miss Carmie foaled an attractive filly who was purchased by Carl Rosen.

There is a tendency for horses named for people to disappoint both the namer and the namesake. The 1971 Swoon's Son—Miss Carmie filly was a noteworthy exception. She was named for the tennis champion Chris Evert, with whom Rosen was associated in producing a line of sports clothing.

		Ben Brush, 1893	Bramble Roseville
	Sweep, 1907		
		Pink Domino, 1897	Domino Belle Rose
THE PORTER, b, 1915			
		St. Leonards, 1890	St. Blaise Belladonna
	Ballet Girl, 1906		
		Cerito, 1888	Lowland Chief Merry Dance
TWO BOB, **ch m, 1933**			
		Spearmint, 1903	Carbine Maid of the Mint
	Chicle, 1913		
		Lady Hamburg II, 1908	Hamburg Lady Frivoles
BLESSINGS, b, 1925			
		Friar Rock, 1913	Rock Sand Fairy Gold
	Mission Bells, 1919		
		Sanctuary, 1911	Broomstick Vespers

TWO BOB, ch, 1933-1953. Bred by C.V. Whitney (Ky.). Raced 5 yrs, 94 sts, 12 wins, $22,170. Won Kentucky Oaks; 2nd Governor's H; 3rd Washington H, Christmas H, Miami Beach H, Lady Baltimore H, E. Phocion Howard Memorial H. Dam of 7 named foals, 7 rnrs, 7 wnrs, 3 sw.

1942: TWOSY, b f, by Bull Lea. Raced 4 yrs, 52 sts, 21 wins, $101,375. Won Colonial H, Sagamore S, Carroll H; 2nd Matron S, Cleopatra H, Correction H, Princess Pat S, Arlington Lassie S; 3rd Modesty S. Dam of 6 foals, 5 rnrs, 4 wnrs, including **Smileytown** ($31,201). Granddam of **TWO RELICS, MISS CARMIE, Coloquill**. Died 1975.

1944: Great Spirit, ch g, by Sun Teddy. Raced 10 yrs, 88 sts, 15 wins, $31,135.

1946: TWO LEA, b f, by Bull Lea. Raced 4 yrs, 26 sts, 15 wins, $309,250. Champion 3yo filly and older female. Won Hollywood Gold Cup, Santa Margarita H, Cleopatra H, Vanity H, Princess Doreen S, Artful S, Ramona H, Children's Hospital H (NTR, BM, 8½ furlongs in 1:41.60), San Mateo H; 2nd Modesty S, Santa Anita Maturity, Bay Meadows H, Milady H; 3rd Santa Anita H. Dam of 8 foals, 6 rnrs, 5 wnrs,

including **TIM TAM** ($467,475, champion 3yo colt), **ON-AND-ON** ($390,718), **PIED D'OR** ($152,513). Granddam of **TARBOOSH, SON ANGE, HE'S AN ANGEL, SEW FOR FOUR, Turn Here, Twin Buttes**.

1947: Mostest, ch c, by Blenheim II. Raced 7 yrs, 94 sts, 16 wins, $61,775. Died 1956.

1950: Bob Away, ch g, by Whirlaway. Raced 7 yrs, 102 sts, 15 wins, $25,684. 2nd Rodeo H.

1951: MIZ CLEMENTINE, b f, by Bull Lea. Raced 4 yrs, 36 sts, 16 wins, $267,100. Won California Derby (NTR, Tan, 9 furlongs in 1:49), Hollywood Oaks, New Castle S, Cinema H, Sea Breeze S, Las Flores H, Vagrancy H, Pollyanna S, California Oaks, Goose Girl S, Yerba Buena H (NTR, Tan, 8 furlongs and 70 yards in 1:40.80); 2nd Santa Anita Maturity, Arlington Lassie S, Santa Margarita H, San Fernando S, Clang H. Dam of 2 foals, 2 rnrs, 2 wnrs. Granddam of **BEST TURN**. Died 1962.

1953: Captain Morgan, b c, by Bull Lea. Raced 4 yrs, 37 sts, 2 wins, $10,875. Sire of 32 foals, AEI 0.45. Died 1975.

The equine Chris Evert was a champion, too. She won the New York Filly Triple Crown among ten wins in fifteen career starts to reign as Eclipse Award-winning three-year-old filly of 1974.

In the stud, Chris Evert produced a pair of stakes-winning fillies in Six Crowns and Wimbledon Star. Six Crowns was named in recog- nition that both sire and dam had won Triple Crowns, for she was by Secretariat. (The dam's Triple had a non-pejorative asterisk, since one of the races, the Acorn, was run in two divisions.) For Rosen's family, Six Crowns produced the noble Chief's Crown, named for the late Carl Rosen's nick- name. Chief's Crown, by Danzig, was champion two-year-old of 1984, when he won the first of all Breeders' Cup races. At three, Chief's Crown won the Marlboro Cup, Travers Stakes, and Flamingo, and placed in all three of the Triple Crown races. His successes in the stud included a prestigious addition to the legacy when his son Erhaab won the Epsom Derby of 1994. Chief's Crown was also the sire of Chief Bearhart, 1997 Breeders' Cup Turf winner and champion grass horse.

In addition to Chief's Crown, Six Crowns foaled Classic Crown, a Mr. Prospector filly who won the grade I Frizette and Gazelle in the late 1980s.

In 1973, Miss Carmie (great-granddaughter of Two Bob) foaled another stakes winner by a stallion who had been a high-class race horse but disappointing sire. The stallion in this case was Bold Hour, and the filly was All Rainbows, who won the Poquessing, Mademoiselle, and Bi-Centennial Pageant among seven wins in seventeen races. Returned to Echo Valley, All Rainbows in 1985 foaled a roan filly by the French Two Thousand Guineas winner Caro. The filly grew into a large, leggy, powerful type.

Named Winning Colors, she dominated males in the Santa Anita Derby. Trained by D. Wayne Lukas and racing for the immensely successful stable of Eugene Klein, Winning Colors made history in the spring of 1988 when she led from the start and held off Forty Niner to win the Kentucky Derby by a neck. She followed Regret (1915) and Genuine Risk (1980) as the third filly to win the Derby. The win came thirty years after the Derby victory of a grandson of Two Bob, Tim Tam. Winning Colors was the champion three-year-old filly that year, and she concluded her season with a stunning effort in the Breeders' Cup Distaff, in which the unbeaten older filly Personal Ensign barely caught her at the wire.

Two Lea and Miz Clementine had seemed to typify the family in earlier years, as rugged Amazon sorts of mares at the races, able to take on the best

colts of their times. Winning Colors was a compelling repetition of her own family history.

Among other stakes winners tracing in the female line from Twosy have been Delay of Game, Hometown Queen, Revasser, Spicy Award, Classic Fame, Exbourne's Wish, Hiwaya, Beyton, Preakness third-place finisher Paristo, Two Timing, South African group I winner Lambent Light, 1990s Japanese star Silk Phoenix, Green Means Go, Missed the Storm, and 1998 Frizette Stakes winner Confessional.

Champion Mare, Champion's Dam

Twosy had been the first foal of Two Bob. In 1943, Two Bob was barren, then in 1944 she foaled Great Spirit, a gelding by Sun Teddy. While not of high class, Great Spirit had the family durability. He made eighty-eight starts from three through twelve, won fifteen races, and earned $31,135. In 1945, Two Bob had no foal.

Returned to Bull Lea, Two Bob produced the filly Two Lea in 1946. Two Lea had as tough a constitution as one could wish, but she had bad feet from the beginning, and her lengthy, albeit interrupted, career was a masterpiece from the hands of Calumet trainers Ben A. Jones and his son Jimmy. She was born with an imperfect left foreleg and was beset at one time or another by a range of maladies from ringbone to pus pockets to a splint.

Two Lea won once from three races at two in 1948, then at three came on to win six of seven, including the Cleopatra, Princess Doreen, and Artful Stakes. Typical of Calumet of the time, a stablemate, Wistful, swept the old filly Triple Crown of the Kentucky Oaks, Pimlico Oaks, and Coaching Club American Oaks. Off those records the two fillies were voted co-champions of their age and sex for 1949. This voting result is difficult to fathom from our current vintage and vantage point, even though Wistful was third behind Two Lea in the Cleopatra Handicap in her final start.

Two Bob

The following year, Two Lea received another oddity of a championship, although an admirable one. She won only one stakes, but it was the Santa Margarita. However, she was widely accepted to have been the best in the Santa Anita Maturity, in which she was eased to allow stablemate Ponder to win. Then, again versus the highest class of males, Two Lea was used as Citation's pacemaker in the Santa Anita Handicap and wound up third behind him and the winner, Noor. Such achievements were adjudged by voters to merit an unorthodox championship among older fillies and mares.

Two Lea was away from the races for more than a year, and she came back sporting an alarming knot on the front of the left fore ankle after being fired. Nevertheless, she was as good at six, possibly better, than ever. If her two championships were somewhat anomalous, so was her non-championship of 1952. She won six of eleven and earned $174,550. In a Calumet battalion also including Wistful and A Gleam, she rounded back into form to win the Vanity and several other stakes against other distaffers, carrying up to 127 pounds victoriously. Against males, Two Lea scored in the $100,000 Hollywood Gold Cup. The nomenclature of voting divisions at the time included "handicap" fillies and mares, not older fillies and mares, per se. So, she was in competition with her three-year-old stablemate Real Delight, who took one poll, while the stellar older filly Next Move won the other.

Two Lea was retired with fifteen wins in twenty-six races and earnings of $309,250. Throughout its glory years, Calumet had a preponderance of handsome names, but Two Lea's first foal was not an inspiration for Mrs. Gene Markey, the former Mrs. Wright who had a brief widowhood before marrying Adm. Gene Markey. The 1954 Count Fleet filly was named Two Lea's Girl. She was unraced and was not a notable producer.

Two Lea's next three foals were all stakes winners: Tim Tam, On-and-On, and Pied d'Or. All three were by non-Calumet stallions.

Tim Tam was in the first crop by Greentree Stable's champion Tom Fool. Ben A. Jones gave him plenty of time, raced him once at two, then had to play catch up. By the time of the Kentucky Derby of 1958, Tim Tam had made ten starts and had soared to the top of his division, winning the Everglades, Flamingo, Fountain of Youth, Florida Derby, and Derby Trial. (The Flamingo came via disqualification of Jewel's Reward.) Second choice at 2-1 in the Kentucky Derby, Tim Tam wore down his persistent, though never successful, rival Lincoln Road to win by a half-length, becoming Calumet's seventh Derby winner and the eighth (combined) for the Joneses.

After a similar triumph in the Preakness Stakes, Tim Tam seemed poised to end a decade-long drought of Triple Crown winners by taking the Belmont Stakes to complete the first sweep since Calumet's Citation in 1948. It was not to be. Tim Tam was badly outrun by Cavan in the stretch and came out of the race with fractured sesamoids which quickly brought his retirement. He had won ten of fourteen and earned $467,475. He was the champion three-year-old of the year. Tim Tam was a good stallion without approaching greatness, and he begot the champion filly Tosmah.

Two Lea's second stakes winner was On-and-On, a Nasrullah colt who defeated a superb field including Bald Eagle, First Landing, and Sword Dancer in the 1960 Brooklyn Handicap. He also won the McLennan and Tropical Park Handicaps, plus the Ohio Derby, and three other stakes. On-and-On blazed six furlongs in 1:08 4/5 in winning the Sheridan Stakes. On most days, On-and-On could not handle the very best like he did in the Brooklyn, but he won a dozen races and earned $390,718. He sired Calumet's eighth Derby winner, Forward Pass, who won the 1968 Run for the Roses after prolonged court battles eventually upheld the disqualification of Dancer's Image. Forward Pass won the Preakness without court help and would have been a Triple Crown winner with a cumbersome footnote but for his defeat by Stage Door Johnny in the 100th Belmont Stakes.

In 1957, Two Lea foaled another colt by the Claiborne Farm stallion Nasrullah. Named Pied d'Or, he got the obligatory look as a Derby horse that any Calumet colt attracted, but was not of that caliber. He did wind up winning eighteen races, including three stakes: the Camden, Paumonok, and Princeton Handicaps.

Two Lea had a total of eight foals. Six raced, and five won. After Pied d'Or, she had no further stakes winners, but her 1962 foal, Mon Ange, a full sister to Tim Tam, produced the added-money winners Tarboosh, Son Ange, and He's an Angel. Mon Ange also became the second or third dam of several stakes winners from California to Trinidad and Tobago to France to Japan.

To return to Two Bob: In 1947, she had foaled the Blenheim II colt named Mostest, who again had the family's sturdiness, winning sixteen of ninety-four races from three through seven and earning $61,775. Two Bob was barren in 1948 and 1949 and then in 1950 foaled the Whirlaway gelding Bob Away. He fit the mold, winning fifteen of 102 races from two through eight and earning $25,684. Bob Away set a track record and was stakes-placed, but not in the context Calumet was seeking. He was second in the Rodeo Handicap and set his mark sprinting at Cranwood Park.

Returned to Bull Lea, Two Bob came through

again, producing the high-class filly Miz Clementine in 1951. Miz Clementine did not match full sister Two Lea in the way of championships, but she was not far off in quality. The filly won sixteen of thirty-six races from two through five and earned $267,100. Her eleven stakes wins included the California Derby, Hollywood Oaks, Vagrancy Handicap, and New Castle Stakes. In the New Castle, she defeated Searching and Myrtle's Jet. Miz Clementine's signature race, however, was the Santa Anita Maturity of 1955. Facing the previous year's Kentucky Derby winner, Determine, going one and a quarter miles, Miz Clementime fought off the colt to cross the wire first, but was disqualified for bearing out. (Mrs. Markey changed Calumet's winter base from Santa Anita to Florida the next year.)

Miz Clementine had no stakes winners, but her 1960 Swaps filly, Sweet Clementine, foaled the useful stakes winner and important stallion Best Turn (sire of Cox's Ridge).

Two Bob was barren in 1952, then the following year produced her last, a Bull Lea colt named Captain Morgan. The mare died soon after foaling at the age of twenty and the colt was placed on a nurse mare. Captain Morgan had two wins from thirty-seven races and earned $10,875.

Two Bob had produced seven foals, all winners, and three had been exceptional. Calumet was sometimes wrongly assumed to have relied too much on Bull Lea when, in fact, other farm stallions and many outside stallions were always used. Ironically, the case could be made that Two Bob's record would have been enhanced by taking the obvious, and easy, path. Mated to Bull Lea she foaled three important daughters and then they in turn thrived when crossed with outside stallions. ❖

Vagrancy

Years before many sportsmen sought to leave their mark on international racing, William Woodward Sr. was among the handful of Americans who frequently took aim at racing in the Thoroughbred's birthplace, England. In Vagrancy, he bred a filly who was not only one of his legion of outstanding runners at home in America, but also produced Black Tarquin, perhaps the best of Woodward's horses abroad.

Since Thoroughbred racing is no more immune to the ebbs and flows of human politics and ego than is any other aspect of life, Vagrancy's role carried some ironies. Two of the male antecedents on her bottom side were the great Man o' War and the wonderful sire Hamburg. Those two seemingly peerless examples of the Thoroughbred breed sprung from strains not documentable as pure enough for inclusion in the English Stud Book. Known as the Jersey Act, the policy which excluded them affected a great many American-breds. The doctrine had, by no coincidence one assumes, been developed early in the century after the banning of gambling on racing in New York and other states prompted fears in the English of a stampede of American horses to their shores. (Meanwhile, in France, another descendant of Frizette had produced the influential stallion Tourbillon.)

England's Jersey Act was lifted late in Woodward's life, 1949, and, as chairman of The Jockey Club in America and an honorary member of England's Jockey Club, he was instrumental in finally having the issue resolved. Woodward's horses still raced in silks of white with red polka-dots, but the equine version of the Scarlet Letter was removed from the American Thoroughbred.

Some racing aficionados of today will recognize the name Frizette primarily because of the grade I race for two-year-old fillies which keeps the word current. In addition to foaling Princess Palatine, second dam of Vagrancy, Frizette was the dam of Frizeur, whose daughter Myrtlewood launched another lasting line of mares and runners. Thus, Mr. Prospector also carries a drop of the once-tainted blood of Frizette.

Princess Palatine, by Prince Palatine, foaled the Man o' War filly Valkyr in 1925, and Valkyr in turn produced four stakes winners: Vicar, Vicaress, Vagrancy, and Hypnotic. This was a high-class group. Vicar was a moderate sort of stakes winner, but the others won in top-level company. Vicaress won the Spinaway Stakes, Ladies Handicap, and Delaware Handicap, and Hypnotic won the Coaching Club American Oaks and Alabama Stakes, two races also won by Vagrancy in her championship three-year-old season of 1942.

Vagrancy was sired by Sir Gallahad III, who had been imported to Claiborne Farm by a partnership involving Woodward, Claiborne owner Arthur

Hancock Sr., Marshall Field, and R. A. Fairbairn (see chapter on Marguerite). Like most other Belair Stable horses bred and owned by Woodward, Vagrancy was turned over to trainer James (Sunny Jim) Fitzsimmons. Storied in American racing, Fitzsimmons was a former jockey whose crooked posture eventually became so pronounced that it dominated the image of the man, even though the keen eye and horseman's judgment persevered in concert. Jimmy Breslin's book *Sunny Jim* assigned some blame for this deformity to the young Fitzsimmons' sweating at a brick kiln in order to keep off weight. This was in a time before he conceded that his days as a race rider were over. By the 1940s, Fitzsimmons was training for a pair of the most distinguished stables in America, Woodward's Belair and Mrs. Henry Carnegie Phipps' Wheatley Stable. He ranks with Ben A. Jones as the only trainer of two Triple Crown winners (Gallant Fox and Omaha). Sunny Jim did not retire until 1963, three years before his death.

Woodward did not breed horses hoping for some big scores at two and an early exit to the stud. Anything his young horses did at the age of two was a sort of prelude to what he hoped for them, which was success in the most important races for three-year-olds and later the handicaps or stayers' Cup races. Vagrancy behaved as if she not only had been bred for this scenario, but also bought into the idea personally.

At two, Vagrancy developed well enough to win three races, and she placed in one of the big autumn events for juvenile fillies, the Selima, behind the whimsically named Ficklebush. At three, Vagrancy emerged as the dominant runner among three-year-old fillies and also was adjudged the champion distaff handicapper of the year, denoting superiority over older females as well. Of the many outstanding horses Woodward bred and raced, Vagrancy was the only filly or mare to be voted a champion. (Voting did not begin validating championships as official until 1936; however, historians regarded Woodward's Happy Gal, ex post facto, as the best two-year-old filly of 1932.)

Fitzsimmons was not of a school — in education or practice — to pamper horses. At three, Vagrancy ran twenty-one times. She won eleven races, including nine stakes, at least seven of which would have been anointed as grade I were the modern grading style in effect at the time. Of her ten defeats, six occurred when she ventured out of her gender division to face colts, and the male division's champion Alsab was among them. While such matters always must be recognized as subjective, it seems fair to say that her general lack of inclusion in discussions of the very greatest of racing fillies and mares stems from her not having crossed this gender line successfully. Certainly, she had every chance to add a unisex triumph to her slate, a distinction achieved by the likes of Miss Woodford, Regret, Princess Doreen, Twilight Tear, Busher, Lady's Secret, and Personal Ensign.

Vagrancy, however, flaunted a toughness even some of those were not asked to prove. Her twenty-one races at three were spread from April through October, and she won the Coaching Club American Oaks, Beldame Handicap, Ladies Handicap, Pimlico Oaks, Delaware Oaks, Gazelle Stakes, Queen Isabella Handicap, Test Stakes, and Alabama Stakes. These races ranged from seven furlongs to one and a half miles. In the one and one-eighth-mile Beldame, she as a three-year-old was giving three pounds in actual weight to the older Barrancosa and dead-heated for the win. At one and a half miles in the Ladies Handicap, Vagrancy carried 126 and defeated the older Dark Discovery, who carried eighteen pounds less. Jimmy Stout was Vagrancy's regular rider, as he was for many of the Belair stars of the time.

The reality of life for many brilliant fillies is that

		Ajax, 1901	Flying Fox / Amie
	Teddy, 1913		
		Rondeau, 1900	Bay Ronald / Doremi
SIR GALLAHAD III, b, 1920			
		Spearmint, 1903	Carbine / Maid of the Mint
	Plucky Liege, 1912		
		Concertina, 1896	St. Simon / Comic Song
VAGRANCY, dk b m, 1939			
		Fair Play, 1905	Hastings / Fairy Gold
	Man o' War, 1917		
		Mahubah, 1910	Rock Sand / Merry Token
VALKYR, ch, 1925			
		Prince Palatine, 1908	Persimmon / Lady Lightfoot
	Princess Palatine, 1919		
		Frizette, 1905	Hamburg / Ondulee

VAGRANCY, dk b, 1939-1964. Bred by Belair Stud (Ky.). Raced 3 yrs, 42 sts, 15 wins, $102,480. Champion 3yo filly and handicap female. Won Beldame H, Ladies H, Coaching Club American Oaks, Pimlico Oaks, Delaware Oaks, Gazelle S, Queen Isabella H, Test S, Alabama S; 2nd Acorn S, Diana H, Ladies H, New England Oaks, Lawrence Realization; 3rd Selima S, Beldame H, New York H. Dam of 8 named foals, 6 rnrs, 6 wnrs, 3 sw.

1945: BLACK TARQUIN, br c, by Rhodes Scholar. Raced 3 yrs in Eng, 15 sts, 8 wins, $73,487. Champion 3yo colt in Eng. Won St. Leger S, St. James's Palace S, Burwell S, Gimcrack S, White Rose S, Royal Lodge S, Derby Trial S; 2nd Richmond S, Newmarket S, Ascot Gold Cup, Queen Elizabeth S. Sire of 380 foals, AEI 0.85.

1946: Truancy, br f, by Isolater. Unraced.

1947: HYVANIA, b g, by Hypnotist II. Raced 9 yrs, 90 sts, 15 wins, $84,275. Won Forget Hurdle H, Midsummer Hurdle H, Amagansett Hurdle H (twice), Rouge Dragon Hurdle H; 2nd New York Turf Writers Cup H (T), Aqueduct National Maiden Hurdle, Amagansett Hurdle H, Rouge Dragon Hurdle H; 3rd Forget Hurdle H (twice), Saratoga National Maiden Hurdle, Rouge Dragon Hurdle H, Brook Stp H, Bushwick Hurdle H, International Stp H (twice), Charles L. Appleton Memorial Stp.

1948: VULCANIA, ch f, by Some Chance. Raced 2 yrs, 32 sts, 6 wins, $54,815. Won Diana H, Test S; 2nd Selima S, Alabama S, Demoiselle S; 3rd Acorn S, Discovery H. Dam of 11 foals, 10 rnrs, 7 wnrs, including **NASCANIA** ($84,100), **FIRERULLAH** ($21,119). Granddam of Banja Luka (Broodmare of the Year in 1987), **FIDDLE ISLE**, **TALLAHTO**, **CONGA MISS**, **LE CLE**, **CHANCEY BIDDER**, **BILL'S EXPRESS**, **Pedrinho**, **Pit Bunny**, **Lullabey**. Died 1970.

1952: Natasha, b f, by Nasrullah. Raced 2 yrs, 7 sts, 1 win, $3,900. Dam of 9 foals, 9 rnrs, 8 wnrs, including **NATASHKA** ($151,673, Broodmare of the Year in 1981). Granddam of **TRULY BOUND**, **TROVE**, **GREGORIAN**, **ITSAMAZA**, **IVORY WAND**, **ARKADINA**, **BLOOD ROYAL**, **Royal Sister II**, **Ribarbaro**, **Saracen Summer**.

1954: Barren.

1955: Liberty Ruler, b g, by Nasrullah. Raced 3 yrs, 19 sts, 2 wins, $16,717. 3rd Jamaica H, Everglades S. Died 1962.

1956: Tramp, dk b f, by Tom Fool. Unraced. Dam of 3 foals, 2 rnrs, 1 wnr. Granddam of **PELLILIEU**.

1957: Slipped.

1958: Rambling, dk b f, by Shut Out. Raced 2 yrs, 9 sts, 1 win, $2,460. Dam of 5 foals, 5 rnrs, 4 wnrs. Granddam of **SPIDERMAN**, **FAR AWAY**, **Sardana**. Died 1970.

1959: Not bred.

---

they do not train on from one year to the next with the same exuberance, or quality. In Vagrancy's case, she won only one race at four. Although she placed in such familiar features as the Beldame and Ladies, she added no further stakes victories. She was retired to Woodward's broodmare band, boarded at Claiborne Farm in Kentucky, with a record of forty-two races, fifteen wins, and earnings of $102,480. At the time of Woodward's death a decade later, one of his achievements widely noted was that he had bred ten individual runners which had earned $100,000 or more, which helps place Vagrancy's achievement in perspective for her time.

Classics and Close Calls

As is discussed in the chapter on Marguerite, Woodward took an interest in England and English customs. Years before Paul Mellon more or less perfected the art of fostering the status of English landscape and portrait painters, Woodward lent his own contribution to that field. He registered his colors in England in 1928 and also acquired an interest in British sporting artists. Eventually, a wing of the Baltimore Museum of Art would include a fine collection of paintings he purchased, and trophies his horses won, including portraits by such as George Stubbs and J. F. Herring. The collection also houses a self-conscious, but touching, volume in which Woodward set down his opinions and motives about his sporting art collection. Woodward also supported artists of his own time, commissioning portraits of his notable horses on both sides of the Atlantic by Percy Earl, Martin Stainforth, Franklin Voss, and others.

The ultimate goal of anyone with a leaning toward English racing is the Epsom Derby. That one and a half-mile spring test for three-year-olds across the meandering and undulating course of hallowed Epsom Downs was central to his thinking when Woodward began sending a few young horses each year to Cecil Boyd-Rochfort at Freemason Lodge, Newmarket. Woodward never achieved a Derby win, although his Prince Simon was beaten but a head by Galcador after seeming to have the 1950 Derby in hand.

Earlier that spring, Prince Simon had been beaten a head by Palestine in another of England's five classic races, the Two Thousand Guineas. In a similar vein, Woodward's 1935 American Triple Crown winner, Omaha, lent his name to the lasting lore of

England's Ascot Gold Cup via a narrow loss to the filly Quashed. Those results might direct the reader toward the conclusion that it was a fortunate thing that Woodward seldom actually traveled to England to see his horses run. On the contrary, considering that he sent only a few colts to Freemason Lodge in any given crop, his record in the English classics was exceptional. He won two runnings of the St. Leger, with Boswell and Black Tarquin, plus one running of the Epsom Oaks with Hycilla and a One Thousand Guineas with Brown Betty. Moreover, his Flares avenged full brother Omaha by winning the greatest of all English stayers' races, the Ascot Gold Cup. At the other end of the distance/stamina scale, Woodward's Foxbrough was the champion two-year-old in England in 1938.

Black Tarquin, the St. Leger winner of 1948, was Vagrancy's first foal. He was sired by Rhodes Scholar, who for Lord Astor won the Eclipse Stakes of 1936. Prior to the advent of the King George VI and Queen Elizabeth Stakes in 1951, the Eclipse was the most important middle-distance race in England for three-year-olds and upward. Rhodes Scholar, sired by Pharos and foaled from the St. Leger winner Book Law, stood three seasons in England. He then was imported to Claiborne in a transaction in which farm owner Hancock joined with two of his major clients, Woodward and Mrs. Henry Carnegie Phipps.

Black Tarquin was typical of the sort of horse Woodward tried to breed. He was intended for the classics, but even classic three-year-olds need speed and some degree of early maturity. The colt won the Gimcrack Stakes at two and was weighted below only Lerins (re-named My Babu) on the English Free Handicap for two-year-olds of 1947. The following spring, Black Tarquin won the Lingfield Derby Trial Stakes, but finished eighth in the Derby itself.

Redeeming himself admirably, Black Tarquin won the St. James's Palace Stakes during the Royal

Vagrancy

Ascot meeting and was beaten only a head by Italian champion Tenerani in the one and a half-mile Queen Elizabeth Stakes. The next target was the oldest and longest of the five English classics, the one and three-fourths-mile St. Leger, founded during the same year the Americans and English were at odds, namely 1776.

England's *Bloodstock Breeders' Review* paid tribute to Black Tarquin's appearance and to trainer Boyd-Rochfort in its description of the St. Leger scene: "Black Tarquin never looked better in his life, and was delivered by his trainer trained to the hour…there are few, if any, trainers in this country who know more about the art of preparing stayers than he…"

Black Tarquin made a prolonged run from behind to pass a rising star among stayers, Alycidon, winning the St. Leger by one and a half lengths. The first three places were filled by individuals representing owners at the top of the sport in their respective countries: Woodward owned the winner; runner-up Alycidon carried the historic colors of England's renowned Earl of Derby; and third-placed Solar Slipper was owned by prominent Irish Turfman Joseph McGrath. Moreover, the field included Angelola, carrying the royal colors of King George VI, as well as the Aga Khan's Epsom Derby/Grand Prix de Paris winner My Love. Although out of a mare named Vagrancy, the American-bred colt put his breeder-owner in high company, indeed.

The following year, Black Tarquin won three races before the Ascot Gold Cup. Then, in that grand old event, he could not come to terms with Alycidon, who had improved into a very distinguished stayer. Black Tarquin was retired to stud at Claiborne.

It is often said of a brilliant horse who manages to win at one and a quarter miles or one and a half miles that he does not truly "stay" but wins "on

class." (This is admittedly a splitting of linguistic hairs, but is no more difficult to accept than the widely held observation that sports teams sometimes play "above themselves.") The opposite of the non-stayer/class equation, although seldom expressed, also appears to be true: A horse whose main proclivity is stamina can sometimes be an important winner as a two-year-old and later at medium distances because of inherent class. Such a horse is ill-suited to the stud, especially if he exists in a time and place where emphasis on stamina in high fashion racing is waning.

The fast horse with enough class to get an extended distance does not have to impart that outward limit of ability to his offspring in order to be successful. Conversely, the natural distance horse who somehow has enough lick to win a sprint race is unlikely to succeed unless, somehow, that added fillip in his own makeup is passed along.

In Alycidon and Black Tarquin, this anecdotal observation had both a proponent and opponent from the same arena: Alycidon was that rare character, i.e., a great stayer whose offspring inherited sufficient speed to make him a leading sire of flat runners; Black Tarquin, on the other hand, fell more into the expected mode. Of his fourteen stakes winners, eleven succeeded in Europe, where emphasis on speed is — or at least was — less pronounced than at home. Perhaps most supportive of the notion that Black Tarquin would have been more beneficially placed in England, siring potential stayers, than in Kentucky, competing with Bull Lea, Heliopolis, and Nasrullah, was the career of his son Trelawny. After he fractured a cannon bone, Trelawny's insurance representatives recommended euthanasia, but they were resisted, and by the end of 1963, the horse had placed in a series of jump races before returning to the flat. By the time of his Goodwood Cup victory in 1963, according to the

Bloodstock Breeders' Review, he had won so many two-mile and plus races that he had "established himself as the most popular horse in England."

Vagrancy and Versatility

Vagrancy herself had won major sprints as well as major events at up to one and a half miles. Her offspring likewise resisted being pigeon-holed. The mare's third foal was Hyvania (by Hypnotist II), who won or placed in eighteen steeplechase stakes. Vagrancy then foaled Vulcania (by Some Chance), who won the seven-furlong Test Stakes and the one and one-eighth-mile Diana Handicap (over Marta and Adile).

Vulcania became one of the primary vehicles of Vagrancy's lasting influence. Vulcania's 1957 foal was Nascania, who was to be one of the mainstays in the breeding and racing operation of another important Claiborne client, Howard B. Keck, and his wife Libby (singly and in partnership, as racing lingo has it). To the cover of the great stallion Nasrullah, Vulcania foaled Nascania, winner of four stakes on the West Coast, where the Kecks based their racing operation. Nascania in turn foaled one of the more distinguished grass-course runners to campaign in California in Fiddle Isle, whose eight major triumphs in California included one course record at a mile and two at one and a half-miles. Fiddle Isle's victory in the San Juan Capistrano at one and three-fourths miles harkened back to the career of Black Tarquin. Vulcania also produced a moderate stakes winner named Firerullah.

In 1956, Vulcania foaled a filly by Kentucky Derby winner Dark Star. The foal was named Legato, and she became the dam of major winners Tallahto (by Nantallah) and Le Cle (by Tom Rolfe). Both of those fillies also produced stakes winners, Tallahto following her career of three grade I wins by foaling grade I winners Prince True and Hidden Light.

Legato, daughter of Vulcania and granddaughter of Vagrancy, also foaled Banja Luka (by Double Jay), who in turn produced Ferdinand. In 1986, jockey Bill Shoemaker pushed Ferdinand through along the rail at Churchill Downs to score in the Kentucky Derby. It was the fourth Derby win for Shoemaker, then in his fifties, and the first for Ferdinand's trainer, Charlie Whittingham, then in his seventies. Ferdinand, a Nijinsky II colt who raced in the name of Mrs. Keck, defeated Alysheba in the Breeders' Cup Classic the next season and was named Horse of the Year. Ferdinand was but one of a half-dozen stakes winners foaled from the prolific Banja Luka.

The Alabama Revisited

The chapter's subject mare, Vagrancy, had no registered foal between Vulcania in 1948 and a Nasrullah filly of 1952, who was named Natasha. Woodward died in 1953 and when Natasha was three, William Woodward Jr. was killed, leading to the sale of the Belair horses. A moderate winner, Natasha produced George Getty's grand filly Natashka, she by Dedicate. In 1966, Natashka won the historic Alabama Stakes, which had been so prominent on the escutcheon of her female family. Natashka also won the Monmouth Oaks, Santa Maria Handicap, Las Flores Handicap, and Miss Woodford Stakes.

Natashka produced five winners of stakes races in the United States and Europe. They were American grade II winner Truly Bound, a filly by In Reality; Irish group I winner Gregorian, a colt by Graustark; Arkadina, a Ribot filly who won a stakes race in Ireland and placed in both the Irish One Thousand Guineas and Irish and English Oaks (and foaled Irish St. Leger winner Dark Lomond); Blood Royal, a Ribot colt who won two group III races in England; and Ivory Wand, a Sir Ivor filly who won the Test Stakes and placed in two runnings of the Spinster.

Several from the generation represented by Natashka's daughters also carried on the line of producing stakes winners, among them Ivory Wand, dam of English group winner and German/Italian champion Gold and Ivory. In 1986, Ivory Wand foaled a Hero's Honor filly, Touch of Greatness, who to the cover of Gone West foaled Elusive Quality. In 1998, Elusive Quality, among representatives of yet another generation descending from Vagrancy, set the world record for a mile when he won the Poker Handicap on grass in 1:31 3/5.

Other distant descendants of Vagrancy's foal Natasha include the two-time Juddmonte International winner and Eclipse winner Ezzoud

Vagrancy

and English group I winner Distant Relative.

Vagrancy had no reported foal of 1953 or 1954, then foaled the stakes-placed Nasrullah gelding Liberty Ruler in 1955. Vagrancy's 1956 Tom Fool filly, Tramp, was unraced, and the mare slipped her 1957 foal. Vagrancy's last foal, Rambling, a filly by Shut Out, was foaled in 1958; she, too, produced the dams of some stakes horses.

Vagrancy's ancestry, her racing record, and generations of her progeny defy most generalizations. They won sprints and European classics and set a contemporary mile record. There, was, however, a meandering commonality, and that was a frequent sharing of abundant class. ❖

TAIL FEMALE LINES

In addition to the family notes contained in each chapter, more detailed information about the subject mares is provided on the following pages. Tail female lines chronicle a mare's influence through her daughters to the present day. The influence of La Troienne, for example, extends over eight generations and is manifested in an incredible 815 stakes winners through mid-April, 1999. Several subject mares of more recent vintage have comparably abbreviated tail female lines, but their influence undoubtedly will extend into the new century.

Scores of familiar names abound in these tail female lines, as do some new ones destined to achieve their own renown. Stakes winners are noted in bold face type.

Alcibiades
(by Supremus)

Hipparete (by Pharamond II)
  OUT TALK (by Ambiorix)
    Brag (by Bold Lad)
      REVIVALIST (by Advocator)
      Terminal Blush (by Silent Screen)
      IT'S OVER (by Stop the Music)
    Constant Talk (by Cornish Prince)
    ISLAND CHATTER (by Island Whirl)
    Flyitoff (by Forli)
      Year of the Cat (by Cougar II)
      PALACE OF ICE (by Pledge Card)
  PILLOW TALK (by Mr. Trouble)
    Ave Valeque (by Bold Ruler)
      CIAO (by Silent Screen)
        BY YOUR LEAVE (by Private Account)
        HADIF (by Clever Trick)
        SECRET HELLO (by Private Account)
        SILENT ACCOUNT (by Private Account)
        GOLD CASE (by Forty Niner)
    No Comment (by Nashua)
    HEDGE (by Bagdad)
    Incommunicado (by Double Jay)
      In Absentia (by Believe It)
        DEFREEZE (by It's Freezing)
        FROST FREE (by It's Freezing)
      KOLUCTOO BAY (by Creme dela Creme)
      Sunshine Law (by Tisab)
        Molloy (by Shecky Greene)
        SHADY DEAL (by Quack)
    Mum (by Buckpasser)
      Pass the Mums (by Inverness Drive)
        Coldallthetime (by It's Freezing)
        IMPERIAL PASS (by Imperial Falcon)
        FREEZING DOCK (by It's Freezing)
    Pillow Dreams (by Hillsdale)
      Sabana Queen (by Gray Phantom)
      LA GUASIRITA (by Excalibur III)
      Sueno Vano (by Party Flag)
      TIO ROBERTO C (by Lawgiver)
  RASH STATEMENT (by Ambiorix)
    Bold Angel (by Bold Ruler)
    SERAPHIC (by Up Spirits)
    Herodias (by Bold Ruler)
      Spark Bird (by Sea-Bird)
        Sparte (by Val de l'Orne (FR))
        SORRIENKAL (FR) (by Sorrento (FR))
      SPARTIATE (by Apalachee)
Last of All (by Rico Monte)
  Future Event (by Helioscope)
    Funade (by Royal Serenade)
    INDIAN SERENADE (by Tipont)
    Nevent (by Nasco)
      Candelette (by Candle Stand)
      FIRST STRIKE (by The Very Best)
      MAC'S DANDY (by The Very Best)
LITHE (by Pharamond II)
  Gentle Ruler (by Nasrullah)
    GENTLE KING (by What Luck)
    WHAT A GENT (by What Luck)
  Lithia (by Ambiorix)
    Bold Lithia (by Boldnesian)
      Lithia's Dantan (by Prince Dantan)
      SUNSHINE JIMMY (by Judge Smells)
    LITHIOT (by Ribot)
    Lovey (by Double Jay)
      Love and Live (by Brave Emperor)
        Lover's Faite (by Parfaitement)
        LOOKIN FOR ROMANCE (by Great Prospector)
      Loviana (by Umbrella Fella)
      LORDLY LOVE (by Lord Harry L.)
      LOVE TO LAUGH (by Grimaldi)
      Saving My Love (by Ambehaving)
      HOLDING MY LOVE (by Pocket Park)
    MONOLITH (by Ribot)
    Noble Scale (by Vaguely Noble)
      BRASS SCALE (by Dixieland Brass)
      Madam Schu (by Nureyev)
      VLADIVOSTOK (by Lord Avie)
    NOON BALLOON (by Bold Forbes)
    Queen's Statue (by King's Bishop)
    DIXIE HERO (by Dixieland Band)
    Scathing (by Vitriolic)
    ISMELDA (by Wavering Monarch)

LITHE (continued)
  SUPPLE (by Mr. Trouble)
  Svelte (by Nasrullah)
    Trim Turn (by Turn-to)
      Fine Tuning (by T. V. Lark)
      GRACE'S TUNE (by Mr. Leader)
      ONE IS ENOUGH (by Three Martinis)
      Deep Enough (by Raise a Native)
      CRAB GRASS (by Known Fact)
      EXCLUSIVE ENOUGH (by Exclusive Native)
      MEDIUM COOL (by Conquistador Cielo)
      Once to Often (by Raise a Native)
      BOOM TOWN GIRL (by Unbridled)
    Run for Purse (by Run For Nurse)
    My Girl Mandie (by Dr. Giddings)
    TANZANID (by Tanthem)
  T. V. IMAGE (by T. V. Lark)
MENOW (by Pharamond II)
SALAMINIA (by Man o' War)
  Aegina (by Sir Damion)
    Aerobee (by Menow)
      Martina Jo (by Admirals Pride)
        Gambling Jo (by A Gambler)
        FOREIGN GAMBLER (by Foreign Comet)
    Arta (by Mr. Trouble)
      Yep Yep Yep (by All Hands)
      ALL LAUGHS (by Funny Fellow)
    Royal Gina (by Royal Note)
      Flying Gina (by Flying Relic)
        Gallant Mama (by My Gallant)
        MAGAL (by Hooched)
      MAJESTIC GINA (by Ambiopoise)
      MAJESTICANT (by Exuberant)
  ATHENIA (by Pharamond II)
    Aesthete (by Revoked)
      Aesthetic (by Mr. Trouble)
        Aesthetically (by Sir Gaylord)
          Esthete (by Le Fabuleux)
          Acetylene (by Explodent)
          EXPLOSIVE FLAG (by U. S. Flag)
          SABATINI (by Texas Prospector)
        Aware (by Buckpasser)
        PARK'S POLICY (by Tell)
        Travois (by Navajo)
        ICETRAIN (by Icecapade)
      BAGFULL (by Bagdad)
      Grasse (by Sir Gaylord)
      PRINCE THATCH (IRE) (by Thatch)
      INSISTANCE (by Sir Gaylord)
        Evanescente (FR) (by Pharly)
        THE SHADOW (by Kaldoun)
        Innisfree (FR) (by Crystal Palace)
        INDIGHIRKA (FR) (by Bering (GB))
      SUMMIT (FR) (by High Top)
      Perceptive Lady (by Damascus)
        Broadway Star (by Broadway Forli)
        BROADWAY CHIEF (by Tunerup)
        BROADWAY'S TOP GUN (by Full Pocket)
      TASTE (by Round Table)
      Tastefully (by Hail to Reason)
      BON GOUT (by Dewan)
      Design (by Tom Rolfe)
      CLEAN LINES (by Ack Ack)
      Palate (by Ack Ack)
      LA ALCAPARRA (VEN) (by Inland Voyager)
      Touch (by Herbager)
      ALLUSION (by Mr. Prospector)
      BAG (by Devil's Bag)
      Suave (by Majestic Prince)
      SWANK (by Topsider)
      SWEAR (by Believe It)
    Feeze (by Mr. Trouble)
    SEAWEED (by Admiral's Voyage)
  Affectation (by Citation)
    Fashion Plate (by Cohoes)
      Chic Juliet (by Gallant Romeo)
      SPEND (by Draconic)
      Fashion Dancer (by Dancer's Image)
        Biabela (by Caracolero)
        PLAY FOR (by Baronius)
        Misty Moon (by Baronius)
        VIRGINIE (BRZ) (by Legal Case)
        Oversight (by Baronius)
        VYATKA (BRZ) (by Lucence)
  SWISS CHEESE (by Dotted Swiss)

SALAMINIA (continued)

Attica (by Mr. Trouble)
  Be Careful (by Dedicate)
    Be Ever Careful (by Capacitator)
      BREZO (SPA) (by Chacal)
    To Rib (by Hurry Ribot)
      Copper Rib (by Copper Kingdom)
        PORT KINGDOM (by Portimao)
  Beaumont (by Bold Ruler)
    C'Est Beau (by Quack)
      Comtesse (by Mr. Leader)
        TALKING TOWER (by Irish Tower)
    Invitiate (by Speak John)
      Extenuating (by Extemporaneous)
        CONSEGRITY (by Touch of Ability)
  Indaba (by Sir Gaylord)
    Capulet (by Gallant Romeo)
      DEAREST INDU (by Full Pocket)
      MY BLONDE BEAUTY (by Peteski)
  Lady Attica (by Spy Song)
    Looker (by Stage Door Johnny)
      LADY IVOR (by Superbity)
    Sour Orange (by Delta Judge)
      DYNA ORANGE (JPN) (by Northern Taste)
        CENTER RISING (JPN) (by Hector Protector)
      SHADAI IVOR (by Northern Taste)
        Icy Goggle (by Royal Ski)
          AIR JIHAD (JPN) (by Sakura Yutaka O)
    Tea At Five (by Olden Times)
      Fappy's Brew (by Fappiano)
        MALT (by Zilzal)
      MUGATEA (by Hold Your Peace)
      PATCHY GROUNDFOG (by Instrument Landing)
  McCoy (by Hillsdale)
    Coy Maid (FR) (by Habitat)
      ERUDITE (FR) (by Green Dancer)
      RUSCELLI (by Val de l'Orne (FR))
    Lady Mickey (by Swaps)
      Ela Minnie Mou (by Ela-Mana-Mou (IRE))
        SIBARITO (IRE) (by Viking)
      Ivoronica (by Targowice)
        IVORY BRIDE (GB) (by Domynsky (GB))
          CABCHARGE STRIKER (by Rambo Dancer)
        PUTUNA (GB) (by Generous)
    Princess Mab (by Turn-to)
      PRINCE MAB (by Targowice)
  SIR IVOR (by Sir Gaylord)
GEORGIAN (by Revoked)
Oread (by Rico Monte)
  Othris (by What a Pleasure)
    PRINCESS O'HARA (by Sir Wimborne)
  Regal Note (by Royal Note)
    Bubbling Note (by Syrinx)
      Gamble Bay Girl (by Banners Image)
        TOMMIE LU (by Zulu Tom)
      Gamble Bay Time (by Night Time)
        J T DILLON (by J. T. Hurst)
LIBBA (by Sir Damion)
  ASSEMBLYMAN (by Menow)
  Footstool (by Pied d'Or)
    MAC N' WATER (by Philately)
  Philately's Lady (by Philately)
    FLANKER NINETEEN (by Drouilly (FR))
    HOSTESS LADY (by Chip o' Lark)
Pella (by Pharamond II)
  Pellene (by Revoked)
    Doublene (by Double Jay)
      Double Set (by Resurgent)
        BURGANDY DANCER (by Marshua's Dancer)
        TWICE THE VICE (by Vice Regent)
      NAVAJO (by Grey Dawn II)
    Regal Purple (by Beau Purple)
      BEAU GROTON (by Groton)
      Fuchsia Filch (by No Robbery)
        JOHN CASEY (by Prince John)
        SING SING (by Stop the Music)
        Snitch (by Seattle Slew)
          GRAB (by Danzig)
      LEGAL QUEEN (by No Robbery)
      PRINCELET (by Stage Door Johnny)
    TROUBLEPEG (by Mr. Trouble)
    PLEASURE SEEKER (by Ambiorix)
  Pellita (by Rico Monte)
    Rainy Countess (by Rainy Lake)
      SHARP DUCHESS (by Vitriolic)

SALAMINIA (continued)

Sacrifice (by Pharamond II)
  Dice (by Blue Prince)
    BOLD ROLL (by Bold and Brave)
    IVORY CASTLE (by Irish Castle)
      Esscorrie (by King Pellinore)
        KING CORRIE (by Bold Ruckus)
    New Dice (by Bold and Brave)
      NEW PLAY (by Broadway Forli)
    Poised Dice (by Ambiopoise)
      Pamlico Gal (by Sea-Bird)
        Place in Time (AUS) (by Bletchingly)
          CHURCH STREET (by Cerreto)
          NORTHERN TIME (by Sovereign Red (NZ))
    Poliade (FR) (by Busted)
      PIRAK (by Noir et Or)
  Hecuba (by Priam II)
    Cuba Bonita (by Big Dipper II)
      Cuban Lass (by This Evening)
        DOTS HOT FLASH (by Poggibonsi)
        DOTTIE T. (by Don-Ce-Sar)
        HASTY LASS (by Three Martinis)
      HECUBAS DIAMOND (by Mister Jive)
    Wincuba (by Winning Shot)
      DOC DANYSH (by Arctic Canuck)
      MISS MOLLY (by Lothario)
  Spice (by Blue Prince)
    PINCH OF SPICE (by Bold and Brave)
Salamanca (by Revoked)
  Nashuas Sal (by Nashua)
    EASTERN TOWN (by Bagdad)
  Toms Sal (by Tompion)
    GREY DAWN LADY (by Grey Dawn II)
    MILLION DOLLAR SAL (by Master Hand)
      BOLD RECITAL (by Recitation)
    Molly Bellah (by Roman Line)
      Mystic Warrior (by Iron Warrior)
        Marilyn's Mystique (by Dearest Doctor)
          VON GROOVEY (by Sword Dance (IRE))
      Our Felicity (by Iron Warrior)
        DIRTY MIKE (by Temperence Hill)
    Poke Salad (by Poker)
      LADY TASSO (by Tasso)
    SAL'S HIGH (by Poker)
      She So Slew (by Slew o' Gold)
        DANCE FOR AVERTED (by Averted)
  Trouble Spot (by Mr. Trouble)
    Green Trouble (by Green Ticket)
      FOR YOUR PLEASURE (by What a Pleasure)
      Irish Ballad (by Stop the Music)
        PARIS SONG (by Hurok)
    Queen Trouble (by First Family)
      QUEEN'S FAMILY (by New Prospect)
        LOSTFOREVER (by Gourami)
      QUEEN'S MASTER (by Master Derby)
      SLEW NOT (by Slewacide)
    Silent Running (by Maris)
      RUNNING BO (by Mambo)
      RUNNING RAZOR (by Dr. Geo. Adams)
    Trouble Good (by Approbation)
      Shahpasand (by Barachois)
        Alice Ruth (by Exuberant)
          ALICE'S MAGIC (by Wavering Monarch)
          CONNIE'S FANTASY (by Rhinflo)
          FERVENT AFFAIR (by Formal Dinner)
          PYRITE DINNER (by Formal Dinner)
      WHENYOU'RESMILING (by Explodent)
      LOUISE A LA PLAGE (by His Majesty)
  TURN TO SAL (by Turn-to)
Salvia (by Mr. Trouble)
  DELTA SAL (by Delta Judge)
    Delta Key (by Sauce Boat)
      DELTA LADY (by Fighting Fit)
    RAISE A MAN (by Raise a Native)
    STALWART SAL (by Stalwart)
      ENOUGH SAL (by Exclusive Enough)
    HADIF ONE (by Hadif)
  HAFA ADAI (by Hawaii)
  Sally's Market (by To Market)
    French Nylon (by Flag Raiser)
      AGUA BLANCA (by Stardoric)
    Puzzi (by Dancer's Image)
      NOBLE PEER (by Sir Tristram)
    Spring Market (by Spring Double)
      CATO DOUBLE (by Nodouble)

| **DOUBLE LIZ** (by Nodouble)
Saltu (by Tudor Minstrel)
| **PRINCESS ZEN** (by Zen)
Sister Sal (by Delta Judge)
Asir (by Exclusive Native)
| **SIR COURT** (by Court Trial)
NIPPYINMISSISSIPPI (by Our Native)
PRESIDENTIAL (by Vice Regent)
White Cross (by Revoked)
FIRM POLICY (by Princequillo)
Blue Law (by Tom Rolfe)
Five of Gold (by Irish Castle)
BACKGROUND (by Telefonico)
BACKYARD (VEN) (by Telefonico)
TWELVE MILE LIMIT (by Coastal)
STATUTE (by Verzy)
Firm Defense (by Bold Ruler)
Rainy Reward (by Stage Door Johnny)
| **RAINY SESSION** (by Sir Session)
Maidsmorton (by Bold Ruler)
| **TAPEI TILLIE** (by Pirate's Bounty)
Miss Cevin Levin (by Drone)
| **NO MARKER** (by Grey Dawn II)
Sarinda (by Stop the Music)
CALLEDONS PROSPECT (by Allen's Prospect)
PACIFIC BASIN (by Big Spruce)
PUNCHBOWL (by Two Punch)
Tudor Emblem (by King of the Tudors)
Beaubraun (by Drone)
| **DYNAMO JET** (by Pass the Glass)
Golden Gater (by Stage Door Johnny)
WIMBORNE'S GATER (by Sir Wimborne)
SPARTA (by St. Germans)
Buddy Kenney (by Pharamond II)
Far Pacific (by Polynesian)
Avon Miss (by Double Eclipse)
Avon River (by Stevward)
Caledon Classic (by Vice Regent)
CALEDON ROAD (by Lord At War (ARG))
Avondida (by Stevward)
BOLD AVON (by Bold n Bizarre)
SPARSHOTT (by Police Car)
PASS THE BRANDY (by Round Table)
Honey (by Pavot)
HASTY HONEY (by Hasty Road)
Honey Road (by Hasty Road)
Bee Line Baby (by Fuzzbuster)
| **BEMOMONEY** (by Tilt the Odds)
Honeymon (by Monitor)
Rum Honey (by Nostrum)
| **OLD TERRITORY** (by Big Bold Sefa)
Scissile (by The Axe II)
Mrs. McSnort (by Copy Chief)
HASTY SQUAW (by Prince Gala)
HASTYS BOOK (by Mari's Book)
NAVY BRASS (by Crafty Admiral)
Pitcher (by Shut Out)
Petoskey (by Helioscope)
Back to Michigan (by Bold Sultan)
| **EDUARDO II (PAN)** (by Twist the Axe)
KEOKIS STAR (by Dynastic)
ROYAL FAN (by Royal Gem II)
Fanrigo (by Amerigo)
Ameriturn (by Turn-to)
Ameriangel (by Halo)
HALO AMERICA (by Waquoit)
T. V. HIGHLIGHTS (by T. V. Commercial)
Guest Shot (by Sunrise Flight)
JUSTAGUEST (by Groton)
Hotsie Totsie (by Icecapade)
CARNIVAL PURSUIT (by Jose Binn)
FOUNTAIN LAKE (by Vigors)
FREE HOUSE (by Smokester)
SHOT N' MISSED (by Naskra)
Hem and Haw (by Double Jay)
AMERICAN HISTORY (by Tom Rolfe)
DELAWARE CHIEF (by Chieftain)
Hedging (by Hail to Reason)
BETINHO (by Thru a Straw)
Doble Filo (by White Face)
| **YAGUALERA** (by Erin Bright)
JUST A THOUGHT (by Raised Socially)
Key to Friendship (by Key to the Kingdom)
TOAST THE CROWN (by Magesterial)

King's Wife (by Bold Ruler)
Upon Reflection (by Quadrangle)
FAMOUS LAST WORDS (by Rock Talk)
War Pitch (by Warfare)
Hilda's Pitch (by Prince Khaled)
Bird in Flight (by Mr. Busher)
Savate (by Southern Cream)
DIRCE (by Exalte)
EXALSA (by Exalte)

Almahmoud
(by Mahmoud)

Bubbling Beauty (by Hasty Road)
ARCTIC TERN (by Sea-Bird)
Champagne Cocktail (by Roberto)
Meadow Mist (by Irish River (FR))
| **EISHIN GUYMON** (by Seattle Dancer)
SANGRIA (by El Gran Senor)
Polar Fizz (by Nearctic)
La Spumante (by Drone)
Dulce Vino (by Sauce Boat)
IRISH TWIST (by Torsion)
Vague Bubble (by Vaguely Noble)
Avra (by Mendez)
GRAPHIC (by Scenic (IRE))
COSMAH (by Cosmic Bomb)
Cosmiah (by Olympia)
Fancy Jet (by Nearctic)
BIRD OF COURAGE (by Great Career)
LAURA'S JET (by Wajima)
MURIESK (by Nashua)
BORDER CAT (by Storm Cat)
FATHERS IMAGE (by Swaps)
Flamingo Way (by Third Brother)
Dancing Free (by Dancing Count)
| **I'M OUT** (by Lord Gaylord)
Somerville (by Somerset)
Cosmahgorian (by Gregorian)
COSMO TOPPER (by Compelling Sound)
Via Rica (by Rico Tesio)
GENTLEMAN GENE (by Maribeau)
HALO (by Hail to Reason)
Honor Tricks (by Bold Bidder)
Aseltine's Angels (by Fappiano)
BRANCASTER (by Riverman)
Jo Dan (by Buckpasser)
Jojima (by Wajima)
Sacred Squaw (by Olden Times)
| **ENZO** (by Solford)
SKY HARBOUR (by Far North)
Parfait Royale (by Damascus)
| **IMPORTANT NOTICE** (by Katowice)
La Dame Du Lac (by Round Table)
HEEREMANDI (IRE) (by Royal Academy)
La Confidence (by Nijinsky II)
FLAWLESSLY (by Affirmed)
PERFECT (by Affirmed)
LAKE COMO (by Nijinsky II)
Lake Ivor (by Sir Ivor)
Lovely Nedra (by Irish Tower)
| **LAURA'S PISTOLETTE** (by Big Pistol)
Miss Cross (by Far North)
VOY SI NO (by White Mischief)
MIZNAH (IRE) (by Sadler's Wells)
NAZOO (IRE) (by Nijinsky II)
SINGLE COMBAT (by Nijinsky II)
Love of Learning (by Hail to Reason)
Love for Life (by Forli)
ANNUAL REUNION (by Cresta Rider)
Soft Charm (by Secretariat)
| **FULL MOON MADNESS** (by Half a Year)
Tesio's Love (by Tom Rolfe)
CAT AFFAIR (by Storm Cat)
MARIBEAU (by Ribot)
Perfecta (by Swaps)

COSMAH (continued)

- Bold Casmah (by Cannonade)
  - **ONE OF ZEN** (by Zen)
- Good Contract (by Bold Bidder)
  - Slam Bid (by Forli)
    - **CYDALIA** (by Cresta Rider)
- Professional Dance (by Nijinsky II)
  - **FORLI'S TANGO** (by Forli)
  - **NINJA DANCER** (by Miswaki)
- Suprina (by Vaguely Noble)
  - **L'EMIGRANT** (by The Minstrel)
  - **SALPINX** (by Northern Dancer)
  - **ZALAZL** (by Roberto)
  - **THEATRICIAN** (by Theatrical (IRE))
- Queen Sucree (by Ribot)
  - **CANNONADE** (by Bold Bidder)
  - **CIRCLE HOME** (by Bold Bidder)
  - **DEL SARTO** (by Bold Bidder)
  - Georgica (by Raise a Native)
    - Georgica's Gal (by Raja Baba)
      - **OUR ROYAL HIGHNESS** (by Top Avenger)
    - Rythmique (by The Minstrel)
      - City Ex (by Ardross)
        - **DONKEY ENGINE (IRE)** (by Fairy King)
        - **PETIT POUCET (GB)** (by Fairy King)
  - Kennelot (by Gallant Man)
    - **LOTKA** (by Danzig)
      - **LOTTA DANCING** (by Alydar)
    - Nicole Mon Amour (by Bold Bidder)
      - **CIELAMOUR** (by Conquistador Cielo)
      - **ORBIS** (by Conquistador Cielo)
    - **STEPHAN'S ODYSSEY** (by Danzig)
  - Princess Sucree (by Roberto)
    - **BUROOJ (GB)** (by Danzig)
    - **RASHEEK** (by Topsider)
  - **WASSL TOUCH** (by Northern Dancer)
- Royal Match (by Turn-to)
  - Hardliner (by Buckpasser)
    - Bold Flawless (by Bold Bidder)
      - **GENTILHOMME (GB)** (by Generous)
      - **LIFE AT THE TOP (GB)** (by Habitat)
      - **TIGER SHARK** (by Chief's Crown)
      - **SOUND REASONING (IRE)** (by Known Fact)
    - **JOHN'S GOLD** (by Bold Bidder)
      - Tough as Nails (by Majestic Light)
        - **CATRAIL** (by Storm Cat)
  - Matchless Miss (by Dust Commander)
    - **MATCHLESS DIABLO** (by Diablo)
    - **SUPERVITE (IND)** (by Line In The Sand)
  - **MATCHLESS NATIVE** (by Raise a Native)
  - **REXSON** (by Bold Bidder)
- **TOSMAH** (by Tim Tam)
  - **LA GUIDECCA** (by Royal I. J.)
- **FOLK DANCER** (by Native Dancer)
- Natalma (by Native Dancer)
  - Arctic Dancer (by Nearctic)
    - Danseuse Etoile (by Buckpasser)
      - **DAMPIERRE** (by Lear Fan)
      - **DANSEUR DE CORDE** (by Foolish Pleasure)
      - **DANSEUR ETOILE** (by Spectacular Bid)
      - Dauphine (by Spectacular Bid)
        - **IRISH BOSS (IND)** (by Waajib)
      - **DRAPEAU TRICOLORE** (by Irish River (FR))
    - Feuille d'Erable (by Secretariat)
      - Pris de Fer (by Sir Ivor)
        - **GULLIVIEGOLD** (by Gulch)
      - **LA PREVOYANTE** (by Buckpasser)
      - Quat'sous (by Buckpasser)
        - Abeille (by Tentam)
          - **ALOUETTE** (by Malvado)
        - L'Anse Au Griffon (by Prove Out)
          - **NORTHERN LANCE** (by Sovereign Dancer)
    - **BORN A LADY** (by Tentam)
      - **ARROWTOWN** (by Mr. Prospector)
    - Native Era (by Victorian Era)
      - Barzana (by Icecapade)
        - **BARZANA DANA** (by Dr. Carter)
        - **GRAY NOT BAY** (by Procida)
      - Eranos (by Arts and Letters)

NATALMA (continued)

- Godsrun (by Godswalk)
  - Always Above (IND) (by Malvado)
    - **CAMBRIAN (IND)** (by Excalibur's Lake)
  - **THANKSGIVING** (by Riyahi)
- **MARATHON** (by Runnett)
- **NATIVE VICTOR** (by Victoria Park)
- **NORTHERN DANCER** (by Nearctic)
- Raise the Standard (by Hoist the Flag)
  - Bonita Francita (by Devil's Bag)
    - **ETTERBY PARK** (by Silver Hawk)
    - **JULES** (by Forty Niner)
    - **ORPEN** (by Lure)
  - **COUP DE FOLIE** (by Halo)
    - **COUP DE GENIE** (by Mr. Prospector)
    - **EXIT TO NOWHERE** (by Irish River (FR))
    - **HYDRO CALIDO** (by Nureyev)
    - **MACHIAVELLIAN** (by Mr. Prospector)
    - Salchow (by Nijinsky II)
    - **WAY OF LIGHT** (by Woodman)
- **REGAL DANCER** (by Grey Monarch)
- Spring Adieu (by Buckpasser)
  - Passing Gull (by Arctic Tern)
    - **PASSING TRICK** (by Phone Trick)
  - Razyana (by His Majesty)
    - **DANEHILL** (by Danzig)
    - **EAGLE EYED** (by Danzig)
    - **EUPHONIC** (by The Minstrel)
    - **HARPIA** (by Danzig)
  - You're My Lady (by Roberto)
    - **YOUTHFUL LEGS** (by Explodent)

Aspidistra
(by Better Self)

- **A. DECK** (by First Cabin)
- **CHINATOWNER** (by Needles)
- **DR. FAGER** (by Rough'n Tumble)
- Magic (by Buckpasser)
  - Charedi (by In Reality)
    - Gana Facil (by Le Fabuleux)
      - **CAHILL ROAD** (by Fappiano)
      - Orseno (by In Reality)
        - **MINERY** (by Forty Niner)
      - **UNBRIDLED** (by Fappiano)
    - Magic Blue (by Cure the Blues)
      - **PALIKAR** (by Star de Naskra)
    - **PENTELICUS** (by Fappiano)
  - Magaro (by Caro (IRE))
    - **COOLAWIN** (by Nodouble)
    - Sister Chrys (by Fit to Fight)
      - **SILVER RHAPSODY** (by Silver Hawk)
    - **TAYASU TSUYOSHI** (by Sunday Silence)
  - **MAGNIFICENCE** (by Graustark)
  - Mazurka (by Northern Dancer)
    - Direwarning (by Caveat)
      - **CAVONNIER** (by Batonnier)
- Perplexing (by Esmero)
  - Baffling Queen (by Royal Union)
    - Queens Wonder (by Minnesota Mac)
      - **NALEES WONDER** (by Nalees Man)
- Quit Me Not (by Bold Reason)
  - Eternal Vow (by Nasty and Bold)
    - **MISS PROSPECTOR** (by Crafty Prospector)
  - I'm Pretty (by Secretariat)
    - **JUDGE T C** (by Judge Smells)
- **TA WEE** (by Intentionally)
  - **ENTROPY** (by What a Pleasure)
  - **GREAT ABOVE** (by Minnesota Mac)
  - **TAX HOLIDAY** (by What a Pleasure)
    - Over Issue (by Fappiano)
      - **EXPENSIVE ISSUE** (by Deerhound)
  - Thill (by Iron Ruler)
    - **CINTULA** (by Ramsinga)
    - Parchessi (by Youth)
      - **MORDEKAI JONES** (by Native Uproar)
- **TWEAK** (by Secretariat)
  - Stem (by Damascus)
    - **DINNER AFFAIR** (by Who's for Dinner)
  - Twitch (by Fappiano)
    - **ZANETTI** (by With Approval)

Banquet Bell
(by Polynesian)

CHATEAUGAY (by Swaps)
Jawn (by Graustark)
  True Esteem (by Roberto)
    PICHY NANY (by Gran Zar (MEX))
Luiana (by My Babu)
  Darbyvail (by Roberto)
    TURKISH TRYST (by Turkoman)
  Fair Renown (by Stage Door Johnny)
    Lady of Renown (by His Majesty)
      CUTTING BLADE (by Sharpo)
  LITTLE CURRENT (by Sea-Bird)
  Luv Luiana (by Roberto)
    ALMAZYOON (by Danehill)
  Mighty Spender (by Never Bend)
    Lots a Promise (by His Majesty)
      Lent (by Guilty Conscience)
        COLLATERAL (by Iron Courage)
        GOOD RESOLUTION (by Dinner Money)
    PRAYERS'N PROMISES (by Foolish Pleasure)
      ANJIZ (by Nureyev)
      NABEEL DANCER (by Northern Dancer)
    WATER DANCE (by Nijinsky II)
  Winding Stream (by Swaps)
    On the Straight (by Proud Clarion)
      LITTLE SPEED (by Morespeed)
    Une Soiree Perdue (by Hoist the Flag)
    Recusal (by Raja Baba)
      VITTORIO (by Vittorioso)
PRIMONETTA (by Swaps)
  CUM LAUDE LAURIE (by Hail to Reason)
    Laurie's Angel (by Graustark)
    Desert Angel (by Desert Wine)
      DESERT AIR (by Manzotti)
      DESERT DEMON (by Manzotti)
      SAND SAINT (by Manzotti)
  GRENFALL (by Graustark)
  MAUD MULLER (by Graustark)
  PRINCE THOU ART (by Hail to Reason)
  Sunshine O'My Life (by Graustark)
    DANCE O'MY LIFE (by Sovereign Dancer)

Best in Show
(by Traffic Judge)

BLUSH WITH PRIDE (by Blushing Groom (FR))
  BETTER THAN HONOUR (by Deputy Minister)
  SMOLENSK (by Danzig)
GIELGUD (by Sir Ivor)
MALINOWSKI (by Sir Ivor)
Minnie Hauk (by Sir Ivor)
  AVIANCE (IRE) (by Northfields)
    CHIMES OF FREEDOM (by Private Account)
      TOMISUE'S INDY (by A.P. Indy)
    IMPERFECT CIRCLE (by Riverman)
    SPINNING WORLD (by Nureyev)
  CHIEF CONTENDER (IRE) (by Sadler's Wells)
  Perfect Alibi (by Law Society)
    LIKELY STORY (IRE) (by Night Shift)
MONROE (by Sir Ivor)
  Danthonia (by Northern Dancer)
    ZANTE (GB) (by Zafonic)
  Didicoy (by Danzig)
    DIDINA (GB) (by Nashwan)
  DIESE (by Diesis (GB))
  ILE DE JINSKY (by Ile de Bourbon)
  MASTERCLASS (by The Minstrel)
  XAAR (GB) (by Zafonic)
Nijinsky's Best (by Nijinsky II)
  YAGLI (by Jade Hunter)
Sex Appeal (by Buckpasser)
  Bella Senora (by Northern Dancer)
    D'ARROS (IRE) (by Baillamont)
    NAPOLI (GB) (by Baillamont)
  Carillon Miss (by The Minstrel)

SEX APPEAL (continued)
    BLU CARILLON (IRE) (by Love the Groom)
    TRY MY SEGNOR (GB) (by Tirol)
  EL GRAN SENOR (by Northern Dancer)
  Golden Oriole (by Northern Dancer)
    Sunny Morning (by Law Society)
      SHIROKITA CROSS (JPN) (by Tamamo Cross)
  Russian Ballet (by Nijinsky II)
    DR JOHNSON (by Woodman)
  SOLAR (by Halo)
    Love From the Air (by Deputy Minister)
      LADY PALOMA (by Clever Trick)
      TAKEAWAKATLOVE (by Miswaki)
    Solariat (by Secretariat)
      ALEX NUREYEV (by Nureyev)
      ANGELINA BALLERINA (by Nureyev)
      SEXY SLEW (by Slew o' Gold)
  TRY MY BEST (by Northern Dancer)
Show Lady (by Sir Ivor)
  Dancing Show (by Nijinsky II)
    HURRICANE SKY (by Star Watch)
    Shantha's Choice (AUS) (by Canny Lad)
      REDOUTE'S CHOICE (AUS) (by Danehill)
    UMATILLA (NZ) (by Miswaki)
  GREAT REGENT (by Vice Regent)

Blue Delight
(by Blue Larkspur)

ALL BLUE (by Bull Lea)
BUBBLEY (by Bull Lea)
  Fizzy (by Swoon's Son)
    WHO DUZZIT (by Bold Lad)
  Giggles (by Helioscope)
    FERROUS (by Iron Ruler)
  Ginny's Little Eva (by Taga)
    Deficit Funning (by Nile Delta)
      Fast Funning (by Partez)
        BODABINGBODABOOM (by American Artist)
  Meme Chose (by On-and-On)
    RED CORAL (AUS) (by Red God)
    TARIB (by Habitat)
  Royal Chuckle (by Beau Prince)
    ROYAL PROCTOR (by Proctor)
  Traci's Treat (by Ruffled Feathers)
    SILVER FEATHERS (by Age Quod Agis)
Delidore (by Commodore M.)
  Lady Vogue (by Prince John)
    Liberty Vogue (by Riboronde)
      LORD MUD (by Mud and Water)
      Mischief Mud (by Mud and Water)
      REVILLEW SLEW (by Can't Be Slew)
    Pick Up Your Cards (by Piaster)
      LINDA CARD (by Noble Monk (IRE))
      RARECARD (by Slewpy)
  Tom's Ray (by Seaneen)
    Dumpty Tom (by Dumpty Humpty)
      Pink Room (by Racing Room)
      MANTIC (by Majestic Man)
    Popps Dancer (by Banderilla)
      SHE'S A CHAMP (by Island Champ)
KENTUCKY PRIDE (by Bull Lea)
PRINCESS TURIA (by Heliopolis)
  FORWARD PASS (by On-and-On)
  Maysville Lass (by Bull Lea)
    Country Belle (by Herbager)
      BELLIMBUSTO (by Be My Guest)
  Real Cuno (by Mark-Ye-Well)
    Betty Coed (by No Robbery)
      Irish Betty (by The Irish Lord)
        BIG CREEK BETTY (by In the Woodpile)
    Real Empress (by Young Emperor)
      REAL EMPEROR (by Raise a Cup)
  Tim's Princess (by Tim Tam)
    Balletic (by Nijinsky II)
      Classy Cassie (by Lord Durham)
        ROSES FOR CLASSY (by Son of Briartic)
    Bidders Delight (by Bold Bidder)
      RED CLOUD (by Buckaroo)
    NATIVE HERITAGE (by Raise a Native)

PRINCESS TURIA (continued)
- Speedy Shoes (by Francis S.)
  - Little Fawn Eyes (by Exclusive Native)
    - Trail Bench (by Walker's)
      - **TAY ROB** (by Hoist the Silver)
- Tout de Vous (by Stevward)
  - **FRIVOLOUS MISCHIEF** (by Gaelic Dancer)
- **TURN TO TURIA** (by Best Turn)
REAL DELIGHT (by Bull Lea)
- Heliolight (by Helioscope)
  - Heliogram (by Native Charger)
    - **GREAT HUNTER** (by Chieftain)
  - **LONESOME RIVER** (by Rough'n Tumble)
  - Minnetonka (by Chieftain)
    - **BARRERA** (by Raise a Native)
    - **EMINENCY** (by Vaguely Noble)
    - **KATONKA** (by Minnesota Mac)
      - **GIVE ME STRENGTH** (by Exclusive Native)
      - **INCA CHIEF** (by Mr. Prospector)
      - Legacy of Strength (by Affirmed)
        - **SILENT HAPPINESS** (by Sunday Silence)
        - **STINGER (JPN)** (by Sunday Silence)
      - Montage (by Alydar)
        - **ANDROS BAY** (by Alleged)
        - Mahrah (by Vaguely Noble)
          - **FAHIM (GB)** (by Green Desert)
      - My Prayer (by Hero's Honor)
        - **THE TEXAS TUNNEL** (by Oggygian)
      - **TALAKENO** (by Vaguely Noble)
    - **PHAEDRA** (by Graustark)
  - Roundup Rose (by Minnesota Mac)
    - **CODEX** (by Arts and Letters)
    - Eyes (by Iron Ruler)
      - Crosseyed (by Dickens Hill (IRE))
        - **CROSSEYED DEVIL** (by Devil's Cry)
      - **ERSTWHILE** (by Arts and Letters)
        - **URUS** (by Kris S.)
        - **VILHELM** (by Silver Hawk)
      - Wolf Trail (by Superbity)
        - **DUSTIN'S DREAM** (by Quiet American)
    - Fulfilled (by Le Fabuleux)
      - Nashoba (by Superbity)
        - **DON'S SHO** (by Don's Choice)
    - **RODEO STAR** (by Nodouble)
  - Silken Ripples (by Roberto)
    - **SMOOTH RUNNER** (by Local Talent)
- **NO FOOLING** (by Tom Fool)
- **PLUM CAKE** (by Ponder)
  - **PLUM BOLD** (by Bold Ruler)
  - Plum Plum (by On-and-On)
    - Plum Happy (by Round Table)
      - **FOBBY FORBES** (by Bold Forbes)
      - Silentia (by Silent Screen)
        - **WATERGATE ROAD** (by Gate Dancer)
    - **PRUNEPLUM** (by Olden Times)
    - Right Turn (by Turn-to)
      - **RICH CREAM** (by Creme dela Creme)
      - Right Right (by Noholme II)
        - Darlin Darlene (by Raise a Bid)
          - **JOYOUS GARD** (by Lyphaness)
          - **KOSHARI DANCER** (by Lyphaness)
          - **LYPHS LITTLE DARLN** (by Lyphaness)
  - Plumpon (by Damascus)
    - From Now On (by Raise a Native)
      - **SOAP CREEK SLEW** (by Tsunami Slew)
  - **SUGAR PLUM TIME** (by Bold Ruler)
    - **CHRISTMAS BONUS** (by Key to the Mint)
      - **BONUS MONEY (GB)** (by Chief's Crown)
      - **BRIGHT CANDLES** (by El Gran Senor)
        - **GRAND SLAM** (by Gone West)
        - **LEESTOWN** (by Seattle Slew)
    - **CHRISTMAS GIFT** (by Green Desert)
    - **IRON COUNTY XMAS** (by Cox's Ridge)
    - **SHEBL** (by Green Desert)
    - Yaqut (by Northern Dancer)
      - **ESTIMRAAR (IRE)** (by Bustino (GB))
  - Sultans Favorite (by Bagdad)
    - Harem Slippers (by The Axe II)
      - Judarun (by Raise a Cup)
        - **HALARUN** (by Fast Gold)
  - Sweet Tooth (by On-and-On)
    - 'N Everything Nice (by Damascus)
      - China Bell (by Seattle Slew)
        - **CHINA STORM** (by Storm Cat)

REAL DELIGHT (continued)
- **ALYDAR** (by Raise a Native)
- Gleaming Smile (by Gleaming)
  - **GRIN** (by Danzig)
  - Joyous Pirouette (by Nureyev)
    - **WILDLY JOYOUS** (by Wild Again)
- **OUR MIMS** (by Herbager)
  - Mimbet (by Raise a Native)
    - **ELMHURST** (by Wild Again)
- **SUGAR AND SPICE** (by Key to the Mint)
  - **CINNAMON SUGAR (IRE)** (by Wild Again)
  - **SURE TURN** (by Best Turn)
- Yule Log (by Bold Ruler)
  - **CHRISTMAS PAST** (by Grey Dawn II)
- **SPRING SUNSHINE** (by Nashua)
- **LUCKY SO N' SO** (by Alydar)
- Mawgrit (by Hoist the Flag)
  - **DAZZLE ME JOLIE** (by Carr de Naskra)
  - Mawkish (by Alydar)
    - **RARE PICK** (by Rare Brick)
- Pet Eagle (by Raise a Native)
  - Mirror Bright (by Gleaming)
    - **BRIGHT AGAIN** (by Wild Again)
    - **BRIGHT ASSET** (by Private Account)
- **RAISE A CUP** (by Raise a Native)
Whirling Lark (by Whirlaway)
- Cool World (by Hill Prince)
  - False Dawn (by Double Jay)
    - **JAMILA KADIR** (by Turn to Reason)
- **GO LIGHTLY** (by Faultless)
- Miss Lightfoot (by Sun Again)
  - Farthingale (by Nadir)
    - Fashion Revue (by Tudor Minstrel)
      - **ROSCON** (by Princely Native)
  - Graceful Way (by Nadir)
    - **CARRY THE BANNER** (by Advocator)
    - Certain Appeal (by Norcliffe)
      - **DUSTY APPEAL** (by Dust Commander)
    - Graceful Banner (by Decidedly)
      - **BLACKHAWK'S GHOST** (by Stutz Blackhawk)
- Palm Leaves (by Citation)
  - Famous Flame (by Bagdad)
    - Worthy of Optimism (by Twice Worthy)
      - Neponsit (by True Knight)
        - **LAFITTE (MEX)** (by Fuzzbuster)
  - Leavesumthinking (by Raja Baba)
    - Crimson Leaves (by Crimson Satan)
      - **CRIMSON MEMORY** (by Mountain Native)
    - Leavesum Lucy (by Raise a Cup)
      - **LOVEUMOR LEAVESUM** (by Mountain Native)
- Sophistry (by Dedicate)
  - **JEWEL OF THE NIGHT** (by Pia Star)
  - Sunrise Sue (by Grey Dawn II)
    - **EL SENOR** (by Valdez)
- Stolen Glance (by Spy Song)
  - Guyandot (by Torsion)
    - Silver Torque (by Silver Hawk)
      - **ROSE ROSENBAUM** (by Turkoman)
    - **TALK ABOUT HOME** (by Elocutionist)
  - Miss Roman Song (by Roman Line)
    - **SING QUICK** (by To the Quick)
    - **SMITHQUICK** (by Hopeful Word)
  - Popaway (by Cyclotron)
    - Solar Witch (by Beauguerre)
      - Another Runner (by Speculating)
        - Miz Danus (by Mundanus)
          - **HERE COMES WALTER** (by The Hague)
    - **STOP THE RAIN** (by Rainy Lake)
  - **PRINCE TERRELL** (by Blue Prince)
- Tender Night (by Bagdad)
  - **DYNANITE** (by Dynastic)
    - **DYNAWITE** (by Vigors)
      - **GLACIAL** (by Northern Flagship)
    - **STRAWBERRY WINE** (by Strawberry Road (AUS))
  - **TENDERLY YOURS** (by Irish Castle)

Boudoir II
(by Mahmoud)

Bowl of Roses (by Alibhai)
  Chateau Rose (by Chateaugay)
    NICHIDO ARASHI (JPN) (by Bold and Able)
  Flower Centre (by Jaipur)
    FAHREWOHL (GER) (by Hotfoot)
    Stamen (by Ballymore)
      Florescence (IND) (by Grey Gaston)
        REGAL EQUITY (IND) (by Razeen)
    THE NEUROLOGIST (IRE) (by Ragstone)
      QUADRIGEMINAL (by Mac Diarmida)
  Pride City Gal (by Gallant Man)
    OUI MADAME ROSE (by Oui Henry)
Caluria (by Heliopolis)
  Botany (by Indian Chief II)
    MORISQUETA (by Search Tradition)
    YAMOLAI (ARG) (by Search Tradition)
  Most Magic (by T. V. Lark)
    Mineoath (by Stage Coach)
      Long Way (by Climber)
        GAD BRAIAN (by Ball Fighter)
Flower Bed (by Beau Pere)
  BRAMBLES (by Beau Max)
  FLORAL PARK (by Alibhai)
    Bold Flora (by Bold Favorite)
      Berta Flora (by Roberto)
        SMART TOO (by Smarten)
      ROOTENTOOTENWOOTEN (by Diesis (GB))
        KUKULCAN (by Cox's Ridge)
      Slick Turn (by Best Turn)
        RUSSELLTHEMUSSELL (by American Standard)
      TURN BOLD (by Best Turn)
    Mugwumpery (by Assemblyman)
      MUCKRAKER (by Judger)
    Patriotic Petunia (by National)
      Freedom Flower (by Raise a Man)
        STORMY REGENT (by Archregent)
      Miss Flower Belle (by Torsion)
        PRORUTORI (by Providential (IRE))
      Torsion Belle (by Torsion)
        Beaty Sark (by Deputy Minister)
          SHANANIE'S BEAT (by Shananie)
        CRAFTY DUDE (by Crafty Prospector)
      THAT LADY (by Trust a Native)
  FLOWER BOWL (by Alibhai)
    BOWL OF FLOWERS (by Sailor)
      Royal Bowl (by Royal Gunner)
        Fleet Bowl (by Fleet Nasrullah)
          Glass Fleet (by Pass the Glass)
            DANGER (by Bluebird)
          Glass Tumbler (by Pass the Glass)
            Lift Your Glass (by Pirate's Bounty)
              MAGIC GLASS (by Never Tabled)
      SPRUCE BOUQUET (by Big Spruce)
    GRAUSTARK (by Ribot)
    HIS MAJESTY (by Ribot)
    Yetive (by Ribot)
      Aunt Jenny (by Hail to Reason)
        COUSIN JEN (by Age Quod Agis)
      Bright Trillium (by Raise a Native)
        Berillium (by Good Counsel)
          FLAGS WAVING (by Delta Flag)
        BRIGHT CIDE UP (by Slewacide)
      High Larch (by Bold Ruler)
        Princess Palatine (by Raise a Native)
          Special Fancy (by Hawkin's Special)
            KRAAL (by Slewvescent)
      Migratory (by Sea-Bird)
        Le Clerc (by True Knight)
          SUPERABUNDANCE (by Exuberant)
    Green Finger (by Better Self)
      BLANDFORD PARK (by Little Current)
      FREE HAND (by Gallant Man)
      Green Signal (by Roberto)
        White Feather (by Tom Rolfe)
          SNOWY APPARITION (by Devil's Bag)
        TAKE ME OUT (by Cure the Blues)
      Point Out (by Gallant Man)
        Finisterre (AUS) (by Biscay)
          MANILASTERRE (by Manila)

FLOWER BED (continued)
      OUR POETIC PRINCE (by Yeats)
      Primary Force (by Middleground)
        Noisy Night (AUS) (by Town Crier)
      DANCING POET (by Yeats)
  Multiflora (by Beau Max)
    Bold Flourish (by Bold Lad)
      Exotic Visage (by Tom Rolfe)
        EXOTIC EAGLE (by Beau's Eagle)
        Toppeshamme (by Topsider)
          STRIMMER (by Sharpo)
    GALLANT BLOOM (by Gallant Man)
      Rare Flower (by Graustark)
        Robra (by Roberto)
          KIYO AMY (by Fast Gold)
    Orchid Vale (by Gallant Man)
      BATMAN (by Godswalk)
      LADY'S SLIPPER (AUS) (by Dancer's Image)
      MISTY VALLEY (by Majestic Light)
Royal Hostess (by Alibhai)
  Royal n' Worthy (by Twice Worthy)
    Worthy Times (by Times Rush)
      WILLIS G. (by Crafty Native)
  Spanish Guest (by Alhambra)
    SPANISH JULIE (by Smasher)
  Spes Nostra (by Mr. Busher)
    Miss San-Jo (by Amarullah)
      NATIVE GOAL (by Exclusive Native)
      Plumed Miss (by Military Plume)
        Gato Numero Uno (by Comet Kat)
          ANISHA (by Danski)
          SUNITYA (by North Prospect)
    Paisley Square (by Amarullah)
      Hilarious Square (by Fast Hilarious)
        JON DARK (by Distinctive Pro)
        PRO FLIGHT (by Distinctive Pro)
YOUR HOST (by Alibhai)
Your Hostess (by Alibhai)
  CORAGGIOSO (by Gallant Man)
    ENCOURAGE (by Quack)
    Hoist the Banner (by Hoist the Flag)
      STORMY DEEP (by Diamond Shoal (GB))
    Love Sick (by Raise a Native)
      TRAVELIN LOVER (by Pilgrim)
    Runny Nose (by It's Freezing)
      SHA RUNNER (by Inland Voyager)
  Dancing Hostess (by Sword Dancer)
    Balcony Dancer (by Gallant Romeo)
      EXCLUSIVE NUREYEV (by Nureyev)
    LOOSEN UP (by Never Bend)
    PALLADIUM (by T. V. Lark)
  Etiquette (by Bernborough)
    COMMAND MODULE (by Knightly Manner)
    Many Thanks (by T. V. Lark)
      Love and Kisses (by Viceregal)
        WESTERN RUN (by Providential (IRE))
    MR. POMRANKY (by Cannonade)
    Thank You Note (by Creme dela Creme)
      LISWAKI (by Miswaki)
      LIBRADA'S BRIGADE (by Bet Twice)
    White Lie (by Bald Eagle)
      BAD CONDUCT (by Stalwart)
      Beautiful Mother (by Damascus)
        MOTHER'S TREASURE (by Hoist the Silver)
    HIPPODAMIA (by Hail to Reason)
      GLOBE (by Secretariat)
      Housatonic (by Riverman)
        HOUSA DANCER (FR) (by Fabulous Dancer)
        HOUSAMIX (by Linamix (FR))
      HOYA (by Secreto)
      Synclinal (by Vaguely Noble)
        Taroz (by Capote)
          TAP (by Mari's Book)
      Laurel Lark (by T. V. Lark)
        Number One Lark (by Soy Numero Uno)
          SHARI'S GLORY (by On to Glory)
        Touche (by Blade)
          ASSERCHE (by Assert (IRE))
      Souveraine (by Personality)
        SAINT DESIR (by Saint Cyrien)
        SUPREMATIE (FR) (by Gay Mecene)
    White Moon (by Hail to Reason)
      Cosmic Law (by Delta Judge)
        COSMIC TIGER (by Tim the Tiger)

CHILITO (by Strawberry Road (AUS))
ONCE A SAILOR (by Vice Regent)
EL PERICO (by Drone)
Hawaiian Joss (by Hawaii)
ALPHABULOUS (by Alphabatim)
SILENT WHITE (by Silent Screen)
White Reason (by Hail to Reason)
LINDON LIME (by Green Dancer)
WONDER DANCER (by Raise a Native)
GALLATIA (by Gallant Man)
GALLINA (by Raise a Native)
So Desirable (by Seattle Song)
LOVELORN LADY (by Fit to Fight)
RIGHT CROSS (by Nashua)
Gay Hostess (by Royal Charger)
Betty Loraine (by Prince John)
Betty's Secret (by Secretariat)
Catopetl (by Northern Dancer)
CLOSE CONFLICT (by High Estate (IRE))
NEWTON'S LAW (IRE) (by Law Society)
From Sea to Sea (by Gregorian)
SEALAUNCH (by Relaunch)
INTERREX (by Vice Regent)
ISTABRAQ (IRE) (by Sadler's Wells)
SECRETO (by Northern Dancer)
CARACOLERO (by Graustark)
Magic One (by Secretariat)
Determined One (by Determined King)
NEMURO (by Northrop)
Native Lorraine (by Raise a Native)
Dear Lorraine (FR) (by Nonoalco)
CATCH THE BLUES (IRE) (by Bluebird)
Will Patricia (by Bellypha (IRE))
HOPETOSEEYA (by Moment of Hope)
PRAIRIE MAIDEN (by Badger Land)
Pride of Darby (by Danzig)
BAHAMIAN SUNSHINE (by Sunshine Forever)
BUCKEYE SEARCH (by Meadowlake)
Caronatta (by Raise a Native)
RALLY RUN (by Dixieland Band)
CROWNED PRINCE (by Raise a Native)
LOVELY GYPSY (by Armageddon)
MAJESTIC PRINCE (by Raise a Native)
Meadow Blue (by Raise a Native)
Allegedly Blue (by Alleged)
HAWAIT AL BARR (GB) (by Green Desert)
Mangala (by Sharpen Up (GB))
ALLIED FORCES (by Miswaki)
NUREYEV'S BEST (by Nureyev)
Really Blue (by Believe It)
REAL QUIET (by Quiet American)
Our Queen (by Raise a Native)
Casino Babe (by Golden Act)
CASINO MAGISTRATE (by Magesterial)
Rollabout (by My Babu)
LADY FACE (by Proud Clarion)
Rolling (by Fleet Nasrullah)
Flag Lily (by Raise a Native)
CASA DE KOBI (by Tally Ho the Fox)
La Menina (by Royal Charger)
Consentida (by Beau Max)
Scarlet Ink (by Crimson Satan)
SCARLET BOUQUET (by Northern Taste)
SCARLET RIBBON (by Northern Taste)
Lady Ambassador (by Hill Prince)
Champagne Lover (by Champagne Charlie)
FABIANAZO (by Buckaroo)
Classy Twist (by Twist the Axe)
WITH A TWIST (by Fappiano)
POLICY MATTER (by Topsider)
Lady Nasus (by Gun Shot)
PYRGOS (by Bold and Brave)
MINSTREL GREY (by Tudor Grey)
My Guest (by Mister Gus)
Exclusive Hostess (by Exclusive Native)
I AM ON FIRE (by Forli)
MEMORABLE MITCH (by Mehmet)
NATIVE GUEST (by Raise a Native)
RAISE YOUR SIGHTS (by Raise a Native)
In Your Sights (by Green Dancer)
BRITE ADAM (by High Brite)
Very Best Friend (by Best Turn)
VICE N' FRIENDLY (by Vice Regent)

ROYAL CLIPPER (by Royal Charger)
T. V. COMMERCIAL (by T. V. Lark)
Votre Hotesse (by Nantallah)
AUBERGE (by Hail to Reason)
Our Duckling (by Quack)
Our Crowd (by Al Hattab)
HUSHED GOODBYE (by Secret Hello)
SWAZI GIRL (by Hatchet Man)
SWAZI'S MOMENT (by Moment of Hope)
Small Hotel (by Raise a Native)
Minhah (by Little Current)
RED DRAGON (by Northern Secret)
Spare That Tree (by Hatchet Man)
DANVILLE (by Demons Begone)

Bourtai
(by Stimulus)

AMBASSADOR (by Nasrullah)
BANTA (by Some Chance)
Golden Sari (by Ambiorix)
Royal Folly (by Tom Fool)
Heartbreak (by Stage Door Johnny)
CORRAZONA (by El Gran Senor)
THIRTY SIX RED (by Slew o' Gold)
Labwa (by Lyphard)
BAADERAH (IRE) (by Cadeaux Genereux)
MAJESTIC FOLLY (by Alydar)
MORELIA (by Deputy Minister)
POLSKI BOY (by Danzig Connection)
PRINCE VALIANT (by Stage Door Johnny)
SELARI (by Prince John)
Silver Sari (by Prince John)
BIG SPRUCE (by Herbager)
JABOT (by Bold Ruler)
ENCOLURE (by Riva Ridge)
MANTA (by Ben Lomond)
Andrushka (by Giboulee)
POINCIANA (GB) (by Big Spruce)
Princess Margaret (by Vaguely Noble)
NOBLE PARISTO (by Paristo)
Patola (by B. Major)
Cheeka Lodge (by Tumiga)
SANTU PRETU (by Flag Admiral)
MANDATE (by Prince John)
Poster Girl (by Nasrullah)
Honor Maid (by Prince John)
HONOR MEDAL (by Avatar)
SWEET MAID (by Proud Clarion)
JESTIC (by His Majesty)
PEER PRINCE (by Vaguely Noble)
ILLUSTRIOUS (by Round Table)
Middle Cornish (by Speak John)
CONFORMIST (by Alleged)
Middle Course (by Storm Bird)
SANSKRIT (by Pancho Villa)
RINGSIDE (by Sir Ivor)
TALKING PICTURE (by Speak John)
EASY TO COPY (by Affirmed)
DESERT EASE (IRE) (by Green Desert)
Easy 'n Gold (by Slew o' Gold)
DIXIELAND GOLD (by Dixieland Band)
EASY DEFINITION (IRE) (by Alzao)
TWO-TWENTY-TWO (IRE) (by Fairy King)
EPICURE'S GARDEN (by Affirmed)
LISIEUX ROSE (IRE) (by Generous)
GUARANTEED INCOME (by Saratoga Six)
LOW KEY AFFAIR (by Affirmed)
TRUSTED PARTNER (by Affirmed)
ARCHIVE FOOTAGE (GB) (by Sadler's Wells)
BAYOU (by Hill Prince)
Alluvial (by Buckpasser)
COASTAL (by Majestic Prince)
Dancing Detente (by Nijinsky II)
Ackrimony (by Ack Ack)
CANNONBALL (by Cannonade)
Athenian Princess (by Ack Ack)
BILL'S PILL (by Silver Ghost)
Change Partners (by Ack Ack)

LEVEE (continued)

| | | **JUAN IN A MILLION** (by Ends Well)
| | Pretty Pretender (by Quack)
| | | **KAFIRISTAN** (by Key to the Mint)
| | Take Warning (by Traffic Judge)
| | **FORETAKE** (by Forli)
| | **HEED WARNING** (by Reviewer)
| | **NO BEND** (by Never Bend)
| Raise the Levee (by Raise a Native)
| | Leave Me (by Never Bend)
| | | Gold Heist (by Mr. Prospector)
| | | | **HEISTER** (by Air Forbes Won)
| | | | **SHOTGUN** (by Pancho Villa)
| | | Raise Me (by Mr. Prospector)
| | | | **FAIRLEE WILD** (by Wild Again)
| | | | Stand From Under (by First Albert)
| | | | **ENDSASEEKET** (by Ends Well)
| | | **LIVER STAND** (by Mt. Livermore)
ROYAL GUNNER (by Royal Charger)
SHUVEE (by Nashua)
| **BENEFICE** (by Damascus)
| **SHUKEY** (by Key to the Mint)
| | Heart Beat Away (by Green Forest)
| | **ESKIWAY** (by Eskimo)
| **TOM SWIFT** (by Tom Rolfe)
Sister Shu (by Nashua)
| Lulu Mon Amour (by Tom Rolfe)
| | **ARBUSHA** (by Danzig)
| | Danlu (by Danzig)
| | | **STRATEGIC CHOICE** (by Alleged)
| | **NICHOLAS** (by Danzig)
| **NORDANCE** (by Danzig)
| **SHUDANZ** (by Danzig Connection)
| Shufleur (by Tom Rolfe)
| | **MANZOTTI** (by Nijinsky II)
| | Marsh Maid (by Coastal)
| | | **CRAFTY CASH** (by Crafty Prospector)
| | Shujinsky (by Nijinsky II)
| | | Wandering Lace (by Private Account)
| | | **DRINA** (by Regal and Royal)
| Sister Mint (by Key to the Mint)
| | Danzig's Southside (by Danzig)
| | **DANZATRICE** (by Pancho Villa)
Louisiana (by Nadir)
| Cajun Princess (by Advocator)
| **RAISE A BOY** (by Raise a Native)
Poetic License (by Count Fleet)
| Blue Medley (by First Landing)
| | Exclusive Fir (by Exclusive Native)
| | | **EXIT POLL** (by Seattle Slew)
| | | **WELCOME DAN SUR** (by Magesterial)
| | **WHITE FIR** (by Swaps)
| Spoonerism (by Tell)
| **TELL AGAIN** (by Petrone)
Salaza (by Pilate)
| Songful (by Spy Song)
| | Fantastic Go (by Our Rulla)
| | | Fantastic Run (by Rerun)
| | | **TOVI RUN** (by Kfar Tov)
| | Miss Starlet (by Imbros)
| | **MISTY'S STARLET** (by Misty Day)
| Tondalayo (by Polynesian)
| **WANDERLURE** (by Hill Prince)

Courtly Dee
(by Never Bend)

AISHAH (by Alydar)
| **ALDIZA** (by Storm Cat)
ALI OOP (by Al Hattab)
ALTHEA (by Alydar)
| **ALYSSUM** (by Storm Cat)
| **AURORA** (by Danzig)
| | **ARCH** (by Kris S.)
| **DESTINY DANCE** (by Nijinsky II)
| **YAMANIN PARADISE** (by Danzig)
AQUILEGIA (by Alydar)
| **BERTOLINI** (by Danzig)
Embellished (by Seattle Slew)
| **ISLAND OF SILVER** (by Forty Niner)

| SEATTLE DAWN (by Grey Dawn II)
| **GOLD SUNRISE** (by Forty Niner)
TRUCKEE (by Danzig)
Foreign Courier (by Sir Ivor)
| **GREEN DESERT** (by Danzig)
| **YOUSEFIA** (by Danzig)
| | **MYTHICAL GIRL** (by Gone West)
KETOH (by Exclusive Native)
Maidee (by Roberto)
| **DEFACTO** (by Diesis (GB))
Namaqua (by Storm Bird)
| **NAMAQUALAND** (by Mr. Prospector)
NATIVE COURIER (by Exclusive Native)
PRINCESS OOLA (by Al Hattab)
| **AZZAAM** (by Chief's Crown)
| **BALWA** (by Danzig)
| One Tough Lady (by Mr. Prospector)
| | **BET TWICE PRINCESS** (by Bet Twice)
TWINING (by Forty Niner)
Vireo (by True Knight)
| **CHIEF TURKO** (by Turkoman)
| Mistress True (by Master Derby)
| | **MISS ANGELINA** (by Brilliant Protege)
| Rush for Gold (by Quack)
| | **PRECIOUS GLITTER** (by Danehill)

Fall Aspen
(by Pretense)

BIANCONI (by Danzig)
COLORADO DANCER (IRE) (by Shareef Dancer)
Dance of Leaves (GB) (by Sadler's Wells)
| **CHARNWOOD FOREST (IRE)** (by Warning (GB))
| **MEDAALY (GB)** (by Highest Honor (FR))
ELLE SEULE (by Exclusive Native)
| **ASHRAAKAT** (by Danzig)
| **ELNADIM** (by Danzig)
| **MEHTHAAF** (by Nureyev)
| Only Seule (by Lyphard)
| | **OCCUPANDISTE (IRE)** (by Kaldoun)
| Toujours Elle (by Lyphard)
| | **TOTO LE HEROS** (by Saumarez (GB))
FORT WOOD (by Sadler's Wells)
HAMAS (IRE) (by Danzig)
MAZZACANO (GB) (by Alleged)
NORTHERN ASPEN (by Northern Dancer)
PRINCE OF THIEVES (by Hansel)
Sheroog (by Shareef Dancer)
| **KABOOL (GB)** (by Groom Dancer)
| **SHARAF KABEER (GB)** (by Machiavellian)
TIMBER COUNTRY (by Woodman)

Grey Flight
(by Mahmoud)

BOLD PRINCESS (by Bold Ruler)
| Brave Lady (by Herbager)
| | My Sharp Lady (by Sharpen Up (GB))
| | | **SHARP APPEAL** (by World Appeal)
| | **POPULAR HERO** (by Nijinsky II)
| | To No End (by Affirmed)
| | | **ANCIENT QUEST** (by His Majesty)
| Fantastic Flyer (by Hoist the Flag)
| | Amelia Airhead (by Well Decorated)
| | | **CMDTE PEPE RIOS** (by Leo Castelli)
| | **FORMAL DINNER** (by Well Decorated)
INTREPID HERO (by Forli)
Madame Royale (by Forli)
| **DOUBLY ROYALE** (by Crowned Prince)
| Northern Eclipse (by Northern Answer)
| | **A TASTE FOR LACE** (by Laomedonte)
| | **ECLIPSO** (by Hatchet Man)
| Midnight Eyre (by Irish Castle)
| | **LATE NITE MARTINI** (by Three Martinis)
| **SOLAR LAUNCH** (by Sassafras (FR))

Supremely Royal (by Crowned Prince)
   CAPRICORN BELLE (GB) (by Nonoalco)
  Kick the Habit (by Habitat)
   THREE GREEN LEAVES (IRE) (by Environment Friend)
PREDICTABLE (by Tatan)
PRIMED (by Pronto)
Renounce (by Buckpasser)
  Arraign (by Judger)
   COZZENE'S PRINCE (by Cozzene)
  Baltic Sea (by Danzig)
   PROSPECT BAY (by Crafty Prospector)
  WAITLIST (by Avatar)
BOLD QUEEN (by Bold Ruler)
  Big Player (by Buckpasser)
   Player Princess (FR) (by Crowned Prince)
    Bold Flight (by King of Macedon)
     THUNDER ROAD (by Nikos)
  Instantaneously (by Pronto)
   Princess G. (by His Majesty)
    DO IT A ZEN (by Zen)
  Clear Ceiling (by Bold Ruler)
   Gilt (by Majestic Prince)
    Kiama (by Be My Guest)
     LAW DREAM (IRE) (by Law Society)
   How High the Moon (by Majestic Light)
    Double Sunrise (by Slew o' Gold)
     KONA GOLD (by Java Gold)
   INFINITE (by Majestic Light)
    POLISH TREATY (by Danzig)
   Pure Profit (by Key to the Mint)
    EDUCATED RISK (by Mr. Prospector)
    INSIDE INFORMATION (by Private Account)
   QUICK AS LIGHTNING (by Buckpasser)
   STRATOSPHERIC (by Majestic Light)
FULL FLIGHT (by Ambiorix)
GRAY PHANTOM (by Ambiorix)
MISTY DAY (by Nasrullah)
MISTY FLIGHT (by Princequillo)
MISTY MORN (by Princequillo)
  BEAUTIFUL DAY (by Bold Ruler)
   BRIGHT SUN (by Tatan)
   Hasty Dawn (by Pronto)
    ALL HASTE (by Alleged)
    Ducks and Drakes (by Quack)
     GRAN MORNING (by Gran Zar (MEX))
   Ideal Day (by Buckpasser)
    Beautiful Lady (by Apalachee)
     EYE CANT HEAR YOU (by Hatchet Man)
    Buck's Dame (by Damascus)
     Briesta (by Cresta Rider)
      BRILLIANCE (FR) (by Priolo)
     DICTATOR'S SONG (by Seattle Song)
  BOLD CONSORT (by Bold Ruler)
   Directoire (by Gun Bow)
    LA DORGA (by Northern Dancer)
     L'IRLANDAISE (by Irish River (FR))
     IRISH FLIGHT (by Saint Cyrien)
     LA GROUPIE (FR) (by Groom Dancer)
   Musical Ride (by The Minstrel)
    RUN LADY RUN (by Smarten)
   Queen of Capri (by Forli)
    To the Letter (by Arts and Letters)
     DYNA LETTER (by Northern Taste)
    Tovalop (by Northern Dancer)
     TORREY CANYON (by Gone West)
     TOSSUP (by Gone West)
   QUICK TURNOVER (by Buckpasser)
  BOLD LAD (by Bold Ruler)
  In Succession (by Bold Ruler)
   Fabulous Successor (by Le Fabuleux)
    PEERLESS FORBES (by Air Forbes Won)
    Proven Record (by Elocutionist)
     NIKKI JEAN (by Raise a Man)
  In the Clouds (by Double Jay)
   Miss Betty (by Buckpasser)
    Beware (by Bold Forbes)
     LA SPIA (by Capote)
    EXIT FIVE B. (by Best Turn)
    HICKMAN CREEK (by Seattle Slew)
    PATCHES (by Majestic Light)
    RED ATTACK (by Alydar)
    Samantha Starlight (by Raise a Cup)
     OUT OF FULL (by Full Out)

Lovely Morning (by Swaps)
  Disappear Moon (by Reviewer)
   HILO BOB (by Wavering Monarch)
  Lady of the Dawn (by Bold Ruler)
   Bold Circlet (by King Pellinore)
    MOON LIGHT BOY (by Matchlite)
   Sarcelles (by Little Current)
    HAMMINSKI (by Peterhof)
    LOVELY MELLOW (by Dormello (ARG))
  RESOLVER (by Reviewer)
   ADJUDICATING (by Danzig)
   DISPUTE (by Danzig)
   In My Favor (by Val de l'Orne (FR))
    A GREATER MAGIC (by Slewpy)
   Jurisdictional (by Damascus)
    SECRET SAVINGS (by Seeking the Gold)
   TAX COLLECTION (by Private Account)
   TIME FOR A CHANGE (by Damascus)
  Queen of the Sky (by Bold Ruler)
   Foreign Missile (by Damascus)
    HERON BAY (by Alleged)
    SQUAN SONG (by Exceller)
   RODWELL (by Roberto)
  SUCCESSOR (by Bold Ruler)
  SUNRISE FLIGHT (by Double Jay)
Pleasant Flight (by Bold Ruler)
  Dawn's Meteor (by Grey Dawn II)
   COLCONDA (by Shareef Dancer)
  FLITALONG (by Herbager)
   SOAR TO THE STARS (by Danzig)
  Hop a Jet (by Riva Ridge)
   CASSIDY (by Jolie's Halo)
  Illuminating (by Majestic Light)
   LIGHT OF MINE (by Mining)
   PRIVATE LIGHT (by Private Account)
  ON A CLOUD (by Val de l'Orne (FR))
  Spring Is Sprung (by Herbager)
   Primevere (by Irish River (FR))
    PRIOLO (by Sovereign Dancer)
Quick Flight (by Herbager)
  Never Linger (by Never Bend)
   Johara (by Exclusive Native)
    ASHAL (by Touching Wood)
   Never Spliced (by Silent Screen)
    In One Piece (by Borzoi)
     CHARMING MAN (by Hero's Honor)
     RETSEL (by Sportin' Life)
    PRECAUTION (by With Caution)
  Quick Reason (by Hail to Reason)
   QUICK ICE (by Icecapade)
SIGNORE (by Ribot)
WHAT A PLEASURE (by Bold Ruler)

Hildene
(by Bubbling Over)

First Flush (by Flushing II)
Acantha (by Bossuet)
  Mercy Mine (by Court Martial)
   Exclusiva (by Exclusive Native)
    NORTH DIP (by Explodent)
   NATIVE LOVIN (by Exclusive Native)
   EUATHLOS (by Youth)
   Explodin Love (by Explodent)
    EXPOSE (by Flying Paster)
   TARA GLENN (by Ancestral (IRE))
Akobo (by Bossuet)
  Little Perfect (by Nashua)
   Said Again (by Verbatim)
    ELLS ONCE AGAIN (by Kennedy Road)
    I SAID E (by Hawkin's Special)
  Minmognovich (by Pan Dancer)
   KENTUCKY BLUE (DEN) (by Round Tower)
   Kentucky North (by Northern Ace)
    OUR PLEASURE (by Modern Pleasure)
   KENTUCKY QUEEN (DEN) (by Jammed Red)
   Kentucky Star (by Jammed Red)
    FIJI (by Nicke (SWE))
  Windy Damsel (by Warfare)

FIRST FLUSH (continued)
    PATRIOTAKI (by Mangaki)
    Windy Thelma (by Ramadan)
        WINDY TATE (by Agitate)
            WINDY'S HALO (by Present Value)
Alida (by Doswell)
    Element of Style (by Hill Rise)
        Juliet of Style (by Gallant Romeo)
            JOE'S KATIE BEAN (by Advocator)
        AYE KATIE (by Aye's Turn)
    Flying Cat (by Bryan G.)
        Contrica (Pan) (by Bold Sultan)
            REGALAZO (VEN) (by Guapo)
BOLD EXPERIENCE (by Bold Ruler)
    Aces Full (by Round Table)
        PETITE ILE (IRE) (by Ile de Bourbon)
    All Or None (by Sir Gaylord)
        Give Her the Gun (by Le Fabuleux)
            ANOTHER FELIX (by Miswaki)
        Saturday Matinee (by Silent Screen)
            HAMLET (by Key to the Kingdom)
    MS. ROSS (by Hoist the Flag)
        MAKE THE MAGIC (by Raise a Native)
    UPPER CASE (by Round Table)
Bold Matron (by Bold Ruler)
    Beckley (by Tatan)
        GILGIT (FR) (by Kashmir II)
    Due Dilly (by Sir Gaylord)
        DR. BLUM (by Dr. Fager)
        RING OF LIGHT (by In Reality)
        SPIRIT LEVEL (by Quadrangle)
    Tempest Tost (by First Landing)
        Magic Toss (by His Majesty)
            LADY COFFEE (by Star Choice)
COPPER CANYON (by Bryan G.)
    Cherokee Phoenix (by Nijinsky II)
        CHEROKEE COLONY (by Pleasant Colony)
        RISEN COLONY (by Pleasant Colony)
    Copernica (by Nijinsky II)
        Carmelita (by Mogambo)
            FIVE TIMES A LADY (by Quinton)
        COPPER BUTTERFLY (by Blushing Groom (FR))
        Copperplate (by Secretariat)
            COPPER HORIZON (by Pleasant Colony)
        CRUSADER SWORD (by Damascus)
    Insilca (by Buckpasser)
        SILKEN DOLL (by Chieftain)
            Chief Appeal (by Valid Appeal)
                TURKAPPEAL (by Turkoman)
            JUYUSH (by Silver Hawk)
            MEADOW SILK (by Meadowlake)
            SILKEN CAT (by Storm Cat)
        TURK PASSER (by Turkoman)
    Hunting Pink (by Jacinto)
        Cat Hunt (by Cougar II)
            SR. SERENO (by Lodz)
        LE BAG LADY (by Sauce Boat)
        Pink Screen (by Silent Screen)
            CATIRE BELLO (VEN) (by Inland Voyager)
    Long Stemmed Rose (by Jacinto)
        BRILLIANT ROSE (by Bold Reason)
        Such 'n Such (by Ack Ack)
            KITTY TATCH (by Vigors)
            SUCH CLASS (by Vigors)
    Thetis (by Parnassus)
        Petite Greek (by Beau Purple)
            QUINTAS GREEK LADY (by Quinta)
        Rhiannon (by Beau Gar)
            RHIARADO (by An Eldorado)
        Third Wife (by Hydrologist)
            EXPENSIVE DECISION (by Explosive Bid)
    Trollius (by Ambiorix)
        Amtare (by Petare)
            RACE THE WAVES (by Sailing Along)
        Barclay Belle (by Chieftain)
            Gussie's Chance (by George Lewis)
                WAGERS DELIGHT (CHI) (by Worldwatch)
            SOLO RIDE (by Solo Landing)
    VIRGINIA DELEGATE (by Bold Ruler)
FIRST LANDING (by Turn-to)
HILL PRINCE (by Princequillo)
MANGOHICK (by Sun Beau)
PRINCE HILL (by Princequillo)
Satsuma (by Bossuet)

SATSUMA (continued)
    CICADA (by Bryan G.)
        CICADA'S PRIDE (by Sir Gaylord)
    Countess Mariska (by Mister Gus)
        Space Countess (by Petare)
            COUNTESS INRO (by Inca Roca)
    Sabana (by Bryan G.)
        Accomodating (by Raise a Native)
            Aricia (by Flag Raiser)
                Albala (FR) (by Arctic Tern)
                    UNEXPECTEDLY (by Geiger Counter)
                Albinoua (FR) (by King of the Castle)
                    STAR MAITE (FR) (by Kenmare (FR))
                Arriance (FR) (by Gay Mecene)
                    ARDANA (IRE) (by Danehill)
        Cher Lafite (by Bold Lad)
            CLASSIC AMBITION (by Cyane)
            SONG OF AMBITION (by Relaunch)
        Will Hail (by Hail to Reason)
            Pilferer (by No Robbery)
                SAVANNAH SLEW (by Seattle Slew)
                    ADMIRALTY (by Strawberry Road (AUS))
                    Delma (by Theatrical (IRE))
                        MS VERSATALITY (by Opening Verse)
            State Tax (by Caro (IRE))
                TAX DANCER (by Din's Dancer)
                TAXABLE DEDUCTION (by Prized)
            TELFERNER (by Tell)
                Eventual (by Wajima)
                    Star Event (by Avatar)
                        EGIPTO (PER) (by Good Command)
                        POCO LOCO (by Encino)
            LYIN TO THE MOON (by Kris S.)
THIRD BROTHER (by Princequillo)

Iltis
(by War Relic)

Me Next (by Rough'n Tumble)
    After Me (by Mongo)
        After School (by Arts and Letters)
            French Degree (by Le Fabuleux)
                Lefabuleux's Gold (by Golden Act)
                    DOUBLE DEGREE (by Parfaitement)
            ITS ACEDEMIC (by Sauce Boat)
        After the Mint (by Key to the Mint)
            LUCKY BABA (by El Baba)
        Native Fruit (by Exclusive Native)
            Native Blade (by Blade)
                SCRAMBIES (by Shananie)
    Leave Me Alone (by Northern Dancer)
        REACH THE GOLD (by Slew o' Gold)
    LUCKY OLE ME (by Olden Times)
        KUDZ (by Master Willie (GB))
        LUCKY NORTH (by Northern Dancer)
        Lucky Ole Axe (by The Axe II)
            AXSPECT (by Northern Prospect)
        Lucky Ole Queen (by King's Bishop)
            DIXIE LUCK (by Dixieland Band)
            LUCKY DELIGHT (by Miswaki)
                LIMIT OUT (by Northern Flagship)
            This Ole Queen (by Princely Native)
                COOPER STREET (by Synastry)
                KING OF SYN (by Synastry)
    MIDNIGHT PUMPKIN (by Pretense)
        O My Darling (by Mr. Prospector)
            BLUEBELL DANCER (by Sovereign Dancer)
        TANK'S PROSPECT (by Mr. Prospector)
    You'n Me (by Intentionally)
        SWALK (by Arts and Letters)
MY DEAR GIRL (by Rough'n Tumble)
    Endearing (by Count Fleet)
        CHEERS MARION (by Native Charger)
        Dearest Hope (by Uppercut)
            Cordear (by Accordant)
                ARA RUSSELL (by Feel the Power)
            SUPER RATE (by Superbity)
        KETTLE RIVER (by Vertex)
    Love You Dearly (by Sadair)
        COASTLINER (by Coastal)

MY DEAR GIRL (continued)
        Family Affair (by Honest Pleasure)
        NINES WILD (by Wild Again)
        Lady Darrington (by Drone)
        FOREIGN SURVIVOR (by Danzig)
GENTLE TOUCH (by Chieftain)
  DR. CARTER (by Caro (IRE))
IN REALITY (by Intentionally)
MY DEAR LADY (by Mr. Prospector)
  MY DEAR FRANCES (by Caro (IRE))
  FRANCES IN THE SKY (by Sky Classic)
  NISSWA (by Irish River (FR))
Near and Dear (by Needles)
  Barbie Dear (by The Pruner)
    Near to Me (by Native Charger)
    RITMO CRIOLLO (by Fast Gold)
  CLOSE TO ME (by What a Pleasure)
    Close Enough (by L'Emigrant)
    I'M IN HEAVEN (by Saint Ballado)
    MI VEREDA (by Cahill Road)
  Lady Gueniviere (by Medieval Man)
  BIG PARTNER (by Mehmet)
  Nice and Warm (by Crozier)
    OCALARADO (by Well Decorated)
REALLY AND TRULY (by What a Pleasure)
RETURN TO REALITY (by Intentionally)
SUPERBITY (by Groshawk)
WATCHFULNESS (by Native Charger)
You're Lovely (by Ambehaving)
  My Lovely Girl (by My Dad George)
    BLADE MAID (by Blade)
    HOT POCKETS (by Full Pocket)
MY OLD FLAME (by Count Flame)
Sutton Place Gal (by Needles)
  Double Treasure (by Rough'n Tumble)
    Double Dream (by Forli)
      Party Party (by Farewell Party)
      BIG BRAC (by Le Braconnier)
TREASURE CHEST (by Rough'n Tumble)
Carefully Hidden (by Caro (IRE))
  ENSCONSE (by Lyphard)
  Rimsh (by Storm Bird)
  CRYSTAL DROP (GB) (by Cadeaux Genereux)
Crown Treasure (by Graustark)
  CRYSTAL SPIRIT (GB) (by Kris)
  DIAMOND SHOAL (GB) (by Mill Reef)
  GLINT OF GOLD (by Mill Reef)
DIOMEDIA (by Sea-Bird)
  DIRECT ANSWER (by Honest Pleasure)
  MEDIA STARGUEST (IRE) (by Be My Guest)
  State Treasure (by Secretariat)
    Air and Space (by Tilt Up)
    TIMELESS TWISTER (by Always Run Lucky)
    DOUBLE DIAMOND (IRE) (by Last Tycoon (IRE))
    Verity (by Believe It)
    DANGER CROCODILE (by Herat)
Frontonian (by Buckpasser)
  Armeria (by Northern Dancer)
    ARMIGER (GB) (by Rainbow Quest)
  I WANT TO BE (by Roberto)
    DRACO (IRE) (by Soviet Star)
GOLD TREASURE (by Northern Dancer)
  CROWN SILVER (by Spectacular Bid)
  No More Ironing (by Slew o' Gold)
    SNEAKY QUIET (by Seeking the Gold)
KANZ (by The Minstrel)
Miss Treasure (by Candy Spots)
  FLYING TROVE (by Super Concorde)
  JETTA J. (by Super Concorde)
  Miss Derby (by Master Derby)
    Madame Nureyev (by Nureyev)
    MISS UNIVERSAL (IRE) (by Lycius)
Noble Treasure (by Vaguely Noble)
  Noble Dust (by Dust Commander)
    NOBLE BALLERINA (by Shareef Dancer)
    Proudfoot (IRE) (by Shareef Dancer)
    HEAD OVER HEELS (IRE) (by Pursuit of Love)

Imperatrice
(by Caruso)

IMPERIAL HILL (by Hill Prince)
Chere Yvonne (by Nantallah)
  Chere Leader (by Mr. Leader)
    Cheer for Tom (by Ramirez)
    HERO'S ROYAL FLUSH (by Yesterdays Hero)
    Chere the Leader (by Ramirez)
    BLASTED (by Zuppardo's Prince)
    HIPPIE CHICK (by Collectible)
    LITTLE MISS LEADER (by Yesterdays Hero)
  DON'T JOKE (by Shecky Greene)
  Donna Chere (by Conestoga)
    Nicky's Charm (by Nikoli (IRE))
    BERRY CHARMING (by Turnberry)
    Separate Bedrooms (by Blushing Groom (FR))
    SUE GAIL (by Green Forest)
    Stephie Brown Eyes (by Explodent)
    DANCING WITH RUTH (by Thorn Dance)
    Val Chere (by Val de l'Orne (FR))
    TRICK CARD (by Clever Trick)
  My Mia (by Shecky Greene)
  MY IMPERIAL SLEW (by Slew City Slew)
  NO JOKE (by Shecky Greene)
  SPECTACULAR JOKE (by Spectacular Bid)
  COX ORANGE (by Trempolino)
Colombade (by Boldnesian)
  Minted (by Key to the Mint)
  I. D. MINTED (by Caller I. D.)
Hula Girl (by Native Dancer)
  Bequa (by Never Bend)
    Bequeath (by Lyphard)
    DECORATED HERO (GB) (by Warning (GB))
  BRAVE DANCE (by Chieftain)
  Eastern Dreamer (by Never Bend)
    Eastern Celia (by Ladiga)
    MAYANO PETRUS (by Mouktar)
  HULA CHIEF (by Chieftain)
  MAIKAI (by Never Bend)
  SOVEREIGN DIGNITY (by Mr. Leader)
  Maimiti (by Never Bend)
    Las Manitas (by Faraway Son)
    C B ACCOUNT (by Personal Flag)
Imperial Spirit (by Never Bend)
  Crown and Sceptre (by Affirmed)
  HIGHEST YIELD (by Settlement Day)
  LUMINEUX (by Majestic Light)
Native Imp (by Native Charger)
  Pleasuretoown (by Foolish Pleasure)
  PLEASURE CALLER (by Caller I. D.)
Summer Hill (by Sir Gaylord)
  La Menandiere (by Roi Dagobert)
  BETSY BAY (FR) (by Bellypha (IRE))
  Sainera (by Stop the Music)
    Happy Result (by Diesis (GB))
    HAPPY DANCER (by Seattle Dancer)
    MISCROWN (by Miswaki)
    PATER NOSTER (by Stately Don)
  SOMETHING GORGEOUS (by Full Out)
Imperieuse (by Jack High)
  HI-SAG (by Saggy)
IMPERIUM (by Piping Rock)
Queens Moon (by Hunters Moon IV)
  Bianca Mano (by Saratoga)
    Handy Penny (by Centime)
      Fast Penny (by Fast Hilarious)
      HALEY'S BEAU (by Beau Groton)
      SILENT BUT FAST (by Silent Cal)
    Iron Spur (by Iron Ruler)
      Caught a Pass (by Pass Catcher)
      SET A RECORD (by Upper Case)
      Electric Chair (by Executioner)
      BIG JOLT (by Valid Appeal)
    Passing Situation (by Pass Catcher)
      Casual Date (by Blue Ensign)
      DATING PROSPECT (by Abel Prospect)
    Penny Catcher (by Pass Catcher)
    FRANK AT THE BANK (by Upper Case)
LAKE CHELAN (by Bryan G.)
  A GRAY GHOST (by Native Charger)
  Chelantain (by Chieftain)

QUEENS MOON (continued)
For Certain (by In Reality)
FOR CERTAIN DOC (by Doc Sylvester)
JALTIPAN (by Conquistador Cielo)
Native Chelan (by Native Charger)
LAKE NATIVE (by Mr. Redoy)
SLY PERFECTION (by On the Sly)
Moonbow (by Pelham)
Lady in the Moon (by Beau Gar)
Red's Moonbeam (by Play the Red)
OPRYLAND SPECIAL (by Hawkin's Special)
QUEEN'S DOUBLE (by Double Jay)
Queen's Pawn (by Hill Prince)
Empress Bishop (by King Emperor)
REXSON'S BISHOP (by Rexson)
Quintal (by Heliodorus)
Betchu I Ketchum (by Bold Hitter)
LAFEET LAFAST (by Pirateer)
SCATTERED (by Whirlaway)
DISPERSE (by Middleground)
HERE AND THERE (by Middleground)
Hide and Seek (by Alibhai)
Hiding Place (by Middleground)
KING'S PLACE (by Truxton King)
Under Cover (by To Market)
Cryptic Verse (by Yeats)
GOLD BROSE (by Huntingdale)
Humming (by Poised)
SLY GRIN (by Good Investment)
Somethingroyal (by Princequillo)
Cherryville (by Correspondent)
Good News Cherry (by Intent)
Cerisette (by My Babu)
JOHN CHERRY (ENG) (by Stage Door Johnny)
SILENT INTENT (by Silent Screen)
Inchmarlo (by Nashua)
MARLINGFORD (IRE) (by Be My Guest)
Shee Clachan (by Never Bend)
Avatar Lady (by Avatar)
AVATAR SLEW (by Slew's Royalty)
FIRST FAMILY (by First Landing)
Grand Coulee (by First Landing)
Grandstand Win (by Dr. Fager)
GREAT GORMET (by Wajima)
SECRETARIAT (by Bold Ruler)
SIR GAYLORD (by Turn-to)
Swansea (by Turn-to)
Buck the Tide (by Buckpasser)
Arbulus (by Liloy (FR))
PERSANE (by Tampero (FR))
Chieftain Girl (by Chieftain)
MOMENT OF TRUTH (by Known Fact)
Sea Swan (by Buckpasser)
Sea Cap (by Icecapade)
North Beach (by Nobloys (FR))
WALES (by Worldwatch)
WATCH NOW (by Worldwatch)
Superior Suprise (by Hold Your Peace)
Adocicada (by Crafty Prospector)
FOREST BELL (by Forever Sparkle)
Swan Dance (by Native Dancer)
Angel Clare (FR) (by Mill Reef)
Homeward Angel (by Lyphard)
LEE'S FANTASY (by Lear Fan)
NETTLESOME (GB) (by Tyrant)
Selerina (by Reviewer)
SUMMER PARTIES (by Vaguely Noble)
SYRIAN SEA (by Bold Ruler)
ALADA (by Riva Ridge)
Super Luna (by In Reality)
SARATOGA DEW (by Cormorant)
Lyphia (by Lyphard)
BACANAL (by Spend a Buck)
Swift Syrian (by Tom Rolfe)
Dolly Speed Queen (by Raise a Native)
MARIONNETTE (by Stage Door Johnny)
The Bride (by Bold Ruler)
AT EASE (by Hoist the Flag)
Exquisite Miss (by Nijinsky II)
Dishonesty (by In Reality)
SWEET SARITA (by Gate Dancer)
Fabulous Fraud (by Le Fabuleux)
Duplicit (by Danzig)
NISHINO FLOWER (by Majestic Light)

SOMETHINGROYAL (continued)
HEAVENLY MATCH (by Gallant Romeo)
PERSONAL BUSINESS (by Private Account)
IN CONFERENCE (by Dayjur)
SPEEDWELL (by Bold Ruler)
LULUBO (by Native Charger)
Careful Glance (by Roberto)
LAPSENG (by Seattle Dancer)
Quick Cure (by Dr. Fager)
Candy Bowl (by Majestic Light)
SWEET ROBERTA (by Roberto)
JAH (by Relaunch)
CURE THE BLUES (by Stop the Music)
EVANGELICAL (by Devil's Bag)
Sky Lab (by Conquistador Cielo)
GOLDEN KING (by Vanlandingham)
GOLDEN LAB (by Panoramic (GB))
SI SI YOU (by Native Charger)
Young Look (by First Landing)
Vitriolic Princess (by Vitriolic)
BIRDIE'S ADVOCATE (by Advocator)
MOUNTAIN BAY (by Advocator)
SQUARED AWAY (by Piping Rock)
YEMEN (by Bryan G.)

Key Bridge
(by Princequillo)

Dumbarton Oaks (by Arts and Letters)
Native Barton (by Raise a Native)
IT'S SUZIE (by Far North)
Stagey (by Stage Door Johnny)
Etage d'Or (by Medaille d'Or)
MELISSA'S QUICKIE (by El Raggaas)
FORT MARCY (by Amerigo)
Gliding By (by Tom Rolfe)
CLARE BRIDGE (by Little Current)
Clare Court (by Glint of Gold)
SNAKE SNAP (GB) (by Shareef Dancer)
Clare Garden (GB) (by Shirley Heights (GB))
UVENTO (BRZ) (by Quintus Ferus)
WESSAM PRINCE (GB) (by Soviet Star)
Early Rising (by Grey Dawn II)
MY PATRIARCH (GB) (by Be My Guest)
SILVER PATRIARCH (by Saddlers' Hall (IRE))
SONG OF SIXPENCE (by The Minstrel)
Key Link (by Bold Ruler)
Key to the Edge (by Sharpen Up (GB))
MENSAGEIRO ALADO (by Ghadeer)
Sequence (by Graustark)
Fine Sequence (by Buckfinder)
FINEST SEA (by Sea Aglo)
KEY TO CONTENT (by Forli)
Key to the Heart (by Arts and Letters)
Magic Square (by Quadrangle)
Energy Square (by Air Forbes Won)
SECRET ENERGY (by Alwuhush)
KEY TO THE KINGDOM (by Bold Ruler)
KEY TO THE MINT (by Graustark)
Seven Locks (by Jacinto)
Ahrex (by Dr. Fager)
PAT COPELAN (by Copelan)
Sawmill Dollars (by Our Native)
CLAUSEN EXPORT (by Spend a Buck)
Forli's Song (by Forli)
HE'S A SQUALLING (by Summer Squall)
Seven Arts (by Arts and Letters)
CLASSIC ACCOUNT (by Private Account)
INDOMITABLE (by Pilgrim)
LYKATILL HIL (by Pilgrim)
Tabitha (by County Delight)
Ann Avon (by The Bart)
ARTIC EXPLOSION (by Eskimo)
At Daybreak (by Villamor)
MRS LYON (by Northern Jove)
CANDILEJAS (by El Gran Capo)
Planned Pleasure (by Vertex)
PLEASURE ME MORE (by Villamor)

La Troienne
(by Teddy)

Baby League (by Bubbling Over)
  Betteefarlee (by Jamestown)
    Lovely League (by Lovely Night)
      Do Your Thing (by I'm For More)
        J. RODNEY G. (by Bold Favorite)
        TABAYOUR (by Al Hattab)
        THINGHATAB (by Al Hattab)
        HABAR (by Track Barron)
      Toodie (by Orestes III)
        Jewell's Dream (by Persian Road II)
          Miss Green Brier (by Smoked Salmon)
            RALPH'S TRIUMPH (by Triomphe)
  Bomb Dolly (by Omaha)
    CAROLOS (by Russia II)
    Desert Wheat (by Salmagundi)
      High Wheat (by High Finance)
        BIG BAD TUNE (by Riding Tune)
  BUSHER (by War Admiral)
    Bush Pilot (by Jet Pilot)
      NEEDLE AND BALL (by Tim Tam)
      Whileaway (by Summer Tan)
        FIVE STAR GENERAL (by Lt. Stevens)
        Lady of Night (by What a Pleasure)
          FROSTY AFFAIR (by Icecapade)
          ROSEMONT RISK (by Exclusive Native)
            ISLAND BANKING (by Private Account)
        SUPER PLEASURE (by What a Pleasure)
    JET ACTION (by Jet Pilot)
    Miss Busher (by Alibhai)
      Bushfield (by Jet Pilot)
        Beaufield (by Maribeau)
          BEAU'S EAGLE (by Golden Eagle II)
          Glamorous Beau (by Assert (IRE))
            BEAU JINGLES (by Riverman)
          Promising Girl (by Youth)
            MAN FROM ELDORADO (by Mr. Prospector)
        Heamaw (by Chieftain)
          Runnun Tell (by Tell)
            COUNTRY BORN (by Native Born)
            Loshadka (by Valdez)
              PRINCESS LAO (by Laomedonte)
        Little Tobago (by Impressive)
          PLAY ON (by Stop the Music)
          Why Did I (by Foolish Pleasure)
            JUST CUZ (by Cormorant)
              COME ON GET HAPPY (by Cure the Blues)
        Lorna Doone (by Tom Rolfe)
          HUARALINO (by Habitat)
      Speed Bird II (by Jet Pilot)
        AGOGO II (by Never Say Die)
        GEMINI SIX (by Princely Gift (GB))
        PILOT BIRD (by Four-and-Twenty)
          PILOTSON (by Nantwice)
        Ptarmigan (by Nearctic)
          SHERRIGAN (by Sherry Prince)
  Popularity (by Alibhai)
    BEVY OF ROSES (by Bernborough)
    Popularity Plus (by Ronsard)
      TWAS EVER THUS (by Olden Times)
    RED TULIP (by Jet Pilot)
      Betty's Bet (by Bold Hour)
        BRONZE COURT (by Tobin Bronze)
        COME ON SASSA (by Sassafras (FR))
      Flower Lady (by Fleet Nasrullah)
        Cotteneaster (by Summer Advocate)
          GLORY US (by Northern Score)
          POSITION RYDER (by Pole Position)
        STRAIGHT FLOW (by Going Straight)
      Native Lady (by Raise a Native)
        Our Great Love (by Fleet Nasrullah)
          COLOSO (MEX) (by Imperial Ballet)
        GORILERO (by Kandinsky)
      Shelephant (by Bold Lad)
        Miss Preppy (by Rollicking)
          PREPORANT (by Cormorant)
    TOP CHARGER (by Royal Charger)
  Bushleaguer (by War Admiral)
    Face Lift (by Herbager)
      Major Overhaul (IRE) (by Known Fact)

BABY LEAGUE (continued)
      MAJOR PROCIDA (by Procida)
      Plastic Surgery (by Upper Case)
        Binibini (by Solitary Hail)
          SARANGGANI (by Dazzling Account)
      So Fine (IRE) (by Thatching (IRE))
        NONE SO BRAVE (GB) (by Dancing Brave)
    TAKACHIHO (by Don)
  SHAVETAIL (by Jet Pilot)
Grand League (by Grand Slam)
  Cosmic League (by Cosmic Bomb)
    Miss Big League (by Six Fifteen)
      DARK SATIN (by Captain Courageous)
      Go Lately (by Philately)
        Island Mist (by Pirateer)
          ONE MISTY MORNING (by Sharper One)
        Precursor (by Fiesty Fouts)
          DUBLIN GULCH (by Black Mackee)
      Home Run Queen (by Hitter)
        SCORE FOUR (by Night Time)
      Smart n' Sassy (by Mr. Mustard)
        PAUPER NICKLE (by Reasonably Fair)
    Like Magic II (by Sun Again)
      Magic Goddess (by Red God)
        MODEL SPORT (by Model Fool)
          DYNA ACTRESS (JPN) (by Northern Taste)
          PRIME STAGE (by Sunday Silence)
          STAGE CHAMP (by Real Shadai)
      Midsummer Magic (by Midsummer Night)
        VIVIEN (by Villon)
    Umdoodyed (by War Admiral)
      CAPTAIN BROTHER (by Captain Morgan)
  HARMONIZING (by Counterpoint)
  La Dauphine (by Princequillo)
    Azeez (by Nashua)
      Attract (by Blushing Groom (FR))
        NORTHERN CONDUCT (by Northern Taste)
      AZIRAE (by Raise a Native)
      Cazeez (by Cannonade)
        Nameseeker (by Run the Gantlet)
          LIL SNEEKER (by Lil Tyler)
      EMPEROR REX (by Warfare)
      OBRAZTSOVY (by His Majesty)
      Zeeza (by His Majesty)
        Legal Miss (by Law Society)
          BALI BEAUTY (by Seven Zero)
    Courtesan (by Gallant Man)
      PUNCHLINE PATTY (by Two Punch)
    Dashua (by Nashua)
      Wardasha (FR) (by Warfare)
        Run Wardasha (by Run the Gantlet)
          EMPERORS PRIDE (by Cut Above)
        SON OF WAR (by Pragmatic)
    GUILLAUME TELL (by Nashua)
    JUNGLE ROAD (by Warfare)
  MR. BUSHER (by War Admiral)
  Rocking Horse (by Challenger II)
    Boogooloo (by Nasrullah)
      WA-WA CY (by Tom Fool)
    Flying Fairy (by Hill Prince)
      Flying Baby (by Silver King II)
        Baby Peggy (by Killoqua)
          Yesca (by Croupier)
            VICKHEM (by Unbelievable II)
        VUELO (by Croupier)
      Impatient Ann (by Iron Ruler)
        HARRY 'N BILL (by Amasport)
      MISS HILL (by Silver King II)
    Junior League (by Third Brother)
      PARKRANGLE (by Quadrangle)
    White Horse Girl (by Princequillo)
      CAUGHT IN THE RAIN (by Umbrella Fella)
  STRIKING (by War Admiral)
    BASES FULL (by Ambiorix)
      BOLD AND BRAVE (by Bold Ruler)
      Good Opportunity (by Hail to Reason)
        Better Opportunity (by Prince Regent)
          One Better (by Nebbiolo)
            STACK ROCK (by Ballad Rock)
        Northern Chance (by Northfields)
          GRAND MORNING (IRE) (by King of Clubs (GB))
        NORTHERN PET (by Petorius)
      Good Position (by Bold Ruler)
        LA POMPADOUR (by Vaguely Noble)

BABY LEAGUE (continued)

    OLD MAESTRO (by Irish River (FR))
    Out Distance (by Forli)
    OUT OF THE BID (by Spectacular Bid)
No Opening (by Buckpasser)
   IRISH OPEN (by Irish Tower)
Opening (by Dr. Fager)
   Mimi's First (by Hawaii)
    SNEAKIN JAKE (by Table Run)
Pennant Star (by Bold Ruler)
   Bases Loaded (by Northern Dancer)
    Dancing At Dawn (by Grey Dawn II)
    THE NAME'S JIMMY (by Encino)
   RELIEF PITCHER (IRE) (by Welsh Term (IRE))
   Time for a Hit (by Delta Judge)
    Verbatims Girl (by Verbatim)
      COLONEL BART (by Blazing Bart)
   Slide (by First Landing)
   DONA MARTHA (VEN) (by Text)
Stolen Base (by Herbager)
   ASK CLARENCE (by Buckpasser)
   BASIE (by In Reality)
   JEANO (by Fappiano)
   DONT WORRY BOUT ME (by Foolish Pleasure)
   COWBOY COP (by Silver Deputy)
   I'LL GET ALONG (by Smile)
   PASSING BASE (by In Reality)
   Seems to Me (by Foolish Pleasure)
   Real Doll Dode (by In Reality)
    FOR REAL ZEAL (by Unreal Zeal)
BATTER UP (by Tom Fool)
   Bravissimo (by Bold Ruler)
   Bravo Native (by Restless Native)
   CHEROKEE WONDER (by Cherokee Colony)
   Front Stage (by Prince Taj)
   BRAVERY (by Zephyr Zip)
   BRAVE PRINCE (by Kenmare (FR))
   VALOURINA (by Snippets)
DARING YOUNG MAN (by Bold Lad)
Mudville (by Bold Lad)
   Facial (by Creme dela Creme)
   FACE THE MOMENT (by Timeless Moment)
   IRON FACE (by Iron Constitution)
   REX'S PROFILE (by Rexson)
GLAMOUR (by Nasrullah)
   Artistically (by Ribot)
   ABSOLUTE (FR) (by Luthier)
   Abordable (by Formidable)
   ABOARD (by Hero's Honor)
   ABSURDE (FR) (by Green Desert)
   ALPHABEL (by Bellypha (IRE))
BOUCHER (by Ribot)
Brilliantly (by Hill Prince)
   Bright Machete (by The Axe II)
   CURRENT BLADE (by Little Current)
   GET SWINGING (by Get Around)
   Brilliant View (by Summer Tan)
   September Dream (by American Native)
    SEPTEMBER TEN (VEN) (by White Face)
    Torrestrella (VEN) (by Needles n Pens)
     COLOSAL (by North Parallel)
    RIVIERA (VEN) (by Flag Admiral)
   Heatherglow (by The Axe II)
   An Affinity (by Raise a Native)
   FORUM CLUB (by Shelter Half)
   Canonization (by Native Heritage)
   LADY SHIRL (by That's a Nice)
   Glamorous (by Exclusive Native)
    LITTLE RAISIN (by Little Current)
Instant Beauty (by Pronto)
   Soy Bonita (by Soy Numero Uno)
   Incomprensiva (by Triomphe)
   AZUCAR (by Full Realization)
   CANA DULCE (DR) (by Full Realization)
Intriguing (by Swaps)
   CUNNING TRICK (by Buckpasser)
   Fascinating Trick (by Buckpasser)
   Fast 'n Tricky (by Lomond)
   SHISEIDO (IND) (by Classic Tale (GB))
   Northern Naiad (FR) (by Nureyev)
   GREY WAY (by Cozzene)
   Political Intrigue (by Deputy Minister)
   REDATTORE (by Roi Normand)
   HOW CURIOUS (by Buckpasser)

BABY LEAGUE (continued)

   NUMBERED ACCOUNT (by Buckpasser)
   Confidentiality (by Lyphard)
   CONFIDENTIAL TALK (by Damascus)
   DANCE NUMBER (by Northern Dancer)
   GET LUCKY (by Mr. Prospector)
   ACCELERATOR (by A.P. Indy)
   Oscillate (by Seattle Slew)
   MUTAKDDIM (by Seeking the Gold)
   RHYTHM (by Mr. Prospector)
  PRIVATE ACCOUNT (by Damascus)
   Secret Asset (by Graustark)
   ASSATIS (by Topsider)
   RAZEEN (by Northern Dancer)
   WARRSHAN (by Northern Dancer)
  Playmate (by Buckpasser)
   SINGLE THREAD (by Damascus)
   WOODMAN (by Mr. Prospector)
  Special Account (by Buckpasser)
   Awesome Account (by Lyphard)
   ANGUILLA (by Seattle Slew)
   KASHGAR (by Secretariat)
   Bank On Love (by Gallant Romeo)
   Atyaaf (by Irish River (FR))
    RAISE A GRAND (IRE) (by Grand Lodge)
   WELDNAAS (by Diesis (GB))
  GALLANT SISTER (by Vigors)
   Lyphard Gal (by Lyphard)
    HERITAGE OF GOLD (by Gold Legend)
  GALLANT SPECIAL (by Gallant Romeo)
  Kemp (by Spectacular Bid)
   HEAR THE BELLS (by Deputy Minister)
   DEB'S HONOR (by Affirmed)
   WILD DEPUTY (by Wild Again)
   JAYNE WHALEY (by Deputy Minister)
   PERSONAL BID (by Personal Flag)
  Tara's Number (by Northern Dancer)
   MARY MCGLINCHY (by Pleasant Colony)
  Time Deposit (by Halo)
   TRESORIERE (by Lyphard)
  The Cuddler (by Buckpasser)
   VERIFICATION (by Exceller)
JAUNTY (by Ambiorix)
POKER (by Round Table)
ROYAL ASCOT (by Princequillo)
HITTING AWAY (by Ambiorix)
MY BOSS LADY (by Bold Ruler)
  Artist and Model (by Ribot)
   Fontana (IRE) (by Thatch)
   Twinkling (by Effervescing)
   NANNETTA (by Falstaff)
  His Squaw (by Tom Rolfe)
   RIVER SCAPE (by Riverman)
  How Pleasing (by Tom Rolfe)
   How Pleasant (by Foolish Pleasure)
   HOW RARE (by Rare Brick)
LANDSCAPER (by Herbager)
So Chic (by Nasrullah)
  BEAU BRUMMEL (by Round Table)
  Dress Uniform (by Court Martial)
   DIFFUSION (FR) (by Habitat)
   Tanouma (by Miswaki)
   AZZILFI (GB) (by Ardross)
   KHAMASEEN (GB) (by Slip Anchor)
   TAMNIA (GB) (by Green Desert)
   Diplomatie (FR) (by Val de Loir)
   So Striking (by Storm Bird)
   MILADY (VEN) (by Slew Prince)
  FASHION VERDICT (by Court Martial)
  A Streaker (by Dr. Fager)
   CAPTURE HIM (by Mr. Prospector)
  Best Dressed List (by Buckpasser)
   NORTH VERDICT (by Far North)
  Court Circular (by Ambiorix)
   ASH CREEK (by Manado)
   HIGH COURT (FR) (by Hill Rise)
  Spy Court (FR) (by Snob)
   SOVEREIGN COURT (by Sovereign Red (NZ))
  Fashionable Trick (by Buckpasser)
  A Slick Chic (by Chieftain)
   A SLIM CHIC (by Angle Light)
   HOUSE SPEAKER (by King Pellinore)
  Silk Brocade (by The Minstrel)
   SEMORAN (by Phone Trick)

Mrs. Grundy (by Stage Door Johnny)
Sheckys' Choice (by Shecky Greene)
SHECKY PLEASURE (by Raised Socially)
PLASTIC SURGEON (by Dr. Fager)
REASONABLE CHOICE (by Hail to Reason)
SARTORIALY PERFECT (by Gallant Romeo)
The Garden Club (by Herbager)
BLUSHING CATHY (by Blushing Groom (FR))
Dinner Meeting (by Bold Ruler)
Dinner Music (by Raise a Cup)
ANNIVERSARY WISH (by Beau's Eagle)
APPROVANCE (by With Approval)
WISHES AND ROSES (by Greinton (GB))
EAGLE CROWN (by Beau's Eagle)
Exotic Garden (by Bold Ruler)
Dunbarten Oaks (by Raise a Native)
TEMPERENCE OAKS (by Temperence Hill)
LINES OF POWER (by Raise a Native)
Mareve (by Hawaii)
Evolutionary (by Silent Screen)
WESTERN LIL (by Western Trick)
Hidden Garden (by Mr. Prospector)
JAZZ CLUB (by Dixieland Band)
NOSTALGIA (by Silent Screen)
Tacida (by Vitriolic)
La Passionaria (by Reform)
KENARIA (by Kenmare (FR))
LA CARENE (FR) (by Kenmare (FR))
UP THE FLAGPOLE (by Hoist the Flag)
ALLIED FLAG (by Danzig)
FLAGBIRD (by Nureyev)
FOLD THE FLAG (by Raja Baba)
LONG VIEW (by Damascus)
PROSPECTORS DELITE (by Mr. Prospector)
TOMISUE'S DELIGHT (by A.P. Indy)
RUNUP THE COLORS (by A.P. Indy)
TOP ACCOUNT (by Private Account)
Flirting Lady (by Swaps)
Laddisa (by Sir Gaylord)
LAURIUS (FR) (by Artaius)
Louisville (FR) (by Val de l'Orne (FR))
LE BELVEDERE (by Miswaki)
LOUIS LE GRAND (by Key to the Kingdom)
YPHA (by Lyphard)
Love in Vain (by Buckpasser)
APALACHIAN AFFAIR (by Apalachee)
STRONG AND STEADY (by Steady Growth)
MODRED (by Round Table)
Memsie (by Tulyar)
GERABHER (by Herbager)
House Maid (by Habitat)
MONA LISA (by Henbit)
Sierra Nevada (by Warfare)
Acrobata (by Catullus)
EL PLATINO (by Gordie H.)
BARLOVENTO (by Natidan)
PAS DE DEUX (by Nijinsky II)
Sparkling (by Bold Ruler)
BUBBLING (by Stage Door Johnny)
Lake Mist (IRE) (by Kings Lake)
SHANDON LAKE (IRE) (by Darshaan)
EFFERVESCING (by Le Fabuleux)
Sparkling Account (by Private Account)
Sparkling Dixie (by Dixieland Band)
HOLY HOPE (BRZ) (by Jarraar)
The Sweet Swinger (by Le Fabuleux)
SINOPTICO (by Southern Halo)
BEE ANN MAC (by Blue Larkspur)
Blameless (by Middleground)
Blameless Girl (by Lone Cowboy)
Innocent Victory (by Victory Stride)
VICTORY L. (by Lucky Legend)
Exclusion (by Shut Out)
Clem's Ex (by Clem)
Mischievous Saint (by Explodent)
Victorian Myth (by Huguenot)
BLUEYESNLONGLEGS (by Yesterdays Hero)
Excluding (by Prophets Thumb)
TAIPO (by Ballydonnell)
Let Me In (by Clem)
GUARDS UP (by Cornish Prince)
HOW TO KNOW (by Green Ticket)
One Alone (by One for All)

STOLEN ZEAL (by Unreal Zeal)
Palace Pet (by Call Me Prince)
Pekingese (by Timeless Moment)
DARK DOGGIE (by Water Bank)
Oui Madame (by Parnassus)
Love to Reason (by Hail to Reason)
One Good Reason (by Wise Exchange)
Item Four (by Gray Dancer)
SMOKY POINT (by Basket Weave)
ITEM THREE (by Native Horizon)
SILVER DADDY (by Gray Dancer)
WHITE MOMENT (by Balance of Power)
Say Yes Lady (by Groton)
OUTOFAJOB (by Marshua's Dancer)
OUT THE WINDOW (by Clem)
Play by Play (by On the Mark)
Valenada (by Beau Max)
BALCONY BEAU JIM (by First Balcony)
Belle Histoire (by Blue Larkspur)
Eastern Tale (by Nasrullah)
Duck Blind (by Native Dancer)
Castling (by King's Bishop)
ARRIVED ON TIME (by Codex)
Castle North (by Northern Prospect)
KHALIFA OF KUSHOG (by Air Forbes Won)
JUST ANYTHING (by Laomedonte)
SENOR TOMAS (by El Gran Senor)
Duffy Ducket (by In Reality)
DUXUN LIMITED (by King's Bishop)
Tale Bow (by Gun Bow)
NOW PENDING (by Petrone)
VUELO (by In Reality)
Fiction (by Devil Diver)
Fictional (by Venetian Way)
Fictional Dancer (by Banderilla)
THAT MASS DANCER (by That's a Nice)
ILLUSTRIOUS GIRL (by Illustrious)
Im a Wave (by Sailor's Son)
Our Micho Wave (by Our Michael)
BEN'S DIAMOND (by Dyno Stat)
Twist the Truth (by Torsion)
LETTERS OF TRUTH (by Arts and Letters)
PIERPONTELLA (by Royal Coinage)
Riganda (by Ribot)
CATTLE KATE (by Delta Judge)
Josie Bassett (by Ack Ack)
PUT IT ON MY BILL (by Quack)
Narrative (by War Relic)
BRAVE PILOT (by Jet Pilot)
Tan Pilot (by Summer Tan)
Wing Talk (by Laugh Aloud)
Gilded Connection (by Gilded Age)
CONNECTING TERMS (by Private Terms)
P DAY (by Private Terms)
Diary (by Bold Ruler)
FREE UP (by In Reality)
Narration (by Sham)
BONSHAMILE (GB) (by Ile de Bourbon)
BRIGHT MOON (by Alysheba)
Swan Song (by Ribot)
APPLAUSE (by Shecky Greene)
FAVORED LADY (by Fappiano)
Head Cheerleader (by Nostrum)
WESHTRUM (by Weshaam)
Mary Breckinridge (by Speak John)
Pros in Motion (by Spence Bay (IRE))
STAR PROMOTION (by Racing Star)
PROSPECTIVE RULER (by Northern Prospect)
Trillium Ridge (by Riva Ridge)
BRENTWOOD PASS (by Orbit Dancer)
To the Throne (by Elocutionist)
Allthatyoucanbe (by Fifth Marine)
I'M ALLTHAT (by Orbit Dancer)
ROYAL IMAGE (by Proud Truth)
SPEACH QUEEN (by Caucasus)
KING'S STORY (by Bold Ruler)
AUTOBIOGRAPHY (by Sky High II)
Vita Mia (by Ribot)
LOTS OF FUN (by Cornish Prince)
DR ABRAHAM (by Lord Avie)
MT. PLEASANT (by Vigors)
Vowed (by Dedicate)
Betrothed (by Bold Ruler)

      WEDDING PARTY (by Hoist the Flag)
       Bless You (by Halo)
       CONQUISTADORESS (by Seeking the Gold)
      DEPUTATION (by Deputy Minister)
   PROMISE (by The Irishman)
   TAKE THE PLEDGE (by Funny Fellow)
ROYAL RECORD (by Nasrullah)
Secret Story (by Spy Song)
 CATULLUS (by Roman)
 Keep a Secret (by Never Bend)
  Chiba (by Indian Chief II)
   Foxey Key (by On the Sly)
   FOXEY'S LAST KEY (by Big Bold Sefa)
   TRACK LIGHTNING P. (by List)
  Infantes (by Exclusive Native)
   TEJANO (by Caro (IRE))
  Ten Thousand (by Val de l'Orne (FR))
   LA PIMIENTA (by Goldgalliano (IRE))
 Madame Spy (by Warfare)
  HEAD SPY (by Chieftain)
   SPY LEADER LADY (by Mr. Leader)
 Louisa C. (by Diplomat Way)
  Ambassadora (by Numa Pompilius)
   FOXY ENVOY (by Tally Ho the Fox)
 Needlefish (by Beau Gar)
  FISHY BUSINESS (by Late Act)
 Secret Teller (by Tell)
  SYNFUL SECRET (by Synastry)
 Spynette (by Jabneh)
  RIGHT SIGHT (by George Lewis)
   Noble Sight (by Continuing)
   LOMAXTI (VEN) (by On Retainer)
Mountain Legend (by Jacinto)
 Schwanden (by The Axe II)
  HALO HANSOM (by Sunny's Halo)
 Sissy Sham (by Sham)
  SHAM FRANCISCO (by Temperence Hill)
NO TURNING (by Never Bend)
Secret Cove (by Sea O Erin)
 Secret Princess (by Noble Jay)
  MAY I REQUEST (by My Gallant)
  MY SECRET (by Sabona)
Belle of Troy (by Blue Larkspur)
 Best Side (by Better Self)
  Berlette (by Decathlon)
   Berle Girl (by Sea O Erin)
   SUN 'N SPLASH (by Moonsplash)
   La Victroienne (by Victory Morn)
   ARIAN MORN (by Bold Arian)
  BEST GO (by Mongo)
   Chris McCown (by Hawaii)
   SWEET HAWAII (by Honeyland)
  Good Landing (by First Landing)
   Becky Be Good (by Naskra)
   BAIL OUT BECKY (by Red Ransom)
   BENELLI (by Danzig Connection)
   Landera (by In Reality)
   CUTLASS REALITY (by Cutlass)
   My Locket (by Key to the Mint)
    Good Going Gracie (by State Dinner)
    HARLAN COUNTY (by Tejano)
   SELDOM SEEN SUE (by Lines of Power)
  INTERVENE (by Prince John)
  Mare Calda (by Gaelic Dancer)
   HELD ACCOUNTABLE (by Private Account)
   OWNED BY ALL (by Mitey Prince)
   HOW ABOUT BECKY (by Broad Brush)
   OWNED BY US (by Waquoit)
   PROUD OWNER (by Proud Truth)
  One Chicken Inn (by Gaelic Dancer)
   Chief's Silver (by Jumping Hill)
   Fort Silver (by Fort Calgary)
   ENZO THE BAKER (by Memo (CHI))
   SUPER DIAMOND (by Pass the Glass)
 Joyous Imp (by Johns Joy)
  Jubila (by Novarullah)
   Happy Troubador (by Tudor Minstrel)
    Proud n' Happy (by Proudest Roman)
    Miss Hurricane (by Pronto)
    MASTER CHO (by Sticky Situation)
    PROUD APPEAL (by Valid Appeal)
   Yes Dear Jennifer (by Iron Ruler)
    Obstinacy (by Valid Appeal)

    BEST OF THE REST (by Skip Trial)
    LIGHTING FORCE (by Skip Trial)
   Wincoma Lass (by Admiral's Voyage)
   WINCOMA LAD (by Ramirez)
 Princess of Troy (FR) (by Prince John)
  GAMBOY (FR) (by Gift Card)
 Prosita (by Protanto)
  Leading Light (by Mr. Leader)
  LEADING BALLERINA (by Moscow Ballet)
 The Wife (by Johns Joy)
  Friendly Hand (by Deck Hand)
   DEL DUN GEE (by Bold Dun-Cee)
   My Lucky Hand (by Kentuckian)
   GOLD HAND (by El Sardinero)
  Soft Drink (by Colo Colo)
   FLEET DRINK (by Fleet Mel)
   Soft n' Fleet (by Fleet Mel)
   GREEN PEACE (MEX) (by Rooftree (IRE))
 Vertical (by Vertex)
  Notary Haase (by Ribocco)
  Candice (by Spellcaster)
   ZIG ZAG ALLEY (by Lord Ligonier)
   JIM'S ALLEY DANCER (by I'ma Hell Raiser)
COHOES (by Mahmoud)
Besieged (by Balladier)
Happy Journey (by Adaris)
 Fern (by Underwood (GB))
  Eve's Joy (by We Don't Know (IRE))
  Gay Capri (by Donalbain (GB))
  PAL O'MINE (by Rapier II)
  Frond (NZ) (by Old Soldier)
  FERNOON (by Fiesta Star (AUS))
 Happy Countess (by Count Rendered (GB))
  Te Pari Chat (by Chatsworth II (GB))
  Parachute (by Oncidium (GB))
  ALPINE FLYER (by Pompeii Court)
  I'M IN HEAVEN (by Zamazaan (FR))
 Happy Edition (by Sovereign Edition)
  Merely a Monarch (by Saraceno)
  Merely a Maid (by Bagwis)
  ASPAADE (by Final Card)
HOOK MONEY (by Bernborough)
Mons Meg (by Pharamond II)
 Kansirette (by Stymie)
  Ronsirette (by Ronsard)
   Impressive Diamond (by Lexico)
   SLEW KANDU (by Slew Machine)
   VALID APPRAISAL (by Big John Taylor)
   MS. COMMANDER (by Bold Commander)
   NORTHERN DIAMOND (by Northern Hawk)
   CULLINAN DIAMOND (by Achieved (IRE))
  LISTEN TO REASON (by Hail to Reason)
  PERTSHIRE (by Stymie)
 Sweet Blossom (by Promised Land)
  Sea Bouquet (by Crewman)
  AVENGER'S BOUQUET (by Staunch Avenger)
  KANUSUE (by Kanumera)
  Sweet Tiger (by Paper Tiger)
  TIGRILLO (MEX) (by Tom Tony)
Twitter (by Brookfield)
 Atwitter (by Battlefield)
  AGLIMMER (by Grey Dawn II)
  AFLICKER (by Damascus)
  FOREST GLOW (by Green Forest)
  DUDLEY WOOD (by One for All)
 College Boards (by Thinking Cap)
  College Bold (by Boldnesian)
  BOLDARA (by Alydar)
  Confirmation Class (by Affirmed)
  REBLIN (by Regal Classic)
  NASTY AND BOLD (by Naskra)
  PEMBROKE (by Gone West)
  TOLD (by Tell)
  Colnesian (by Boldnesian)
  Inspire (by Tell)
  INSPIRED PROSPECT (by Woodman)
  Ukud (by Woodman)
  LAW LIBRARY (IRE) (by Case Law)
 Excited (by Etonian)
  Bush Woman (by Grey Dawn II)
  PASSING JUDGEMENT (by Boitron (FR))
  Court Time (by Gallant Romeo)
  COURT SHOT (by Cut Shot)

Be Merry (by Battlefield)
Bustling (by Menetrier)
Golden Spring (by Up Spirits)
NODOUBLERINKER (by Strategic Command)
Hilarious Spirit (by Up Spirits)
MYRTHFUL MYNX (by Lord Vancouver)
Imaglee (by Grey Dawn II)
CURTAIN RAISER (by Theatrical (IRE))
I REJOICE (by Lord Gaylord)
I'M A THRILLER (by Tri Jet)
THINK QUICK (by Thinking Cap)
Big Event (by Blue Larkspur)
Blackball (by Shut Out)
Alice Sit Down (by Alycidon)
Bookworm (by Arts and Letters)
Bobby Sox (by On the Sly)
SUPER SKIRT (by Proud Truth)
Princess Tutor (by Prince John)
ANOTHER DIANA (by Hard Work)
Seek (by Stop the Music)
MS. CHATFIELD (by Hasty Flyer)
VENT DE FRAIS (by Wind and Wuthering)
STRAPHANGER (by Gallant Man)
Foolish Fancy (by Tom Fool)
Pop Art (by Tudor Minstrel)
POP'S SPIRIT (by Red Viking)
Trumpery (by Tudor Minstrel)
TRUMPETER SWAN (by Sea-Bird)
Hester Prynne (by Dedicate)
BOLD CONQUEST (by Bold Bidder)
NOT EVEN (by Sadair)
PERRY CABIN (by Arts and Letters)
Ship's Channel (by Admiral's Voyage)
Screen Shot (by Silent Screen)
BISHOP BOB (by Clever Trick)
MALICIOUS (by Helioscope)
Monkey Business (by Tom Fool)
LUCKY CAPER (by Lucky Debonair)
Violets Are Lucky (by Vitriolic)
Oh So Am I (by That's a Nice)
LADY DULCINEA (by Dawn Quixote)
Me Jane (by Gallant Man)
Gallant Voyage (by Admiral's Voyage)
Gallant Moolah (by Moolah Bux)
MOOLAH SMOKE (by Smoked Salmon)
Nancy Strieter (by Devil Diver)
Ecinreb (by Prospectin)
Ecinreb County (by County Clare)
INNEGABLE S (MEX) (by Swagger)
Mano Chueca (by County Clare)
Devolada (by Going Around)
LINDO SINALOA S (MEX) (by Swagger)
North Branch (by Mr. Tramp)
FORKINTHEROAD (by Hawkin's Special)
Out You Go (by Hail to Reason)
OUT DOOR JOHNNY (by Stage Door Johnny)
Pirate Flag (by Crafty Admiral)
Broadside (by Stage Door Johnny)
Burst of Sound (by Stop the Music)
BURSTING FORTH (by Alwasmi)
Head On (by Naskra)
WORLD CLASS SPLASH (by Bucksplasher)
RIVER ESTATE (by Pirate's Bounty)
Mary Read (by Graustark)
STONE WHITE (by Broadway Forli)
Ravage (by Stage Door Johnny)
Floodgate (by Stop the Music)
MAJOR EXPORTER (by Cougar II)
Sound Alarm (by Stop the Music)
IRISH ALARM (by Irish Castle)
THE AXE II (by Mahmoud)
Blue Eyed Momo (by War Admiral)
Blue Green (by Questionnaire)
Freshness (by Tulyar)
Farce (by Bon Mot (FR))
LINDORO (by Sun Prince)
MAGIC PRICE (by Don Roberto)
STRAIGHT MAN (by Homing)
WHITEHALL BRIDGE (by Auction Ring)
Full of Fun (by In the Corner)
Full of Pep (by Hard to Beat)
AUBISQUE (by R. B. Chesne)
FIOCA (by Balsamo (FR))

FULL CONTACT (by Cadoudal (FR))
PIPER'S SON (by Tom Fool)
FRANCIS S. (by Royal Charger)
Sweet Sixteen (by First Fiddle)
MEJIRO ASAMA (by Partholon)
Sweet Eight (by Gay Time)
Sweet Bern (by Partholon)
Kalista Gallop (by Empery)
VICTORY UP (JPN) (by Assatis)
YUWA JAMES (by Mogami)
Sweet Chanel (JPN) (by Venture)
SAKURA GAISEN (JPN) (by Partholon)
Sweet Cherry (by Partholon)
PURE SYMBOLI (by Speed Symboli)
Sweet Jane (by Silver Shark)
JAMSHID (by Symboli Rudolf (JPN))
Sweet Nice (by Hard to Beat)
DANTSU SIRIUS (JPN) (by Tamamo Cross)
MEINER TRAIT D'OR (by Tamamo Cross)
Sweet Venus (JPN) (by Speed Symboli)
SWEET CARSON (JPN) (by Partholon)
Sweet Four (by Rising Light)
Sweet Fuinikusu (by Fidalgo)
MEJIRO TORANZAMU (by Lombardo)
HALL OF FAME (by Shut Out)
Queen Caroline (by Shut Out)
Saline (by Sailor)
SALT MARSH (by Tom Rolfe)
Salty Candy (by Candy Spots)
Worth My Salt (by Lord Rebeau)
LA SUPERNOVA (by Lac Ouimet)
Zinger (by Swoon's Son)
CORSEQUE (by The Axe II)
Queen Ange (by Son Ange)
GEO'S BIG BEAUTY (by St. Petersburg)
ROYAL GARDENER (by Landscaper)
BIG HURRY (by Black Toney)
Allemande (by Counterpoint)
MARKING TIME (by To Market)
A Pretty Smile (by Honest Pleasure)
San Lo (by Clever Trick)
STAR CITY LIGHT (by Risen Star)
RELAXING (by Buckpasser)
CADILLACING (by Alydar)
STROLLING ALONG (by Danzig)
EASY GOER (by Alydar)
EASY NOW (by Danzig)
Time Note (by Buckpasser)
Tidy (FR) (by Kashmir II)
TIDELIOSK (FR) (by Hellios)
Timing (by Bold Ruler)
Moskee (by Explodent)
DROUTH WILLOW (by Premiership)
TYPE RYDER (by Criminal Type)
Processional (by Reviewer)
RAIN ON MY PARADE (by Little Current)
Sparkle in Her Eye (by Miswaki)
BLU TAXIDOO (by Danzig Connection)
Twitchet (by Roberto)
EVANESCENT (by Northern Jove)
TACTICAL ADVANTAGE (by Forty Niner)
Ambulance (by Ambiorix)
Head Nurse (by Bold Ruler)
Amatilla (by In Reality)
BRIAN'S BLUFF (by Raja Baba)
TIMELY BUSINESS (by Diesis (GB))
ARCTICA (by With Approval)
On Duty (by Sea-Bird)
Arrange the Silver (by State Dinner)
JANE SCOTT (by Copelan)
Bedside (by Le Fabuleux)
BROKEN PEACE (by Devil's Bag)
OPEN GATE (by Dr. Fager)
PORTAGE (by Riverman)
Take My Shift (by Buckpasser)
Shifting Restless (by Restless Wind)
ELECTRIC LADY (by Inland Voyager)
KING OF THE CASTLE (by Bold Ruler)
Nurse's Aid (by Tom Fool)
FOOLISH PRINCE (by Blue Prince)
St. Bernard (by Hill Prince)
Mother Superior (by Bold Ruler)
No News (by Noholme II)

BIG HURRY *(continued)*

- Forget Me Never (by Forever Sparkle)
  - **ST. JUSTI** (by Stack)
- **PASS THE DRINK** (by Swaps)
- Simplon Pass (by Buckpasser)
  - **PASTOURELLES** (by Lypheor (GB))
  - **ZUNO STAR** (by Afleet)
- **BE FEARLESS** (by Burgoo King)
- Blue Line (by Burgoo King)
  - In the Sky (by Heliopolis)
    - In the Heaven (by Intent)
      - Flamingo Pink (by Bold Ambition)
        - **FLAMINGO KID** (by Monetary Gift)
    - In the Sun (by Promethee)
      - Grill (by Sadair)
        - Finally a Dancer (by Dancing Dervish)
          - **ANNETTAS PROSPECT** (by Be a Prospect)
        - **SPOILED ROYAL** (by Regal and Royal)
  - Inaname (by Shut Out)
    - Boo's Babu (by Our Babu)
      - Yessenia Eunice (by Rio Dulce)
        - **MR. MELQUIN** (by Suavecito)
    - Ina Battle (by Battlefield)
      - Delta De (by Delta Judge)
        - **TAYLORS PROMISE** (by Promised City)
      - Inagarden (by Farm to Market)
        - **CHELO** (by Daniel Boone)
    - Inavale (by Royal Vale)
      - **BRASS** (by Fachendon)
    - Manina (by Mangayte)
      - **QUEEN FOR THE DAY** (by King Emperor)
        - **DUKE OF MONMOUTH** (by Secreto)
      - Princess Mum (by Secreto)
        - **FAR EASTER** (by Far Out East)
      - **THE WHEEL TURNS** (by Big Burn)
        - **VANA TURNS** (by Wavering Monarch)
          - **PETIONVILLE** (by Seeking the Gold)
          - **PIKE PLACE DANCER** (by Seattle Dancer)
  - **ISASMOOTHIE** (by Rosemont)
- **BRIDAL FLOWER** (by Challenger II)
  - **BEYLERBEY** (by War Admiral)
  - Boda (by War Admiral)
    - Bee Tree (by Beau Max)
      - Little Kate K. (by Might)
        - **BUDDY BRENTON** (by Brent's Prince)
        - **CORNELIA** (by Bailjumper)
    - Fauchon (by Final Ruling)
      - **CHEROKEE FROLIC** (by Cherokee Fellow)
        - Cherokee Darling (by Alydar)
          - **KATIN** (by Mountain Cat)
        - **FABULOUS FROLIC** (by Green Dancer)
        - **LINDSAY FROLIC** (by Mt. Livermore)
        - Winelight (by Green Dancer)
          - **JELLY ROLL JIVE** (by Prosper Fager)
    - Frolic and Fun (by Jester)
      - **SMASHER** (by Farewell Party)
      - **SNAPPY CHATTER** (by Rock Talk)
    - Vichy (by Restless Native)
      - Prodigious (FR) (by Pharly)
        - **MR. ADORABLE** (by Blushing Groom (FR))
        - **PUBLIC PURSE** (by Private Account)
        - **SUPER STAFF** (by Secretariat)
      - **SHEILA SHINE** (by Full Pocket)
      - **CHANCE TO DANCE** (by Stop the Music)
  - Flower Faces (by Nip and Tuck)
    - Capule (by Middleground)
      - Carioca (by Gala Performance)
        - **CROFTITO (IRE)** (by Crofter)
        - Flower Vase (IRE) (by Auction Ring)
          - **MAYFLOWER LASS** (by Pilgrim)
        - Native Flower (by Tumble Wind)
          - Harmer (IRE) (by Alzao)
            - **AMARETTO BAY** (by Common Grounds)
      - **THE QUIET BIDDER** (by Auction Ring)
    - Wild Flower (by Armageddon)
      - **LAW OF THE LAND** (by Bombay Duck)
      - Sinsemilla (by Senate Whip)
        - **AIR STALKER** (by Royal Pavilion)
        - **FANCY DIANE** (by Royal Pavilion)
      - Violet Vale (by Determine)
        - **CANON LAW** (by Canonero II)
  - Royal Bride (by Princequillo)
    - **FULL REGALIA** (by Middleground)
    - Myrtle Wreath (by Brazado)

BIG HURRY *(continued)*

- Rosal (by Middleground)
  - Rose Reina (by Truxton King)
    - **ROSEY WEST** (by Wilk West)
- Stolen Scepter (by Jacinto)
  - **SHE CAN'T MISS** (by Duck Dance)
    - **HORSAFIRE** (by Hold Your Peace)
    - **INCINERATE** (by Groovy)
    - **PAGOFIRE** (by Island Whirl)
  - Shout the Crowd (by Your Alibhai)
    - **SCAMMS CAN** (by Barachois)
  - Steal the Line (by Smiling Jack)
    - **SMILING NEATLY** (by Neater)
    - **SET TO SIZZLE** (by Miswaki)
    - **SMILE N' DANCE** (by Gate Dancer)
- Dashing By (by Menow)
  - Chicken Little (by Olympia)
    - **A LITTLE AFFECTION** (by King Emperor)
    - **LOVE AND AFFECTION** (by Exclusive Era)
    - **ZOMAN** (by Affirmed)
  - Affecting (by Stevward)
    - **BLACK JACK MACK** (by Barrera)
  - Affection Affirmed (by Affirmed)
    - **DREAMER** (by Zilzal)
    - **RIVER DEEP** (by Riverman)
  - Affirmed Ambience (by Affirmed)
    - **AFFIRMED AND READY** (by Great Above)
  - **SPANISH WAY** (by Roberto)
- Stealaway (by Olympia)
  - Captured Moment (by Graustark)
    - **MATTHEW'S MOMENT** (by Little Current)
  - Darby Dame (by His Majesty)
    - **PROUD N' APPEAL** (by Proud Appeal)
    - **SMART COUPONS** (by Gate Dancer)
  - Kleptomaniac (by Fleet Nasrullah)
    - Anything in Sight (by Round Table)
      - **RIGAMAJIG** (by Majestic Light)
    - Say Anything (by Sovereign Dancer)
      - **SAID ENOUGH** (by Norquestor)
    - Nerves of Steal (by Round Table)
      - Excellent Spirit (by Damascus)
        - **SPIRITUAL STAR** (by Soviet Star)
      - **PUBLIC ACCOUNT** (by Private Account)
    - **SUSPICIOUS** (by Damascus)
      - **ASPIRING** (by Academy Award)
  - **TRUE KNIGHT** (by Chateaugay)
- **GREAT CAPTAIN** (by War Admiral)
- No Fiddling (by King Cole)
  - Miz Carol (by Stymie)
    - Aunt Rose (by Amarullah)
      - **I AMBLICHUS** (by Ribocco)
    - Miz Seabird (by Sea-Bird)
      - Foolish Miz (by Foolish Pleasure)
        - **FLASHING EYES** (by Time to Explode)
        - **GRAUSTARK LAD** (by Graustark)
        - **TON WA KA WA MA NI** (by Hatchet Man)
    - **REGAL GLEAM** (by Hail to Reason)
      - Foreseer (by Round Table)
        - **CAERLEON** (by Nijinsky II)
        - Far (by Forli)
          - **AGO** (by Danzig)
          - **YONDER** (by Seattle Slew)
        - **MERCE CUNNINGHAM** (by Nijinsky II)
        - **PALMISTRY** (by Forli)
          - Conjuror (by Nijinsky II)
            - **WICKED MAMA** (by Devil's Bag)
        - Video (by Nijinsky II)
          - **SCAN** (by Mr. Prospector)
        - **VISION** (by Nijinsky II)
      - Glisk (by Buckpasser)
        - **GLOW** (by Northern Dancer)
        - **LUSTRA** (by Danzig)
        - Wink (by Forli)
          - Dwell (by Habitat)
            - **QUICK ACTION** (by Alzao)
          - Glister (by Topsider)
            - **GLEAMING SKY (SAF)** (by Badger Land)
          - Tabyan (by Topsider)
            - **CAP JULUCA (IRE)** (by Mtoto)
      - Idle Gleam (by Pronto)
        - Gleaming Water (by Pago Pago)
          - **L'EAU VIVRE** (by Fast Gold)
          - **MIDDLEFORK RAPIDS** (by Wild Again)
        - Pucheca (by Tom Rolfe)

    BUCKBEAN (by Buckfinder)
    Gitana (by Spectacular Bid)
      Kaydanna (by L'Emigrant)
        KAYDEE CLASSIC (by Regal Classic)
    Purace (by Forli)
     CHECKPASSER (by Silver Buck)
    Tableaux (by Round Table)
     DEVILED (by Devil's Bag)
     SCUFFLEBURG (by Cox's Ridge)
    TRENDY GENT (by Nijinsky II)
  ROYAL GLINT (by Round Table)
No Teasing (by Palestinian)
  First Release (by First Balcony)
   DOUBLE DINKY (by Nodouble)
  No Luck (by Lucky Debonair)
   Beronaire (by Ribero)
    REIKO (FR) (by Targowice)
     GREENVILLE (by Clever Trick)
     Suva (by Northjet (IRE))
      SURGEON (GB) (by Sharrood)
     TIKKANEN (by Cozzene)
     TURGEON (by Caro (IRE))
    Sweet Annie (FR) (by Pharly)
     LUTE ANTIQUE (by No Lute)
   MOGAMI (by Lyphard)
   Princess Lyphard (FR) (by Lyphard)
   Mejiro Fantasy (by Gay Mecene)
    MEJIRO PALMER (by Mejiro Eagle)
  STOP TEASING (by Nashua)
  STOP DANCING (by Gaelic Dancer)
STRAIGHT DEAL (by Hail to Reason)
  Affirmatively (by Affirmed)
   MAIS OUI (by Lyphard)
   IMPERFECT WORLD (by Carson City)
  BELONGING (by Exclusive Native)
   Bejinsky (by Nijinsky II)
   LOYAL GROOM (by Runaway Groom)
  BELONG TO ME (by Danzig)
  DESIREE (by Raise a Native)
   ADORED (by Seattle Slew)
   COMPASSIONATE (by Housebuster)
  REMINISCING (by Never Bend)
   COMMEMORATE (by Exclusive Native)
   PERSEVERED (by Affirmed)
   PREMIERSHIP (by Exclusive Native)
  So Endearing (by Raise a Native)
   QUALIFY (by Danzig)
SEARCHING (by War Admiral)
  ADMIRING (by Hail to Reason)
   Courting Days (by Bold Lad)
   MAGESTERIAL (by Northern Dancer)
   Fond Recollections (by Arts and Letters)
    State of Grace (by Key to the Kingdom)
    NORTH CARROLL (by Baederwood)
   GLOWING TRIBUTE (by Graustark)
    CORONATION CUP (by Chief's Crown)
    GLOWING HONOR (by Seattle Slew)
    HERO'S HONOR (by Northern Dancer)
    MACKIE (by Summer Squall)
    SEA HERO (by Polish Navy)
    SEATTLE GLOW (by Seattle Slew)
    Victoria Cross (by Spectacular Bid)
    ENGLAND EXPECTS (by Topsider)
   WILD APPLAUSE (by Northern Dancer)
    BLARE OF TRUMPETS (by Fit to Fight)
    EASTERN ECHO (by Damascus)
    ROAR (by Forty Niner)
   Wealth of Nations (by Key to the Mint)
    Printing Press (by In Reality)
    LITE LIGHT (by Majestic Light)
  AFFECTIONATELY (by Swaps)
  PERSONALITY (by Hail to Reason)
  PRICELESS GEM (by Hail to Reason)
   ALLEZ FRANCE (by Sea-Bird)
    ACTION FRANCAISE (by Nureyev)
    ANDROID (by Riverman)
    ASTORG (by Lear Fan)
    Ave France (by Seattle Slew)
    AVEC LES BLEUS (by Miswaki)
    Crillion (by L'Enjoleur)
    FIK EL BARRAKI (by Crystal Glitters)
   French Beauty (by Jim French)
    Allez Beauty (by Trojan Fen)

    ALLANDRO (by Acatenango)
   Lady Winborne (by Secretariat)
    AL MAMOON (by Believe It)
    BORN WILD (by Wild Again)
    LA GUERIERE (by Lord At War (ARG))
    LASTING APPROVAL (by With Approval)
    Lady Lady (by Little Current)
    LOVAT'S LADY (by Lord At War (ARG))
    LOST SOLDIER (by Danzig)
   Priceless Countess (by Vaguely Noble)
    ORDWAY (by Salt Lake)
   Sans Prix (by Vaguely Noble)
    SOLDAT (by Bering (GB))
    SPECIAL PRICE (by Bering (GB))
   Searching Around (by Round Table)
    Searching Magic (by Graustark)
     Buck Magic (by Silver Buck)
      MAGIC ALPHA (by Alphabatim)
   STASHED (by Key to the Mint)
  THE ADMIRAL (by War Admiral)
BIMELECH (by Black Toney)
BIOLOGIST (by Bubbling Over)
BLACK HELEN (by Black Toney)
  Be Like Mom (by Sickle)
   Bim's Blossom (by Bimelech)
    Laughing Mary (by My Host)
    HASTY TRIP (by Oceanus II)
    Lucky Mrs. L. (by Lucky Mel)
     Velvet Luck (by Fleet Velvet)
      LUCKY DESTROYER (by Destroyer (SAF))
      MUDDY PROSPECTOR (by Hurlingham)
    Real Good Mary (by Real Good Deal)
    RALPH'S DEAL (by Dr. Ralph Robbins)
   My Honeybunch (by Old English)
    MY CHARGE (by Spanish Charge)
   Sweet as Pie (by Dogpatch)
    ROMAN FIESTA (by Our Rulla)
  BUT WHY NOT (by Blue Larkspur)
   HOW NOW (by Beau Max)
OEDIPUS (by Blue Larkspur)
RENEW (by Blue Larkspur)
  Refurbish (by Bold Venture)
   BUFFLE (by Zenith)
   De Nuevo (by Poised)
    Lace Curtain (by Cavan)
    LADY JULENE (by Court Recess)
    STRAWSHY (by Count of Honor)
     IRISH SENATOR (by Mickey McGuire)
     Recycled (by Replant)
     LITTLE GRAY WOLF (by Wolf Power (SAF))
    SAY I'M SMART (by Clev Er Tell)
   Puzzesca (by Law and Order)
    HYPNOSIS (by Unconscious)
    MIGHTY MOUSE (by Shecky Greene)
    Parrish Princess (by Drone)
     BOLD PRINCESS (PR) (by Bold Hour)
     PRINCESS ROONEY (by Verbatim)
    Puzzes Times (FR) (by Olden Times)
     Fourth Degree (by Oats)
      FLAGSHIP UBERALLES (IRE (by Accordion)
      GLENSTAL FLAGSHIP (IRE) (by Glenstal)
      VIKING FLAGSHIP (by Viking)
  Broth (by St. Germans)
   OPEN SHOW (by Amphitheatre)
  Choosy (by My Request)
   Chaste (by Dedicate)
    Chaste Girl (by Swaps)
    FANCY N' FAIR (by Break Up the Game)
    Miss Haveago (by Haveago)
     I Know Better (by Iron Ruler)
     CLEAN CUT (by Cut Shot)
    PRIVATE GIRL (by Buck Private)
     LITTLEST SECRETARY (by Secretary of War)
     PRIVATE SECRETARY (by Secretary of War)
   LESTER C. (by Prove It)
  Janannie (by Kauai King)
   AIR FLIGHT (by Travelling Victor)
   Janacan (by Bold Forbes)
   JAN ARTIC (by Son of Briartic)
  Lilly Fair (by Round Table)
   Atomic Lil (by Atomic)
    Bush Party (by Refleet)
     MOOYAH BAY (by Police Car)

FEMALE LINE

BLACK HELEN (continued)

Lily Pure (by Sunday Guest)
  | **PRECIOUS PLATINUM** (by Golden Reserve)
SUPBERLY HONEST (by Police Car)
Medinini (by Police Car)
  | **POLICE RESERVE** (by Golden Reserve)
ROUND MAGIC (by Magic Morn)
  Cruising Round (by Police Car)
  | **YOUR EMINENT SEA** (by Seafood)
Magic Fleet (by Refleet)
  | **FLEET RESERVE** (by Golden Reserve)
TRAVELLING ROUND (by Traveling Dust)
  TRAVELLING VICTOR (by Hail to Victory)
ROUND PEARL (by Round Table)
Perla Fina (by Gallant Man)
  | **ELECTRIC FLASH** (by Fappiano)
  | **FINE N' MAJESTIC** (by Majestic Light)
Setting (by Exclusive Native)
  | **VIVID ANGEL** (by Septieme Ciel)
Hula Hula (by Polynesian)
  Damascene (by Damascus)
  | **DELICATE ICE** (by Icecapade)
  Ice Bid (by Spectacular Bid)
  | **CHANGE FORA DOLLAR** (by Silver Buck)
  Yukiguni (by Caro (IRE))
  | **M.I.BLANC (JPN)** (by Brian's Time)
  HULA BEND (by Never Bend)
  HULA CHIEF (NZ) (by Marceau)
  Hula Dance (NZ) (by Riverton)
  | **LOVE DANCE** (by Kaapstad)
  | **MORVEN WARRIOR** (by Sir Tristram)
  HULA DRUM (NZ) (by Marceau)
  Hula Gold (by Rheingold)
  | **SIR MIDAS** (by Sir Tristram)
  Sunset Beach (AUS) (by Kenmare (FR))
  | **MARDI'S MAGIC (AUS)** (by Kenny's Best Pal)
  Hula Queen (by Round Table)
  Floema (ARG) (by Two Harbors)
  | **ARGENTINA** (by Waikiki Star)
Never Hula (by Never Bend)
  Never Babble (by Advocator)
  | **DON'T SAY HALO** (by Halo)
  | **NEVER BAT** (by Batonnier)
  Never Knock (by Stage Door Johnny)
  | **GO FOR GIN** (by Cormorant)
  Navy Knock (by Bold Navy)
  | **PERCEIVED VALUE** (by Present Value)
  | **PLEASANT TAP** (by Pleasant Colony)
  She Might Hula (by Caucasus)
  | **HULASTRIKE** (by Straight Strike)
Regalita (by Ribot)
  VICEREINE (by Free Ride)
In the Purple (by Burgoo King)
  Has a Heart (by General Staff)
  Flying Shuttle (by Loom)
  Omi Regal (by Viceregal)
  | **BLUE BAY BRIDGE** (by Reefer Madness)
  OMI SHADAI (by Remand)
IMAGEM (by Ace Admiral)
Imprint (by War Relic)
  Florida Print (by Alcibiades II)
  Raise a Scene (by Elevation)
  PACHUTO'S SCENE (by Pachuto)
  | **ORBIT'S SCENE** (by Orbit Dancer)
  | **SCENE IN ORBIT** (by Orbit Dancer)
  POWER SCENE (by Fame and Power)
Hill Princess (by Hill Prince)
  BRINY MARLIN (by Top Charger)
Hildessa (by Bronzerullah)
  Halton County (by Carteret)
  | **DANCE CORPS** (by Dancing Champ)
  HILDESHEIM (by Carteret)
  CENTENARIAN (by Vice Regent)
  Springheim (by Spring Double)
  Canadian Cream (by Rich Cream)
  QUEST MASTER (by Northern Prospect)
Page Book (by Needles)
  Paper Ruler (by Fair Ruler)
  Fic'tious Countess (by Southern Count)
  Malbec (by Southern Slugger)
  | **CHELVIS** (by Buckfinder)
  POCOBELLA (by Whitesburg)
  Le Parvenue (by Southern Slugger)
  | **DIE KATZE** (by Comet Kat)

BLACK HELEN (continued)

POWERLESS (by Southern Count)
  HIGHT LIGHT (by Slewpy)
SISSY'S TIME (by Villamor)
Vittoria (by Your Host)
  Be Nice to the Doc (by Northern Jove)
  | **LOST KING** (by Lord Avie)
BRAVORIA (by Big Brave)
Intoxication (by War Relic)
  Sun Again Gal (by Sun Again)
  Terrible Gal (by Terrible Tiger)
  TERRIBLE DAN (by Do It Again Dan)
Pretty Poesy (by Hafiz)
  Grape Tree (by Tudor Grey)
  Splendid Foliage (by Hawaii)
  | **ACADEMIC AWARD** (by Academy Award)
  Kary Katharine (by Tudor Grey)
  Lady Calvert (by Groshawk)
  UNPREDICTABLE LAD (by Unpredictable)
Pretty Precious (by Admiral's Voyage)
  Raja Magic (by Raja Baba)
  Boldly Precious (by Bold Ruckus)
  BOLD BO JIN (by Dancer's Bo Jin)
SNAKE RIVER (by Catullus)
Resourceful (by Shut Out)
  Efficient (by Princequillo)
  Banning (by Crafty Admiral)
  | **BALOMPIE** (by Pardao)
  CHEM (by The Minstrel)
  Lead Dancer (by The Minstrel)
  | **LUISITA'S CHOICE** (by Sports View)
  Native Banner (by Raise a Native)
  MYSTI'S POEM (by Stalwart)
  Dawn Chorus (by Grey Dawn II)
  FOREVER FAITHFUL (by Bravest Roman)
  | **GLASS CEILING** (by Pirate's Bounty)
  Dunmore (by One-Eyed King)
  Omalette (by Salem)
  BOULABALLY (by Cormorant)
  Erin O'Connell (by Dondeen)
  Erin's Dynasty (by Dynastic)
  | **CAN'T SLOW DOWN** (by Dominated)
  O'DEPUTY (by Deputy Minister)
  SEVERIANO (by Native Royalty)
  Heather Bee (by Drone)
  AIR DISPLAY (by Nikoli (IRE))
  Miss Castle Hill (by Ack Ack)
  Elusive Miss (by Elocutionist)
  | **HONKEY TONK KID** (by Ultramate)
  LADY LISTER (by Lord Lister)
  Peak Performance (by Hillsdale)
  Eastern Ruler (by Young Emperor)
  | **TAFARA** (by Explodent)
  Indicter (by Delta Judge)
  INDICT THE CHIEF (by Little Big Chief)
Hidden Resources (by Turn-to)
  On a Trip (by Unconscious)
  RARELY LAYTE (by Our Native)
Ingenuity (by My Request)
  DESTRO (by Ribot)
  Garden Variety (by Herbager)
  Chili Spice (by Iron Warrior)
  | **MR. G. J. G.** (by Breezing On)
  FINES HERBS (by Iron Warrior)
Hopeful History (by Reflected Glory)
  HOPEFUL BELLE (by Sette Bello)
  DRY BEAN (by Demons Begone)
In Eighty Days (by Globemaster)
  KOFFDROP (by Insubordination)
  DROP A BID (by Dickens Hill (IRE))
  POCKET DROP (by Full Pocket)
Sittin Ona Fortune (by Search for Gold)
  JONS FORTUNE (by Jon Ian)
Martha Brae (by Bold and Brave)
  TINA'S TEN (by Cyane)
  Danzig in the Park (by Danzig)
  | **BOISERIE** (by Irish River (FR))
  FAST MARKET (by Secretariat)
THE IBEX (by Hill Prince)
Businesslike (by Blue Larkspur)
AUDITING (by Count Fleet)
BUSANDA (by War Admiral)
  BUCKPASSER (by Tom Fool)
  BUPERS (by Double Jay)

BUREAUCRACY (by Polynesian)
Finance (by Nasrullah)
  La Mesa (by Round Table)
    Corporate Queen (by Truxton King)
      Cie Canadienne (by Canadian Gil)
        ECUDIENNE (by Cost Conscious)
      Royal Merger (by Princely Native)
        BATROYALE (by Batonnier)
  La Affirmed (by Affirmed)
    CARESS (by Storm Cat)
    COUNTRY CAT (by Storm Cat)
    LOVELIER (by Affirmed)
  OUTSTANDINGLY (by Exclusive Native)
    Outlasting (by Seattle Slew)
      FORTITUDE (by Cure the Blues)
    SENSATION (GB) (by Soviet Star)
Navsup (by Tatan)
  Naval (by Broadway Forli)
    CHARTS (by Mari's Book)
  POLISH NAVY (by Danzig)
Oak Cluster (by Nasrullah)
  MANITOULIN (by Tom Rolfe)
  Oak Leaf Cluster (by Promised Land)
    Prominique (by On the Sly)
      Promise Star (by Star de Naskra)
        STARS AND SON (by Son of Briartic)
  OPEN HEARING (by Court Martial)
    LE NOTRE (by Herbager)
    OUTDOORS (by Herbager)
    Rules of the Game (by Hitting Away)
      By Law (by Drone)
        LAWFUL BEAT (by Spanish Drums)
      Fawncy Daughter (by Forward Pass)
        BALDSKI'S HERO (by Baldski)
        ICE OVER (by It's Freezing)
      ROMAN STARLET (by Proudest Roman)
      Two Up (by Upper Nile)
        ZIAD'S GAME (by Ziad)
      Verna Marie (by Bravest Roman)
        Oh Marie (by Quick Dance)
          READY EDDIE (by Literati)
  Splendid Spree (by Damascus)
    Splendid Ack Ack (by Ack Ack)
      LITTLE BAR FLY (by Raise a Man)
      BABY BARFLY (by Son of Briartic)
      BARFIGHTER (by Wild Again)
      ST. HELENS SHADOW (by Septieme Ciel)
    SPLENDID ANN (by Raise a Man)
    SPLENDID SPRUCE (by Big Spruce)
    SPLENDID WAY (by Apalachee)
  TWICE CITED (by Double Jay)
    Second Ovation (by Le Fabuleux)
      DANCING OVATION (by Northern Jove)
      Humdrum (by Drum Fire)
        ACCUMULATOR (by Swing Music)
  Twin Oaks (by Double Jay)
    FELLOW HEIR (by Diplomat Way)
    Mild Persuasion (by Roman Line)
      Big Mad (by Hail to Reason)
        IDA LEWIS (by Restivo)
      RESTANBEGONE (by Restivo)
    Shade Princess (by Prince Taj)
      Magical Morn (by Impressive)
        MAGIC NORTH (by North Sea)
Busy Whirl (by Whirlaway)
  A Little Giddy (by Beau Gar)
    Too Giddy (by Tamao)
      Fast Mistress (by Northern Jove)
        MYSHIPHASCOMIN (by Premiership)
  Lines Busy (by Alibhai)
    Busy Wave (by Bupers)
      ABADASHA (by Yorkville)
      BORDER RULING (by Court Ruling)
      BUSY RULER (by Orbit Ruler)
    Busy Windsong (by Bold Commander)
      DO THE BUMP (by Marshua's Dancer)
      LI'L ARCH (by Stage Director)
      Rain Crow (by Bosun)
        SUBVERSIVE CHICK (by Bull Story)
  Tushan (by Bimelech)
    Dixie Do (by Deuce II)
      DIXIE JAY (by Praise Jay)

Why Be Busy (by Polynesian)
  Myra R. (by Royal Note)
    Miss Myra (by Ambehaving)
    DR. KROY (by Jolie Jo)
    National Strike (FR) (by Grey Dawn II)
    Scarginski (by Stradavinsky (IRE))
    TEMYR (by Derek)
  Tapa Cloth (by Watch Your Step)
    Nepta (FR) (by Neptunus)
    GAMBAS (FR) (by Shoemaker)
  Tired Out (by Dotted Swiss)
    Tigyr (by Gyr)
    NITZANA (by Northern Treat)
Challenge Like (by Challenger II)
  Ammo (by War Admiral)
    Run Missy Run (by Run For Nurse)
      Actionary (by Swoon's Son)
        GAELIC ACTION (by Agitate)
      Orphan Annie's Act (by Erins Isle (IRE))
        DESERT ISLE DERBY (by Desert Wine)
  Defiant (by Sun Again)
    JEFF D. (by I Will)
    Marjon (by Run For Nurse)
    KING L. B. (by Harry's Secret Joy)
  I Like Blue (by Blue Prince)
    First I Like (by First Landing)
    SECRET HAVEN (by Silent Screen)
Discriminate (by Shut Out)
  Dot's Girl (by Tudor Grey)
    SOAKING SMOKING (by Bucksplasher)
  Weather Mate (by Bagdad)
    Want More Wins (by Three Bagger)
      VIBRANTE (VEN) (by Sun Cross)
    War Path (by Kasteel)
      Guerrilla (by More Light)
        GUEVARA (by Good Taste (ARG))
      WAR CHEST (ARG) (by Consultant's Bid)
His Duchess (by Blenheim II)
  COMIC (by Tom Fool)
  Comic Relief (by Tom Fool)
    Court Jestress (by Crozier)
      CHIEF BANDITO (by Banderilla)
      LUCKY TAURO (by El Centauro)
      ORDER IN COURT (by Banderilla)
      GOOD POTENTIAL (by Relaunch)
      Miss Magistrate (by Tanthem)
        MAGGIES PISTOL (by Big Pistol)
  Duchess Rae (by Hitting Away)
    Cinto Tora (by Jacinto)
      BEAU CENTAVO (by Beaudelaire)
    Duchess dela Trois (by Coastal)
      DUCHESS OF PEKISKO (by Regal Classic)
    EL MORENO (by Noble Table)
  Flighty Duchess (by Sunrise Flight)
    BLUE RIBBON GIRL (by Star Envoy)
  Our First Pleasure (by What a Pleasure)
    JOSH'S JOY (by Dr. Blum)
  So Social (by Tim Tam)
    BANNER GALA (by Hoist the Flag)
    HASTY REPLY (by Pronto)
    Queen's Gambit (by Bold Ruler)
      CHESS MOVE (by Avatar)
      Whiffling (by Wavering Monarch)
        FLITCH (by Demons Begone)
        PRAIRIE BAYOU (by Little Missouri)
    Roberto's Social (by Roberto)
      EXCELLENCE ROBIN (by Polish Navy)
    SNOBISHNESS (by Forli)
      OH SO CHOOSY (by Top Command)
      OH SO SNOBISH (by Quadratic)
      Pretty Special (by Riverman)
        FOREVER COMMAND (by Top Command)
        MY BIG BOY (by Our Hero)
      Quexine (FR) (by Sir Gaylord)
        QUEXION (by Young Generation (IRE))
        QUEXIOSS (FR) (by Ardross)
    SOCIAL BUSINESS (by Private Account)
      SQUIRE JONES (by Seeking the Gold)
    WARD MCALLISTER (by Bold Ruler)
  Topolina (by Tropical Breeze)
    GOODBYEYOUALL (by Good Behaving)
Rivers End (by Challenger II)
  Busy Flow (by Hairan)

208

BUSINESSLIKE (continued)
| **NATURAL FLOW** (by Windy City II)
Mac-Nervy (by Tenacious)
Nervy Anchor (by Sheet Anchor)
Pan Anchora (by Crest Pan)
| **UNGIDO** (by The Taka Mahaka)
Spice Bandit (by Bandit)
Pappa's Spice (by Pappa Steve)
| **STEP'N** (by Barbizon Streak)
Pass the Pepper (by Carry Back)
FIRE IN YU WIRE (by Element)

Marguerite
(by Celt)

Anastasia (by Wrack)
| Galleria (by Sir Gallahad III)
| One Man Show (by Princequillo)
| Show Boss (by Boss)
| **BRANDY CREEK** (by Royal Ascot)
| Pomana (by Pompey)
| Fenny Poppers (by Fenelon)
| Arabella Allen (by Yildiz)
| | **PRINCE TIMOTHY** (by Trojan Monarch)
| | Proud Arabella (by Right Proud)
| | **THE POET'S VAMP** (by Terrible Tiger)
| Happy Lagoon (by Trojan Monarch)
| Penrage Blitzen (by Jet Traffic)
| **BOLD RELIC** (by Bold Monarch)
| Penrage Queen (by Road At Sea)
| **QUEEN LETIZIA** (by El Raggaas)
| Flamona (by Flares)
| Gretel (by Third Degree)
| **JOSE F.** (by Devils Brew II)
| **MARINERO** (by Eurasian)
Sunana (by Sun Edwin)
| Fidgety Miss (by Okapi)
| Louise Bell (by Yankee Hill)
| Breakwater (by Cyane)
| | **KEBEA'S BRAKEATER** (by Staff Writer)
| Widow Susan (by Royal Coinage)
| **SORRY LOOKIN** (by Farewell Party)
| Tasarinan (by Farewell Party)
| | **ASK MIKEY** (by Funny Fellow)
| | Party Widow (by Proud Appeal)
| | **SARATOGA SUNRISE** (by Personal Flag)
| Watta Widow (by Step Nicely)
| **MISSHOLLYGOLIGHTLY** (by Tiffany Ice)
| Lady Argyle (by Tintagel)
| Main Deck (by First Cabin)
| Dover Jay (by Billy Bluejay)
| **BUT WHAT** (by Liberty Hall)
| **BUT JIM** (by Rise Jim)
FIGHTING FOX (by Sir Gallahad III)
FOXBROUGH (by Sir Gallahad III)
GALLANT FOX (by Sir Gallahad III)
Maraschino (by Sir Gallahad III)
| Mara Miss (by Our Scholar)
| Me a Native (by Restless Native)
| | **RESTLESS NAVAJO** (by Navajo)
| Nifty Native (by Native Dancer)
| A Real Native (by Mr. Prospector)
| **BOUNTIFUL NATIVE** (by Pirate's Bounty)
| **TRUE AND BLUE** (by Hurry Up Blue)
Maranon (by Prince Simon)
| Skip Deck (by Admiral Drake)
| Warrullah (by Nalur)
| **PRINCE ASTRO** (by Dancing Dervish)
| St. Bella (by Prize Silver)
| **BELLA STAT** (by Doctor Stat)
Marapania (by Devil Diver)
| **AMBER DIVER** (by Ambiorix)
Ida T. (by Jet Flight)
| **BICENTENARY** (by Lurullah)
Mari Quest (by Prince Quest)
| Mari Delta (by Delta Judge)
| **HOLLYWOOD GIRL** (by Banderilla)
REINZI (by Some Chance)
Rosy Finch (by Prince Simon)
| **BALLET ROSE** (by Native Dancer)

MARASCHINO (continued)
| Nellie B. (by Bold Bidder)
| **B. HOEDOWN** (by Hoedown's Day)
| **HOEDOWN B. GOOD** (by Hoedown's Day)
| **NELLIE'S BARGAIN** (by Bargain Day)
| **RIBORONDE** (by Ribot)
Shallow Lake (by War Relic)
| **AMBER STONE** (by Amber Morn)
| **BRUCE SOUTH** (by Speak John)
| Shallow Well (by Well Mannered)
| **MOSTLY MANNERS** (by Sir Jason)
| **MANITOBA DANCER** (by Flare Dancer)
THE SENATOR (by Isolater)
Marguery (by Sir Gallahad III)
| First Flower (by Nasrullah)
| Bunch (by Endeavour II)
| Bet a Bunch (by Social Climber)
| Personal Gain (by Naskra)
| | **CHARLIE (PAN)** (by El Gran Capo)
| | **WINCHESTER** (by El Gran Capo)
Fleet Vixen (by Count Fleet)
| Fleet's Choice (by Stymie)
| Carlin B (by Tronado)
| | **LADY VERNALEE** (by Hold Your Peace)
| | Peace Holdings (by Hold Your Peace)
| | **GREAT PEACE** (by Great Above)
| **FLEET ADMIRAL** (by Ace Admiral)
MARULLAH (by Nasrullah)
| **BLESSING ANGELICA** (by Beau Gar)
| Dancing Angelica (by Native Charger)
| | **BOLGER'S DANCE** (by Bolger)
| She's Confirmed (by Native Charger)
| Sounds Great (by Stop the Music)
| **LUCIFER (VEN)** (by Slew Prince)
| **HANDSOME BOY** (by Beau Gar)
Lullah (by Beau Gar)
| Lullah Lullah (by Native Dancer)
| Chalk Lullah (by Peace Corps)
| Marianne Theresa (by John's Gold)
| **KELLY KIP** (by Kipper Kelly)
Med Coed (by Dr. Fager)
| **BISHOP'S DELIGHT** (by Sawbones)
| Just Dance (by Duck Dance)
| **SHADOW CASTER** (by Future Storm)
Umbrella Tree (by Beau Gar)
| **TOWER ABOVE 'EM** (by Irish Tower)
Russ Elaine (by Count Fleet)
| **MR. BROGANN** (by Ridan)
Ridell (by Ridan)
| Andrea Lynn (by My Dad George)
| | That's Right (by Jatski)
| | **DANCER'S BEST** (by Flare Dancer)
| Delso (by More So)
| Del Sovereign (by Sovereign Dancer)
| | **DENIED ACCESS** (by Cryptoclearance)
| **FLUTTERBUTT** (by Run For Nurse)
| | **MAGERBUTT** (by Magesterial)
| **ROMAN FLIGHT** (by Proudest Roman)
| **ISAYSO** (by Valid Appeal)
| **NURSO** (by Run For Nurse)
| **BIG RUCKUS** (by Bold Ruckus)
Dolcie (by Dr. Fager)
| Dolcie Doll (by Soy Numero Uno)
| **SOY JUBILO** (by Churning Current)
Talahi (by Ridan)
| **MR. RED WING** (by Tropical Breeze)
Russ-Marie (by Nasrullah)
| I'm All (by Noholme II)
| I'm in Focus (by For The Moment)
| **WISHFUL NICKLE** (by Plugged Nickle)
Lady Marguery (by Tim Tam)
| **BOBBY MURCER** (by Indian Chief II)
| **PARTEZ** (by Quack)
| Redpath (by Indian Chief II)
| Garden Grove (by Exclusive Native)
| | **MATAJI** (by Best Turn)
| **RACE THE WILD WIND** (by Sunny's Halo)
MARGARETHEN (by Tulyar)
| Doff the Derby (by Master Derby)
| **GENEROUS** (by Caerleon)
| **OSUMI TYCOON (IRE)** (by Last Tycoon (IRE))
| **STRAWBERRY ROAN (IRE)** (by Sadler's Wells)
| **WEDDING BOUQUET (IRE)** (by Kings Lake)
| **WINDY TRIPLE K.** (by Jaklin Klugman)

Hail Maggie (by Hail to Reason)
Hail the Dancer (by Green Dancer)
MANDARINO (by Trempolino)
SABONA (by Exclusive Native)
MARGRAVINE (by Hail to Reason)
Margie Belle (by Vaguely Noble)
MILDE (by Desert Wine)
KUROKAMI (by Caerleon)
Noble Chick (by Vaguely Noble)
NORDAVANO (by The Minstrel)
Prix (by Vaguely Noble)
Vintage (by Foolish Pleasure)
IN EXTREMIS (by Sharpen Up (GB))
JUVENIA (by Trempolino)
TRILLION (by Hail to Reason)
BARGER (by Riverman)
BAYA (by Nureyev)
Trevilla (by Lyphard)
Sine Labe (by Vaguely Noble)
TAMARISK (IRE) (by Green Desert)
TREBLE (by Riverman)
TRIPTYCH (by Riverman)
Tim Marie (by Tim Tam)
Heart a Dancer (by Raise a Native)
Curried Favor (by Raja Baba)
SPICY FACT (by Known Fact)
Nothing to Do (by Nijinsky II)
BRAVE WARRIOR (by Cossack Warrior)
REPUTED DANCER (by Alleged)
LIFE'S HOPE (by Exclusive Native)
LITTLE HAPPINESS (by Raise a Native)
A Little Love (by J. O. Tobin)
A LITTLE KISS (NZ) (by Sackford)
HAPPY BID (by Spectacular Bid)
WHIRLING FOX (by Whirlaway)
Marigal (by Sir Gallahad III)
LONE EAGLE (by Isolater)
Margaret (by Rhodes Scholar)
Lucky Lonie (by Isolater)
Miss Poppycock (by Summer Tan)
ED'S DELIGHT (by Royal Surrender)
MY EMMA (by Isolater)
SIR RULER (by Nasrullah)
UNCLE SEAWEED (by Jacopo)
PETEE-WRACK (by Wrack)

Missy Baba
(by My Babu)

CHOKRI (by Herbager)
DROMBA (by Droll Role)
GAY MISSILE (by Sir Gaylord)
Dry Fly (FR) (by Mill Reef)
FOTITIENG (by Nureyev)
GALLANTA (FR) (by Nureyev)
GAY GALLANTA (by Woodman)
SPORTSWORLD (by Alleged)
GALLAPIAT (by Buckpasser)
GAY MECENE (by Vaguely Noble)
LASSIE DEAR (by Buckpasser)
Charming Lassie (by Seattle Slew)
BRULAY (by Rubiano)
LEMON DROP KID (by Kingmambo)
FOXHOUND (by Danzig)
Lassie's Lady (by Alydar)
BITE THE BULLET (by Spectacular Bid)
SHUAILAAN (by Roberto)
Run for Lassie (by Fappiano)
MADISON'S CHARM (by Capote)
SPECTACULAR SPY (by Spectacular Bid)
WEEKEND SURPRISE (by Secretariat)
A.P. INDY (by Seattle Slew)
SUMMER SQUALL (by Storm Bird)
WOLFHOUND (by Nureyev)
Kindegartn Dropout (by Dunce)
Sandbox Graduate (by Lucky Fleet)
Forget the Rain (by Forget the Showers)
CHASIN'RAIN (by Creekarosa)
MASTER BOLD (by Bold Ruler)

Pennyworth (by Key to the Mint)
WORTHEROATSINGOLD (by Naskra)
DAYLIGHT SAVINGS (by Sky Classic)
RAJA BABA (by Bold Ruler)
SAUCE BOAT (by Key to the Mint)
Sooni (by Buckpasser)
BLACK CASH (by Deposit Ticket)
MY MARCHESA (by Stately Don)
Toll Booth (by Buckpasser)
Banker's Favorite (by Lyphard)
LIBOR (by Sir Ivor)
CHRISTIECAT (by Majestic Light)
IDLE GOSSIP (by Lyphard)
IDLE SON (by Sharpen Up (GB))
KEY TO THE BRIDGE (by Key to the Mint)
ISLEFAXYOU (by Storm Bird)
PETROSKI (by Polish Navy)
PLUGGED NICKLE (by Key to the Mint)
TOKENS ONLY (by Youth)
TOKEN DANCE (by Sovereign Dancer)
GATOR DANCER (by Pleasant Colony)
TOLL FEE (by Topsider)
TOLL KEY (by Nodouble)

Myrtlewood
(by Blue Larkspur)

Crepe Myrtle (by Equipoise)
Kilfane (by Whirlaway)
Crimson Glory (by Citation)
Court Gem (by The Pie King)
REGAL STONE (by Native Royalty)
MYRTLE CHARM (by Alsab)
Fair Charmer (by Jet Action)
MY CHARMER (by Poker)
ARGOSY (by Affirmed)
Clandestina (by Secretariat)
DESERT SECRET (IRE) (by Sadler's Wells)
LOMOND (by Northern Dancer)
SEATTLE DANCER (by Nijinsky II)
SEATTLE SLEW (by Bold Reasoning)
Jet's Charm (by Jet Pilot)
Bright Jetty (by Sensitivo)
Ice Jetty (by Icecapade)
VIVI AWARD (by Wander Kind)
Pocket Charm (by Pocket Ruler)
Gold Charmer (by Gold and Myrrh)
National Charmer (by National Zenith)
DANCE FOR JAN (by Citidancer)
Wings of Charm (by Bald Eagle)
Ruth's Charm (by Tisab)
SIMPLY SO (by Gold Ruler)
Victorian Charm (by Victoria Park)
Bettor Be Bold (by Bold Laddie)
BETTER AND BOLDER (by Wander Kind)
FRANWORTH (by Envoy)
MYRTLE'S JET (by Jet Pilot)
Quiet Age (by Bald Eagle)
ALISAGE (by Adios (GB))
Modest Lass (by Mystic II)
STRATE MYSTIC (by Strate Stuff)
Spinosa (by Count Fleet)
MASKED LADY (by Spy Song)
RAISE A LADY (by Raise a Native)
WHO'S TO KNOW (by Fleet Nasrullah)
All Too True (by Caro (IRE))
TRULY MET (by Mehmet)
ANGEL ISLAND (by Cougar II)
Danzig Island (by Danzig)
SECRET BEAUTY (by Mt. Livermore)
ISLAND ESCAPE (by Slew o' Gold)
OUR REVERIE (by J. O. Tobin)
SHARROOD (by Caro (IRE))
Confirmed Affair (by Affirmed)
THIS ONE'S FOR US (by Cox's Ridge)
Jolie Jolie (by Sir Ivor)
COUGARIZED (by Cougar II)
JOLIE'S HALO (by Halo)
MISTER JOLIE (by Valid Appeal)
Northern Jolie (by Northern Jove)
COOL SLEWPY (by Slewpy)

210

CREPE MYRTLE (continued)
> **PLEASANT JOLIE** (by Pleasant Colony)
> Tokyo Princess (by Wajima)
>> Highest Carol (by Caro (IRE))
>>> **YANKEE VICTOR** (by Saint Ballado)

Dragona (by Bull Lea)
> Dragonfly (by Mahmoud)
>> Dragon Queen (by Blue Prince)
>>> Tropic Magic (by Drone)
>>>> **FOR THE GIPPER** (by Commanding Lead)
>>> Rosey Roan (by Northern Bay)
>>>> **KLINT'S KOMET** (by Nice Catch)
> **ROYAL ATTACK** (by Royal Charger)

DURAZNA (by Bull Lea)
> Manzana (by Count Fleet)
>> **JOURNALETTE** (by Summer Tan)
>>> **SOCIETY COLUMN** (by Sir Gaylord)
>>>> Lady Lavery (by Northern Dancer)
>>>>> **FAVOURED NATIONS** (by Law Society)
>>>> **LEADING COUNSEL** (by Alleged)
>>>> **PRESENT THE COLORS** (by Hoist the Flag)
>>>> Sarah Gamp (by Hoist the Flag)
>>>>> **ESTRELLA FUEGA** (by Lypheor (GB))
>>>>> Sly Sarah (by On the Sly)
>>>>>> **SALLY GIRL** (by Fain)
>>>> **SYLPH** (by Alleged)
>>>>> Nesaah (by Topsider)
>>>>>> **ORFORD NESS (GB)** (by Selkirk)
>>>>> **PRIVITY** (by Private Account)
>>>>> **ZINDARI** (by Private Account)
>>>> Take Your Mark (by Round Table)
>>>>> **CHARMER** (by Be My Guest)
>>> **TYPECAST** (by Prince John)
>>>> **PRETTY CAST** (by Cover Up Nisei)
>> La Morlaye (by Hafiz)
>>> Indian Call (by Warfare)
>>>> Cheyenne Birdsong (by Restless Wind)
>>>>> **COMPELLING SOUND** (by Seattle Slew)
>>>>> **CRESTON** (by Flying Paster)
>>>>> **SEQUOYAH** (by Gummo)
>>>>> **SHYWING** (by Wing Out)
>>>> **DANCING PARTNER** (by Exclusive Native)
>>>> **ERWIN BOY** (by Exclusive Native)
>>>> Play Around Honey (by Exclusive Native)
>>>>> **LONDRINA** (by Vice Regent)
>>>> **SIBERIAN EXPRESS** (by Caro (IRE))
>>>> **LADY TRAMP** (by Sensitivo)
>>>> Love Bunny (by Exclusive Native)
>>>>> **LE FANTOME** (by Fairway Phantom)
>>>> Myrtlewood Mona (by Raise a Native)
>>>>> Myrtlewood Kitten (by Cougar II)
>>>>>> **OUR KITTEN** (by Our Michael)
>>>> **POPULAR DEMAND** (by Sensitivo)
>> Maori Moon (by Polynesian)
>>> Galivant (by Nahar)
>>>> Whoppin (by War Trouble)
>>>>> **HAPPY FELLOW** (by Northern Legend)
>> Melon (by Heliopolis)
>>> **HAND TO HAND** (by Warfare)
>>> Jet Stratus (by Jet Pilot)
>>>> Dels Bolero (by Bolero)
>>>>> Aquarian Magic (by Full Out)
>>>>>> **MAGIC CRUISER** (by Monetary Gift)
>>>> Mares Tail (by Gallant Romeo)
>>>>> **MARSHUA'S ROMEO** (by Marshua's Dancer)
>>>> **SPIRIT ROCK** (by Selari)
>>> Mouse Club (by Clem)
>>>> Beach Talk (by Sensitivo)
>>>>> **BEACH PARTY** (by Proud Clarion)
>>>>> Pat Priscilla (by Zip Pocket)
>>>>>> **ZIPPEROO** (by Old Chronicle)
>>> Rock Dove (by Sky High II)
>>>> Magma Lass (by Drum Fire)
>>>>> **E.'S EGO** (by Empire Glory)
>>> **STRAIGHT AS A DIE (ENG)** (by Never Bend)
>> Myrtle's Song (by Spy Song)
>>> Lotofspysong (by Irongate)
>>>> **ALABAMA ACE** (by Native Over Tilt)
>>> Palisades Girl (by Sunrise County)
>>>> **FUN AND TEARS** (by Hempen)
>>>>> **FUN FLIGHT** (by Full Pocket)
>>>>>> **FLIGHT FORTY NINE** (by Forty Niner)
>>>>>> **PINK SHOES** (by Phone Trick)
>>>>>> **TOUR** (by Forty Niner)

DURAZNA (continued)
> **IT'S A DONE DEAL** (by Upper Nile)
> **TRICKY FUN** (by Phone Trick)
> The Stage Is Set (by Stage Director)
> **DARK STAGE** (by Strike Gold)
>> Tuzana (by Tudor Minstrel)
>>> War Folly (by Warfare)
>>>> Molalla (by Gallant Man)
>>>>> **ARMIN** (by Bold Forbes)
>>>>> Bold Stunner (by Bold Forbes)
>>>>>> **EVANS TALORY** (by Rajab)
>>>>> Flaming Gold (by Storm Bird)
>>>>>> **LULU'S RANSOM** (by Red Ransom)
> Myrtlemoud (by Mahmoud)
>> Caution (by Windsor Serial)
>>> **AMBER LIGHT** (by Coursing)
>>>> **KNIGHT OF GOLD** (by Tell)
>>>> **TABLE TORCH** (by Tell)
>> Dance With Care (by Gaelic Dancer)
>>> Snapshot (by Gummo)
>>>> **PRIZE SHOT** (by Cajun Prince)
>>>> **SOFTSHOE SURE SHOT** (by Bolger)
> Querida (by Alibhai)
>> Dear April (by My Babu)
>>> **APRIL DAWN** (by Gallant Man)
>>>> Aveshur (by New Policy)
>>>>> **OUR NEW LUCK** (by What Luck)
>>>> **SHARM A SHEIKH** (by New Policy)
>>>> **PROFIT KEY** (by Desert Wine)
>>>> **VINNIE THE VIPER** (by Raise a Man)
>>> **HIGHEST TRUMP** (by Bold Bidder)
>>>> **DANCE BID** (by Northern Dancer)
>>>> **NORTHERN PLAIN** (by Northern Dancer)
>>>> Wasnah (by Nijinsky II)
>>>>> **BAHHARE** (by Woodman)
>>>>> **BAHRI** (by Riverman)
>>>> **WINGLET** (by Alydar)
>>>>> **AJINA** (by Strawberry Road (AUS))
>>> **HURRY UP DEAR** (by Dark Star)
>>> Mademoiselle Molly (by Nashua)
>>>> Easily Romanced (by Solford)
>>>>> **MY LADY SILK** (by Don't Blush)
>>>> **JAMINE** (by Monteverdi (IRE))
>>> My Dear Joan (by Quadrangle)
>>>> **ROYAL AND MAJESTIC** (by Majestic Prince)
>>> Ninita Refinada (by Mongo)
>>>> **EYE'S REFINED** (by Eye of the Morn)
>>>> **GYOKO SAN** (by Golden Eagle II)
>>>> Splendidly Blended (by Hand of Glory)
>>>>> **ATLANTIS BLEND** (by Lost Atlantis)
>>>>> **SPLENDID LANNY** (by Lost Atlantis)
>>> **MR. HINGLE** (by Bald Eagle)
>> Quebabu (by My Babu)
>>> **BOLD MOVE** (by Bold Hour)
>>> Love That Girl (by High Echelon)
>>>> Ivor's Love (by Sir Ivor)
>>>>> **FORMAL TANGO** (by Dynaformer)
>>>> Winthataway (by Blushing Groom (FR))
>>>>> **LE LINGOT** (by Northern Jove)
>>> **QUEEN JANINE** (by Tompion)
>> Royal Dowry (by Royal Charger)
>>> **CHARGER'S STAR** (by Pia Star)
>>> **TUDOR QUEEN** (by King of the Tudors)
> Gallawood (by Sir Gallahad III)
>> Feronia (by Heliopolis)
>>> Font (by Double Jay)
>>>> Duck Fit (by Quack)
>>>>> Duck the Issue (by Judger)
>>>>>> **DUCK THE FALLS** (by Taylor's Falls)
>>>>>> **DUCKLORE** (by Implore)
>>> **JERONIA** (by Johns Joy)
>>> Lady Brick (by Johns Joy)
>>>> Lady Jilsie (by Fleet Nasrullah)
>>>>> **JILSIE'S GIGALO** (by Gallant Knave)
>>> **MR. BRICK** (by Johns Joy)
>>> My Devotion (by Crozier)
>>>> L'Amourette (AUS) (by Indian Conquest (IRE))
>>>>> **STRIKE RATE (AUS)** (by Beau Sovereign)
>>>> **TRUE DEVOTION (AUS)** (by Beau Sovereign)
>>>> **CENTREFOLD** (by Centro)
>>>> **SMART KID (NZ)** (by Kaapstad)
>> Privy Council (by Johns Joy)
>>> Amahlic (by Impressive)
>>>> **ANGEL'S HALO** (by Wing Out)

    OUT LICKED (by Wing Out)
Gala Galla (by Royal Charger)
  Baby Babu (by My Babu)
    Fledgling (by Bold Lark)
      MR. FLEDGLING (by Wolfgang)
  Favorite Gal (by Night Invader)
    Noble Dame (by Native Royalty)
      LADY K. T. (by Bear Hunt)
    SIR NEW MY (by Weekend Guest)
  Princess Tudor (by King of the Tudors)
    Dame d'Argent (by Warfare)
      Dame de Matin (by Proud Birdie)
        CLASSIC ASHLEE (by Regal Classic)
        MARIA'S BROWN EYES (by Jig Time)
      Fleur de Nord (by Far North)
        ALASKAN FROST (by Copelan)
        FROSTY BID (by Explosive Bid)
      SPOKESWOMAN (by Elocutionist)
        TWOUNDER (by Beau's Eagle)
    PROFOUND CINDY (by Apalachee)
    WARDLAW (by Decidedly)
Smooth Run (by Alibhai)
  Twilight Empress (by Dark Star)
    WAHOO WAHOO (by Mr. Deep Well)
MISS DOGWOOD (by Bull Dog)
  Amiga (by Mahmoud)
    ALERT PRINCESS (by Raise a Native)
      NYMPH OF THE NIGHT (by Magesterial)
      SHAM'S PRINCESS (by Sham)
      ETERNITY'S BREATH (by Nureyev)
      Sweet Shampagne (by Sham)
      A BID LACY (by Spectacular Bid)
    CARRIER X. (by Count Fleet)
    DEDIMOUD (by Dedicate)
    Palta (by Mr. Busher)
      Autumn Haze (by Bernborough)
        AUTUMN'S END (by Ambernash)
        Bedbug (by Ring for Nurse)
          Gala Goldie (by Jungle Savage)
            GALA DE ORO (by Shelter Half)
              WISE ONE (by Smarten)
            GALA GOLD DIGGER (by Rollicking)
            GALA GOLDILOCKS (by Shelter Half)
          GALA JUBILEE (by Rollicking)
        Hazy Truth (by Your Alibhai)
          Sunny and Hazy (by Sunny North)
            JOAN KATHERINE (by Fenter)
        Tropical Haze (by Tropical Breeze)
          Tropical Dancer (by Marshua's Dancer)
            EXOTIC DANCER (by Exotic Traveler)
            LATIN TEMPO (by Studdish)
    TUMIGA (by Tudor Minstrel)
  BELLA FIGURA (by Count Fleet)
    Lindisima (by Nashua)
      Trojan Gold (by Trojan Bronze)
        Run Jolene Run (by Daring Damascus)
          DEMASCUS SLEW (by Seattle Sun)
BERNWOOD (by Bernborough)
Ellenwood (by Shannon II)
  Arctica (by Arctic Prince)
    BEMO (by Maribeau)
    North Flow (by Upper Nile)
      SIZZLIN SUNSHINE (by Sunshine Forever)
    Polar Crest (by Far North)
      POLAR RIDGE (by Cox's Ridge)
    PRINCE HAGLEY (by Hagley)
    Varina (by Swoon's Son)
      Affectionate Air (by Silky Baby)
        ANA BELEN (CHI) (by Nijinsky Model)
  Diane W. (by Jet Jewel)
    PARCHMENT (by Royal Note)
  Miss Boxwood (by Mr. Busher)
    GREEK ROAD (by Greek Money)
    La Villita Lady (by Yorky)
      LA VILLITA KID (by Real Petty)
    Miss Norahs (by Delta Judge)
      Palamiss (by Wage Raise)
        OZARK (by Bold Laddie)
        PALIZZIA (by Bold Laddie)
      PALICA (by Our Michael)
  PENINSULA PRINCESS (by Crewman)
Miss Fleetwood (by Count Fleet)
  Cold Morning (by Mr. Busher)

  Cold Dead (by Dead Ahead)
    Ahchoo (by Hold Your Peace)
      CHOOBLOO (by Bolger)
    BAY DIPLOMAT (by Sr. Diplomat)
    Dead Crow (by Jerry Crow)
      TEETERBOARD (by Menocal)
  CUT CORNERS (by Good Investment)
  Exclusive Evening (by Creme dela Creme)
    SEND MORE MONEY (by Great Mystery)
  Seldom Seen (by Cornish Prince)
    BOLTRICK (by Clever Trick)
Egret (by Tudor Minstrel)
  BOMBAY DUCK (by Nashua)
Sea Myrtle (by Swoon's Son)
  Crepe Myrtle (by Native Royalty)
    JULIO ANDRE (by Spicy Story)
  SEA ROYALTY (by Native Royalty)
  SEMI PRINCESS (by Semi-pro)
    AEROSTATION (by Prince John)
Myrtle Lane (by Royal Charger)
  Mountain Path (by Hill Prince)
    Fair Mountain (by Warfare)
      TRUCKIN HAROLD (by Truxton King)
SEQUENCE (by Count Fleet)
  Bold Sequence (by Bold Ruler)
    Bold Mermaid (by Sea-Bird)
      Bold and Dandy (by Dancing Count)
        ETA CARINAE (by John Alden)
      CHATEAU GOLD (by Strike Gold)
      Halomer (by Halo)
        HALO LANDING (by Assault Landing)
    BORN TO LEAD (by Mr. Leader)
    Oughtness (by Buckpasser)
      Louisiana Flash (by Future Hope)
        LACQUARIA (by Bertrando)
        WILD LIGHTNING (by Wild Again)
    Sable Linda (by Graustark)
      Furs for My Lady (by Lt. Stevens)
        A FUR PIECE (by Contare)
    Surgery (by Dr. Fager)
      LEFT COURT (by Valdez)
      SEWICKLEY (by Star de Naskra)
      SHARED INTEREST (by Pleasant Colony)
        FORESTRY (by Storm Cat)
GOLD DIGGER (by Nashua)
  Gold Mine (by Raise a Native)
    ETIQUETTE (by Raja Baba)
    Heart of America (by Northern Jove)
      AMERICAN CHAMP (by Jolie's Halo)
    Tutta (by In Reality)
      QUEEN TUTTA (by Kris S.)
  GOLD STANDARD (by Sea-Bird)
  LILLIAN RUSSELL (by Prince John)
    Kentucky Lill (by Raise a Native)
      LIL'S BOY (by Danzig)
    Slew Princess (by Seattle Slew)
      IGOTRHYTHM (by Dixieland Band)
      SLEW GIN FIZZ (by Relaunch)
  MR. PROSPECTOR (by Raise a Native)
  Myrtlewood Lass (by Ribot)
    Amelia Bearhart (by Bold Hour)
      CHIEF BEARHART (by Chief's Crown)
      EXPLOSIVE RED (by Explodent)
      RUBY RANSOM (by Red Ransom)
HERMOD (by Royal Charger)
Inviting (by My Babu)
  INTRIGUING HONOR (by Sham)
    SHAHRA BAY (by Shahrastani)
  Lovely to Look At (by Creme dela Creme)
    TALL GRASS WALKER (by Navajo)
  Nutmeg Native (by Raise a Native)
    CLAXTON'S SLEW (by Seattle Slew)
      ESCENA (by Strawberry Road (AUS))
      HUMBEL (by Theatrical (IRE))
    MOTEE (by Hopeful Word)
    Nutmeg Lady (by Poison Ivory)
      BARNSBORO (by Sir Harry Lewis)
      HE'S O K (by Schaufuss)
  WITHOUT PEER (by Creme dela Creme)
NOORSAGA (by Noor)
Moonflower (by Bull Dog)
  MOON GLORY (by Norseman)
    AQUA VITE (by Nashua)

212

MOONFLOWER (continued)
- Objectivity (by Bald Eagle)
  - Objective (by Hitting Away)
    - Hope Fulfilled (by Kinsman Hope)
      - **STEADY HOPE** (by Steady Growth)
- Moon Princess (by Princequillo)
  - **FINAL RETREAT** (by Yorktown)
- Irish Moongirl (by Irish Ruler)
  - **MOONDOWN** (by Downing)
- Moon Minstrel (by Tudor Minstrel)
  - Flexi Gal (by Paul A.)
    - **TIMEGLO** (by Sea Aglo)
- Nashua Mia (by Nashua)
  - **SCOTTIE WILL** (by Joey Bob)
- Moon Relic (by War Relic)
  - **MOON SHOT** (by Jet Pilot)
- Timepiece (by Eight Thirty)
  - Frequently (by Decidedly)
    - **JUMPING HILL** (by Hillary)
  - Right Moment (by Noor)
    - Silver Hill (by Hillary)
      - **FLAG SARGENT** (by Tibaut Two)
    - Summit Party (by Hill Rise)
      - L'Natsum (by L'Natural)
        - **STANSUM** (by Stanstead)
      - **NATURAL SUMMIT** (by L'Natural)
- Spring Beauty (by Sir Gallahad III)
- Sonata II (by Hyperion (GB))
  - Brushwork II (by Botticelli)
    - A Royal Brush (by Royal Saxon)
      - **HELEN'S DANCER** (by Orbit Dancer)
        - **VIMY'S SECRET** (by Secret Claim)
    - Drawn Out (by Royal Saxon)
      - **DUN DRAWN OFF** (by Dunstable)
      - **STRETCH MOVE** (by Native Tactics)
  - Danza Nativa (by Kauai King)
    - **TRES JOLIE (VEN)** (by White Face)
      - Jolie's Dream (by Key to the Mint)
        - **SCOTT GORDON** (by Velcro Fly)
  - **LYFORD CAY** (by Alcide)
  - Mossata (by Mossborough)
    - Vam Paree (NZ) (by Perpetual)
      - **LADY PAREE** (by Tights)
  - Silly Sonata (by Silly Season)
    - **PORPOURIE** (by Vice Regent)
- Spring Tune (by Spy Song)
  - Aparoma (by My Babu)
    - Myrtlewood Beauty (by Never Bend)
      - Angel Rouge (by Crimson Satan)
        - **ANGEL'S APPEAL** (by Valid Appeal)
        - **HOLST** (by Explodent)
      - **LOCUST BAYOU** (by Majestic Prince)
      - Nymphe des Bois (by Caro (IRE))
        - Summernights Dream (by General Assembly)
          - **NIGHT IN RENO** (by Bet Big)
    - Rare Fragrance (by Nashua)
      - **ACTOR'S AROMA** (by An Act)
  - **LADY WAYWARD** (by Dedicate)
    - **NEVER ASK** (by Never Bend)
    - Village Gossip (by Buckpasser)
      - **LIGHT OF NASHUA** (by Nashua)
    - Wayward Native (by Raise a Native)
      - **FORCE OF ONE** (by Exuberant)
  - Village Beauty (by My Babu)
    - **CROWN THE QUEEN** (by Swaps)
      - **HUGGLE DUGGLE** (by Never Bend)
        - **AL MUNDHIR** (by Seattle Slew)
      - **SILENT BEAUTY** (by Creme dela Creme)
      - **CATAHOULA** (by Never Bend)
        - **SUGAR CHARLOTTE** (by Wajima)
      - **SQUABBLE** (by Never Bend)
      - **VILLAGE SASS** (by Sassafras (FR))
- **YOUNG MAN'S FANCY II** (by Alycidon)
  - Thoughts of Love (by Prince John)
    - Temple Bells (by Marshua's Dancer)
      - **APPEALING GIRL** (by Valid Appeal)
        - **FASTY AND NASTY** (by Nasty and Bold)
        - **HOPEFUL APPEAL** (by Hopeful Word)
        - **VALIBASQUE** (by Bounding Basque)
      - Dancer's Protege (by Brilliant Protege)
        - **BATCHWOOD** (by Baederwood)
        - **CHAMPION JAY** (by Clever Champ)
      - **MISSY DEAR** (by Deerhound)

No Class
(by Nodouble)

ALWAYS A CLASSIC (by Deputy Minister)
CLASSIC REIGN (by Vice Regent)
CLASSY 'N SMART (by Smarten)
- **DANCE SMARTLY** (by Danzig)
  - **SMART STRIKE** (by Mr. Prospector)
GREY CLASSIC (by Grey Dawn II)
REGAL CLASSIC (by Vice Regent)
SKY CLASSIC (by Nijinsky II)

Rose Leaves
(by Ballot)

BOIS DE ROSE (by Negofol)
BULL LEA (by Bull Dog)
DOGPATCH (by Bull Dog)
ESPINO (by Negofol)
RUDDY (by McGee)
NECTARINE (by Bull Dog)
- **APPLEKNOCKER** (by Reaping Reward)
- Bramble Bug (by Display)
  - Pandora (by Unbreakable)
    - Flower Bonnet (by Johns Joy)
      - Chapeau Fleur (by Dress Up)
        - **DUSTY COUNTY** (by Dusty Canyon)
        - **DUSTY FLOWER** (by Dusty Canyon)
        - Phil's Chapeau (by Philately)
          - **BEAULAHLAND** (by Drum Fire)
        - Fleur Du Regal (by Regal Bearing (GB))
          - **DOC ART** (by Wayne's Crane)
          - **FLOWERFOOL** (by Fool the Experts)
          - **MAXREGAL** (by Society Max)
      - Jolie Chapeau (by Nashua)
        - **DIORISSIMO** (by Triple Bend)
          - **SCENTED ROYAL** (by Royal Prerogative)
        - Her Chapeau (by Herbager)
          - **HER FLING** (by Northern Fling)
        - Nice Bonnet (by Royal Levee)
          - Little Prema (by Cloudy Dawn)
            - **GRACE AVE.** (by Nostrum)
        - **ROSIE'S SEVILLE** (by List)
        - Stiff Competition (by Amberoid)
          - Competitive Leader (by Mr. Leader)
            - **MR. BRILLIANT** (by Brilliant Sandy)
          - President's Asst. (by One for All)
            - **NO COMPETITION** (by Honey Jay)
  - **JOY TO TELL** (by Tell)
  - Mountain Laurel (by Black Mountain)
    - **CASTELLI MOUNTAIN** (by Leo Castelli)
- Gay Rig (by Turn-to)
  - **GAY SAILORETTE** (by Sailor)
    - Sincerity (by Tom Rolfe)
      - Grass Roots (by Hawaii)
        - **LEMON GRASS** (by Slew the Coup)
  - Gay Sonnet (by Sailor)
    - Pretty Sonnet (by Stop the Music)
      - **PLENTY CHILLY** (by It's Freezing)
    - Special Charm (by Verbatim)
      - **CASSALERIA** (by Pretense)
    - **SWEETEST CHANT** (by Mr. Leader)
      - **DANZIG'S BEAUTY** (by Danzig)
        - **DANCING GULCH** (by Gulch)
        - **DISTORTED HUMOR** (by Forty Niner)
  - Let's Be Gay (by Bagdad)
    - Be Sassy (by Olden Times)
      - **OLD STORIES** (by Cox's Ridge)
    - Keep Her Happy (by Sham)
      - **HAPPY GINI** (by Ginistrelli)
        - **HAMOND (GER)** (by Acatenango)
        - **HAPPY BOY** (by Time for a Change)
        - **HAPPY CHANGE (GER)** (by Surumu)
      - **PRIVATE THOUGHTS** (by Pretense)
- **GOLD BOX** (by Heliopolis)
- **MACEDONIA** (by Olympia)

Mount Dora (by Olympia)
Liberty Dora (by Sir Gaylord)
Raja Dora (by Raja Baba)
DORADORADORA (by Runaway Groom)
SKY DANCER (JAM) (by Robin's Song)
Play Possum (by Fighting Fox)
Champagne Toast (by Prince Khaled)
CHAMPSVILLE (by Nashville)
Cool Snooze (by Nearctic)
DREAM OF SPRING (by Pleasure Seeker)
Jillary (by Hillary)
JILLARY JILL (by Native Royalty)
Jingling Pocket (by Full Pocket)
PICK POCKET MIKE (by Ruthie's Native)
MODUS VIVENDI (by Rising Market)
Sykophantes (by Misrepresentation)
PAST AGES (by Flying Paster)
Winter Sleep (by Rising Market)
RELIGIOSITY (by Irish Tower)
DIAL A SONG (by Mining)
FOR ALL SEASONS (by Crafty Prospector)
Sleep Thru Dinner (by State Dinner)
Mabuhay (by Avatar)
MYLITTLEVIC (by Vying Victor)
WINTER SOLSTICE (by Acroterion)
LOON'S CRY (by Lear Fan)
EMPRESS OF INDIA (by Victoria Park)
FLOW LINE (by Khaled)
Interloper (by Venetian Way)
Little Maryperkins (by Swoon's Son)
JACK DRAWBAUGH (by Cuff Link II)
RECORDING (by Don B.)
Victorine (by My Babu)
My Own Beau Peep (by Beau Purple)
La Belle Grecque (by Isle of Greece)
Grecian Luck (by Run of Luck)
GRECIAN GLAMOUR (by Arctic Action)
Lady Eileen (by Diplomat Way)
MINIGHOSTA (by Silver Ghost)
PLEASANT BROOK (by Intentionally)
Sleek Dancer (by Northern Dancer)
NORTHERN PROSPECT (by Mr. Prospector)
SHARP BELLE (by Native Charger)
Regal Feeling (by Clever Trick)
GRAND CHARMER (by Lord Avie)
RING MY BELL (by Idabel)
Sleek Belle (by Vaguely Noble)
CHIC BELLE (by Mr. Prospector)
Bandoline (GB) (by Top Ville)
STERLING HEIGHTS (by Royal Academy)
Society Bride (by Blushing Groom (FR))
SOCIETY DREAM (FR) (by Akarad)
Listen Here (by Never Listen)
HIGHLAND HAPPENING (by Highland Blade)
SLEEK FEET (by Seattle Slew)
SLEEK GOLD (by Mr. Prospector)
WITWATERSRAND (by Mr. Prospector)
CHOKAI CAROL (by Brian's Time)
NELSON (by Seattle Slew)
Sleek Street (by Native Admiral)
Street Native (by Mr. Prospector)
SLEEK WORLD (by Will Win)
SUE BABE (by Mr. Prospector)
Champagne Babe (by Alleged)
CHAMPAGNEFORASHLEY (by Track Barron)
CYRANO (by Seattle Slew)
SIR HARRY LEWIS (by Alleged)
SIR RICHARD LEWIS (by Carr de Naskra)
PASSADO (by Roman)
Ripper-Do (by Rippey)
Belle Biz (by Crimson Satan)
FIESTY BELLE (by Naskra)
Josephine Saxa (by Plum Bold)
Linkage Love (by Linkage)
OSCAR MAGIC (by Recognized)
Hastings Song (by Spy Song)
Fran's Song (by Gladwin)
SONG CATCHER (by Sun Catcher)
Larchmont Miss (by Crafty Admiral)
Saralima (by The Big Boss)
JESSE JIM (by Jim J.)
Ripper Did (by Crafty Admiral)
ADMIRAL'S SHIELD (by Crozier)

Vicious Tongue (by Malicious)
Barking Brass (by Lt. Stevens)
KEEWATIN (by Slewpy)
Rive Gauche (by Star Envoy)
AMERICAN DREAMER (by Premiership)
FRENCH GOLD (by Northern Prospect)
GREATSILVERFLEET (by On to Glory)
Stone Rock (by Mr. Prospector)
ASTRO (by Five Star Flight)
Super Starlz (by Super Concorde)
PRECOCITY (by Aferd)
WILD NOTE (by Royal Note)
Accipitress (by Accipiter)
WISE ACRE (by Wise Times)
B'S Overdraft (by Damascus)
BRIGHT PENNY (by Vice Regent)
FOR ONCE'N MY LIFE (by Key to the Kingdom)
TOP OF MY LIFE (by Topsider)
VIRTUOUS REGENT (by Vice Regent)
Ideal Design (by Raise a Native)
Golden Garden (by Golden Eagle II)
AVENUE OF GOLD (by Avenue of Flags)
LUDICROUS (by Droll Role)
NOTED (by Buffalo Lark)
WILD TOM (by High Echelon)
Sweet Woman (by Roman)
I'M FOR MORE (by Olympia)
LADY SWAPS (by Swaps)
Lady Accipiter (by Accipiter)
REGAL LAD (by Regal Search)
She's Very Ultra (by Olympia)
When and If (by Dr. Fager)
MACHALSTVA (by Stage Door Johnny)
WITH APLOMB (by Dr. Fager)
Svidhod (by Priam II)
Iron Woman (by Iron Peg)
Iron Talk (by No Back Talk)
ARTIC WOMAN (by Son of Briartic)
Parrott's Polly (by Royal Serenade)
Pretty Polly Wog (by Beau Gar)
BILL MONROE (by Brent's Prince)
ROSE OF WENDOVER (by Brent's Prince)
KENATHENA (by Cryptoclearance)
ROBADAN (by Prince John)
Full of Mere (by Full Out)
TILT GATE (by Tilt Up)
Gay Robber (by Sir Gaylord)
T. V. CAPER (by T. V. Lark)
T. V. RESIDUAL (by Pirate's Bounty)
SINGULAR VISION (by Never Tabled)
WARNING LABEL (by Never Tabled)
Mandy's Gray (by Drone)
ALWAYS UP (by Buck's Bid)
OWENS TROUPE (by For The Moment)
Stay Up Late (by Aloma's Ruler)
CARA REGINA (by Fit to Fight)
Marymobill (by Kauai King)
Vitrina (by Pass the Glass)
ELITE'S BULLY (by Elite Syncopation)
That Potts Girl (by Blue Prince)
GREAT POINT (by Jig Time)
SWEET PATOOTIE (by Alquest)
Tweetsie (by Noor)
TWEEBER (by Berseem)
Orange Leaves (by Hard Tack)
YING AND YANG (by Basileus II)
Yuno Sumthin (by Basileus II)
Really Sumthin (by Jet Master)
Donut Hole (by Donut King)
COLONEL'S ALPHA (by Colonel Power)
Donut's Image (by L'Enjoleur)
IMAGE OF PROSPECT (by Northern Prospect)
DONUT'S PRIDE (by Nodouble)
AFINE PASTRY (by Afleet)
LAST VICE (by Vice Regent)
Summer Time (by Bull Dog)
Big Harvest (by Reaping Reward)
Grand Season (by On Trust)
Forever Agnes (by Real Supreme)
SONIC GRAY (by Double Sonic)
Grand Relation (by Correlation)
DANCING RELATION (by Dancer's Image)
Medieval Season (by Medieval Man)

214

    | **MEDIEVAL PROSPECT** (by Diamond Prospect)
Oil Princess (by Errard)
  OIL RICH (by Phalanx)
    Lemos (by Sea-Bird)
    | **LOINTAINE** (by Lyphard's Wish (FR))
    Merry Mama (by Prince John)
      BLOWING ROCK (by Fair Ruler)
      How Dear (by Iron Ruler)
      | **PAPA KOO** (by Judger)
      So What (by Iron Ruler)
        AAMOO (by Megaturn)
        What Gin (by Ginistrelli)
          TEERRIFIC SUE (by Turkoman)
          UDRIVEMEHOME (by Torcher)
    Method Actress (by Round Table)
    | **MODERN PLEASURE** (by What a Pleasure)
    Rich Reserve (by Swaps)
      Discourse (by Speak John)
        Great Dialogue (by Illustrious)
          BEAR TRUTH (by Double Sonic)
      Refining (by Prince John)
        SUGAR SHARP (by Sharpen Up (GB))
    Sweet Heaven (by Olympia)
      Our Sweet Heaven (by Search for Gold)
      | **LOOKING FOR HEAVEN** (by Encino)
      Road to Heaven (by Kennedy Road)
        CASTLE PARK (by Slady Castle)
        HELLO MOM (by Caveat)
  OIL ROYALTY (by Greek Song)
    Barbsie (by T. V. Lark)
    | **BARBERY** (by Empery)
    T. V. BARB (by Empery)
    Mrs. Got Rocks (by Bold Bidder)
      Gale Bridge (by Vaguely Noble)
        NAEVOG (by Ela-Mana-Mou (IRE))
        TRIVIAL PURSUIT (by Ela-Mana-Mou (IRE))
    Nancy Wynne (by Bold Bidder)
      BEAR CAT (by Cougar II)
      DELAYER (by Fappiano)
Oil Show (by Ponder)
| **FUEL QUEEN** (by Bolinas Boy)
Princess Diane (by Phalanx)
  CHARMING DIANE (by Alhambra)
  Dianette (by Thorn)
    IRISH ACTRESS (by Seattle Song)
Rich Royalty (by Prince John)
  AIDE TO ROYALTY (by Native Aid)
  Major Play (by B. Major)
    Morning Games (by Grey Dawn II)
      Afternoon Winner (by Text)
      | **ANN'S WINNER** (by Personal Flag)
      ALPHABATIM (by Verbatim)
      GRAN ALBA (by El Gran Senor)
      MAGICAL RIVER (by Riverman)
      PUZZLE BOOK (by Text)
        BROCK STREET (by Afleet)
        MYSTERIOUSLY (by Afleet)
  | **ROYAL VILLA** (by Villamor)
Strike Oil (by Prince John)
  Everglow (by Jacinto)
    COMEDY ACT (by Shecky Greene)
    | **ZIGGY'S ACT** (by Danzig)
    Empty Nest (by No Robbery)
      KING'S NEST (by Rollicking)
      MISTER S. M. (by Rollicking)
    HOLDFAST (by Crewman)
    RED EMBER (by Crimson Satan)
    Sunset Hour (by Tumiga)
      QUEEN OF THE HOUR (by Hail Bold King)
  OIL POWER (by Crimson Satan)
  PRESS NOTICE (by Creme dela Creme)
  Saw Oil (by Ace of Aces)
    FRENCH OIL (by L'Enjoleur)
    NIGHTCAPPER (by Sunshine Forever)
  Scarlet Gold (by Crimson Satan)
    Five Red Stars (by Five Star Flight)
      SAYSTAR (by Oh Say)
    STARS KNOCKOUT (by Two Punch)
  SPOUT (by Delta Judge)
Blue Petal (by Blue Larkspur)
  BLUE BALLAD (by Balladier)
  | **BORDONE** (by Botticelli)
  STEVE'S LARK (by Landing)

Easy Living (by Heliopolis)
  Angel Food (by Shut Out)
    Delicious II (by Requested)
      Dea (by Midsummer Night)
      | **DEIMOS** (by Canisbay)
      Delicious Night (by Midsummer Night)
      GAY CLEMENTINE (by Some Hand)
  Appalachia (by Hill Prince)
    Dee's Might (by Might)
      MATTHEW T. PARKER (by Rock Talk)
    Julie Pink (by Young Emperor)
    | **SWIFT ARREST** (by No Robbery)
    QUIET BAY (by Mo Bay)
  Lady Whileaway (by Princequillo)
    Hope Renewed (by Never Bend)
      Hopeico (by Amerrico)
        MAGNIFY (by Contested Colors)
    Interstellar (by Mongo)
      Redeeming Feature (by Sea Songster)
      ROAD ROCKET (by Voom Voom)
    Lady Elegant (by Seaneen)
      DONNA LUCIA (by Red Fox)
      IT'S A BEAR (by Impressive)
RILEY (by Hill Prince)
ROYAL LIVING (by Hill Prince)
Save Time (by War Admiral)
  CAPTAIN VANCOUVER (by Never Bend)
  DOROTHY GLYNN (by Northern Dancer)
    Disastrous (by Fleet Nasrullah)
    | **EARTHQUACK** (by Quack)
    HALO DOTTY (by Halo)
    | **LEGENDARY PRINESS** (by Gone West)
    Orcadia (by Sir Ivor)
      Northern Obsession (by Trepan)
      CANADIENNE (by Overskate)
  Jungle Dance (by Graustark)
  MAJESTIC KAT (by Majestic Prince)
Tides Out (by Shut Out)
  Fia Fia (by Beau Gar)
    NANCY'S BIRTHDAY (by Rattle Dancer)
    Petteget (by Pet Bully)
      Ariannie (by Bushido)
        That's a Annie (by That's a Nice)
          ZAPPIE ONE (by Thumbsucker)
      BILLY ONWARD (by Mr. Billy B.)
      OCEAN DRIVE (by Campion Kid)
    TIMJIM DANDY (by Pet Bully)
  Tides In (by Traffic Judge)
    Evon Rapacka (by Fathers Image)
    GOHRUDEN BOHTO (by Shinzan)
  Time to Play (by Neke)
    Playful Princess (by Hail the Prince)
    PLAYFUL LINAN (by Banderilla)
Reaping Time (by Reaping Reward)
  Gay Reaper (by Bimelech)
  BERKLEY CORNER (by Seven Corners)

Rough Shod II
(by Gold Bridge)

GAMBETTA (by My Babu)
  Aphonia (by Dunce)
    Aphonita (by Greek Sky)
    | **BIBLIONIC** (by Notebook)
    GEORGE SPELVIN (by Nantallah)
  MESSINA (by Secretariat)
  Nosey Nan (by Nantallah)
    Flying Rumor (by Alydar)
    | **GRAND JEWEL** (by Java Gold)
    NO CABEZA (by Executioner)
    Arcadienne (by Barrera)
      Royale Satin (by Upper Nile)
      PHILISIMO (by Potentiate)
    REGAL RUMOR (by Damascus)
    BAYOU HEBERT (by Hoist the Flag)
    Thruthegrapevine (by Sir Ivor)
    MR. VICIOUS (by Kerosene)
    TIGHANTUIR (by Bayou Black)
  Secret Rumor (by Damascus)

GAMBETTA (continued)

```
           Jennifer's Bid (by Spectacular Bid)
              MISS BID FLASH (by Horse Flash (FR))
           Spectacularsecret (by Spectacular Bid)
              HOT WAY (by Robbama)
        TABLE THE RUMOR (by Round Table)
           Pure Speed (by Gulch)
              MAKE HASTE (by Cure the Blues)
              QUICK LAP (by Nicholas)
           Rally Around (by Hoist the Flag)
              PRIMETIME NORTH (by Northern Dancer)
     SITZMARK (by J. O. Tobin)
GAMELY (by Bold Ruler)
     CELLINI (by Round Table)
     Gambling (by Round Table)
        Bettor (by Conquistador Cielo)
           FUERO JUZGO (by Ghadeer)
STARETTA (by Dark Star)
     Brilliant Girl (by Globemaster)
        Radiant Splender (by Penowa Rullah)
           Splendor Lady (by Winged Step)
              DANCER ON WINGS (by St. Petersburg)
     LADY BRILLIANCE (by Globemaster)
        Brilliant Dancer (by Dancer's Image)
           SUDDEN FLARE (by Robellino)
        Winter Breeze (by Nearctic)
           Frozen Expression (by In a Trance)
              CABRINI EXPRESS (by Cabrini Green)
           Whitesburg Express (by Whitesburg)
              HIGHLAND GOLD (by Slew o' Gold)
     Star Strewn (by Native Dancer)
        ASTEROID FIELD (by Forli)
        Star of Araby (by Damascus)
           Star of the North (by Cold Reception)
              Estrella Surena (by Prince Thatch (IRE))
                 CALESITA (by Alamour)
        Trebor's Choice (by Damascus)
           FITZ (by Waquoit)
     Superiority (by Bold Ruler)
        Strobe (by Bagdad)
           Master Switch (by Master Derby)
              SOUTHERN SWITCH (by Red Attack)
           Strobe's Song (by Bravest Roman)
              MILKSHAKE (by Quadratic)
                 HOWLIN WOLF (by Wolf Power (SAF))
     Zonah (by Nasrullah)
        DRUMTOP (by Round Table)
           Battle Drum (by Alydar)
              BRIGADE OF GUARDS (by Eastern Echo)
           BROGAN (by Nijinsky II)
           Kyra's Slipper (by Nijinsky II)
              HEAVENLY DANCE (by Halo)
              Klompen (by Halo)
                 STARQUESTER (by Norquestor)
           TOPSIDER (by Northern Dancer)
           WAR OF WORDS (by Arts and Letters)
        Georgie (by Damascus)
           SURELY GEORGIE'S (by Alleged)
              GEORGE AUGUSTUS (by El Gran Senor)
              MONGOL WARRIOR (by Deputy Minister)
              SURELY SIX (by Saratoga Six)
        Julia B. (by Herbager)
           Veiled Prophet (by Damascus)
              SAFE TO SAY (by Naskra)
        TAKE YOUR PLACE (by Round Table)
        Zeal (by Round Table)
           Coaxing (by L'Enjoleur)
              COAX CLASSIC (by Caveat)
           Grande Vogue (by Vaguely Noble)
              GRANDE COUTURE (by Miswaki)
           Lady Hardwick (by Nijinsky II)
              AIR BAG (by Devil's Bag)
              MISS HARDWICK (by Honest Pleasure)
           Zealous Cat (by Cougar II)
              CAKE N' STEAK (by Sensitive Prince)
        Zone (by Tulyar)
           Ribot Babe (by Sir Ribot)
              INDIGO STAR (by Star Envoy)
        Zonely (by Round Table)
           Diamond Field (by Mr. Prospector)
              NEW FRONTIER (IRE) (by Sadler's Wells)
              WAFAYT (IRE) (by Danehill)
           Native Zone (by Exclusive Native)
              TANK (by Tank's Prospect)
```

GAMBETTA (continued)

```
           TIJUANA NATIVE (by Assert (IRE))
        Sharp Zone (by The Axe II)
           Music Zone (by The Minstrel)
              STRIKE ZONE (by Time for a Change)
              WILD ZONE (by Wild Again)
        Super Zone (by The Minstrel)
           Super Baba (by Raja Baba)
              PRANKSTER (by Clever Trick)
           VICTORY ZONE (by Val de l'Orne (FR))
LT. STEVENS (by Nantallah)
MOCCASIN (by Nantallah)
     APALACHEE (by Round Table)
     Aztec (by Tom Rolfe)
        TOLTEC (by L'Emigrant)
     BELTED EARL (by Damascus)
     BRAHMS (by Round Table)
     FLIPPERS (by Coastal)
        HAIL ATLANTIS (by Seattle Slew)
           MR. KATOWICE (by Katowice)
           STORMY ATLANTIC (by Storm Cat)
     INDIAN (by Round Table)
     NANTEQUOS (by Tom Rolfe)
     Sandal (by Damascus)
        Huaraches (by Buckfinder)
           SHOOT TO KILL (by L'Emigrant)
     SCUFF (by Forli)
        EBROS (by Mr. Prospector)
RIDAN (by Nantallah)
Thong (by Nantallah)
     ESPADRILLE (by Damascus)
        Pump (by Forli)
           CLASSIC SPORT (by Nijinsky II)
           FILAO BEACH (by Alysheba)
     Handsewn (by Sir Ivor)
        FESTIVAL HALL (IRE) (by Sadler's Wells)
     KING PELLINORE (by Round Table)
     LISADELL (by Forli)
        FATHERLAND (IRE) (by Sadler's Wells)
        Glenveagh (by Seattle Slew)
           Saddlers Gal (IRE) (by Sadler's Wells)
              EL CONDOR PASA (by Kingmambo)
        GOLDEN DOME (by Golden Fleece)
        Lisaleen (by Northern Dancer)
           White Wisteria (GB) (by Ahonoora (GB))
              BODYGUARD (GB) (by Zafonic)
              WHITE GULCH (GB) (by Gulch)
        Rosa Mundi (by Secretariat)
           CORREGGIO (IRE) (by Sadler's Wells)
           La Joyeuse (by Northern Dancer)
              ENDLESS JOY (by Law Society)
           Quarter Deck (IRE) (by Storm Bird)
              HANA (FR) (by Alleged)
           SWORD DANCE (IRE) (by Nijinsky II)
        YEATS (by Nijinsky II)
     Special (by Forli)
        BOUND (by Nijinsky II)
           LIMIT (by Cox's Ridge)
        Fairy Bridge (by Bold Reason)
           FAIRY GOLD (by Northern Dancer)
           PUPPET DANCE (by Northern Dancer)
           SADLER'S WELLS (by Northern Dancer)
           TATE GALLERY (by Northern Dancer)
        Kilavea (by Hawaii)
           KILINISKI (IRE) (by Niniski)
           Nakterjal (GB) (by Vitiges)
              BIENAMADO (by Bien Bien)
              Minimal Surface (by L'Emigrant)
                 EXPEDICIONARIA (VEN) (by Inland Voyager)
           Puget Sound (GB) (by High Top)
              NINOTCHKA (by Nijinsky II)
              Thong Thong Thong (by El Gran Senor)
                 HOT THONG (BRZ) (by Jarraar)
        NUMBER (by Nijinsky II)
           Add (by Spectacular Bid)
              INFLATE (by Forty Niner)
              Multiply (by Easy Goer)
                 DESERT HERO (by Sea Hero)
           CHEQUER (by Mr. Prospector)
           JADE ROBBERY (by Mr. Prospector)
           NUMEROUS (by Mr. Prospector)
        NUREYEV (by Northern Dancer)
THATCH (by Forli)
```

Two Bob
(by The Porter)

MIZ CLEMENTINE (by Bull Lea)
 Sweet Clementine (by Swaps)
  BEST TURN (by Turn-to)
  Honeysuckle Vine (by Tom Fool)
   Honey Dreamer (by Dewan)
    Dream Vision (by Northern Taste)
     ALOHA DREAM (JPN) (by Creator (GB))
    Dyna World (by Huntercombe)
     National Flag (by Dictus)
      INTER FLAG (JPN) (by Northern Taste)
      MARUKA KOMACHI (JPN) (by Sunday Silence)
   Honey Wama (by Wajima)
    Honey Gun (by Ack Ack)
     AIR FORES GUN (by Air Forbes Won)
  MISS TOKYO (by Dewan)
  Spring Memories (by Riva Ridge)
   CONSUMING PASSION (by Jackie Fires)
   Shattered Dreams (by Explodent)
    ARISTIE (by Loustrous Bid)
TWO LEA (by Bull Lea)
 Eskimo Love (by Arctic Prince)
  Scorer (by Prince John)
   Pebeanjays (by Beau Brummel)
    DAILY DESIRE (by Cuchillo)
  SEW FOR FOUR (by Needles)
 Mon Ange (by Tom Fool)
  Angel Chile (by Herbager)
   BALLYMACARNEY (by Habitat)
   BEULAH LAND (by Targowice)
   GORKY PARK (FR) (by Gorytus)
   Sweet France (FR) (by Exclusive Native)
    Angelet Sweet (JPN) (by Colonel Symboli (JPN))
     Sweet Angelet (by Mogami)
      Sister Mill (by Mill George)
       SEIUN SKY (JPN) (by Sheriff's Star)
      SWEET MITHUNA (by Mr C B (JPN))
     SWEET NATIVE (JPN) (by Partholon)
    WILD SURF (IRE) (by Mill Reef)
   HE'S AN ANGEL (by Raise a Cup)
   Margot Verre (by Tom Rolfe)
    ALY MAR (by Alydar)
   SON ANGE (by Raise a Native)
   TARBOOSH (by Bagdad)
 ON-AND-ON (by Nasrullah)
 PIED D'OR (by Nasrullah)
 TIM TAM (by Tom Fool)
 Two Lea's Girl (by Count Fleet)
  Quasi (by Barbizon)
   Twin Lea (by Prove It)
    NAT'S LEA (by L'Natural)
TWOSY (by Bull Lea)
 Twice Over (by Ponder)
  Family Fame (by Droll Role)
   CLASSIC FAME (by Nijinsky II)
  MISS CARMIE (by T. V. Lark)
   ALL RAINBOWS (by Bold Hour)
    All Dance (by Northern Dancer)
     CAREZZA (by Caro (IRE))
     RULING (by Alleged)
    WINNING COLORS (by Caro (IRE))
   Ann Stuart (by Lyphard)
    BEYTON (by Alleged)
   Barbara Schurgin (by Droll Role)
    PARISTO (by Buckpasser)
   Charmie Carmie (by Lyphard)
    FAAZ (by Fappiano)
    Himmah (by Habitat)
     HIWAYA (GB) (by Doyoun (IRE))
   CHRIS EVERT (by Swoon's Son)
    Center Court Star (by Secretariat)
     BEST STAR (by Seattle Slew)
     LAMBENT LIGHT (by Capote)
    Nijinsky Star (by Nijinsky II)
     HOMETOWN QUEEN (by Pleasant Colony)
     REVASSER (by Riverman)
     VIVIANA (by Nureyev)
    SIX CROWNS (by Secretariat)
     CHIEF'S CROWN (by Danzig)
     Chosen Crown (by Forli)

TWOSY (continued)
      Chosen Slew (by Slew o' Gold)
       SKYWALKER'S CHOICE (by Skywalker)
     CLASSIC CROWN (by Mr. Prospector)
     Jeweled Crown (by Seattle Slew)
      SILK PHOENIX (JPN) (by Adjudicating)
    Tournament Star (by Nijinsky II)
     Wimbledon (by Blushing Groom (FR))
      DELAY OF GAME (by Summer Squall)
     TOP SEED (by Wild Again)
    WIMBLEDON STAR (by Hoist the Flag)
   Missed the Wedding (by Blushing Groom (FR))
    GREEN MEANS GO (by Green Dancer)
    MISSED THE STORM (by Storm Cat)
   Search Committee (by Roberto)
    FIRST STAGE (by Relaunch)
   Social Column (by Vaguely Noble)
    HARD NEWS (by Lyphard)
    LIAISON (by Blushing Groom (FR))
    Mrs. King (by Icecapade)
     R. B.'s Spicy (by Private Account)
      SPICY AWARD (by Black Tie Affair (IRE))
    Social Wish (by Lyphard's Wish (FR))
     EXBOURNE'S WISH (by Exbourne)
    TWO TIMING (by Blushing Groom (FR))
   Whisper Who Dares (by Green Dancer)
    CONFESSIONAL (by Holy Bull)
    GOSSIP (by Pleasant Colony)
 My Jerce (by War Admiral)
  Hex (by Gray Phantom)
   Pride of Piazza's (by Zingalong)
    DONTFORGETHISNAME (by Illuminate)
 Phil's Jest (by Jester)
  Jest Innocent (by Vigors)
   JEST NO CENTS (by Torsion)
  TWICE FOOLISH (by Native Admiral)
   ALL NONENSE (by Hall of Reason)
   STRAWBERRY ROAD (by Kennedy Road)
TWO RELICS (by War Relic)

Vagrancy
(by Sir Gallahad III)

BLACK TARQUIN (by Rhodes Scholar)
HYVANIA (by Hypnotist II)
Natasha (by Nasrullah)
 Mazaca (by Pappa Fourway)
  ITSAMAZA (by Limit to Reason)
   ITSAMAZING (by The Minstrel)
  Mrs. Witt (by Alleged)
   Hagley's Miss (by Hagley)
    THANKS FRANKS (by Herat)
  Score Baby Score (by Limit to Reason)
   Iambic Pentameter (by Arts and Letters)
    CLARIFY (by Eastern Echo)
 TROVE (by Key to the Mint)
  SIMPLE TASTE (by Sharpen Up (GB))
NATASHKA (by Dedicate)
 ARKADINA (by Ribot)
  DARK LOMOND (IRE) (by Lomond)
  ENCYCLOPEDIA (by Reviewer)
  FORLENE (IRE) (by Forli)
   GLORIA'S DANCER (by Northern Dancer)
   SAGE WELLS (IRE) (by Sadler's Wells)
  Gold and Purple (IRE) (by Golden Fleece)
   JULIE LA ROUSSE (IRE) (by Lomond)
  Salvatico (by Sir Ivor)
   MIRAFLORA (by Forli)
   WHITE TIE 'N TAILS (by Fred Astaire)
  SOUTH ATLANTIC (IRE) (by Mill Reef)
 BLOOD ROYAL (by Ribot)
 Graceful Gal (by Key to the Mint)
  DULUTH (by Codex)
  I REALLY WILL (by In Reality)
  REAL COURAGE (by In Reality)
  RYTHMICAL (by Fappiano)
   CAPOTE BELLE (by Capote)
  The Time to Bet (by Foolish Pleasure)
   Hurdy Gurdy (by In Reality)
    POOLMAN (by Notebook)

218

Index

Index

Acknowledgments

Matriarchs: Great Mares of the 20th Century was produced with assistance from special projects editor Jacqueline Duke, assistant editor Judy L. Marchman, artist Brian Turner, senior technical staff member Dave Overton, copy editors Tom Hall, Diane L. Viert, and Pat Dolan, research director James A. Cox, and researchers Jay Wallace, Jo McKinney, Linda Manley, and C. Mark Cooper. Pedigree information was provided by The Jockey Club Information Systems.

A B O U T T H E *Author*

EDWARD L. BOWEN is considered one of Thoroughbred racing's most insightful and erudite writers. A native of West Virginia, Bowen grew up in South Florida where he became enamored of racing while watching televised stakes from Hialeah.

Bowen entered journalism school at the University of Florida in 1960. The next summer he worked at Ocala Stud Farm, then spent the following summer working for trainer Kenny Noe at Monmouth Park and Atlantic City. Bowen transferred to the University of Kentucky in 1963 so he could work as a writer for *The Blood-Horse*, the leading weekly Thoroughbred magazine. From 1968-70, he served as editor of *The Canadian Horse*, then returned to *The Blood-Horse* as managing editor. He rose to the position of editor-in-chief before leaving the publication in 1993.

Bowen is president of the Grayson-Jockey Club Research Foundation, which raises funds for equine research. In addition to *Matriarchs: Great Mares of the 20th Century*, Bowen has written seven books, including The Jockey Club's *Illustrated History of Thoroughbred Racing in America*. He is a frequent contributor to various racing publications and also writes the script for the annual Eclipse Awards. Bowen has won the Eclipse Award for magazine writing and other writing awards. He lives in Lexington, Kentucky, with his wife, Ruthie, and four-year-old son George. Bowen has two grown daughters, Tracy Bowen and Jennifer Schafhauser, and one grandchild, Emily Schafhauser.